ALL MUSIC GUIDE REQUIRED LISTENING

CONTEMPORARY COUNTRY

All Music Guide Required Listening Series, No. 3

All Music Guide

Chris Woodstra, Vice President of Content Development
Stephen Thomas Erlewine, Senior Editor, Pop Music
John Bush, Senior Managing Editor, Pop Music

Pop Editors

Heather Phares, Associate Editor
Tim Sendra, Associate Editor

Marisa Brown
Alvin Campbell
Matt Collar
David Jeffries
Thom Jurek

Andy Kellman
Andrew Leahey
Steve Leggett
Jason Lymangrover
J. Scott McClintock

Gregory McIntosh
James Christopher Monger
Margaret Reges

Copy Editors

Jason Birchmeier
Ann Holter
David Lynch

Contributors

Greg Adams
Rick Anderson
Jason Ankeny
Rodney Batdorf
Jason Birchmeier
John Bush
Bryan Buss
Becky Byrkit
Al Campbell
James Chrispell
Rick Cohoon
Dan Cooper
Mike DeGagne
Mark Deming
Charlotte Dillon
Maria Konicki Dinoia
Robert L. Doerschuk
Bruce Eder
Stephen Thomas Erlewine
John Floyd
Megan Frye
Michael Gallucci
Daniel Gioffre

Shawn M. Haney
Brett Hartenbach
Alex Henderson
Hal Horowitz
Mark A. Humphrey
Vik Iyengar
Zac Johnson
Liana Jonas
Thom Jurek
Rudyard Kennedy
Cub Koda
Brad Kohlenstein
Jack Leaver
Steve Leggett
Johnny Loftus
James M. Manheim
Brian Mansfield
Stewart Mason
Michael McCall
Kelly McCartney
James Christopher Monger
Martin Monkman
Chris Nickson

Thom Owens
Roch Parisien
Jana Pendragon
Heather Phares
Lindsay Planer
j. poet
Larry Powell
Vince Ripol
Tom Roland
William Ruhlmann
K.A. Scott
Tim Sendra
Jeff Tamarkin
Mark Vanderhoff
Joe Viglione
Philip Van Vleck
Brian Wahlert
Jonathan Widran
Kurt Wolff
Deborah Wong
Jim Worbois
Ron Wynn

ALL MUSIC GUIDE REQUIRED LISTENING

CONTEMPORARY COUNTRY

Edited by

Chris Woodstra
John Bush
Stephen Thomas Erlewine

Backbeat
Books

An Imprint of Hal Leonard Corporation
New York

Published in 2008 by Backbeat Books
An Imprint of Hal Leonard Corporation
19 West 21st Street, New York, NY 10010

Printed in the United States of America

Book design by Snow Creative Services

Library of Congress Cataloging-in-Publication Data is available upon request.

All Media Guide has created the world's largest and most comprehensive information databases for music, videos, DVDs, and video games. With coverage of both in-print and out-of-print titles, the massive AMG archive includes reviews, plot synopses, biographies, ratings, images, titles, credits, essays, and thousands of descriptive categories. All content is original, written expressly for AMG by a worldwide network of professional staff and freelance writers specializing in music, movies, and games. The AMG databases—**All Music Guide®**, **All Movie Guide®**, and **All Game Guide™**—are licensed by major retailers, Internet sites, and other entertainment media providers and are available to the public through its websites (www.allmusic.com, www.allmovie.com, www.allgame.com) and through its published works: *All Music Guide, All Music Guide to Rock, All Music Guide to Country, All Music Guide to Jazz, All Music Guide to the Blues, All Music Guide to Electronica, All Music Guide to Soul, All Music Guide to Hip-Hop,* and *All Music Guide to Classical Music.*

All Media Guide, LLC, 1168 Oak Valley Drive, Ann Arbor, MI 48108
T: 734/887-5600. F: 734/827-2492
www.allmediaguide.com, www.allmusic.com, www.allgame.com

ISBN: 978-0-87930-918-3

www.backbeatbooks.com

CONTENTS

INTRODUCTION

It's not hard to argue that contemporary country is the Rodney Dangerfield of modern music: it gets no respect. Even among country fans, there are plenty of listeners who claim to only like the old stuff, since the new stuff doesn't sound like country. Or some listeners claim to like new stuff only if it's Americana—the rigidly rustic music that goes out of its way to sound traditional but never gets played on the radio, never really rubs shoulders with the big names of country music. Americana—or as it's sometimes called, alt-country—is a cult then, where contemporary country is the sound of the mainstream and, at its best, the pulse of America's heartland. Of course, any good popular (or populist) music by its very definition should be music for the masses, and if *any* music has ever been about a wide audience, it's country music. From way back before Hank Williams, country dealt with the concerns of the average man, just as it does today. If Big & Rich and Shania sound a bit different than Merle Haggard and Loretta Lynn, well, they didn't sound exactly like Hank, either.

Hag may not sound like Hank, but there is a definite connection from Hank to Merle, as there is from Merle to George Strait to Alan Jackson to Brad Paisley—a through line that keeps history as a vital part of country music while also keeping it contemporary, as the music subtly shifts its sounds and attitudes to match the times. The hits of Toby Keith may sound and feel different from the hits of Willie Nelson and Waylon Jennings, but they are certainly within the same tradition—both in their spirit and how they play to a vast audience. As a matter of fact, in the new millennium (and for the last decade of the 20th century, for that matter), no other pop music speaks to modern life in quite the same way as contemporary country. Sure, rap and rock may place a greater emphasis on explicit innovation, but they never talk about what it is to be a modern man or woman in America, and there are few corollaries to Tim McGraw's songs for working men or Shania Twain's reversing the role and asking for a cold one after a tough day at the office.

It's not just that contemporary country is about modern life, but it *sounds* like modern life in how it blurs the borders between genres. Contemporary country encompasses old-time rock & roll and classic arena-rock, the melodic craft of classic pop songwriting plus the slick radio-ready gloss of adult contemporary pop. It touches on folk and even hip-hop, all sounds that are commonplace in the nation, and blends them together, providing a lush representation of current America. As modern as it sounds, contemporary country is still rooted in traditional country, and some of its biggest stars are, at their core, traditionalists, whether they adhere closely to the sound and feel of the past, as do Alan Jackson and George Strait, or whether they play with history, as do Toby Keith and Brad Paisley.

With artists like these, there is as much variety within contemporary country as in any other kind of modern pop music, as *All Music Guide Required Listening: Contemporary Country* vividly illustrates. Within this book, we don't reach back any further than the founders of modern country: Alabama and George Strait, who helped push the modernist/traditionalist schools with their hits of the '80s and whose music still sounds contemporary, still informing the sound of the radio. We spend some time there, along with genre-bending mavericks like Dwight Yoakam and Lyle Lovett who successfully cut into the country charts in the late '80s. But where this book really kicks in is in the revolution of the early '90s, when Garth Brooks reshaped what country music sounds like, and how many records it could sell. After Garth's record-busting success, there was a flood of similar-sounding hat acts, but also came Shania Twain, who, along with her husband, Robert John Mutt Lange, gave country arena-rock flair that made it more pop than ever. Between Garth and Shania, country had firmly become the sound of mainstream America—particularly since rock abdicated any claims on the throne by retreating into niches, and adult contemporary pop played it too safe. Taken as a whole, contemporary country swung for the fences without alienating its broad audience—a tricky thing to do but often it was quite thrilling, as the music documented within this volume of All Music Guide Required Listening proves.

Not all the hit albums from the '90s and the new millennium are included between these covers. There are big albums that didn't make the cut, and, conversely, we've included some that should have been hits but weren't, for whatever reason. We've only concerned ourselves with the best of the breed. Sometimes, this means full-lengths from artists—including albums that might not be as strong from beginning to end (such as *Ropin' the Wind*, *Come On Over*, or *Shockin' Y'All*), but are still worth hearing. Other times, it means greatest hits albums because, after all, country music has always been driven by the hit single, the kind of hit that sounds good on an album, on a compilation, on a jukebox, on the radio, or on an MP3 player (and for help with your own MP3 players, see our playlists). Taken as a whole, the albums in this volume of All Music Guide Required Listening provide a comprehensive primer of contemporary country. If you already love the music, you'll discover plenty here, from infectious mega-hits to overlooked treasures. And if you have never given the genre a fair shake, this is the book that will introduce you to a music that is richer than you might think—and after flipping through this, you might even start to give contemporary country some well-earned respect.

ALL MUSIC GUIDE REQUIRED LISTENING

CONTEMPORARY COUNTRY

CONTEMPORARY COUNTRY ALBUM DIRECTORY

Trace Adkins

Dreamin' Out Loud
1996, Capitol

Trace Adkins' debut *Dreamin' Out Loud* illustrates that he does indeed have a powerhouse voice, one that's big and strong and capable of handling both honky tonk and ballads. It's a voice that makes singers into stars, and his producers must have realized this. Unfortunately, they wanted to ensure that Adkins became a star, so they gave *Dreamin' Out Loud* a production that's a little too clean and songs that are a little too predictable, when it's clear that he is capable of so much more. Even so, *Dreamin' Out Loud* remains a satisfying debut. Adkins sings his heart out on even the lesser songs, and when he does have a good number ("That's a Bad Way of Saying Goodbye," "There's a Girl in Texas"), he sounds like one of the finest new traditionalists of the late '90s.

Thom Owens

More . . .
November 1999, Capitol

More . . . is a very apt title for Trace Adkins' third album, since it essentially offers more of the same. For some artists, this would be a harsh criticism, but not in the case of Adkins, since he's proving himself to be one of the more reliable neo-traditionalists of the late '90s. Unlike some of his peers, Adkins doesn't pattern his singing after any of his idols; he absorbs his influences, creating his own distinctive sound that has elements of classic honky tonk as well as blues and rock. He sounds equally convincing on heartbreak songs ("Don't Lie"), rockers ("Can I Want Your Love," "More"), honky tonk ("I'm Gonna Love You Anyway," "I Can Dig It"), and Western swing ("All Hat, No Cattle"). *More . . .* may drag a little bit in the middle, but overall, it achieves a nice balance of performance and song, proving along the way that not only does Adkins have and individual voice, but that he's more purely country than many of his peers.

Stephen Thomas Erlewine

Greatest Hits Collection, Vol. 1
July 2003, Capitol

Released four albums and seven years into Trace Adkins' career, *Greatest Hits Collection, Vol. 1* summarizes the first part of his career quite nicely. During this time, he had 13 singles on the *Billboard* country charts—including the Top Ten hits "Every Light in the House," "I Left Something Turned On at Home," "The Rest of Mine," "More," "I'm Tryin'," and the number one "(This Ain't) No Thinkin' Thing"—and this contains all but one, the minor hit "I'm Gonna Love You Anyway." The other two cuts on this 14-track collection are new, and one—the sentimental "Then They Do," which finds Adkins watching his kids grow up—also went to number one, making this a good collection of Adkins at his best. He may not have been one of the flashiest country singers of the '90s, but thanks to his deep baritone, his music was sturdy and reliable, as is this fine collection.

Stephen Thomas Erlewine

Comin' on Strong
December 2003, Capitol

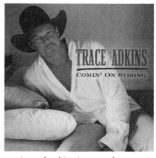

Trace Adkins had reached his mid-30s by the time his debut album, *Dreamin' Out Loud*, was released in 1996. By the time his fifth disc, *Comin' on Strong*, appeared in 2003, he was over 40. So, it is perhaps appropriate that the overall tone of the lyrics in the 11 songs written for him is one of romantic maturity. That starts with the leadoff track and first single, the up-tempo "Hot Mama," in which a husband reassures his wife that she remains attractive to him, even though she can no longer fit into the jeans she wore at 17. "Hot Mama" has a frisky appeal and, with its erotically charged tag line, "You wanna?" a novelty quality, as does the album's closer, "Rough & Ready," a tongue twister with a Western Swing flavor that details a particular type of country male's taste: "Cold beer/Hot wings/Wranglers/Skoal ring," and so on. The nine songs in between are the usual Nashville product, songs about love lost and found. Adkins' distinctive yet traditional baritone brings out the best in this material, whether leaning on the metaphor of the ballad "I'd Sure Hate to Break Down Here" or reflecting on the physical pleasure of "One of Those Nights." *Comin' on Strong* is at its best right at the beginning, and there isn't another song as impressive as "Hot Mama." But it's a sturdy collection of reasonably good country songs given effective interpretations by a veteran talent.

William Ruhlmann

Songs About Me
March 2005, EMI

It's not entirely a coincidence that Trace Adkins sounds like a streamlined Toby Keith on his sixth album, *Songs About Me*, since Keith was the biggest country star of the 2000s, or at least the biggest star who shares Adkins' low, deep voice and taste for traditional country. But it's not entirely fair to peg Adkins as a Keith wannabe, either, since Trace has been around as long as Toby, and has mined a similar neo-traditionalist vein for just as long. Still, *Songs About Me* has the self-conscious air of a Nashville studio product, one that's tailored to a specific sensibility and sound—one that's not far removed from either Adkins' previous work or Keith's current music, but still feels like it was made with the rough, ready, red-state mentality of the mid-2000s in mind. This sober professionalism has its drawbacks—everything from the production to the lyrics is a little too studied, and it can't help but pale in comparison to Keith's bawdy, robust redneck anthems—but it also has its advantages, particularly because Adkins is an assured, professional singer who can sell this material even when it's at its most generic.

That he can't quite make it transcend the generic is nothing to fault him for—if he had better songs, a livelier setting, or a looser production, he might have been able to make this take off—and even if *Songs About Me* isn't much more than a solid piece of craftsmanship, it's quite enjoyable at that level.

Stephen Thomas Erlewine

Alabama

Feels So Right
1981, RCA

On Alabama's second album, *Feels So Right*, you can hear the band becoming comfortable with their sound and finding their niche. Unlike their first release, *My Home's in Alabama*, they don't sound like they're testing out various tempos, selections, and styles. This session has a flowing consistency which resulted in three hit singles: the mellow pop of "Feels So Right" and "Love in the First Degree," along with traditional country on "Old Flame."

Al Campbell

Mountain Music
1982, RCA

On their third album, 1982's *Mountain Music*, Alabama hit their stride, streamlining the rough edges out of their sound and turning into a well-oiled hit machine. Here, when they stretch out it's on the nearly seven-minute "Changes Comin' On," which doesn't jam like Southern rock but instead has a smooth groove that veers close to soft rock. Of course, that soft rock quality was not only a large reason why Alabama crossed over to the pop charts ("Take Me Down," one of three number one country singles here—the other two being the anthemic title cut and "Close Enough to Perfect"— crossed over into the pop Top 20, which is no small feat), it was also instrumental in defining the group's own brand of "mountain music." If their country music didn't sound too down-home—it didn't twang, it didn't have mandolins, it was built on electric guitars—it was nevertheless pure country in its own modern way, borrowing on Western mythos ("Words at Twenty Paces" has an implied swagger, even if it is never menacing) and early Americana-rock (a strong cover of Creedence Clearwater Revival's "Green River"), playing up both sentiment (both the slow devotional "You Turn Me On" and the family celebration "Never Be One") and revelry ("Gonna Have a Party") to create the template for contemporary country. If there's just a touch too much of the slow stuff here, it's all expertly executed and almost all the songs click, with the best (all the aforementioned tracks, minus "Never Be One") standing among the band's best material, helping to make *Mountain Music* not only one of their best albums, but a record that—despite its big, slick production—still sounds like modern country even decades after its initial release.

Stephen Thomas Erlewine

The Closer You Get . . .
1983, RCA

On their fourth album *The Closer You Get*, Alabama gets further away from the country roots and down-home charm responsible for their incredible chart success. One may be surprised at the unusual number of ballads, but popular country in the early '80s, in hindsight, seems more suited to adult easy listening than country with the popularity of Kenny Rogers, Crystal Gayle, and Dolly Parton. The songwriting is strong, and the vocal harmonies still blend unlike any other country band—in fact, the members of Alabama trade lead vocal roles throughout the album. However, this album suffers from glossy production and the use of synthesizers. The use of a drum machine on the opening title track is nearly unforgivable, and the arrangement distracts the listener from an otherwise good song. However, Alabama shines when they use more traditional country arrangements. Upbeat songs like "Red River" and "Dixieland Delight" are great additions to their catalog and demonstrate how they became one of country's most successful groups. This is not the place to start, but most fans should eventually own this album.

Vik Iyengar

40 Hour Week
1985, RCA

Opening with the driving title track, *40 Hour Week* encapsulates why Alabama was the top country group of the '80s. Alternating between restrained rockers and well-crafted ballads, it captures the band at its peak. Nevertheless, it isn't quite as strong as their first albums—the performances and production are a bit too mannered—but its professionalism is appealing. And that professionalism made *40 Hour Week* the group's most popular album, as it crossed over into the pop Top Ten.

Stephen Thomas Erlewine

The Essential Alabama
May 2005, RCA

RCA/Legacy's 2005 double-disc release *Essential Alabama* should not be confused with RCA's 1998 single-disc release *The Essential Alabama*, which may have had the same title but boasted a different track listing. However, the 2005 *Essential Alabama* should be confused with the 1998 double-disc set *For the Record: 41 Number One Hits*, since it has the same track listing as that album. At least the back cover of *Essential* acknowledges that it was "formerly available" as *For the Record*, so most fans will likely not be duped into buying the same album a second time. For the rest of us, *Essential Alabama* keeps everything good about *For the Record: 41 Number One Hits* and eliminates its one flaw: the misleading subtitle that claimed all of the songs on the album hit number one, which was not true (it also implied that the album had 41 songs when it really had 44). This means that *Essential Alabama* is now the definitive Alabama collection, containing every one of their big hits—including such contemporary classics as "Tennessee River," "Mountain Music," "The Closer You Get," "Forty Hour Week (For a Livin')," "Jukebox on My Mind," and "Down Home"—in one concise, entertaining package.

Stephen Thomas Erlewine

Livin' Lovin' Rockin' Rollin': The 25th Anniversary Collection
January 2006, RLG Legacy

There have been plenty of Alabama compilations over the years, ranging from a surplus of budget-line quickies to the excellent double-disc *For the Record*, which was reissued in 2005 under the title *The Essential Alabama*. Despite this, there has never been a career-spanning box set until RCA/ Legacy's 2006 *Livin' Lovin' Rockin' Rollin': The 25th Anniversary Collection*, which tells the group's tale over the course of 51 songs and three discs. If you're counting, you'll notice that this is only seven songs more than *For the Record/ Essential*, which isn't a whole lot to justify an expansion to a triple-disc set, but *Livin' Lovin' Rockin' Rollin'* has a very different feel than that comp, which is the gold standard in Alabama hits albums. While there is certainly a fair share of overlap in song selection, this isn't precisely a collection of hits. As a matter of fact, huge hits like "The Closer You Get" are missing entirely, which makes this set of less interest to casual fans looking to get all the big hits in one place. Those fans should stick with *For the Record/Essential*, since this is intended as an aural biography of a band. Sure, most of the hits are here, but sometime they're present in live versions or alternate takes, and they're supported by album tracks, along with eight previously unreleased cuts (which are mostly live recordings). This provides for a good overview of the group's history, even if it's not as smooth a listen as the double-disc set, primarily due to the fact that the live tracks don't sit easily next to the studio sides. That said, for the serious Alabama fan looking for a trip down memory lane, *Livin' Lovin' Rockin' Rollin'* is a good bet, since it does provide a thorough chronicle of the band's history, complete with a time line and rare photos in the liner notes. Less dedicated fans may prefer the concise, hit-filled nature of *For the Record/Essential*, but this will suit the tastes of the converted just fine.

Stephen Thomas Erlewine

Gary Allan

Smoke Rings in the Dark
October 1999, MCA

Gary Allan grows better and more assured with each album, and his third record, *Smoke Rings in the Dark*, is his best effort yet. Similar to the Mavericks, Allan stylishly blends a number of roots styles, from his signature Bakersfield country to dusty folk and pop crooning, into a neo-traditionalist sound that is curiously out of time. Allan is considerably more mainstream than the Mavericks, which means that the production is more polished and he doesn't really take musical risks. Even if he doesn't quite hold his own against some Americana artists, he certainly is stronger than many contemporary country artists, especially since he tries many different styles and sounds throughout *Smoke Rings in the Dark*. Not every song works, but even those that don't have still something recommendable in their performance or production. It's a fine album from an artist that keeps getting better.

Stephen Thomas Erlewine

Tough All Over
October 2005, MCA Nashville

Gary Allan has been all over the country map since he began recording in 1996. He's made slick Nash Vegas records, hard honky tonk records, and ballad records. With *Tough All Over*, he's made enough of a mark that he gets to release the album he's wanted to make all along. Evidence is in the title cut, which opens the set. Written by Odie Blackmon and Jim Lauderdale, it's a hard roots rocker in the vein of the Blasters' more adventurous moments, with edgy electric guitars, hard, clipped snare drums, a harmonica, and even a Hammond B-3. Yeah, there's a fiddle here, but it's hardly of consequence. This is rock & roll complete with shaking tambourines. "Just Got Back from Hell," driven simply by a National Steel before the guitars start to roar and the pedal steel and B-3 start to whine and whinny, is a gorgeous country song that keeps its focus on tradition while looking toward the future. The shape-shifting early '60s rock at the heart of "Ring" (written by Kostas) wouldn't be out of place on an Everly Brothers or Del Shannon record had they used a pedal steel to carry the backdrop of the tune. The Fender Telecaster is trebly and raw and stands in sharp contrast to the slick on-the-spot vocals. But that's not to say that Allan has abandoned the ballads that have made his name—far from it. "Promises Broken," "Life Ain't Always Beautiful," and "What Kind of Fool," with its finger-plucked single banjo line, are tight, full of emotion and romantic pathos. But it's the rockers, which also include the 21st century rockabilly of "Nick Jack Caver" and the roiling, guitar-wailing, Southern rock-driven "He Can't Quit Her," that hold the most attention. The album's closer, "Putting My Misery on Display," begins simply as a ballad and becomes a rock power ballad. Whether the public will receive Allan's offering is another question, but musically and artistically, it's the most consistent—yet slick—record he's ever done.

Thom Jurek

Greatest Hits
March 2007, MCA Nashville

Gary Allan's *Greatest Hits*, released in 2007 by MCA Nashville, compiles 15 key songs from his back catalog. Most of the inclusions were bona fide hits, including a pair of number ones: "Tough Little Boys" and "Nothing on But the Radio." There are also two new songs, one of which, "A Feelin' Like That," was a number 17 chart hit at the time of the album's release. *Greatest Hits* thankfully includes only a song apiece from Allan's first two albums, *Used Heart for Sale* (1996) and *It Would Be You* (1998), which were released by Decca and are minor works in his discography. This leaves plenty of space on *Greatest Hits* for Allan's subsequent, notably better work for MCA: *Smoke Rings in the Dark* (1999), *Alright Guy* (2001), *See If I Care* (2003), and *Tough All Over* (2005). Each of these latter albums includes songs not included here that are worth hearing. Fans consequently will want to check out those MCA albums in full. As for casual fans who just want the radio hits without any filler, *Greatest Hits* has almost all of them and is an economical choice. Plus, it has "A Feelin' Like That," which can't be found elsewhere. Taken as a whole, *Greatest Hits* showcases Allan's accomplishments to date, which, with the exception of his early albums for Decca, are fairly impressive. He's carved out a respectable place for himself among contemporary country males.

Jason Birchmeier

John Anderson

John Anderson 2
1981, Warner Bros.

His second album (obviously), this traditionally minded package contrasted with the bulk of the material released in the same *Urban Cowboy*-influenced time period. His cover of Lefty Frizzell's "I Love You a Thousand Ways" shows his roots nicely, and "I'm Just an Old Chunk of Coal (But I'm Gonna Be a Diamond Someday)" is simply classic.

Tom Roland

Wild & Blue
1982, Warner Bros.

The occasional use of strings in this album was probably master-minded by former Don Law protege Frank Jones, who co-produced it. Twin fiddles and steel guitar dominate, though, especially in a remake of Ferlin Husky's "The Waltz You Saved for Me," featuring Emmylou Harris. It includes "Swingin'" and a new version of Lefty Frizzell's "Long Black Veil"—the very last track recorded in the legendary Columbia Studio B.

Tom Roland

Seminole Wind
1992, RCA

As his comeback, John Anderson didn't just stumble upon a couple of hit singles, he produced a solid album, full of twangy rubble raisers and moving, yearning ballads. Including the number one hit "Straight Tequila Night," the environment-inspired title cut, and the tender, pleading "Let Go of the Stone," this album catapulted Anderson back to the forefront of country music. Of course, he wasn't just riding the crest of new country; he was harking back to its more traditional roots. But while able to bridge the gap between old and new, he also demonstrates his ability to meld the two as he mourns the poppification of country in "Look Away" and then turns around and puts a honky tonk spin on the Tina Turner cut "Steamy Windows." Being able to be faithful to both while fluidly combining them is true artistry and testament to his voice, his material, and his arrangements. This is contemporary country at top form.

Bryan Buss

Solid Ground
June 1993, BNA

Solid Ground is a fitting title for this album, as John Anderson was surely in his stride when he recorded this follow-up to his comeback, *Seminole Wind*. Anderson's strongest point is that he comes across as an honest-to-God good ol' boy—which many posers of contemporary country only claim to be—and nowhere is this more evident than on the first track, "Money in the Bank." He turns the thankful tune into gold with his trademark twang, then turns right around and nails

an ode to regret for what his success has cost him on "I Wish I Could Have Been There." Though there aren't any tracks as immediately accessible as "Straight Tequila Night," "Let Go of the Stone," "Look Away," or the title track, the cuts on this album are more assured, finding Anderson maturing as both a vocalist and a producer. Though he co-wrote only four of the ten tracks, he owns all of them, making this a classic country album of the early '90s.

Bryan Buss

Anthology
October 2002, Audium

This is an excellent two-disc compilation of John Anderson's Warner Bros. recordings. These 30 tracks consist of all the radio favorites, including "I'm Just an Old Chunk of Coal," "1959," "Straight Tequila Night," "Black Sheep," and the huge country/pop crossover tune from 1982, "Swingin'." Also featured are several cuts that received radio attention but weren't officially "hits," like Mark Knopfler's "When It Comes to You" and Anderson's "Seminole Wind."

Al Campbell

Easy Money
May 2007, Warner Bros./Raybaw

Like many veteran country stars, John Anderson didn't retire so much as fade from the spotlight as his new records slowly started to sell less and less. After an early '80s peak, his hits started to dry up after the mid-'90s and while he continued to work, cutting records and playing shows, he slowly fell off of Nashville's radar. Cut to the middle of the 2000s, when Big & Rich were major players in the Music City, and their key songwriter, John Rich, approached Anderson with the offer of producing and collaborating on a new record. Anderson accepted and the resulting album, *Easy Money*, saw the singer returning to his first major label, Warner, and a homecoming in another sense, too, because it's the biggest, boldest, and best record he's made in a long, long time. Some of this is surely due to Rich, but not because he's the driving force on the album. Yes, he collaborates but he doesn't force his personality on Anderson; instead, he gives Anderson room to be himself, letting the singer veer from wry humor to sentiment. Humor is a crucial part to Anderson's music, and it makes a welcome return here, which is why *Easy Money* is quite a bit different than Anderson's recent comebacks. It's easy to forget that in 2001 he released a big record, *Nobody's Got It All*, on Columbia, produced by Blake Chancey and Paul Worley, the team responsible for the Dixie Chicks' breakthrough hit, and that Keith Stegall helmed 1997's *Takin' the Country Back*, so *Easy Money* isn't his first big-budget, high-profile comeback, but it is the best because Rich really understands Anderson. There may be a moment or two when the album gets a little too close to the gargantuan gonzo country of Big & Rich's Muzik Mafia for comfort—"Funky Country" suits the duo, or perhaps their protégée Cowboy Troy better than it does Anderson—but they're fleeting moments that nevertheless fall within Anderson's comfort zone, so he pulls it off with ease. Most of *Easy Money* feels natural and unforced, whether Anderson is singing the barroom weeper "Something to Drink About," the riotous George Jones tribute "Brown Liquor," or the lovely "You Already Know My Love." This gives the music a richness that separates it from his admirable, but occasionally stilted, recent records, and this is due to both the expertly chosen material and Anderson's re-emergence as a writer here. Just over half the record was co-written by Anderson—along with such collaborators as Rich, Shannon Lawson, and Cowboy Troy, who reveals a previously unheard sensitivity on "Bonnie Blue"—and his songs stand proudly alongside such standards as "Swingin'" and "Seminole Wind," boasting the same kind of subtle craft; these are songs that are so laid back and enjoyable, it's easy to take for granted just how well-written they are. The same could be said for *Easy Money* as a whole—Anderson makes it all look so easy here that it's hard to believe that he hasn't made a record this good in years, but he hasn't since at least the early '90s, possibly the early '80s.

Stephen Thomas Erlewine

Jessica Andrews

Heart Shaped World
March 1999, DreamWorks

When a 15-year-old Jessica Andrews debuted with *Heart Shaped World*, the most obvious comparison was LeAnn Rimes. The parallels were certainly there—like Rimes, Andrews was a teenage country-pop singer with a wholesome, clean-cut, all-American girl image and the usual Nashville hype to go with her debut. But like Rimes, Andrews had some talent, charisma, and substance to go with the hype. Though *Heart Shaped World* isn't brilliant, the Tennessee native usually has decent material to work with. No one's going to mistake this CD for hardcore, Bakersfield honky tonk—like Rimes and Shania Twain, Andrews specializes in a sleek, commercial blend of pop, country, and rock. But as much sweetness as she projects, Andrews isn't bubblegum—when she digs into "You Go First," "I've Been Waiting for You," and "James Dean in Tennessee," you know that the singer isn't without an edge. And on Billy Burnette's ominous, bluesy "Hungry Love"—the tale of a girl who has to grow up much too fast—it's clear that Andrews is capable of depth. A few of the tunes are bland, but *Heart Shaped World*'s best moments indicate that Andrews is someone to keep an eye on.

Alex Henderson

Who I Am
February 2001, DreamWorks

Jessica Andrews delivers an impressive sophomore album. Upon first listen, it's easy to recognize her very maturing talent. Her vocals are strong and convincing, her songs are snappy and infectious, and there's little sign of her being just 17 years of age. Producer for the second time around, Byron Gallimore (Jo Dee Messina, Tim McGraw) says "age is never an issue with her because of the depth in her voice." Truer words were never spoken. Everything from vocal delivery to production redefines what she gave listeners on 1999's *Heart-Shaped World*. Andrews' appealing new confidence comes through in just about all of the album's 12 songs, but the title track "Who I Am," "Every Time," "These Wings," and the vivacious "Never Had It So Good" make it worth setting the CD player for continuous play.

Maria Konicki Dinoia

Now
April 2003, DreamWorks

Facing 20, Jessica Andrews decides to open her music on her third album, *Now*. Her hold to country was always a little tentative, particularly because it seemed like she was signed partially because she was a teenage girl who could really sing during the height of LeAnn Rimes' popularity. Like Rimes, Andrews wants to leave strict country behind as she leaves her adolescence, but unlike LeAnn, Jessica sounds in control, having a clear idea of who she is musically and where she wants to go. *Now* is grounded in country, along with other American roots music, but it's held together with an inclusive pop sensibility and a polished, professional production that nevertheless retains its identity and keeps the focus on Andrews, whose voice sounds stronger and better than ever. If initial comparisons to Rimes did not fall to her favor, she now sounds more versatile and assured than her peer, but she goes even further with *Now*, crafting an album that straddles the country-pop and adult-pop line as alluringly as the best of Faith Hill, whose *Cry* pales in comparison to this record. Why? Because this is never stifled by diva ambitions. Because this has up-tempo and mid-tempo songs with character and color, along with catchy hooks. Because the ballads, while slick, still have substance. Ultimately, because Andrews is a hell of singer, finding her own distinctive voice and coming into her own, somewhere between Faith Hill and Sheryl Crow. If the production ever so slightly is a little too mature, a little older than her years, it's only appropriate because her voice sounds older than her years. But even if this does have an adult-pop bent, it's still done better than nearly any other adult-pop in 2003, and the times that *Now* does loosen up offer tantalizing possibilities of where Andrews could go next. And, no matter which way you cut it, as of this writing *Now* is one of the best mainstream pop albums of 2003, with only Kelly Clarkson's *Thankful* rivaling it in consistency and quality.

Stephen Thomas Erlewine

David Ball

Thinkin' Problem
1994, Warner Bros.

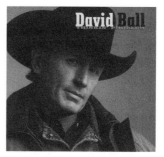

This hard country album has a cerebral twist, as the title song suggests. David Ball, 41 when this album came out, had a craggy Texas face and a voice to match. When he has material to match, such as with "Thinkin' Problem" or the ballad "When the Thought of You Catches up with Me," he's the kind of singer neo-traditionalist country fans dream about.

Brian Mansfield

Starlite Lounge
June 1996, Warner Bros.

Starlite Lounge is another set of gritty, contemporary honky tonk from David Ball, highlighted by his gutsy vocals and no-holds-barred approach. Ball doesn't treat honky tonk as a museum piece, but he has respect for its roots, as well—he just tears through the songs with energy and conviction, which means *Starlite Lounge* is simply an invigorating listen.

Thom Owens

Super Hits
July 2000, Warner Bros.

Country singer David Ball was born in South Carolina. While still in school he learned to play the guitar, tried his hand at songwriting, started his own band, and began performing regularly. A few years later he moved to Texas and formed a new group, Uncle Walt's Band. After a couple of albums, Ball got the chance to go solo in 1994 with a self-titled offering that went gold. Three other full-length recordings followed during the '90s. It's from these that the tunes for *Super Hits* were selected. This best-of collection carries fan favorites like "Watching My Baby Not Coming Back," "Thinkin' Problem," "When the Thought of You Catches up With Me," and "Look What Followed Me Home." All are songs that Ball either wrote or co-wrote. David Ball's music is country, even honky tonk and touching ballads, but many of his tunes are full of rock and pop flavor, paced out with snare drums and electric guitar. The mixture has been a successful one and gives him a chance to reach country music lovers from different generations.

Charlotte Dillon

Amigo
2001, Dual Tone

When honky tonk singer/songwriter David Ball took country programmers (and hence country listeners) by surprise back in the late '90s—because unless the country programmers (Nash Vegas' fascist culture police) can unplug their payola-ed ears long enough for something to penetrate, no one *ever* gets to hear anything new—with "Thinkin' Problem," and got himself nominated for every single award a new artist can, he's since dropped off the screen. Why? *Amigo* may provide an answer. Rather than follow up his hit with another track just like it and an album full of them, which is what the majors and country programming geeks want, Ball stayed true to his muse and his own idea of what country music was supposed to be. As a result, *Amigo* is the finest record he's ever done and the one least likely to get him anywhere out of Nash Vegas in terms of radio. However, the alterna-country fans out there, and that guy Michael Elta who runs BikerBar Internet Radio, should get hip to him. If they did, Ball's record might get the hearing it truly deserves. This is real country music, full of honky tonk memories, easy Western swing blues, and tough, lean-hearted stories peopled with broken heroes, shattered love affairs, and the determination to never give up in the face of defeat. And what's weird, there isn't anything on this album that isn't "commercial" enough to connect with people if they ever had the opportunity to hear it. OK, enough of the manifesto—the songs on *Amigo* are stellar. There's the opening title track (written with country giant Kostas) with its fiddle lines, steel guitar wranglings, and slippery horns. Then there's the awesome "She Always Talked About Mexico," with its killer Buck Owens' melody and mariachi band backing. And then there's the solid Merle Haggard/Bob Wills-ish shimmy of "Swing Baby," one of the finest party songs of the last ten years with a gorgeous Andrews Sisters-styled chorus in the background. And as far as badass old Texas tunes, there's "New Shiner Polka," with the accordion blaring and the pedal steel whipping up a storm of atmosphere on an instrumental break in the midst of the carousing, heartbreak, and regret that is *Amigo*. There

isn't a weak moment here, as Ball has given listeners one of the purest, most solid, and most accessible (largely because of his gorgeous, mellifluous tenor) country & *western* records in over a decade. And, as much as one might love the Hag, this disc blows his *If I Could Only Fly* away.

Thom Jurek

Mandy Barnett

Mandy Barnett
1996, Elektra

Tennessee native Mandy Barnett had already been busy bringing Patsy Cline back to life by playing (and singing the songs of) the rowdy, legendary vocalist in the stage production *Always . . . Patsy Cline*. Then Barnett, not yet even 21 years old, took that experience and used it to power her self-titled debut album for Asylum Records. Cline's influence is out front on Barnett's handling of Willie Nelson's 1962 classic "Three Days" and the brand-new Kostas/Richard Bennett song "I'll Just Pretend." The downside of Barnett's album is that the production tends toward clean and safe territory (such as the overabundance of strings on the syrupy "Rainy Days"). The upside is that, even during her album's most middle-of-the-road moments, Barnett's voice remains strong, smooth, and confident. And a few of the songs shine with real promise—Barnett's delicate handling of Jim Lauderdale's "Planet of Love," for example, and the traditional "Wayfaring Stranger," which closes the album on a comfortable, unhurried note.

Kurt Wolff

I've Got a Right to Cry
April 1999, Sire

If ever there was a singer who was born to sing the torch and twang style that Patsy Cline created, it is Mandy Barnett. A soft-spoken performer who belts 'em out with all the guts and grit of the founding mothers of traditional country mu-

sic, Barnett is amazing. Producer Owen Bradley, a legend himself, is known for his classic production style for country music's true stars like Cline, Bill Monroe, Ernest Tubb, and Brenda Lee. Working at his studio, Barnett was given the kind of support an artist of her caliber deserves. However, Owen Bradley passed away suddenly during the course of production, leaving the project unfinished. Barnett, along with Owen's brother and longtime partner, Harold, as well as Harold's son, Bobby, forged ahead; the result is a lasting and honorable tribute to Owen Bradley's distinguished career, as well as the harbinger of a great career about to blossom. Songs as traditional as the title cut and jazz-infused as "Who" show off Barnett's talents. Able to rip and roar with the boys, Barnett distinguishes herself on the pure honky tonk of "Trademark" while being very cool as she performs "Falling, Falling, Falling." Barnett pays homage to Cline on "Mistakes" and swings hard on "Don't Forget to Cry." A remarkable feat in the face of Owen Bradley's passing, Mandy

Barnett is most certainly one of the few women recording as a country artist who can actually sing country music. She does so with flair and with a sense of history, while still being firmly grounded in who she is and the music she wants to make. *I've Got a Right to Cry* is lush and breathtaking, fulfilling the promise of the country & western genre and providing the listener great satisfaction.

Jana Pendragon

Jeff Bates

Rainbow Man
May 2003, RCA

I have no idea if Nashville is looking for a Barry White to call their own, but judging from his debut album, it seems as if Jeff Bates wants to be the new multiracial love man of country music. *Rainbow Man* features a five-song stretch of romantic tunes in which Bates does his best to put some vocal moves on the lady in his life; and he even sinks into a deep-voiced spoken-word routine on "Long, Slow Kisses" in which he explains the details of the seduction ritual he has planned for the evening (Mr. Love Unlimited himself would probably approve). As background music for that "special night" at home, at very least this album beats Toby Keith's body of work; and while songs like "My Inlaws Are Outlaws" and "Country Enough" are by-the-numbers modern country radio fodder, at least "Rainbow Man" (in which he explains and celebrates his diverse ethnic heritage) and "My Mississippi" boast a personal touch that puts Bates a notch or so above most of his competition. While the slick-as-Teflon production and Bates' overly wavering voice don't flatter this material, at least on *Rainbow Man* Jeff Bates shoots for something slightly to the left of Nashville's radar, a direction he'll hopefully pursue with more vigor on his second album.

Mark Deming

Dierks Bentley

Dierks Bentley
August 2003, Capitol

There is apparently no limit to the number of *Opry*-friendly, down-home, good-looking crooners that Nashville can wrap in jeans and put forth in any given year. Like most of these, Dierks Bentley seems amiable enough, and, on this debut album, he makes each required stop on the stardom trail: rascally, boot-scoot humor ("Bartenders, Etc."), gauzy nostalgia ("My Last Name"), honky tonk swagger ("I Bought the Shoes"), boozy self-pity ("Whiskey Tears"), goofy outtake endings ("How Am I Doin'"), and, in "Distant Shore," an actually fairly complex purée of romantic revenge, poetic intoxication, and Biblical allusion. Aside from strident patriotism, which somehow slipped through the net, that pretty much

covers all the bases. Bentley pulls it all off with a rawboned delivery that skims the surface of the genre without leaving a ripple of individualism in its wake. The last number, "Train Traveling," provides an unexpected jolt by pairing Bentley with the Del McCoury Band, whose intensity is evident from the artful accelerando that kicks off the song. But on every other track, Bentley is backed by competent and undistinguished players who know how to breeze through songs that value the deft lick and clever wordplay more than suggestions of depth or insight. This young singer clearly deserves whatever success he achieves for making all the right moves and offending no one aside from the odd disgruntled critic.

Robert L. Doerschuk

Modern Day Drifter
May 2005, Capitol

There's little question that Dierks Bentley has good taste, as well as a burning desire to be part of the tradition of rough, rugged, and sensitive hard country singers. In particular, he styles himself after Merle and Waylon, two influences that were apparent on his eponymous 2003 debut but come to the forefront on his 2005 follow-up, *Modern Day Drifter*. Even the title of the record signals Bentley's intention to be a ramblin' man for the 2000s, and the music consciously echoes not just the past, but ramblin' man classics—the first single, "Lot of Leavin' Left to Do," is styled after Waylon's "This Time," and "Good Man Like Me" deliberately mimics Hank Snow's "I'm Movin' On." This isn't a drag on the record—if anything slows it down, it's the occasional too-tasteful ballad, as well as such cloying, product placement-filled stabs at contemporary country as "Cab of My Truck"—because Bentley has a nice, strong country croon and delivers this straight-ahead neo-traditionalist sound pleasantly and earnestly. He doesn't have much flair, though, as either a singer or writer. Instead of being a true ramblin' man and forging his own direction, he follows the path that Merle and Waylon created, never stamping it with much of his own personality. This makes for some good music, of course, but it's a bit of a mixed blessing that Bentley is at his best when he's following the blueprint of his heroes to a tee. Next time around, maybe he can draw inspiration from the spirit of his idols and put his own unmistakable personal stamp on his music instead of just crafting his record to sound like something they might have recorded.

Stephen Thomas Erlewine

Long Trip Alone
October 2006, EMI

It's a sign of Dierks Bentley's increasing stardom and clout that he has a writing credit on all 11 songs on his third album, 2006's *Long Trip Alone*. Not every country singer/songwriter gets a chance to do that, but not every singer/songwriter scores a bona fide hit with his sophomore set, and Bentley's 2005 *Modern Day Drifter* was that, reaching the top of the *Billboard* country charts and spawning several hits, including the number one "Settle for a Slowdown." Such success allows an artist to set his own pace, at least a little bit, and Bentley was already showing signs of being a headstrong troubadour on *Modern Day Drifter*, consciously referring—both lyrically and musically—to such classic country mavericks as Waylon Jennings and Merle Haggard throughout the record. Given these deliberate allusions to such musical rebels, it would made some sense if Bentley followed their path and crafted a third album that was tougher, wilder, rougher than his breakthrough, but *Long Trip Alone* isn't that at all: it's a slick, streamlined version of his hit album. Keep in mind that slick and streamlined aren't the same thing as soulless; rather, the polish of *Long Trip Alone* is a sign of Bentley's increased confidence and professionalism, and how he wants to stay at the top now that he's gotten there. As such, the album is so clean it sparkles—all the better for it to fit into mainstream country radio—but beneath that sheen, Bentley remains a little restless, even risky. He'll bring the Grascals to play on "Prodigal Son's Prayer," letting them steer the duet toward their bluegrass roots; he'll explain that "The Heaven I'm Headed To" has a place for both priests and prostitutes; and he'll play tribute to his honky tonk beginnings, on "Band of Brothers," which isn't only a musical tip of the hat to hardcore country, but also a sly salute to his fellow road-warriors. But the main impression of *Long Trip Alone* isn't that restlessness; it's how Bentley can come across as a entirely mainstream country act without losing his sense of self. He's a savvy songwriter, particularly when he's slyly incorporating elements of rock or pop into his country (check out the anthemic opening of "Trying to Stop Your Leaving" for the former, "Free and Easy (Down the Road I Go)" for the latter), managing to be commercial without being crass, coming across as sentimental, not saccharine, on his earnest ballads. At times, it seems like he could use a little bit more heft or grit in his voice, yet his simple, straight-ahead singing enhances his Everyman qualities and helps make him and his music all the more likeable. Perhaps *Long Trip Alone* may disappoint fans who were looking for his next album to be an unapologetic hard country record, but in a way, this is more interesting: Dierks Bentley has kept that spirit and put it within the confines of mainstream country, resulting in one of the livelier and better country records of 2006 and one that proves he is indeed a major talent.

Stephen Thomas Erlewine

Matraca Berg

Sunday Morning to Saturday Night
September 1997, Rising Tide

After spending several years fighting with RCA over how they should market her, Matraca Berg left the label and signed with the emerging indie Rising Tide. Her first effort for the label, *Sunday Morning to Saturday Night*, rivals her previous masterwork, *Lying to the Moon*. Between her debut and *Sunday Morning*, she had immense success as a songwriter, penning such hits as "Strawberry Wine" for the likes of Deana Carter. During that time, however, RCA was more concerned in trying to

make Berg fit into conventional contemporary country musical styles, when her eclecticism is a large part of what makes her special. Rising Tide fortunately gave her an opportunity to reclaim that exciting eclecticism with *Sunday Morning to Saturday Night*. Nearly every song on the record either sparkles with wit or is impeccably observed and affecting. Similarly, the music is fresh and alive, ranging from hard-rocking honky tonk to country-folk to country-rock to moving ballads. It's a terrific, individual album that fully captures everything Berg is capable of achieving.

Thom Owens

Lying to the Moon & Other Stories
August 1999, RCA

Joe Galante at RCA was the moving force behind this re-issue of Berg's splendid RCA debut album "Lying to the Moon," recorded in 1990. Berg has added several new tunes to the original tracks, resulting in a sort of hybrid re-release that recalls old favorites while introducing some outstanding new material. Berg is one of the premier tunesmiths in Nashville, having authored hits for the likes of Deana Carter, Reba McEntire, Pam Tillis, and Suzy Bogguss. Berg is, however, quite capable of delivering her own material in a convincing fashion. As the listener will hear, these aren't just cool tunes; they're cool tunes performed by a pretty cool singer. Special moments include the elemental blues of "I Got It Bad," the melancholy, mountain soul of "Appalachian Rain," the marvelous rollercoaster metaphor of "Along for the Ride," the witty, easy-going groove of "Eat at Joe's," and the sexual semantics of "Back in the Saddle." This is a welcome reincarnation of an excellent album from an artist whose level of talent is way beyond her level of recognition.

Philip Van Vleck

John Berry

Wildest Dreams
September 1999, Hollywood

Listeners won't be able to notice it in the vocals on this 1999 album, *Wildest Dreams*, but only a short year before this recording was made, award-winning artist John Berry was facing one of the most horrible waking nightmares a singer can—the urgent need for throat surgery. If this offering is the end result, then he came through the operation in fine form. The songs on *Wildest Dreams* can lean a little more toward soft pop and rock than country at times. This includes a lot of guitar action on some numbers, but Berry's tenor voice is a powerful match. Both country and pop fans will find plenty to like here with tracks like "Rivers in the Clouds," "Love Is for Giving," "You'll Be in My Heart," "Where Would I Be," and "Salvation."

Charlotte Dillon

Big & Rich

Horse of a Different Color
May 2004, Warner Bros.

Like many professional country musicians, the duo of Big & Rich—Big being Kenny Alphin, while Rich is John Rich, a former singer for Lonestar—are based in Nashville, but that doesn't mean they follow all the conventions of Music

City. In fact, they throw conventions out the window on their 2004 debut album, *Horse of a Different Color*. They can certainly craft a kicking country song, as the backwoods ballad "Deadwood Mountain" proves, but they don't settle for that, preferring to spike predictable song structures with considerable doses of goofy humor or, better still, to fly beyond genre and concoct gonzo amalgams of country, arena rock, and rap. All of this makes Big & Rich hard to peg, particularly because they come across as a big-boned, country variation of Tenacious D or Ween—talented musical pranksters who treat everything as a lark, but have the musical skills to back up their boasts. Like the D, they even have a theme song in "Rollin' (The Ballad of Big & Rich)"—which bizarrely enough sounds a bit like Tenacious D, which isn't nearly as bizarre as how the melody of "Wild West Show" recalls Nirvana's "Frances Farmer Will Have Her Revenge on Seattle"—and they have no compunctions about being flat-out silly, which is good, since that silliness brought them a big novelty hit in "Save a Horse (Ride a Cowboy)," a song designed for drunken shout-alongs in sports bars. Much of *Horse of a Different Color* plays to that audience, but the surprise is that the rowdiness is tongue-in-cheek and that Big & Rich are musically clever, filling the record with big hooks and unbridled weirdness. Not that all of this is successful—it can sound too goofy at points—but it's wilder and stranger than most contemporary country albums of 2004, and a whole lot more fun, to boot.

Stephen Thomas Erlewine

Comin' to Your City
November 2005, Warner Bros.

At the end of a year where Big & Rich seemingly had a hand in every other record coming out of Nashville—and when their past was dredged up in the form of Big Kenny's ignored 1999 album *Live a Little*—the gonzo country duo unleashed *Comin' to Your City*, the highly anticipated follow-up to their surprise blockbuster 2004 debut, *A Horse of a Different Color*. Their omnipresence in 2005 illustrates just how thoroughly Big & Rich, along with their protégée Gretchen Wilson, changed the course of contemporary country in the middle of the decade, helping to usher in music that was bigger, funnier, rowdier, and looser than what was on country radio in the wake of Garth's retirement. Everybody wanted a piece of Big & Rich, including such mainstream divas as Faith Hill, and they had their own pet projects like inept country rapper Cowboy Troy, and they didn't turn down an opportunity to work, so they just flooded the charts. And while such success is a vindication in and of itself, it also raised the stakes for the duo's own record—a challenge they embrace with their trademark goofball humor on *Comin' to Your City*. Opening with a perhaps inadvertent salute to Shel Silverstein on the careening "The Freak Parade," the album immediately delves into territory that's weirder than anything on the debut, and the duo continues to push its music to extremes for the rest of the record. This doesn't mean that this is all a freak show—the stranger moments are stranger, often exhilaratingly so, but the ballads are slicker and the pop tunes are less apologetic

than before. Since the gonzo rebel shtick was always an act put on by two Music City pros, this pursuit of the weird and the normal in equal measure benefits the album since they can pull off both attitudes with slick flair. And it doesn't get slicker than "I Pray for You," a slice of anthemic MOR pop that would sound by-the-books in the hands of another act, but the duo gives the song an insistent, assured arrangement that not only places it above most contemporary country-pop of 2005, but makes it better than nearly all adult contemporary of its year, as well. It's not the only straight-ahead moment that works here, either—"Never Mind Me" has a sweetness straight out soft rock's late '70s/early '80s peak, while "Leap of Faith" is underpinned by a genuine melancholy ache that's a little surprising coming from this pair of pranksters. These moments don't dominate the album, however: they anchor a record that's otherwise a pretty wild ride. Sometimes, the partying is a little obvious—as on the travelogue title track—but that doesn't mean it's not effective; Big & Rich have the hooks and the studio smarts to make the formula sound infectious. Besides, when there are songs as mind-bending and odd as Big Kenny's old-timey mariachi "20 Margaritas" or his country-psychedelia excursion on "Blow My Mind," it's hard to complain about the occasional glimpse of formula—and that's not even taking into account such gems as the silly, self-referential "Filthy Rich," the absurd "Jalapeno," or the gleefully annoying "Soul Shaker," nor does it quite convey how the awkwardly jingoistic military tale "8th of November" (proof that *every* mainstream country album in 2005 needs a patriotic anthem) is subverted by "Our America," where Big & Rich, Gretchen Wilson, and Cowboy Troy cut-and-paste American tunes, slogans, and clichés into a freak-pack national anthem. It's things like this that make up for the lack of a flat-out stunner along the lines of "Save a Horse (Ride a Cowboy)." After all, when an album has so many hooks, good and bad jokes, real and affected weirdness, it's hard to complain; it's better just to sit back and enjoy the show, especially since, for better or worse, there are no better showmen in country or pop in 2005 than Big & Rich.

Stephen Thomas Erlewine

Clint Black

Killin' Time
1989, RCA

Clint Black's accessible brand of Texas country burned up the charts upon its release, selling two million copies and yielding the hit singles "Better Man," "Killin' Time," "Nobody's Home," "Walkin' Away," and "Nothing's News."

Brian Mansfield

Put Yourself in My Shoes
1990, Collectables

Put Yourself in My Shoes never approaches the perfection of Clint Black's debut, but it still produced a number of singles, including "Put Yourself in My Shoes," "Loving Blind," "Where Are You Now," and "This Nightlife."

Brian Mansfield

The Hard Way
1992, RCA

Back to form, Clint Black put some of his most exciting singles on his third album. "We Tell Ourselves" rocked without resorting to Southern boogie, and "When My Ship Comes

In" contained a masterful chorus. The album also included the hit "Burn One Down."

Brian Mansfield

No Time to Kill
July 1993, Collectables

Clint Black's albums seems to alternate between the remarkable and the merely pretty good. *No Time to Kill*, which plays off the title of his first album, is one of the latter. All of this is acceptable, though little matches quality of the title track. Black does a duet with Wynonna Judd called "A Bad Goodbye."

Brian Mansfield

One Emotion
1994, RCA

One Emotion continued Clint Black's streak of uneven albums, featuring a handful of exemplary tracks, including the Merle Haggard collaboration "Untanglin' My Mind," but just as many mediocre songs, like "You Made Me Feel," which was written with Michael McDonald. Nothing on *One Emotion* is particularly bad, but it doesn't sound like Black is pushing himself into new territories, either.

Stephen Thomas Erlewine

Ultimate Clint Black
September 2003, RCA

There have been a few Clint Black compilations—an initial *Greatest Hits* in 1996, a sequel in 2001, two identically titled *Super Hits* with different track listings—prior to 2003's *Ultimate Clint Black*, but this is the first to take full stock of  his ten-year stint at RCA Records. Appropriately, this was released at the end of that run, a few months before he released his first record on Equity, so it was perfectly timed to summarize his peak years as a popular recording artist. Does it do a good job? More or less, yes. It's a mixed blessing that it covers so much ground, since it does wind up giving a full portrait of his '90s stardom, but at the expense of his better, earlier harder country, as well as several country Top Ten singles. Nevertheless, this has the bulk of his biggest hits, from the timeless "Killin' Time" to the Steve Wariner duet "Been There," making it a satisfying retrospective from one of the best new traditionalists of the '90s.

Stephen Thomas Erlewine

BlackHawk

Strong Enough
September 1995, Arista

After their debut album became a platinum success, Blackhawk decided to follow the same formula for their follow-up, *Strong Enough*. Not merely a reproduction of their self-titled debut, *Strong Enough* finds the group consolidating their

strengths as songwriters and performers. Throughout the album, the group turns in first-rate songs and tight performances, distinguished by their strong harmonies.

Stephen Thomas Erlewine

The Sky's the Limit
September 1998, Arista

Blackhawk, like many of their contemporary country peers, struggle to have it both ways. They want to have the hits, but they also want to keep country. At times, the scales have tipped toward the pop end, but with *The Sky's the Limit*, they move back toward country, coming up with a record that harks back to their organic debut. There is a difference, however. Here, they have more confidence, not only in their performances but in the way they merge their pop songwriting instincts with more authentic country instrumentation. It's a combination that works terrifically, enlivening even the weaker songs. Unfortunately, there are a few of those here, but that's part and parcel for a contemporary country album. What counts are the moments that work, and there enough of those— "There You Have It," "Think Again," "Nobody Knows What to Say"—to make it rank as one of their better efforts.

Thom Owens

Platinum & Gold Collection
January 2004, RCA Nashville/BMG Heritage

The 12 tracks in this collection offer an intimate and striking portrait of BlackHawk, the mainstream country trio comprised of Henry Paul, Van Stephenson, and Dave Robbins. This set collects the band's hits from their inception and first single in 1993 through the period when Van Stephenson had to leave the band in 2000 because of a cancer that killed him. While Blackhawk never issued an album that was solid from start to finish, they are one of the most consistent singles acts to emerge from mainstream country in 1990s. With their infectious three-part harmonies, glorious acoustic guitar and piano-dominated arrangements, and endearing heartfelt delivery, they are indeed closer to traditional country music in spirit if not in sound than some of their more "authentic" peers. Collected here are the smashes "Postmarked Birmingham," "Every Once in a While," "I'm Not Strong Enough to Say No," "Hole in My Heart," "Goodbye Says It All," and "Let 'Em Whirl," with a mess of other tunes, all of which charted in the *Billboard* Top 50. For the price, this collection cannot be beat.

Thom Jurek

Suzy Bogguss

Somewhere Between
1988, Liberty

A fabulous, truly surprising debut, this album firmly plants one foot in the past and the other in the Nashville mainstream. The best songs here come from country legends. Merle Haggard penned the powerhouse title cut "My Sweet

Love Ain't Around" came from Hank Williams, and "I Want To Be a Cowboy's Sweetheart" was an old Patsy Montana tune. The new stuff was pretty danged good, too: "Cross My Heart," written by Verlon Thompson and Kye Fleming, was the album's highest-charting single.

Brian Mansfield

Aces
1991, Liberty

Employing such A-listers as Vince Gill, Beth Nielsen Chapman, and Mark O'Connor helped make this a strong outing, but Suzy Bogguss' appealing girl-next-door approach, her choice to straddle the fence between contemporary and traditional C&W and her perfectly pitched voice are what helped this album be the catalyst for making her a household name among country music fans. Whether she's handling the parting of mother and daughter in "Letting Go," the sorrowful heart-break of "Part of Me," or the spunky "Outbound Plane," she expresses such sincerity you never doubt an emotion. Additionally, not many mainstream artists have the nerve to take on a subject that doesn't involve boy-girl love. But Bogguss' choice in the compelling title track shows just how savvy she is. Concerning envy of success between friends, Cheryl Wheeler's "Aces" is smart and hits just the right nuances without ever being as cloying or manipulative as many adult contemporary singles are in their need to be touching. Immediately following that emotional twister is the album's second strongest cut, "Someday Soon." A twangy, yearning tune of a girl longing for a boy who loves "his damned old rodeo" as much as he loves her, Bogguss elicits youthful hope that hasn't leaned toward jaded frustration quite yet. Not many singers can make riding the rodeo sound like the most romantic thing in the world, but that's what makes Bogguss an artist and not just a vocalist.

Bryan Buss

Something Up My Sleeve
September 1993, Liberty

Something up My Sleeve is one of Suzy Bogguss' finest and most consistent albums. Exercising her crystal-clear vocals in ways she hadn't heretofore, she touches the heart in the most earnest way, whether it's the simplicity of "Diamonds and Tears," the skewering of America in "Souvenirs," or the hopelessness of "Something up My Sleeve." Always a step ahead of her peers, Bogguss also always has a firm foot embedded in her roots, and she has a knack for straddling both contemporary and classic country so that they mesh seamlessly. She employs some A-list female writers and vocalists on this album; Matraca Berg, Martina McBride, and Beth Nielsen Chapman all make contributions, showing how respected she is as an artist. With a keen eye on contemporary society ("Hey Cinderella") or an accusing "You Wouldn't Say That to a Stranger," Bogguss puts young upstarts to shame.

Bryan Buss

20 Greatest Hits
September 2002, Capitol

Arguably, Suzy Bogguss did more than anybody to change the role of the female vocalist during the 1990s. Certainly she racked up her share of hits—which are chronicled without fault on this collection. But more than that, she was a singer who weathered the Nash Vegas storms with grace, took control of her own career, and became producer of her own recordings. She selected material rather than having Jimmy Bowen—the cohort in the producer's chair—select it for her. She broke all the rules regarding genres from Western Swing yodels (Patsy Montana's "I Wanna Be A Cowboy's Sweetheart") to cowboy songs (Ian Tyson's "Someday Soon"), modern Americana (John Hiatt's "Drive South" and Nanci Griffith's "Outbound Plane"), to recording the work of cutting-edge Nashville songwriters such as Matraca Berg and Gary Harrison ("Diamonds And Tears" and "Eat At Joe's"), as well as Kim Richey's "From Where I Stand," to songwriting "One More For The Road" and "Far And Way" with Doug Crider, to interpreting the classics (Jimmie Rodgers' "In The Jailhouse Now"). It's one thing to record songs of a different stripe and to break down the barriers between genres; it's quite another to make hit records while doing so, which is exactly what Bogguss did at Capitol in the 1990s. She and Pam Tillis made it possible for singers like Martina McBride, Shania Twain, Bobbie Cryner, and Deana Carter to arrive—and even eventually eclipse them—due to the fickle nature by which Nashville's radio geeks (yes, *geeks*) dictate what the populace wants to hear rather than something that might actually be considered incredible and groundbreaking country music. These 20 cuts offer a vivid and extremely pleasurable look at a run that has succeeded n making Suzy Bogguss one of the rare ones—an artist in full control of her destiny. When she walked away to concentrate on her family, she did so from the top. Now that she's back, *20 Greatest Hits* serves as a guidepost to wherever she's moved to now musically. This is '90s country at its very best, and the only thing that might be finer than this collection is to possess the actual albums these songs came from so that one can search for more of Bogguss' hidden gems.

Thom Jurek

Swing
June 2003, Compadre

On her third self-released album, Suzy Bogguss, one of the finest female vocalists living and working in Nashville, allows one of her many passions to come to the surface on *Swing*. With Asleep at the Wheel's Ray Benson in the producer's chair, Bogguss kicks out 12 classy pop, jazz, and swing tunes with a smoking band making a timeless sound. Benson knows the feel of this music inside and out (and brought his violin player, the Stephane Grappelli-inspired Jason Roberts, along for the ride), and Bogguss, whose mom is a big Sinatra and Ella Fitzgerald fan, can sing virtually anything—but has a special affinity for the swing book—with a twist. There are nuggets of the repertoire here, such as Nat King Cole's "Straighten Up and Fly Right" and Duke Ellington's "Do Nothing 'Til You Hear From Me" as well as "Comes Love"—closely associated with Billie Holiday—and the great Ken Burgan tune "Sweetheart." But there's plenty of new material, too; there are five cuts by Nashville songwriter and jazz singer April Barrows, who writes in the Nat King Cole idiom with smart, modern lyrics; inventive melodies; and a wondrous sense of rhythm. Bogguss and husband and songwriter Doug Crider contributed one and Paul Kramer offered a pair. The jump in these tunes is fresh and new; there are no tired Diana Krall readings of the same old tunes here that had been better-recorded long before. The feel is jumping and smooth, such as on "Burning the Toast" by Barrows, in cut time with Roberts and pianist Floyd Domino floating with clarinetist John H.R. Mills against a popping double-bassline by Spencer Starnes and Benson's guitar. Recorded in Austin, TX, *Swing* feels loose, fancy free, and focused on exploration, bringing the essence of a song out into the idiom in which it was written. "It's New to Me" by Bogguss, Crider, and Kramer has a bluesy truth to it that is underscored by sax and clarinet wafting so warm from the fringes as Domino's right hand fills and comps slip in between lyric and horn arrangement to make the track just shine. The duet with Benson, "Cupid Shot Us Both With One Arrow," features Roberts doing the gypsy swing thing with passion and fervor, yet never takes away the sprightly tempoed tune form the singers. In all, *Swing* is the strongest Suzy Bogguss record ever—yes, ever. This is not a novelty record, not some trendy acclimation to the times, but a way of revealing, as she has, the depth and dimension of her artistry in a new way. Hopefully there are some triple-A jazz and Americana radio programmers out there—as well as a few visionary public-radio DJs—who will play this slab once or twice. That's all it will take. This is the most elegant pop-jazz record of the year thus far, and it will be tough to beat. *Swing* will only delight Bogguss' legion of time-honored fans and win her plenty of new ones as well.

Thom Jurek

BR5-49

BR5-49
September 1996, Arista

BR5-49 was hardly the first retro-country act to emerge in the 1990s, but as one of the first trad-style C&W bands to gain a following (and a major label contract) in Nashville for nearly 20 years, they suggested that in the midst of Garth-mania there

Featuring CHEROKEE BOOGIE, CRAZY ARMS, HICKORY WIND *and more!*

were still folks in Music City hungry for some down-home twang in the classic style, which made country music a phenomenon in the first place. BR5-49's self-titled debut album may lack a bit of the grit and high spirits of their live show (either as witnessed in person or as preserved on the *Live at Robert's* EP), but it does a great job of capturing this band's spunky attitude and superb chops, and makes clear they can write original songs just as well as they can give new life to classics by Moon Mullican and Ray Price. While a few tunes like "Little Ramona (Gone Hillbilly Nuts)" play to the slightly kitschy side of the group's collective personality, "Even if It's Wrong," "One Long Saturday Night," and "Lifetime to Prove" testify that BR5-49 truly respect classic country music, and write songs as smart and heartfelt as the classics they cover. And boy, can they play—Don Herron shines on every instrument he touches (including fiddle, steel guitar, and mandolin), Shaw "Hawk Shaw" Wilson and Smilin' Jay McDowell are a superbly uncluttered rhythm section, and Gary Bennett and Chuck Mead can pick just as well as they harmonize (and that's mighty fine indeed). Adding a here-and-now energy and drive to classic styles of the past,

BR5-49 proves you can not only have it both ways, but have a great time to boot.

Mark Deming

Big Backyard Beat Show
July 1998, Arista

When BR5-49 was first signed by a Nashville major, eyebrows were raised on both sides of the country music border. Traditionalists wondered what it would cost the hillbilly boys who gained fame while playing in the window of *Robert's Western Wear* on Lower Broad in Music City. On the other side of the fence, the cats in the suits were shaking their heads, predicting that BR5-49 would be a short-lived novelty act. With some moderate success, no thanks to country-pop radio, and several years on the road, BR5-49 endured. This, the band's third release, shows a maturing quintet ready to come into its own. With their integrity intact, the boys have learned a thing or two about writing songs, and display their own material proudly. Sandwiched between a Buck Owens cover, "There Goes My Love," and Billy Joe Shaver's forever powerful "Georgia on a Fast Train," Gary Bennett and Chuck Mead provide the band with some worthy tunes. "Storybook Endings (If You Stop Believin')," "My Name Is Mudd," "You Are Never Nice to Me," and "Change the Way I Look" all score big. "Goodbye, Maria" is the band's effective salute to the Tex-Mex sound of country & western music. They even present listeners with a fast-movin' truck-drivin' song, "18 Wheels and a Crowbar." With Don Herron's magnificent musicianship providing steel, fiddle, dobro, mandolin, and almost anything else that is required, BR5-49 deserves more than just a modicum of respect for hanging in there despite predictions. If the infinitely listenable *Big Backyard Beat Show* is any indication of their future, they should be around for a long time.

Jana Pendragon

Coast to Coast Live
April 2000, Arista

For all their acclaim and genuine talent, retro-country act BR5-49 struck some listeners the wrong way—namely, fans of the honky tonk, Bakersfield country, Western swing, country boogie, and rockabilly that BR5-49 revitalized with their studio records. To these listeners, the quintet may have had the chops, but they were just a bit too knowing—they weren't playing with a smile, but a smirk. Reasonable enthusiasts could disagree on this point, and they did, but there still remained a significant portion of would-be fans that couldn't get with the band, because what some perceived as good humor seemed like condescension to others. Those listeners may be surprised by the group's first live album, *Coast to Coast*. Recorded in the summer of 1999 (at five different locations), the album finds the group in their element, passionately knocking out tunes in front of an appreciative audience. They're tight, energetic, and musically deft, effortlessly switching genres and spitting out high-octane solos. It's pretty intoxicating, actually, especially since the band has great taste—not only do they revive Don Gibson's overlooked "Sweet Sweet Girl!" and Bob Wills and Tommy Duncan's standard "Brain Cloudy Blues," but they are no elitists, choosing to cover Gram Parsons ("Big Mouth Blues") and the far less hip Charlie Daniels ("Uneasy Rider") as well. Some fans of pure country music may find Chuck Mead's voice just a little jive, but he's a hell of a guitar player in a crackerjack band, and if you only concentrate on that, *Coast to Coast* doesn't just come alive—it crackles. Not enough credit can be placed on the live setting; its kinetic excitement is the reason why *Coast to Coast* is the BR5-49 album for listeners who aren't already fans, while still being a delight for diehards.

Stephen Thomas Erlewine

Paul Brandt

Calm Before the Storm
June 1996, Reprise

Paul Brandt's debut *Calm Before the Storm* introduces a neo-traditionalist singer/songwriter of considerable potential, with an ability to skillfully bridge vintage honky tonk with a contemporary country sound; along with the chart-topping "I Do," the album also includes the much-acclaimed "My Heart Has a History," Brandt's first Top Five hit.

Jason Ankeny

Outside the Frame
November 1997, Reprise

Paul Brandt's second album, *Outside the Frame*, is a successful continuance of the neo-traditionalist formula that made his debut, *Calm Before the Storm*, such a success. Again working with producer Josh Leo, Brandt finds the middle ground between traditional honky tonk and contemporary country pop and while the songwriting is occasionally uneven, the conviction and passion of the performances make the weaker moments glide by. All in all, the album—from the ballad "What's Come Over You" and the rocker "Yeah!" to "A Little in Love"—proves that Brandt is one of the better mainstream contemporary country vocalists of the late '90s.

Thom Owens

Brooks & Dunn

Brand New Man
1991, Arista

An impressive debut that proudly proclaims its country roots without being afraid to dip its toes into pop and rock, *Brand New Man* is an entertaining listen. Like most Nashville records from the early '90s, *Brand New Man* is short, barely clocking in over 30 minutes, but Brooks & Dunn have clearly brought their A material to the table. The voices of the leaders blend well, and they are backed by a crack Nashville band that handles the all-original material with ease. Highlights include the insanely catchy title track and the almost Springsteen-esque "Lost and Found." Fairly traditional country songs such as "Cheating on the Blues" cohabitate peacefully with more pop-oriented fare like "Neon Moon" and "Still in Love With You." Thankfully, these latter tracks do not follow in the all-too-common mold of over-production that would bury the charms of these songs beneath string orchestras, rock guitars, and huge drums. As individual vocalists,

both Brooks and Dunn are competent and expressive, although they do lack something in originality and distinctiveness. Although it's probably too much to ask from this kind of record, it would still be great to hear this great band really letting loose in extended fashion; such small tastes as at the end of "Cool Drink of Water" make the listener thirsty for more. Occupying the middle ground between Johnny Cash and the Eagles, Brooks & Dunn have put together a terrific group of songs that are memorable, hummable, and, most importantly, fun. Despite the diversity in the material, the album works well as a coherent whole. All in all, *Brand New Man* is a fine, fine collection of pop-country songs, masterfully played.

Daniel Gioffre

Hard Workin' Man
1993, Arista

As with most second albums, the successful traits started to isolate themselves on *Hard Workin' Man*: macho stuff like "Hard Workin' Man" and "Rock My World (Little Country Girl)" rocked harder than anything on *Brand New Man*, though Brooks & Dunn made sure their women came off as good as they did (catch the "and women too" tag on "Hard Workin' Man"). The slower songs ("That Ain't No Way to Go," "She Used to Be Mine") tended toward the sort of evocative images that ran all through their debut. The pair never put all the elements together they way they did their first time out, but they came close enough that few people noticed.

Brian Mansfield

Waitin' on Sundown
September 1994, Arista

Waitin' on Sundown didn't depart from Brooks & Dunn's formula much, but the fans didn't mind—it sold over three million albums anyway. By this point, the duo's albums have become a handful of solid singles—this time out, they were "Little Miss Honky Tonk," "She's Not the Cheatin' Kind," and "You're Gonna Miss Me When I'm Gone"—surrounded by filler, but the hits will make the fans forgive the filler.

Thom Owens

Greatest Hits
September 1997, Arista

Greatest Hits is a thorough overview of one of the most popular country acts of the '90s, containing 11 of Brooks & Dunn's biggest hits—including "Brand New Man," "My Next Broken Heart," "Boot Scootin' Boogie," and "She Used to Be Mine"—plus three new songs that are nearly as good as their older hits. It's an excellent summation of the first part of their career, and an ideal place to become acquainted with the duo.

Thom Owens

If You See Her
June 1998, Arista

The studio formula that melded vocalist Ronnie Dunn with Kix Brooks is still in effect on cuts like "Your Love Don't Take a Backseat to Nothing" and a duet with country-pop diva Reba McEntire ("If You See Him, If You See Her"); there are some good moments here. Dunn's cover of Roger Miller's "Husbands and Wives" displays his abilities nicely, while Brooks comes to life as a rock 'n' roller on "Way Gone." Also good are "Brand New Whiskey" and "Born and Raised in Black and White." However, the final cut, a gospel-kissed tune ("You're My Angel") that shows just how strong Dunn's voice is, evokes the most emotion. Dunn, when allowed to free himself from trite material and heavy production practices, is amazing.

Jana Pendragon

Tight Rope
September 1999, Arista

Brooks & Dunn have always seemed more traditionalist than they actually were. Even with their first album, they had a clear commercial mind behind their rootsiest material, and it's undeniable that they were not only one of the driving forces behind the line-dance craze, but that they had some of the better mainstream country ballads of the decade. Their trick was not just strong vocals, but keeping the music lean and direct, so it sounded like straight-up country even when it had pop aspirations. They retained that illusion up until the end of the '90s, when they not only increased their pop quotient, but they started to feel like a collective instead of a duo. That's a roundabout way of saying that 1999's *Tight Rope*, while a solid album, isn't quite up to their old standards. For instance, such blatant radio crossover moves as covering John Waite's New Wave-era classic "Missing You" feels wrong, even if it's done as well as it possibly could be. That's obviously a misstep, but the really strange thing about *Tight Rope* is how the alternation between a Brooks song and Dunn song feels like two solo albums pieced together, which is something that's never happened before. That these pieces are musically in line with the duo's previous efforts only hammers home the fact that this record is competent, occasionally enjoyable, but not particularly inspired. Parts of the record work quite well, such as "Temptation #9" or the closer "Texas and Norma Jean," but there are large stretches that either feel contrived or a little too generic. Since Brooks & Dunn are professionals, *Tight Rope* is always listenable, but the combination of bland material and the disjointed feeling of the record leaves it a little unsatisfying.

Stephen Thomas Erlewine

Steers and Stripes
April 2001, Arista

Ronnie Dunn told *Country Weekly* magazine that "Country music is more diversified than ever, so you can really do more styles and different things." Lucky for Brooks & Dunn, who've obviously used the state of country music to their advantage, making album number nine something undoubtedly worth hearing. Or maybe it's the year they spent working on it. Whatever it is, *Steers and Stripes* is one of the finer albums from the eight-time winners of CMA's Vocal Duo of the Year. It seems to recapture everything likable about Brooks & Dunn that's been missing from the last few albums. The 14-track collection offers up a bevy of beauties from hardcore country to some penetrating rock. The slow, agonizing conviction in "The Long Goodbye," the Latin-flavored "My Heart Is Lost to You," the reassuring sentiment in "Unloved," and the rockabilly revelry of "See Jane Dance" are

just a few tunes on this eminent song-packed album that really make a lasting impression.

Maria Dinoia

Red Dirt Road
July 2003, Arista

Emboldened by the positive reaction to 2001's *Steers and Stripes*, where the venerated veteran country duo stretched their musical chops, Brooks & Dunn followed with a record that pushed even further and garnered greater musical achievement. Released in the summer of 2003, *Red Dirt Road* is a bit of a concept album, with Brooks & Dunn sketching out a nostalgic trip through their past and a tribute to their roots and upbringing. This isn't just conveyed by the lyrics, which contain offhanded references to '70s icons, including *Born to Run*; the music touches on a bunch of the duo's formative influences, whether it's the Keith Richards homage that kicks off the album opener, "You Can't Take the Honky Tonk Out of the Girl," or the Stax horns that punctuate "Believer." Instead of sounding bound to tradition, Brooks & Dunn sound as musically invigorated as they did on *Steers and Stripes*, demonstrating nuance and muscle in equal measures; after all, they not only do modern country-rock better than their peers, they can pull off a dobro-driven honky tonk song like "My Baby's Everything I Love" with equal aplomb, and then dive into wry satire with the uncredited gospel satire "Holy War" that closes the album. It's not just the amalgam of styles that impresses, but it's the writing, which is as wide-ranging as the performances and just as convincing. Plus, the loose concept gives the album structure and focus, and this, added to the fine songwriting, means that *Red Dirt Road* is not just one of Brooks & Dunn's most ambitious records, it's also one of their best.

Stephen Thomas Erlewine

The Greatest Hits Collection, Vol. 2
October 2004, BMG

Brooks & Dunn's *Greatest Hits Collection, Vol. 2* picks up where their first hits compilation left off: in 1998, with the album *If You See Her*, and runs until 2004, when *Vol. 2* was released. During this time, the duo's popularity never waned, although the quality of their output fluctuated a little bit, before they made an artistic comeback in the early 2000s, culminating with the fine 2003 album, *Red Dirt Road*. *Greatest Hits, Vol. 2* camouflages this erratic output by concentrating on their biggest hits from this era, adding three solid new songs to the mix. This doesn't contain all their hits from these six years—singles like "Beer Thirty" and "You'll Always Be Loved By Me" are missing—but it does contain such big hits as "Husbands and Wives," "I Can't Get Over You," "Ain't Nothing 'Bout You," and "Only in America," which makes this a more consistent listen. While some of those smaller hits are indeed missed, the hits on this fine compilation are enough to provide an accurate overview of this stint of Brooks & Dunn's career, and will likely satisfy most of their fans.

Stephen Thomas Erlewine

Hillbilly Deluxe
August 2005, Arista

During the first half of the 2000s Brooks & Dunn broadened their horizons, incorporating stronger elements of pop and rock to their neo-traditionalist country. As its title suggests, 2005's *Hillbilly Deluxe* finds the duo returning to their roots, creating a lean, tight collection of 13 straight-ahead country songs. This may be a reaction to the romanticization of rednecks in recent country music, but *Hillbilly Deluxe* doesn't sound crass or commercial. It sounds like a logical back-to-basics move after the rock flirtations of 2001's *Steers and Stripes* and 2003's *Red Dirt Road*. Brooks & Dunn don't hide their intentions at all: not only does the album boast a proudly hillbilly title, but the album kicks off with the anthemic "Play Something Country," where a redneck woman implores the DJ to play some "Kenny, Keith, Alan, and Patsy Cline," and Brooks & Dunn follow that advice for the rest of the album, never straying far from country, even when they're covering Nicolette Larson's early '80s hit "Building Bridges" with Sheryl Crow on backing vocals. Most of this direction seems to come from Ronnie Dunn, who provides the great majority of original material here: six of the 13 songs are from Dunn (all but one co-written with Terry McBride), and his tunes are the purest country here, whether it's barroom tales like "Whiskey Do My Talkin'" or weepers like "I May Never Get Over You." That's not to say that Kix Brooks doesn't have a presence here. With the exception of the poppier "One More Roll of the Dice," he also devotes himself to straight-ahead country, highlighted by the sweetly melancholy "Her West Was Wilder" and the rocking closer, "She Likes to Get out of Town." Brooks might not write as much here as he normally does, but the covers he sings are expertly chosen, and the album as a whole gels as well as either *Steers and Stripes* or *Red Dirt Road*. Even though *Hillbilly Deluxe* isn't quite as ambitious as either of those records, it's just as satisfying and further proof that Brooks & Dunn are one of the most reliable, consistently enjoyable acts in modern country music.

Stephen Thomas Erlewine

Garth Brooks

Garth Brooks
April 1989, Liberty

On Garth Brooks' self-titled debut, his fusion of rock & roll and traditional country genres like honky tonk and Western swing is already fully formed as is his gift for extended metaphors. One listen to his signature song and breakthrough hit, "The Dance," proves that, which is why he broke away from the hat acts that he was initially grouped with. Nevertheless, *Garth Brooks* is the most straightforward of all of his albums; Brooks sticks with neo-traditional country on about half of the tracks. He sings traditional country quite well—"Not Counting You" is a particularly effective honky tonk number, demonstrating a debt to both George Jones and George Strait—but what makes the album an exciting debut are songs like the genre-bending ballads "The Dance" and "If Tomorrow Never Comes"; and that is the style that would bring him mass success with his next album, *No Fences*.

Stephen Thomas Erlewine

No Fences
August 1990, Liberty

Essentially, Garth Brooks' second album, *No Fences*, follows the same pattern as his debut, but it is a more assured and risky record. Brooks still performs neo-traditional country, such as the honky tonk hit "Friends in Low Places," but now he twists it around with clever pop hooks. Those pop/rock influences are most apparent on the ballads, which alternate between sensitive folk-rock and power ballad bombast. But what makes *No Fences* such a success is how seamlessly he blends the two seemingly opposing genres, and how he chooses a set of material that makes his genre-bending sound

subtle and natural. Of course, it doesn't hurt that the songs are consistently entertaining, either.

Stephen Thomas Erlewine

Ropin' the Wind
September 1991, Capitol

With *Ropin' the Wind*, Garth Brooks begins to make his '70s rock influences more explicit. Naturally, that is most notable in his reworking of Billy Joel's "Shameless," which he transforms from a rock power ballad into contemporary country. But that influence is also evident on ambitious epics like "The River" and even the honky tonk ravers of "Papa Loved Mama" and "Rodeo." Some might say that those rock influences are what make Brooks a crossover success, but he wouldn't be nearly as successful if he didn't have a tangible country foundation to his music—even when he comes close to standard arena rock bombast, there are gritty steel guitars or vocal inflections that prove he is trying to expand country's vocabulary, not trying to exploit it.

Stephen Thomas Erlewine

The Chase
September 1992, Liberty

The Chase is Garth Brooks' most ambitious and personal album. Not coincidentally, it is one of his least popular releases, selling about half of what the previous *Ropin' the Wind*. But in its own way, *The Chase* is more rewarding and deeper than *Ropin' the Wind*. That's

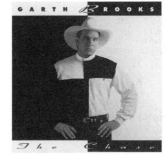

partially due to Brooks' naked ambition; not only does he record "We Shall Be Free" with a gospel choir, but he tackles deeper social and personal issues than he has before. However, the true key to the album is Brooks' conviction; even when his musical experiments don't quite work, it's easy to admire and respect his ambition. Although there are light moments like "Night Rider's Lament" and a cover of Little Feat's "Dixie Chicken," *The Chase* is a more somber, reflective record than his previous three albums; but given a bit of time, it's as satisfying as anything he's ever recorded.

Stephen Thomas Erlewine

In Pieces
August 1993, Liberty

After the relative commercial disappointment of *The Chase*, Garth Brooks toned down his experimental eclecticism on *In Pieces*. Alternating between heavily rock-influenced numbers, dramatic ballads, and revamped honky tonk, *In Pieces* appeals to the audience that found *The Chase* too pretentious and overly serious. That doesn't mean Brooks abandoned his desire to bend the rules—he's just masked his more ambitious material with crowd-pleasing up-tempo numbers like "American Honky-Tonk Bar Association" and "Ain't Going Down (Til the Sun Comes Up)." *In Pieces* is an album that was made for the fans, and it shows—it is one of Brooks' most energetic and exciting collections.

Stephen Thomas Erlewine

The Hits
1994, Liberty

The Hits is exactly what it says it is—18 of Garth Brooks' biggest hits, including his first 14 number one singles. Although he has good album tracks on each of his records, this is the essential Garth Brooks album—it gives a good sense of the singer's talents, especially his underappreciated eclecticism. The Hits was only in print for a year, but it sold in excess of eight million copies, so it hardly can be called a limited edition.

Stephen Thomas Erlewine

Fresh Horses
November 1995, Capitol

Garth Brooks had to move forward in a dramatic way with Fresh Horses, his first new album since 1993. Following the massive successive of The Hits—which effectively recapped why the singer became the single most popular American performer of the '90s—Brooks positioned himself for a new direction with Fresh Horses. The problem is, he doesn't know which way he should go. Throughout the album, he swings back and forth between country and rock without any sense of purpose. Brooks tries to rework Aerosmith's "The Fever" into a rowdy rodeo country-rocker, but the end result is forced and half-hearted. The Aerosmith cover illustrates the problems of Fresh Horses: Brooks is trying too hard to cover new territory and restore hardcore honky tonk grit to his slick country-rock. When he lets his guard down—such on as the melancholy ballad "The Beaches of Cheyenne" and the sassy, suggestive "It's Midnight Cinderella"—he can still come up with winners, but those moments don't come frequently on Fresh Horses.

Stephen Thomas Erlewine

Sevens
November 1997, Capitol

Despite a massive publicity campaign, Fresh Horses failed to match the success of its predecessors, which meant that its successor, Sevens, had to return Garth Brooks to his superstar status in order to be considered a hit. Part of the problem with Fresh Horses is that it embraced arena rock instead of merely flirting with it; as a result, large portions of his audience refused to follow him. Sevens corrects that misstep by retreating to traditional country territory and establishing a new, folky country-pop direction. Theoretically, it sounds like the perfect move, but Sevens doesn't quite play as smoothly as it should. The music never catches fire and often sounds weary instead of hushed and intimate. There are no sweeping epics, no rockers, no steps forward; there's none of the risk-taking that made his early albums so successful. Instead, Sevens is an album of small, subtle pleasures, whether it's the swinging "Longneck Bottle" or the moving ballad "She's Gonna Make It." These aren't great leaps forward, but they're well-written and performed, making for solid additions to his catalog. Unfortunately, there aren't enough of these moments on Sevens. Only a handful of songs match the level of those two, and since the filler itself lacks power, the end result is an album that is surprisingly lackluster.

Stephen Thomas Erlewine

Scarecrow
November 2001, Capitol

Garth Brooks had a real hard time in the latter half of the '90s, running through a couple of muddled near-crossover records before diving off the deep end with the extraordinary In the Life of Chris Gaines. Following that historic belly-flop—few albums in history have been as misconceived as widely rejected—Brooks took some time off, retreating from the spotlight (which was particularly helpful when he divorced his high-school sweetheart) and laying low until late fall of 2001, when he returned with Scarecrow. The extended time off turned out to be a blessing, since it seemed to help him focus for Scarecrow, his strongest album since he delved into unabashed crossover with Fresh Horses. Sure, there's still a healthy dose of pop here—he does cover America's fine Californian folk-rock "Don't Cross the River," for instance—but this is a clean, spare record that never overplays its hand and, in turn, it showcases Brooks' talent for synthesizing popular music styles particularly well. Really, there are no new twists here, but that's part of what's good about the record: He's returned to his strengths, whether it's boozy barroom ravers like the deliriously good George Jones duet "Beer Run" or the preponderance of dramatic, portentous ballads like "The Storm." On paper, this may sound like a retreat, but it plays like a revitalization since it plays to Brooks' strengths—a country boy raised on Eagles who likes country when it rocks, but pumps up power ballads with fiddles and twang. This is no surprise, of course, but it's refreshing to hear him in such a simple, unadorned context, performing good songs with conviction—performances good enough to prove that there's more soul here than on most alt-country records. The friskier songs, from "Beer Run" to "Big Money," fare better than the ballads, but those ballads still work, and overall Scarecrow proves that mainstream modern country doesn't have a better singer than Brooks at his best. And it's good to have him at his best again.

Stephen Thomas Erlewine

The Lost Sessions
2005, Pearl

Garth Brooks signed an exclusive contract with Wal-Mart in the summer of 2005, a pact that guaranteed that the megastore would be the only retailer selling Garth's catalog. The first release under that contract was the second volume of The Limited Series, a six-disc box that gathers all the albums Brooks released since his 1998 installment: two studio albums, 1997's Sevens and 2001's Scarecrow, 1998's live double album Double Live, a DVD called All Access, and The Lost Sessions, which gathered together various odds and ends recorded during the time the box set covered. In that incarnation, The Lost Sessions was a mere 11 tracks, which was enough to produce Brooks' first hit single in a few years with "Good Ride Cowboy," his rollicking, good-natured tribute to his idol Chris LeDoux. But a few months after the release of this second Limited Series—after "Good Ride Cowboy" finished its ride on the country charts—The Lost Sessions was spun off as its own separate release. As its own release, the album not only had a different track sequencing, it was greatly expanded with the addition of no less than six songs, most notable among these a duet with his wife Trisha Yearwood, "Love Will Always Win." In either incarnation *The Lost Sessions* is stronger than most records Garth has made since *In Pieces*, carrying over the back-to-basics feel of *Scarecrow*, but feeling a lot looser than that return to form, especially on the 17-track version of the album, which is one case of more truly being more. Of course, collections of outtakes always tend to be looser than finished albums—particularly finished albums by superstars like Garth who polish their records so they satisfy every part of their audience—but it's a true pleasure to hear Brooks so relaxed. Not only is his sense of humor apparent on many of these tracks—particularly on the appealingly silly "Cowgirl's Saddle" and the ramshackle "My Baby No Esta Aqui"—but even on straight-ahead numbers like "Allison Miranda" he sounds like he's having a good time, which wasn't always the case on *Fresh Horses* and *Sevens*. That looser spirit is evident even on ballads like "For a Minute There" or "Last Night I Had the Strangest Dream," but the most appealing thing about *The Lost Sessions* is that it's not devoted to slow songs like these; they're balanced by driving, anthemic modern country like "I'd Rather Have Nothing," barroom ballads like "Under the Table," ragged singalongs like the terrific "She Don't Care About Me," modern-day western tunes like "That Girl Is a Cowboy," and the aforementioned "Cowgirl's Saddle" and "My Baby No Esta Aqui." Garth hasn't had a record this consistent or compulsively listenable in years, which means that this rarities collection is far from being something just for diehards: this is for anybody who's ever enjoyed his music. No wonder it's been released independently of the box set: *The Lost Sessions* deserves to be heard on its own terms, since it's one of Brooks' best albums of the last 15 years.

Stephen Thomas Erlewine

Kix Brooks

Kix Brooks
October 1993, Capitol

Kix Brooks lone full-length solo effort was originally issued in 1989, the thinking being that the successful songwriter would find just as much stardom as a solo act. Well, it didn't quite work out that way, and despite the charting of the single "Sacred Ground" and a clutch of good-timin' country-pop songs like "Way Up North Around Shreveport," the album tanked. *Kix Brooks* does wilt a bit under its late '80s sheen—the synths on "There's a Telephone Ringing" are a wash out. And its reliance on easy lyrical devices concerning cold beer and lovelorn teenage wanderlust mires portions of the album in Forgettableville. However, it should have no trouble appealing to Brooks & Dunn fans, since its best moments ("Baby When Your Heart Breaks Down," "The River") cleverly mix Brooks' soulful croon with hearty honky tonk and warm acoustic instrumentation.

Johnny Loftus

Junior Brown

12 Shades of Brown
1993, Curb

Brown's debut deck shines like gold with standout original material like "They Don't Choose to Live That Way," "My

Hillbilly Hula Gal," and "My Baby Don't Dance to Nothing but Ernest Tubb" being particular noteworthy. Possessing a voice that will curl the hair on the back of your neck while picking both single-string picking and slide stylings on his twin neck "guit-steel," this is a mighty-talented fella, neo-traditionalist or not.

Cub Koda

Guit with It
August 1993, Curb

Junior Brown's rumbling, strikingly deep voice, tasty electric and steel guitar playing, and splendid honky-tonk and Western swing songs have made him a sensation in country circles. There's nothing phony or cliché about Brown's music; this is the genuine, untutored, undiluted article. Brown can sing tunes requiring sincerity, ache or irony with equal flair. The CD's 12 cuts include the nearly 12-minute "Guit-Steel Blues," and a sharp cover of Hank Garland's "Sugarfoot Stomp," and the bittersweet "Doin' What Comes Easy to a Fool," and "Holding Pattern." Brown is as vital and refreshing as early John Anderson or Randy Travis.

Ron Wynn

Semi-Crazy
May 1996, Curb

On *Semi-Crazy*, Junior Brown's third full-length album, the suit-and-tied Texas singer's clever lyrics, Ernest Tubb-like voice, and virtuoso guitar playing (on his custom-made, double-necked "guit-steel," which allows him to switch quickly between picking and steel playing) are once again intact and on the mark. *Semi-Crazy* may not bowl Brown fans over immediately—he offers no new twists as either a writer or player. On the other hand, because Brown is one of country music's most stunning guitarists (imagine Ornette Coleman crossed with Speedy West)—not to mention possessing a truly original sound—it's hard not to fall for the classic Brown sound of "I Hung It Up" (a standout for the guitar work), "Gotta Get Up Every Morning," and the fun-loving title track (his duet partner, Red Simpson, penned Brown's earlier song "Highway Patrol").

Kurt Wolff

Long Walk Back
August 1998, Curb

Just as much fun and as satisfying as he always is, Junior Brown once more gits gone with all the energy and punch that has come to be expected of this hardcore honky tonker. While the title cut is good, he really revs things up on the all-instrumental "Peelin' Taters" and "I'm All Fired Up." "Stupid Blues," "Just a Little Love," and "Read 'Em and Weep" display the interesting blend of Brown's own Texas swing/Bakersfield/honky tonk brand of country & western music. For a little spice, Junior adds a cover of the Elvis hit

"Rock-A-Hula Baby" and the Hunter/Vincent tune "(I'm Just) Looking for Love." As always, Tanya Rae provides the complementary backing vocals that make the Brown sound so unique. One of traditional country music's favorite good ol' boys, Junior Brown hits the nail directly on the head once again.

Jana Pendragon

Marty Brown

High & Dry
1991, MCA

If everything here were as pure a hillbilly distillation as the title track or the loopy "Old King Kong," Brown might come off like a simple hick with limited nostalgia appeal. But his range is surprisingly wide. Brown's ballads—"I'll Climb Any Mountain" and "Wildest Dreams"—though simple, build to stunning, emotional climaxes. "Every Now and Then" is the equal of many of The Everly Brothers' best. And "Nobody Knows" is surely one of the most lonesome wails in a long, long time.

Brian Mansfield

Wild Kentucky Skies
1993, MCA

One of the best things about Marty Brown's music is that it possesses the qualities that people both love and hate about country music. Brown takes a sure-fire hit song, "I Don't Wanna See You," then sings it in a voice that won't let folks forget just how backwoods country music can be. Songs like "It Must Be the Rain" and "Let's Begin Again" have soaring choruses that recall The Everlys at their best. On the other hand, "No Honky Tonkin' Tonight" and "I'd Rather Fish Than Fight" put to shame the lip service some singers pay to Hank Williams, Sr. and Jimmie Rodgers. With the eerie "She's Gone," Brown takes the country death ballad into territory it's never seen before, and he follows it with the sentimental "Kentucky Skies." Brown is pure country without being purist. Flatly put, he's a hillbilly and proud of it.

Brian Mansfield

Cryin', Lovin', Leavin'
1994, MCA

By his third album, Brown and producer Richard Bennett could be pretty confident they weren't going to get any radio play, so they just cut loose and made as pure an album as Brown was had in him. "You Must Be Mistakin' Me" and "Too Blue to Crow" possess a country sound so hard, they make most New Traditionalists sound like Muzak. Brown cuts Moon Mullican's "Cherokee Boogie," sings "Shameless Lies" with Melba Montgomery, shamelessly cops from Buddy Holly's "Crying, Waiting, Hoping" with the title cut,

and finishes with a gorgeous duet with Joy Lynn White on "I Love Only You."

Brian Mansfield

Shannon Brown

Corn Fed
February 2006, Warner Bros.

Shannon Brown is the latest in a long line of Big & Rich protégés—and the close association with John Rich, who produced her 2006 debut, *Corn Fed*, and had a hand in writing just over half of its songs, at least separates her from the pack of singers who pattern their sound after Big & Rich without actually working with the gonzo duo. Her closest comparison within the Big & Rich stable would be Gretchen Wilson, the stylized redneck woman who kicked up a storm in 2004, around the same time Big & Rich started making waves with their debut, *Horse of a Different Color*. But if Wilson is a deliberate hell-raiser—half Tanya Tucker and half Shania Twain—Brown is the girl next door, sweet and friendly, with just a little bit of sex and sass. And she might be a better straight-up singer than Wilson, too, boasting a greater range and a sense of subtlety—which isn't necessarily a plus for a singer tackling John Rich material. Like a lot of his work, his songs for *Corn Fed* are often contrived and cutesy, and what once sounded fresh and fun is creeping toward the formulaic, particularly on self-congratulatory cuts like "High Hopes," where Rich confronts critics who don't call this new breed of country "country." In the hands of a vocalist without charisma, this could be deadly, but Brown is a thoroughly appealing singer, filled with down-home charm but a vocal power that you don't hear every day. Shannon had been kicking around Nashville for a while before she finally had this opportunity to record a full-length debut—she had a song on the soundtrack for Miramax's 1999 overhyped indie comedy flop *Happy Texas*, and sang some backup vocals on records by Chely Wright, Richard Marx, Lorrie Morgan, and Kenny Chesney—and the skills she developed during those years in the trenches are evident in how she sounds equally convincing on the searching, introspective ballad "Small Town Girl," the funny, swaggering "Big Man," the gospel-inflected "Can I Get an Amen," and the terrific title track. She's good enough that when the Rich originals veer toward formula, she can wring something interesting out of them, but the really promising thing about *Corn Fed* is that the seven songs she had a hand in writing are the best here, suggesting that not only does Brown have a fine debut on her hands, but she has a bright future as well.

Stephen Thomas Erlewine

Tracy Byrd

No Ordinary Man
1994, MCA

No Ordinary Man, Tracy Byrd's second album, was his breakthrough record and its easy to see why. While he was still sorting out the ins and outs of recording on his debut album, Byrd sounds raw, vibrant, and confident throughout *No Ordinary Man*, which is clear from the record's first single, "Lifestyles of the Not So Rich and Famous" and the first-rate weeper "The Keeper of the Stars." Byrd plays ballads and up-tempo dance numbers equally well and his set of material on the album is fairly consistent, making the album his best to date.

Thom Owens

Big Love
October 1996, MCA

Tracy Byrd doesn't change his formula much with *Big Love*. He still works the same new-traditionalist ground that he did with his debut album, only with more confidence—his voice is more assured and, more impressively, his selection of material is stronger and more adventurous. On the whole, *Big Love* is the equal to *No Ordinary Man*.

Thom Owens

I'm from the Country
May 1998, MCA

With *I'm from the Country*, Tracy Byrd continues his streak of sturdy, well-crafted neo-traditionalist contemporary country. With each album, Byrd grows more confident in his delivery and choice of material, which naturally makes the albums stronger. There are still a couple of filler numbers on *I'm from the Country*, but the key to the record's success is that he takes pains in proving the title true—and by the end of the record, you have no question that he is indeed from the country.

Thom Owens

It's About Time
November 1999, RCA

On *It's About Time*, his first album for RCA Records, Tracy Byrd slyly adds some pop flourishes to his neo-traditionalist style. Some longtime followers may be surprised how smoothly the opening track "Put Your Hand in Mine" goes down, but Byrd straightens things out with the next two cuts, "It's About Time" and "Can't Have One Without the Other," which glide along with mildly twangy guitars and his rich baritone. From that point on, *It's About Time* follows a strange path, bouncing between good, neo-traditionalist country and music that seems a little too smooth for Byrd. That's not really a problem, since he's a very good singer and he sounds good no matter what he's singing, but the pace of the album nevertheless is a little awkward, mainly due to the fact that the pop-tinged material isn't quite as strong as the straight country. Still, Byrd is a classy, professional performer, which makes sorting through the chaff to find the wheat a worthwhile experience.

Stephen Thomas Erlewine

Ten Rounds
July 2001, RCA

Tracy Byrd seems to have a knack for recording well-penned songs that pack an emotional punch using just the right words. *Ten Rounds* is no exception, but don't expect Byrd to drag you down with the "tear jerkers"; there's plenty of fun on this one too. Straying away from the pop sound that was infiltrating the music coming out of Nashville at the time of this album's release, Byrd's *Ten Rounds* is a traditional country album, but it isn't filled with the preachiness of the staunch traditionalists. Even "A Good Way to Get on My Bad Side," Byrd's duet with fellow Beaumont, TX, native Mark Chesnutt, doesn't cut completely to the quick when the two lambaste "boy band crap." The same song hails the music of the great Rolling Stones. Byrd's power ballad delivery is present too on cuts such as "Needed" and the Spanish-flavored "Just Let Me Be in Love." Playing the philosopher on

"How Much Does the World Weigh," Byrd chronicles many of life's laments, reminding you to count your blessings. As always, Byrd lets the music speak his heart in *Ten Rounds*, and that's probably at least part of what makes him one of country music's most stable artists.

Rick Cohoon

The Truth About Men
July 2003, RCA

Tracy Byrd is a bit of a goofball, which is a compliment. Unlike his second wave new traditionalist brethren, he realizes that a good part of country music is having a good time, and he refuses to take things too seriously. Add to that a good taste in songwriters—something that can be particularly difficult for his peers, especially in terms of ballads—and you have somebody who's a reliable record maker, somebody who always has a good joke and a good ballad at hand. Since he's so consistent, he's easy to underrate, because he makes it all seem easy and he does it with a smile. A smash hit like "Ten Rounds with Jose Cuervo" can provide an opportunity to reassess an artist, or at least to take stock of what he has to offer, and that happened with Byrd's 2001 album, *Ten Rounds*, yet another solid record that stood out from the pack due to that great song. For his follow-up, 2003's *The Truth About Men*, Byrd could have used that big hit to try something else, but he doesn't. He sticks to his tried and true neo-honky tonk and contemporary country ballad formula. But if a formula works, why try to change it? And *The Truth About Men* proves that the formula does work, offering smiles and slow dances in equal measure, all delivered with an offhand, guy-next-door charm from Byrd. Sometimes the slow tunes get a little too slow, sometimes the up-tempo numbers are a little too silly (the title track has a good premise but some of the jibes don't quite work, not least because the Die Hard 4 mentioned in the second verse as a film preference doesn't even exist), but these are minor quibbles since this is a fun record. It has good-time party songs like the cheerful "Drinkin' Bone" (which is connected to the "party bone," after all) and "How'd I Wind Up in Jamaica," which does Jimmy Buffett better than "It's Five O'Clock Somewhere," Buffett's duet with Alan Jackson that was a smash hit the summer *The Truth About Men* was released, as well as good ballads like Rodney Crowell's "Making Memories of Us." By the time the record closes with a live version of "Ten Rounds with Jose Cuervo," you're beyond wondering why it's here and just enjoying the ride. True, this album doesn't offer much different than other Byrd records, but song for song, it's one of his finest efforts and a hell of a lot of fun.

Stephen Thomas Erlewine

Definitive Collection
March 2007, MCA Nashville

This is the fourth hits compilation devoted to the recordings of Tracy Byrd, but it is the first one to contain tracks from both his MCA/Universal and RCA/BNA Records affiliations, which gives it a leg up on MCA's *Keepers: Greatest Hits* and

BNA's *Greatest Hits* (not to mention the Byrd entry in MCA's discount-priced *20th Century Masters - The Millennium Collection* series). Thus, it spans Byrd's entire major-label career, which lasted from 1992 to 2004. And unlike those earlier sets, none of which contained more than 12 tracks, this one stretches out to 18 songs and nearly an hour. Even better, those 18 selections constitute all of Byrd's Top 20 country hits in chronological order, from the chart-topping "Holdin' Heaven" to "Drinkin' Bone," including his other number one hit, "Ten Rounds with Jose Cuervo." This foolproof track list and sequencing turns out to present an excellent representation of Byrd, a talented country singer operating in the same neo-traditionalist realm as George Strait who is equally at home with a sentimental ballad or a honky tonk singalong, with a taste for two-step and Western swing tunes. He isn't particularly original, which may be why the hits dried up after a decade, but this album provides a reasonable portrait of what the more traditional side of country music sounded like from the mid-'90s to the mid-2000s. It is also what it claims to be, the definitive collection of Tracy Byrd.

William Ruhlmann

Chris Cagle

Play It Loud
October 2000, Virgin

Like many young country music artists, Chris Cagle didn't grow up with country music so much as he did country-influenced pop and rock; his touchstones are the Eagles and Lynyrd Skynyrd, not Hank Williams and Merle Haggard. While his debut album *Play It Loud* unquestionably deserves to be filed under country, it's best to think of it just as much in the Southern rock category. Listening to it, music fans will be reminded most frequently of the Marshall Tucker Band and, especially, the Charlie Daniels Band. Cagle is most at home on up-tempo tracks like "Country by the Grace of God," "Rock the Boat," and the title track, also showing an affinity for swamp rock on "Love Between a Woman and a Man." Hence the leadoff track, "My Love Goes on and On," released months ahead of the album as Cagle's first single, is a good representation of his style, since it is another driving country-rocker. Necessarily, Cagle mixes in a few ballads, but they are not among the album's most impressive tracks. It may be that, with slower tempos and more emphasis on lyrics, such songs reveal Cagle's formulaic songwriting approach less flatteringly. The cliché-ridden, stereotypical declarations of romantic devotion would require a more distinctive balladeer to put it over successfully. The chief exception is the heart-rending "I Breathe In, I Breathe Out," actually Cagle's first song to be recorded (David Kersh cut it in 1997), which was added to the album for its Capitol Records reissue in June, 2001, along with another bonus track, "Are You Ever Gonna Love Me," and some multi-media content including the video for "Laredo," the album's second emphasis track and second chart hit. Cagle is an enthusiastic and engaging performer on his first album, but not yet a fully developed talent.

William Ruhlmann

Chris Cagle
April 2003, Capitol

Though there are moments when he's clearly trying a little too hard, *Chris Cagle* delivers a generally agreeable set on his sophomore release. There are a few problems: the extremely crisp production has almost too much presence and the artist

and his musicians seem to be emoting about an inch in front of the listener's nose. And Cagle's writing leans too often on the creaky formula of hanging the song on the hook of a knee-slap punch line. This can work as long as the language feels natural, like something someone in the country demographic might actually say—which is why "we're not growing old, we're growing love" misses the mark on "Growin' Love," for example. (Cagle's decision to rhyme "change" with "change" in the same song is even more awkward.) Elsewhere, though, his earnest, nasal singing and overall exuberance sell even the weaker material, and where he comes up with a writing gimmick that's actually fresh, such as the chronological breakdown of a happy relationship on "What a Beautiful Day," he hits a clean home run.

Robert L. Doerschuk

Anywhere But Here
October 2005, EMI

On his third album, *Anywhere But Here*, Chris Cagle's rock influences shine stronger than ever. Not only does he cover Bon Jovi's "Wanted Dead or Alive" and name-drop Lynyrd Skynyrd, but "Hey Ya'll" has a defiant, hard-rocking swagger and he favors anthemic mid-tempo tunes built on classic rock to honky tonk ravers. But in a time where Big & Rich and their Muzik Mafia cohorts are rewriting contemporary country music as a flashy, ironic lark, this devotion to classic and Southern rock makes Cagle a bit of a traditionalist, and he wears it well on *Anywhere But Here*. While some of the power ballads veer a little bit toward the generic, there are a bunch of strong songs here, ranging from the opening "You Might Want to Think About It," where Cagle takes a stand for Middle America, to the soaring "Maria," which may be his best fusion of modern country and AOR. Throughout it all, Cagle remains an appealing singer—his voice may be a little thin, but it's friendly, and it can help sell his tales of love, loss, and living. *Anywhere But Here* may not be a knockout, but it's a thoroughly likeable, engaging record that proves Chris Cagle is something of a country everyman for 2005, which not only makes him endearing, but a little refreshing next to such oversize personalities as Big & Rich and Toby Keith.

Stephen Thomas Erlewine

Mary Chapin Carpenter

State of the Heart
1989, Columbia

Carpenter, a folkie, eventually turned to the country market, especially on her third album, *Shooting Straight in the Dark*. On this, her second, she's still in transition, which makes her more thoughtful than the average country singer and catchier than the average folkie, especially on her breakthrough country hit, "Never Had It So Good." The album also includes "Quittin' Time," "Something of a Dreamer," and "How Do."

William Ruhlmann

Shooting Straight in the Dark
1990, Columbia

Although Mary Chapin Carpenter's second album yielded two Top Ten hits, it was the release of 1990's *Shooting Straight in the Dark* that confirmed her talents as an artist who could easily stage a crossover without relinquishing her country roots. With an even stronger infusion of folk and pop, Carpenter opened herself up to a wider market, taking the Cajun-tinged "Down at the Twist and Shout" (with the help of Beausoleil) to number two on the country charts, a song that also netted her a Grammy for best country vocal performance by a female. Both "You Win Again" and Gene Vincent's "Right Now" were also released as singles, expanding Carpenter's exposure even more so, but the other tracks from the album also reveal her lyrical strength and attentive songwriting prowess. "Halley Came to Jackson" is a wonderful tale about a small town's fascination with and misconception about Halley's comet back in 1910, while tracks such as "What You Didn't Say" and "When She's Gone" are also fresh-sounding country efforts that shine a light on her delicate but hearty singing style. Carpenter gets some help from Shawn Colvin on a few of the cuts and, because their collaboration worked so well, she and a number of other artists appeared on her next album and on 1994's *Stones in the Road*, expanding her material to an even greater extent. *Shooting Straight in the Dark* was indeed a breakthrough album for Carpenter, not only in a commercial sense but at a personal level as well, and its progressive repercussions helped in making 1992's *Come on Come On* an even stronger effort, spawning a myriad of hit singles.

Mike DeGagne

Come On Come On
1992, Columbia

Come on Come On proved that even with two previous hit albums under her belt, Mary Chapin Carpenter was still as hot as could be. This album serves as one of the signposts that contemporary country would not only aspire to, but actually become in the 21st century. One need only to stack this slab up against 2006 recordings by Little Big Town and Sugarland to see the roots of Carpenter's blend of sophisticated pop, folk, and soft rock with country. This disc climbed all the way to number six on the country charts, yielding an astonishing seven hit singles, fully revealing Carpenter's meld of aesthetics, skill, and marketing savvy, and she established herself not only as one of her chosen genre's top artists, but crossed over into the then-burgeoning Americana and AAA radio formats as well. With friends such as Rosanne Cash, Joe Diffie, Shawn Colvin, and the Indigo Girls lending a hand, there's a full range of country, folk, and pop-styled songs strewn across the album, helping it and Carpenter herself gain enormous recognition from other audiences outside of country music. "He Thinks He'll Keep Her," a title keeping with country music's tradition of double entendres, became Carpenter's first number one hit, while the confident "I Feel Lucky" peaked at number four and netted her another Grammy. Lucinda Williams' "Passionate Kisses," with its

beautiful guitar arrangements, also made it to number four, and Carpenter's vocal enthusiasm makes Dire Straits' "The Bug" one of the album's most spirited efforts. These songs, along with the title track's compelling folk essence, gave *Come on Come On* a well-rounded sound and exposed her talent for reaching slightly beyond the genre's long-established niches. Not only is Carpenter's music extendable, but her writing rescues country music from its familiar themes of "love 'em and leave 'em" conventionality while still managing to portray maturely the perils of romance and heartbreak from a female perspective. Carpenter repeated much of *Come on Come On*'s full-ranged charm for 1994's *Stones in the Road* release, which garnered her yet a third Grammy in as many albums.

Mike DeGagne & Thom Jurek

Stones in the Road
1994, Columbia

Stones in the Road was an eagerly awaited album from Mary Chapin Carpenter; the runaway success of *Come on Come On* established her as a bona star in the country and up-and-coming AAA radio formats. For this offering, she tipped her sound down to its basics and returned to the core of her music—namely, her folkier singer/songwriter roots. Although the lyrics are among her best and the songs thoroughly memorable and beautifully literate, Carpenter cut back on the number of hooks in her melodies, creating a palette that required closer listening to appreciate. There were no immediately radio-friendly hits to be found here—though radio did indeed pick up on it and the album did exceptionally well. Previously, she found a balance between the lyrical and musical aspects of her writing, walking a tightrope between words and hooks. Here, she concentrates on lyrics, giving the listener something that might require working a bit to appreciate—but also something to hold on to. And craft never leaves Carpenter's songs; these are as finely wrought as anything she's ever done and better than most. There are up-tempo tracks here, such as "House of Cards," the dreamy "A Keeper for Every Flame," the retro pop/rock sound of "Tender When I Want to Be" (a song Bruce Springsteen could have written and most likely deeply influenced), the single "Outside Looking In," and the barroom rocker "Shut Up and Kiss Me." But even these are lyrically more involved than those on earlier records. The moodier pieces here include the title track, the transcendent "John Doe No. 24," and the brilliant "The End of My Pirate Days." Carpenter and producer John Jennings hired a crack band that included drummer Kenny Aronoff, keyboardist Benmont Tench, guitarists Lee Roy Parnell and Steuart Smith, and backing vocalists Trisha Yearwood, Linda Williams, and Shawn Colvin. The sound of *Stones in the Road* is moody and very introspective at times, but it is never less than engaging and even pleasant. This is a worthy if startling entry in Mary Chapin Carpenter's catalog.

Thom Jurek

A Place in the World
October 1996, Columbia

Mary Chapin Carpenter's heady star continued to rise with 1994's *Stones in the Road*, one of her most introspective collections, as searing in its way as Rosanne Cash's *Interiors*. In order to consolidate that success with her follow-up, *A Place in the World*, Carpenter returned to the looser, more rock-sounding *Come on Come On* for inspiration—a record that netted seven hit singles. Carpenter and longtime bandmate and producer John Jennings hired studio aces like guitarist Duke Levine, keyboardist Benmont Tench, Fairport

Convention drummer Dave Mattacks, bassist Bob Glaub, and a host of backing vocalists including Shawn Colvin and Kim Richey, as well as a small string section. This collection still touches on reflective adult folk, but returns to hooky, catchy, radio-friendly country-rock for balance. On the whole, *A Place in the World* doesn't offer the deep reflective rewards of *Stones in the Road*, nor is it quite as kinetic as *Come on Come On*. Still, the record is exceptionally well-crafted and boasts several excellent songs that reflect on the desire for romance and the willingness to risk virtually everything for it. There's the old-time soul feel of "Let Me into Your Heart" with its backing chorus, the bubblegum pop/rock of "I Want to Be Your Girlfriend," the poignant rocker "Hero in Your Hometown"—which is a tracing-paper image for the way contemporary country singles sound in the 21st century—and the anthemic country-rock of "Keeping the Faith." The title track that closes the record is one of several more poignant and introspective tunes, offering a look at the kind of changes Carpenter was going through in her personal and professional life. Any real fan will want to own this one as well as the aforementioned others, but those new to her music may want to seek out the earlier recordings first.

Thom Jurek

Time* Sex* Love*
May 2001, Columbia

The asterisks following the words in the title to Mary Chapin Carpenter's seventh album of new material, *Time* Sex* Love**, hide more words: the full title is *Time Is the Great Gift; Sex Is the Great Equalizer; Love Is the Great Mystery*. If that sounds a bit overdone, it accurately introduces a collection given over to big statements. After four and a half years, Carpenter weighs in with a 73-plus-minute disc that thoughtfully examines important issues. Songs like "Simple Life" and "Maybe the World" take on the uncertainty of life at midstream, a subject also addressed in specifically careerist terms in "The Long Way Home" and philosophically in "Late for Your Life." But if that's the "time" part of the record, "sex" and "love" take primary place. Simply put, the better part of the album consists of torch songs that depict romantic and sexual obsession. Titles like "Swept Away" and "Slave to the Beauty" reveal the theme, and even attempted recoveries like "This Is Me Leaving You" reinforce it. The narrator of that song sounds like she'd be happier singing, "This is me crawling back to you." Working against the theme are the musical elements. Recording in Sir George Martin's Air Studios, Carpenter harks back to the Beatles' *Rubber Soul* for the album's sound, which lightens the mood. And her singing never supports the victimization in her lyrics, always maintaining its calm, murmuring tone. But the point is unmistakable. It's hard to see what any of this has to do with country radio, which, in any case, has been increasingly resistant to Carpenter. This album may not be a country blockbuster, ending the sleight of hand by which an artist who is essentially a folk-rock singer/songwriter has succeeded in Nashville, but it is a mature examination of life and love.

William Ruhlmann

Between Here and Gone
April 2004, Columbia

Early in her career, songwriter Mary Chapin Carpenter was marketed as a country artist, but strangely, it took ten albums before she would record in Nashville. On her first recording of new material since *Time* Sex* Love** in 2001, Carpenter surrounds herself with old friends and new faces. Carpenter co-produced the set with Matt Rollings and John Jennings, two musicians who have regularly appeared on her recordings over the years. Newcomers include fiddler Stuart Duncan, bassist Viktor Krauss, guitarist Dean Parks, Rob Ickes on Dobro, and vocalists Mac McAnally and Garrison Starr. Carpenter's musical palette is much wider than ever before; it is a record full of textures and shapes rather than musical frameworks for lyrics. While the songs are still the most important construct, the manner in which they emerge is far more expansive. And even though there is more steel guitar and fiddle here than on any of her previous recordings, and the record was done in Nash Vegas, it's about as far from a country record—in the modern sense of that word—as can be. Carpenter's cosmopolitanism is certainly a sound for its time.

The concerns experienced by the protagonists of her songs are those of everyday life at the dawn of a new century in the aftermath of September 11. That's not to say her melodies aren't timeless or that these songs do not transcend the present era (only time will reveal that to be true or false), but they tell the truth in a present tense we all recognize. There is an interesting fissure in these songs. As a body, they reflect transition and travel interior as well as actual byways, and impart the emotional sensibilities of being adrift, not in the present or in the past (though recollection of the previous is constant, if fleeting), while the future is still a blurry impression on the horizon. These songs are fissures; they exist in the gaps where real emotions are allowed to articulate themselves quietly and insistently before being blotted out by changes in circumstance and location as they appear like mirages, shimmer, and disappear. While there are standout tracks—"Luna's Gone," "Goodnight America," "My Heaven," "Beautiful Racket," "Grand Central Station" (the most devastatingly beautiful cut on the album), and "Elysium"—the entire record holds together like a narrative mosaic; bits and pieces show up again and again, from song to song, without exact repetition.

Between Here and Gone will hopefully garner some singles and get radio play, but it's hardly that kind of outing. In fact, one has to wonder if radio is brave enough to deal with the complex yet nearly universal emotions Carpenter explores in these gorgeous songs. Musically, this is a sophisticated but very accessible recording, pleasant in its tempos and in its lush presentation. But there is no ear candy here, nothing to while away idle moments by; it is not a "dark" or "melancholy" record, but it is a serious one. *Between Here and Gone* quietly demands the listener's attention and dives deeply into a labyrinth of emotions before emerging as a validating, affirmative, and instructive experience; it is an album not only to experience, but to hold on to. That's a lot for a pop album to promise, let alone deliver, and *Between Here and Gone* is marvelous; it does both.

Thom Jurek

The Calling
March 2007, Zoe

One thing is certain: Mary Chapin Carpenter has heard the sound of the new Nashville. She brings the electric guitars and she brings her Martin; she allows the mix to bring up those drums and basslines. She's no longer afraid of rock & roll as long

MARY CHAPIN CARPENTER   THE CALLING

as it blends with her brand of folkish country. After years of walking the outside, despite a hit record or two, seemingly afraid to really let it rip, she has arrived here, on *The Calling*. Oh yeah, yeah, that's a good thing; it may even be a great thing. Carpenter has always allowed her songwriting to take precedence over her recorded performances, and even though her album performances have sometimes been stellar, they've also been just a little too restrained. The title track that opens *The Calling* and "We're All Right" rock harder than any-thing she's ever cut. The beautiful thing is that with the bigger volume and the loosed electric six-strings, her big voice has more room and those killer hooks she writes don't disappear in the mix. They come off sounding like the anthems they should be. Carpenter has a hell of a way of looking at life from all sides, from behind the closed doors, from the empty lanes and the darkening countryside. She has always had a special way of looking at fate and destiny from the perch of those lives that hold on with only a shred of hope but refuse to give up or let go. That eagerness to survive in the face of all odds, or to affirm the essential goodness of a moment where one of her protagonists can simply breathe, has been her art. She does this better than most and is second to none in her picaresque narratives of the wish to be free, and of embracing freedom as an alternative to despair. And while the music has never matched the tautness of her lyrics, it does here. That doesn't mean the gentleness is all gone. On "Twilight" (a song James Taylor or Nanci Griffith should beg her to cover), the acoustic guitars, vibraphone, cajon (by Russ Kunkel, no less), and electrics blend gently but empathically. "On and On It Goes" is another ballad, loaded with emotion but delivered with the empathy of an old friend imparting a story. The huge drums on "It Must Have Happened" are, along with the title cut, sure bets for videos and singles. This cut just rocks in the way Sugarland rock, straight up, fat, with a message and enough heart to fill a Bruce Springsteen record. The refrain is utterly gorgeous. The jangling Rickenbackers on "Your Life Story" is another candidate for a single. The bottom line, as the album unfolds—whether it's "On with the Song," (written for the Dixie Chicks during their season in hell and an actual anthem), the sweet electric ballad "Why Shouldn't We," or the whispering closer "Bright Morning Star"—is that it never ceases not only to please, but to pull the listener deeper into Carpenter's wide-ranging poetic world. Time will tell, of course, but in *The Calling*, Carpenter may have her finest moment yet; it also feels like an artistic rebirth. These songs come from her marrow and the conviction she sings them with proves it. Carpenter and her co-producer Matt Rollings should be awfully proud of this one.

Thom Jurek

Jason Michael Carroll

Waitin' in the Country
February 2007, Arista Nashville

On the cover of his 2007 debut, *Waitin' in the Country*, Jason Michael Carroll certainly looks like a hunk—and not just a country hunk, either; he looks like Samantha's main man Smith during the waning days of *Sex & the City*, which means he's marketable not just to the country audience but perhaps to the crossover audience as well. So, he looks the part of a country idol and, with his warm, rounded baritone, he sounds like one too, a picture-perfect definition of what a modern country singer should be, so it should come as no surprise that *Waitin' in the Country* also sounds perfectly tailored toward country conventions in the mid-2000s. Carroll never shies away from cliché on this album—he feels at home in the country, will sleep when he's dead, has "Honky Tonk Friends," lives in "Anywhere USA," and finds "No Good in Goodbye"—and the music is a blend of familiar arena rock riffs and new traditionalism swagger, tempered by more than its fair share of treacly sentiment on the ballads. But if *Waitin' in the Country* never defies convention, it never does it badly, either. Sure, some of it can be silly—whether it's the prefabricated rowdy shout-alongs on the chorus of "Honky Tonk Friends" or the line "The people trust the steeple/And the steeple don't lie" on the title track—but Carroll comes across as a likeable, ingratiating guy next door: he may look like a model, but there's an ordinariness in his voice that's endearing. It also suits his friendly, ordinary country and helps make *Waitin' in the Country* an enjoyable first album despite its occasional lapses into saccharine pop and a slight lack of truly memorable material.

Stephen Thomas Erlewine

Carlene Carter

Carlene Carter
1978, Warner Bros.

By recording her debut album in England, Carlene Carter served notice that despite coming from a legendary American country music family, she intended to make her own way in the biz and establish her own musical identity. So while there's a strong country-rock vibe throughout *Carlene Carter*, it's filtered through the British pub rock sensibilities of the Rumour, whose members produce, arrange, and play on all of the tracks on this album (with occasional cameo appearances from pub rock icons Graham Parker, Terry Williams, and Nick Lowe). The results of this transatlantic crossbreeding are generally winning, if a little uneven; on a few tracks, it seems as if both Carter and the Rumour are keeping some of their energy in check as they try to feel each other out. For the most part, though, the performances on *Carlene Carter* are bright and enthusiastic, and the songwriting contributions of Alex Call, Graham Parker, and Carter herself are all quite good, even if their subject matter is generally nothing more complex than love gone wrong. To top it all off, Carter had the good sense to call in at least one family member to help out—and brother-in-law Rodney Crowell did not disappoint, contributing "Never Together but Close Sometimes," a bouncy rocker that's the album's clear highlight.

K.A. Scott

Musical Shapes
1980, F Beat

This is Carter's masterpiece to date—great songs and production that could easily fit into today's climate of country radio.

Cub Koda

Blue Nun
1981, F Beat

Carter's American label passed on this one, and it's too bad. While it's not one of her best albums, when she's on, she's dead on. It's interesting from a historical point because it somewhat chronicles her musical associations with former-husband Nick Lowe and Paul Carrack (ex-Ace, Squeeze, Mike + the Mechanics).

Jim Worbois

I Fell in Love
1990, Reprise

Carlene Carter spent much of her recording career waging a good-natured war between her rock & roll instincts and her country breeding before she signed with Reprise Records in 1989. With *I Fell in Love*, her first album for Reprise, Carter's music suggested she was finally willing to play ball with Nashville . . . but only just. *I Fell in Love* was a more polished set than Carter had recorded up to that time, and sounded like her version of a mainstream country record. But beneath the smooth veneer, Carter's spunky attitude still shines through, and here she claims a thoroughly enjoyable middle ground between Music City traditionalism and roughhouse honky tonk rock. With Tom Petty bassist Howie Epstein in as producer, *I Fell in Love* boasts a savvy studio sound and a legion of top-shelf pickers (including Albert Lee and James Burton on guitars and Benmont Tench on keyboards), but Carter lights a fire under nearly every tune on this set, and even the low-key love songs generate some sparks. And with June Carter Cash and Levon Helm joining her on backing vocals, the country accents ring out with an honesty and purity that cuts through the radio-ready mix. *I Fell in Love* may have been an effort to play nice on Carter's part, but it doesn't sound like a compromise so much as proof she was enough of a talent to have her cake and eat it, too. And in this case, the cake is pretty tasty stuff.

Mark Deming

Little Love Letters
1993, Giant

This is the album fans always dreamed she would make. While it shows off her love of, and ability to handle, various styles of music, she never loses her direction.

Jim Worbois

Little Acts of Treason
October 1995, Giant

Carlene Carter's *Little Acts of Treason* doesn't break much new ground for the singer, but that's not necessarily a bad thing. While she continues in the same vein as *Little Love Letters*, the music is done well, even if the album isn't as infectious and catchy as her previous album.

Stephen Thomas Erlewine

Hindsight 20/20
September 1996, Giant

Hindsight 20/20 is a comprehensive overview of Carlene Carter's career, concentrating on country hits like "Every Little Thing" and "I Fell in Love," but also touching on her earlier recordings like "Never Together But Close Sometimes." The compilation offers an excellent introduction and encapsulation of one of the finest female country singers of the '80s and '90s.

Stephen Thomas Erlewine

Deana Carter

Did I Shave My Legs for This?
1995, Capitol Nashville

Deana Carter's debut album may have seemed like the arrival of an overnight sensation, but that was hardly the truth. Carter cracked it finally at 30, after trying since she was 17 as the daughter of kicking country guitar picker Fred Carter. With its ironic odd title and its mix of singer/songwriter folk, new traditionalist country, and pop, Carter came up with a winner. Produced by Chris Farren and Jimmy Bowen, Carter's album features six originals, including the title track, "Count Me In," the amazing opener, "I've Loved Enough to Know," with its hooky guitars, shimmering fiddles, and cascading pianos, the gorgeous "Love Ain't Worth Making" and "Before We Ever Heard Goodbye," and "How Do I Get There." These are the album's strongest tunes, full of passion and sincerity regarding love, its fulfillment and impossibility, as well as its mystery. And the woman can write a hook. There's a radio-friendly rock and pop feel to tracks such as Mac Wiseman's hard country tonkin' "If This Is Love" and Matraca Berg's pedal steel-ringing "Strawberry Wine." That she sold a few million copies of this record to country fans is not surprising at all; that she sold a few million more to AAA radio fans and to those whose musical tastes are dictated by NPR is. Most of these folks bitch like crazy about "young country," and Carter defined it with her very first record in all the best ways: using the country tradition to make fine, well-crafted music that appeals to a broad range of tastes.

Thom Jurek

Everything's Gonna Be Alright
October 1998, Capitol Nashville

Deana Carter's debut album, *Did I Shave My Legs for This?*, was a surprise hit, considering that its grace, subtlety, and wit were largely qualities unheard of in contemporary country in 1996, the year it climbed up the charts. It immediately marked her as a major artist, placing great expectations on her second album, *Everything's Gonna Be Alright*. Lacking the surprise element of *Legs*, *Everything's Gonna Be Alright* is nevertheless in many ways its equal, since Carter has chosen to expand its sound, not to replicate it. There are more laid-back rock and pop elements to her style this time around, which fits well with her folky, melodic country. Even the presence of Lynyrd Skynyrd as the support band for "The Train Song" (earthy, not rowdy), works better than it reads. Furthermore, her songwriting is melodic and memorable, and her choice of covers, including Melanie's "Brand New Key," is inspired. As long as Carter continues to deliver albums as enchanting as *Everything's Gonna Be Alright*, things are going to be just fine for her and her fans.

Thom Owens

I'm Just a Girl
March 2003, Arista

Deana Carter had a hard time following up her acclaimed debut, 1995's *Did I Shave My Legs For This?*, stumbling with 1998's *Everything's Gonna Be Alright* before leaving Capitol Records and re-emerging nearly four and a half years later on Arista Nashville with *I'm Just a Girl*. A lot had happened in country music in the years that Carter sat out, including shifts toward both pop (in Shania Twain and Faith Hill) and roots (the *O Brother Where Art Thou?* phenomenon), and Carter continues to run outside the path by not pursuing either direction. Instead, she aims straight toward the heart of adult pop (slightly ironic, given the album's title and its *Seventeen* magazine-styled artwork), which really isn't too far off from where she was with on her first record. Still, there are telling differences: the production, apart from the closing raver "Girls' Night," is all smooth and polished, sweetened with pop and lacking nearly any hint of country, as well as the clear sense of humor. There's a keener eye toward a broader audience, right down to the cheesecake photos inside the liner notes, and the product placement in "I'm Just a Girl" sits uneasily (particularly since closing the chorus with "I'm a Chevy girl" makes it sound like an unofficial commercial). Those may seem disarming to those looking for the organic feel of *Did I Shave My Legs?*, but Carter does this pleasing adult pop better than nearly any of her peers, partially because her ambitions are modest and her songwriting is sturdy and tuneful. At times, the production is so even, the music simply flows out of the speaker without distinction between tracks, but the result is a record that holds together as a nice mood piece while holding up as individual songs. True, it doesn't deliver a knockout punch upon the first listen, but it wasn't designed to. It's a quiet grower, filled with easy listening and sunny vibes. It might not earn quite the same audience as her debut, but this is about as good as adult-oriented pop gets in 2003.

Stephen Thomas Erlewine

Johnny Cash

Rockabilly Blues [Koch]
1980, Koch

While stepdaughter Carlene Carter was hanging out with then-husband Nick Lowe and his British roots rock mates Dave Edmunds, Martin Belmont, and Pete Thomas, Johnny Cash decided to see what they thought about the font they claimed for inspiration: rockabilly and roots country. Lowe got to produce one track on *Rockabilly Blues*, as did old pal and rockabilly co-conspirator Cowboy Jack Clement. Earl Pool Ball did the other eight, but Cash held the reins tight. *Rockabilly Blues*, along with *Johnny 99*—also reissued by Koch—is one of the great lost Cash records. Not only does it feature two of his finer songs from the period, the title track and the bitter love song "Cold Lonesome Morning," it features Cash singing a pair of gems by Billy Joe Shaver, "The Cowboy Who Started the Fight" and "It Ain't Nothing New Babe," as well as one by Cash acolyte Kris Kristofferson, "The Last Time" (which, incidentally, is one of the last times a new Kristofferson tune was recorded by anyone). Cash's "Rockabilly Blues (Texas 1955)" is not essentially a rockabilly tune, though Edmunds' guitar playing certainly embodies its feel—but then, Cash was never a rockabilly singer, either. "One Way Rider," with its horns and staccato pacing, is the perfect song for Lowe to produce. June Carter is wailing on the duet, and the slide guitar parts ring like jagged bells through the heart of the mix. The only problem with this set is how quickly it blazes by. Why Columbia wasn't interested in Cash in 1980 is as confusing now as it was then. All the kids they groomed to come up after him, including newbies Montgomery Gentry, would have killed to make a record this fine.

Thom Jurek

American Recordings
1994, American

There are few artists who possess the seemingly unlimited crossover appeal of Johnny Cash. With *American Recordings*, the country legend somehow introduced himself to a modern rock audience by releasing a folk record. Of course, the Man in Black isn't your typical country musician, and *American Recordings* encompasses several different genres, but the folk label was applied chiefly because the songs feature Cash's vocals, acoustic guitar, and nothing else. Universally acknowledged as a country music icon, Cash found himself struggling to get any sort of support from country radio in the '90s as it became dominated by younger, pop-influenced acts. Not one to be discouraged by being shunned by the industry he helped to create, Cash signed with Rick Rubin's American Recordings, which was known for its hard rock and rap acts. Rubin, who had cut his teeth as a producer by working with Run-DMC and the Beastie Boys, was at the controls for the *American Recordings* album and comes off looking like a genius for simply giving Cash a mic and getting out of the way. The album opens with "Delia's Gone," a Cash original about murder that is both haunting and humorous. Several deftly chosen covers also appear, and Cash effortlessly makes each of them his own. One would be hard-pressed to think of a more perfect song for Cash to cover than Nick Lowe's "The Beast in Me." There is no one more qualified to perform a song asking God for salvation from one's inner demons than Johnny Cash. The diverse list of writers who also contribute songs includes Leonard Cohen, Kris Kristofferson, Glenn Danzig, and Tom Waits. Cash deftly applies his signature baritone and rhythmic guitar work to each track and creates what is ultimately a stark, foreboding, and supremely enjoyable album. For some reason, two tracks are live recordings from a performance at L.A.'s ultra-trendy *Viper Room*. The audience offers a few hoots and hollers, but it's unclear if it's because they're having a good time or because they think that's what country audiences are supposed to do. Taking Cash to the hipsters ultimately worked, as *American Recordings* was embraced by the alt-rock audience. "Delia's Gone" popped up on MTV and college radio, and Cash was a hit with a generation of listeners who had yet to be born when he had his first hit. *American Recordings* also garnered the 1995 Grammy Award for Best Contemporary Folk Album.

Mark Vanderhoff

Unchained
November 1996, Warner Bros.

For all of its critical praise, the all-acoustic Rick Rubin-produced *American Recordings* was slightly listless. For the follow-up, Cash and Rubin wisely decided to ditch the minimalist approach of *American Recordings* and set the Man in Black in front of a full band—namely, Tom Petty & the Heartbreakers. The pairing is surprisingly inspired, as the Heartbreakers prove to be a loose and muscular supporting band, giving Cash the opportunity to invest himself completely in the songs. Cash is more than up to the task, bringing life not only to classic country songs from Jimmie Rodgers and the Louvin Brothers, but also classic pop by Dean Martin ("Memories Are Made of This"), alternative rockers (Soundgarden's "Rusty Cage," Beck's "Rowboat"), and several made-to-order songs from the likes of Petty himself. Occasionally, the pairings are a little forced, but more often than not *Unchained* consists of remarkably vibrant and inspired music that lives up to Cash's status as a legend.

Stephen Thomas Erlewine

Rosanne Cash

Right or Wrong
1979, Columbia

On her debut American release (she'd done a record in Germany that she now disowns), Rosanne Cash may not have shaken the money tree or the *Billboard* charts, but she and husband/producer/collaborator Rodney Crowell began to change the face of contemporary country music forever. Recorded in L.A. and not Nash Vegas, *Right or Wrong* still utilized talent synonymous with Music City, but the sound that took country and merged it with the rock and pop styles of the day was a winning formula. Crowell and Cash made the song selections while Rodney called in Emmylou Harris's band (of which he was an alumnus) and some up and comers and created a sonic palette that accented the brave new world of stripped-down mixes and songs that came from the left field of country or pop (the European version of the album featured a Lennon/McCartney tune). Here are nods to the past and heritage in her father's "Big River," a couple of outlaw tunes from Keith Sykes (the title track and "Take Me, Take Me"), as well as the stunning ballad "Couldn't Do Nothing Right" by Karen Brooks and Gary P. Nunn. Here Jerry Jeff Walker recorded a hell of a version in the early '70s, but the crooning sorrow and ache in the grain of Cash's voice and the faux Caribbean rhythm behind a pedal steel-driven melody line make it an entirely different song. Speaking of voice, Cash is most comfortable singing searing ballads such as her own "This Has Happened Before," and Crowell's

"No Memories Hanging' Round," "Seeing's Believing," and "Anybody's Darlin." But Crowell's "Baby, Start Turnin' 'Em Down" is perhaps the strongest track on the album as it combines a restless country shuffle, a rocker's minor key blues riff, and a deliberate nod to Marvin Gaye's "Heard It Through the Grapevine" and Motown. *Right or Wrong* only got to number 42 on the Billboard chart, but it did make radio take notice that something new was about to happen, and on *Seven Year Ache*, the follow-up to this fine album, the floodgates opened.

Thom Jurek

Seven Year Ache
1981, Columbia

Blame whomever you want to for Garth Brooks and Shania Twain, but the bottom line is that Rosanne Cash's masterpiece *Seven Year Ache* paved the way for all of those folks as well as for Mary Chapin Carpenter, Shawn Colvin, and then some. Proclaimed by Cash and her husband/producer/collaborator, Rodney Crowell, as "punktry," the album adds an entirely new twist on the Nashville sound. Perhaps it is because this is L.A. country and reflects the cocaine bliss sound of the era as well as Fleetwood Mac's *Tusk* does. Utilizing everything from synthesizers and rock arrangements to pop ballad-styled charts and plenty of attitude, *Seven Year Ache* yielded three number one singles and songs by rock musicians such as Tom Petty and singer/songwriters like Keith Sykes and Steve Forbert. Of the singles, Cash penned two; the title track, which is a sorrowful indictment of her husband's philandering ways, and the shattering ballad "Blue Moon With Heartache." The third, the smash "My Baby Thinks He's a Train," was written by Asleep at the Wheel's Leroy Preston. Musically, the band included many of the same players from the *Right or Wrong* sessions, with the emerging vocal talent of former Pure Prairie League member Vince Gill. Forbert's "What Kinda Girl" is almost rockabilly in its shuffling intensity and punk bravado. It dares the listener to define the protagonist just to shatter the preconception. There's also a nod to tradition here in Cash's beautifully updated read of the Merle Haggard/Red Simpson nugget "You Don't Have Very Far to Go," complete with whinnying pedal steels and a honky tonk backbeat. In "My Baby Thinks He's a Train," Cash and Crowell very consciously offer a new generation interpretation of dad Johnny's sound. This rocks harder yet is smooth as silk and full of that desolate want Johnny offered in his delivery. But unlike her father's, this isn't a forlorn yearning want, it's a pissed off anthemic want. For the ambulance chasers, this record with its songs of infidelity and broken promises may indeed be the first crack in a marriage and collaboration that ended a decade later. The tempo borrows the old Tennessee Three rhythm, but sped up into the stratosphere, with a shifting Western swing line near the refrain. Over 20 years after it was first issued, *Seven Year Ache* sounds as fresh and revolutionary as it did when it was issued. Any album that stands that test of time in a field like country deserves to be regarded as a classic. Yes, this is the one that changed everything.

Thom Jurek

Somewhere in the Stars
1982, Columbia

Somewhere in the Stars followed by one year the wildly successful *Seven Year Ache*, Rosanne Cash's breakthrough record. Once again with husband Rodney Crowell in the producer's chair and acting as a full collaborator, Cash pushed the Nash Vegas envelope to the breaking point for the time. A listen to Shania Twain's *Come on Over* and *Up!* will point, in a winding manner, back to *Somewhere in the Stars*. Here are guitars ringing through with influences from Dire Straits to Graham Parker & the Rumour. Give a listen to Susanna Clark's "Oh, Yes I Can," and listen to Albert Lee's Mark Knopfler cop. Interestingly, Cash, while writing a great deal during this period, only recorded one of her own songs and co-wrote another with Crowell. The feel has British new wave, country, and L.A. rock blended into a seamless whole. Listen to the chug and tug of "Ain't No Money," written by Crowell, that opens the album. Linda Ronstadt in her prime could have cut this, but only Cash could bring the solid country gutbucket pout in her delivery.

The horn charts on "It Hasn't Happened Yet," a John Hiatt composition, are deep rooted in the Memphis soul tradition of Stax. Given Cash's voice, though, the track comes off at odds with traditions that have little in common except for being heartfelt articulations of the unspeakable. But the longing in Cash's voice stands at odds with the normally reserved slickness of Nash Vegas productions. Tom T. Hall's "That's How I Got to Memphis" feels out of place here, with its slim production and relatively straight country feel, but Cash doesn't skimp on her vocal; it's believable if not overly inspired, and her read of the song is true to Hall's—and the appearance of Johnny Cash on the last verse adds depth and mystery. The most angular track on the album is "I Look for Love," also by Hiatt, which seems like it was written after hearing Joe Jackson for the first time. With its odd lead line and funked-up bass, it feels like the track from outer space here, but in the grain of Cash's deeply passionate delivery it fits right in. The set closes with the title track. In its intimacy and shimmering surfaces, it points directly at records like *Interiors* and *The Wheel* that would come a decade later, though it's a love song, not a dark paean to something lost. As a follow-up to a smash album, *Somewhere in the Stars* was more than worthy and stands the test of time as a pillar in Cash's catalog.

Thom Jurek

Rhythm & Romance
1985, Columbia

Rhythm & Romance was recorded in 1984 and issued in 1984, almost three years after *Somewhere in the Stars*. *Rhythm & Romance* is significant in a number of ways—besides its obvious quality as a piece of popular art. Foremost, it's the first recording that really showcases Rosanne Cash as a songwriter. Of the ten tracks here, she wrote six and co-wrote two others. This is the beginning of a new path in her career, which remains to this day, where she writes all of her own material. Secondly, it's the first record she

made without producer/husband/songwriting partner Rodney Crowell (who was busy making his own breakthrough record, *Diamonds & Dirt*), David Molloy, and David Thoener. Thirdly, even after a nearly three-year absence and with a radical—by country standards—cover, the album topped the charts and charted two singles (in those days almost unheard of). Lastly, she used musicians who were from the L.A. studio scene rather than Nash Vegas stalwarts, guitarist Waddy Wachtel and keyboard ace Benmont Tench from Tom Petty's Heartbreakers among them. Vince Gill also began to emerge from the shadows on this set as a solid singer and guitarist in his own right.

But it's the material that makes any record. First there's Cash's sultry, sexual "Hold On" (which hit the number one spot) with its loping vocal and wanton ache, then there's "Second to No One," with its gorgeous melody, scathing autobiographical lyric, and shimmering acoustic guitars. The keyboard-driven "Halfway House," with its '50s rock melody filtered through '80s new wave riffing, where the guitars move into overdrive on the refrains, is a startling exercise in pushing the envelope. The stunning "Never Gonna Hurt," all hard rock guitars playing a Warren Zevon-esque "Werewolves of London"-type riff, is remarkable in how tough and snotty it is. A cover of John Fogerty's classic "Feelin' Blue" closes the album. It's Memphis funky and full of jagged angles where soul meets the blues meets rock & roll, in a context that is pure modern country. Cash's vocal is thoroughly convincing. Where the original is full of fear and spooky realization, Cash's is full of bravado and resignation to meet the rough stuff on the horizon head-on. Remarkable in every way, *Rhythm & Romance* stands the test of time as an expertly conceived and executed collection of songs that reveals a songwriter in full command of her talent and a singer at the peak of her powers—for whom the restraints of Nashville had become to tenuous to contend with for much longer.

Thom Jurek

King's Record Shop
1987, Columbia

Rosanne Cash's catalog on Columbia is nothing if not formidable. Her pioneering meld of country, rock & roll (with an emphasis on "rock"), folk, and even blues, her topical concerns (which went deeper than most songwriters who came before her in taking on the tough topics of life), and her insistence on working outside the Nashville box scored her a number of hits and blazed the trail for many women who came later. *King's Record Shop* followed by two years her flirtation with the kind of pop coming out of England in droves, the radically underappreciated *Rhythm & Romance*. *King's Record Shop*—produced by her then-husband and longtime collaborator Rodney Crowell—is a granite-solid collection of covers and originals that delve deeply into the traditions that informed her life and created her as an artist, while revealing the trouble in her marriage to Crowell. The opening track, Eliza Gilkyson's "Rosie Strike Back," is a real feminist country anthem, and contain killer backing vocals from Patty Smyth (of Scandal) and Steve Winwood. Her read of John Hiatt's "The Way We Make a Broken Heart" is the kind of torch and tang ballad that will stand the test of time simply for its gender-bending take on relationships. Her collaboration with Hank DeVito, "If You Change Your Mind," is a jangly folk-rock ballad that expresses romantic longing in the face of a wayward lover; in its choruses one hears need as well as generosity. "The Real Me," a song that offers the vulnerability, truth, and flaws of a life in the process of transformation, is a preview of the type of material that would appear on the nakedly revealing *Interiors*.

And it just goes deeper, from her rollicking and rebellious rocker "Somewhere Sometime" to the stellar cover of John Stewart's heart-wrenching "Runaway Train" to the straight-ahead country of her father Johnny's "Tennessee Flat Top Box." With its faux soul R&B chorus, Crowell's "I Don't Have to Crawl" is as full of want, cracked-heart honesty, and determination to keep standing as anything in country music. Ultimately, *King's Record Shop* is Rosanne Cash's classic, a work that transcends production and songwriting styles and the pop and country music of the time.

Thom Jurek

Interiors
1990, Columbia

On Rosanne Cash's final recording for Columbia's Nashville division she pulled out all the stops. Already known for her unflinching honesty, she took it to its most poignant and searing extreme on *Interiors*. Cash produced the record herself and wrote or co-wrote all the material here. A country record it's not, but that hardly matters. This is a pop record with teeth and ache and broken hearts strewn all over the place. In fact, *Interiors* has the feel of a battlefield emptied of everything but its ghosts. The album is a collection of ten songs linked thematically by the chronicling of the tension, dysfunction, and ultimate dissolution of Cash's marriage to Rodney Crowell caused by dishonesty, infidelity, substance abuse, and physical distance; and she owns her side of the street with courage without laying blame. Carefully wrought with subtle instrumentation surrounding her fearless, yet wavering vocals. Acoustic guitars, pianos, brushed drums, an occasional organ, a bass almost hidden under layers of ethereal grace—these are the musical trappings that frame Cash's voice as she sets about a task so seemingly painful it's almost uncomfortable to listen to. It's as if the listener is granted a private audience with her heart and innermost thoughts. Everything is here: the disillusionment, the anger, the vain hope of reconciliation, and finally the acceptance and resignation that endings are a part of life and serve their purpose. While these ten tracks are virtually inseparable from one another, there are standouts such as "Dance With the Tiger" written with John Stewart, "Real Woman" written with Crowell, "Mirror Image," "I Want a Cure," and the harrowing closer, "Paralyzed," where Cash is accompanied only by a piano. Here she lets her current position be known, that seeing the end of this relationship leaves her in the clutches of being unable to move from the emotional space she is in. This album is full of a truth that most would rather not acknowledge, but it is morally and spiritually instructive in terms of its lyrical content, and musically it is her masterpiece. In fact, it's proof that art can redeem what cannot be in human terms.

Thom Jurek

The Wheel
January 1993, Columbia

Like the dark, cathartic *Interiors*, *The Wheel* is an introspective, soul-searching set of confessional songs revolving around love and relationships. While many of the themes and emotions of *Interiors* are repeated on *The Wheel*, Roseanne Cash hasn't repeated herself, either lyrically or musically. Working from the same combination of folk and country that has fueled her songwriting throughout her career, she has created an album of subtle, melodic grace that helps convey the deep feelings of her lyrics. It's an immaculately-produced album, but that never detracts from the emotional core of Cash's music.

Stephen Thomas Erlewine

Rules of Travel
March 2003, Capitol

At every level, *Rules of Travel* distinguishes itself. A latecomer to songwriting, Rosanne Cash delivers plenty of compelling material, fully comparable in quality to the album's two non-original cuts. She comes up with fresh and intriguing chord changes to end verses and choruses on the title track, and images whose rugged eloquence perfectly fits the early-morning mumble of Steve Earle on "I'll Change for You." On "September When It Comes," she switches to a more homespun, folkloric imagery that suits her father's weathered, timeless rumble. The production values change very subtly according to what best suits each song, from the Wallflowers-oriented roots rock saunter of "Hope Against Hope" to the shadowy urban swing of "Will You Remember Me" to the stark acoustic setting of "Western Wall." Though her voice is hardly the most impressive instrument in country music, Cash knows how to compensate by using an understated approach to more quietly highlight the essence of a song. Given the quality of what she gives herself to work with on *Rules of Travel*, it's a method that can't miss.

Robert L. Doerschuk

Black Cadillac
January 2006, Capitol

In the 22 months that passed between the release of Rosanne Cash's wonderfully articulated *Rules of Travel* and *Black Cadillac*, she became an orphan. She lost her stepmother, June Carter Cash, in May of 2003; her father, Johnny, passed away in September of that same year; and in May of 2005, her mother, Vivian Liberto Cash Distin, left this world as well. According to Cash, she began writing the songs for *Black Cadillac* in spring 2003 and ended in spring 2005. She began recording in November 2004. In other words, the album is the aural documentation of a process of grief, loss, and acceptance. And though her family was not the typical American family, this set is universal in its concepts. Certainly, it is an elegy; her father's presence is everywhere here. It is also more than that; it is a reckoning, with memory, anger, love, joy, grief, pain, and resolve. The set opens with Johnny's disembodied voice calling her: "Rosanne, c'mon." And the title track kicks into gear with a rumbling bass, a drum kit, and guitars emerging sparsely, surrounding her voice as she sings, "It was a black Cadillac/That drove you away . . . Now one of us gets to go to heaven/While one has to stay here in hell." The guitars explode into the mix, carrying the refrain, breaking open not only the tune, but her heart: "It was a black Cadillac/Like the one you used to drive/You were always rollin'/But the wheels burnt up your life/It's a black heart of pain I'm wearin'/That suits me just fine/'Cause there was nothin' I could do for you/While you were still alive." These lyrics, the swirling six strings, a funky Fender Rhodes, the crashing of drums, and the distant, tinny horns quoting their place in "Ring of Fire," as the track ends, while it opens up the focus of the rest of the disc—it becomes the mission statement for the heart-rendering that follows.

Cash has a history of searing honesty; *Interiors* and *The*

Wheel are just two examples. But *Black Cadillac* engages it in a different way. She disguises nothing. There are no extended painterly metaphors. These are open and direct songs without self-pity, without artifice. Writing about her parents, she expresses regret, but doesn't ask for more time; there is only the open, unbowed humility of gratitude and the weight and burden of history, and experience that results in wisdom. In "I Was Watching You," she recounts her history from youth to age 50 with Johnny, and amid the atmospheric arrangements, she states plaintively, "Long after life/There is love." It's the crack in the record that becomes the catalyst for her search for meaning after these experiences. There are rockers, too, such as "Burn This Town Down," which struts its country, rock, and roots simultaneously. Yet it's all beside the point. From "God Is in the Roses," a nearly straight-up country tune that re-engages faith in God not as a concept, but as a place for the soul to find solace and rest in life's most difficult occurrences, the question of faith looms large on *Black Cadillac*. In "World Without Sound" she states, "I wish I was a Christian/And knew what to believe/I could learn a lot of rules/To put my mind at ease." "Like Fugitives" indicts religion—and a few other things—to a slippery trip-hop rhythm track and expresses anger purely and simply. The rocking "Dreams Are Not My Home" feels like it were written for Dire Straits. The poetic lyric is offered authoritatively against acoustic and electric guitars. This tune is a manifesto. Its refrain digs against the illusions of the past and the many temptations to escape the difficult present: "I want to live in the real world/I want to act like a real girl/I want to know I'm not alone/And that dreams are not my home." The bluesy country-rock in "House on the Lake" (referring to the old Cash home in Hendersonville, TN) evokes memory and the notion of place as a metaphor for passage and return. The guitars turn and wind around mandolin passages that underscore the determined declaration in Cash's voice.

Cash has always been a pioneer and experimented freely. Since the release of 1990's *Interiors*, she has distanced herself—on records—from her family's country roots; in the process, she's carved a small niche in the nebulous adult alternative "genre." *Black Cadillac* shows the songwriter coming full circle without compromise. Her signature brand of country music has become part of her mix again. She has always employed rock and pop sounds even on her early outings. Cash embraces country here as a part of the sonic tapestry that includes every kind of music she's interested in. This set was recorded in Los Angeles with Bill Botrell (the odd numbered cuts) and in New York with husband-producer John Leventhal (the even numbered ones), and it's an album that CMT and even country radio can warm to. (This is interesting, because in 2006 the music the genre consciously employs and strives to include is something Cash helped to pioneer as far back as the 1980s.) This album is extraordinary. It is brave, difficult, and honest. It is utterly moving and beautiful. Because it so successfully marries all of her strengths as a songwriter, singer, and musician, *Black Cadillac* may be the crowning achievement of her career thus far.

Thom Jurek

Kenny Chesney

All I Need to Know
June 1995, BNA

Kenny Chesney's second full-length, *All I Need to Know* was his breakthrough record, the first to spawn country Top Ten singles, here in the form of the slow slick title track and the sprightly "Fall in Love," both of which go a long way toward

illustrating how much more assured he sounds throughout the album. Chesney may sound more confident, but that sometimes can lead him down dark paths, such as the sticky sentiment of "Grandpa Told Me So." But by and large this is the first time that Chesney sounds like a genuine country star, whether he's easily negotiating the Western swing lilt of the excellent "The Bigger the Fool (The Harder the Fall)" or the rapid rhythms of "Someone Else's Hog," plus the good-natured boogie of "Paris, Tennessee." But the post-Garth punch of "Honey Would You Stand by Me," the slow yet cheerful blues of "Between Midnight and Daylight," and the skillful heartache ballad "The Tin Man"—which deftly reworks a cliché—really pointed the way to the future, capturing the blend of country instrumentation and anthemic pop that became his signature and made him a star.

Stephen Thomas Erlewine

Me and You
1996, BNA

With his second album, *All I Need to Know*, Kenny Chesney began to make inroads onto the charts, a position he consolidated on its 1996 successor, *Me and You*. While he bears no songwriting credits here, these 11 tracks showcase a more  fully rounded Chesney, where the rockers pack more punch and the ballads don't seem quite as big and glossy. For instance, "When I Close My Eyes" is a great soft rock crossover, tuneful and easy but never forced and not dripping with sentiment. Not that he totally avoids sap here, either on the nostalgic hometown tune "Back Where I Come From" or the slow-dance title track, but he's developed into an old pro in spinning this corn convincingly, and when that new trait is balanced by the crackerjack country-rockers that dominate this album—the opening one-two punch of "Back in My Arms Again" and "Ain't That Love," the superb "(Turn Out the Light And) Love Me Tonight"—it makes this his most entertaining record to date.

Stephen Thomas Erlewine

I Will Stand
July 1997, BNA

Building upon the bright, cheerful punch of *Me and You*, Kenny Chesney widened his musical vision on his fourth album, 1997's *I Will Stand*. This is partially due to his own pen—he has two songwriting credits here and none on the predecessor—but it's more down to the music he's chosen to sing and the persona he conveys here. He's relaxed, friendly, and assured, never trying too hard, which gently draws listeners in on both his ballads and rockers—and, what is turning increasingly into his specialty, the sunny mid-tempo tunes, equally suited for the beach or the bar. This is typified by the breezy "She Gets That Way" and the hazy '70s soft rock vibe of his co-written original "You Win, I Win, We Lose," and even the snappier songs (such as "She's Got It All" and "Steamy Windows") don't push too hard—which is fine, because the slower songs don't get mired in sappy sentiment, as "That's Why I'm Here" makes clear. It never sounds like Chesney would belong to either the hillbilly heaven or honky tonk hell that he sings about on the purest country song here—the one that also features verses by Tracy Lawrence and George Jones—but that's the appeal of Kenny Chesney: he doesn't live in the past, but he doesn't disrespect it, either. He's merely in the present, trading upon modern sounds and the tunes that he grew up with, making contemporary country that feels country in how he mixes up country-rock, soft rock, and pop, and it's down so casually that it's easy to take for granted how good he is on this record, the first that really brought his star persona to the forefront.

Stephen Thomas Erlewine

No Shoes, No Shirt, No Problems
April 2002, BNA

Kenny Chesney has a voice that'd be perfect for hard country, but he just doesn't have his heart in it. He likes the sweet melodies and smooth production that come with crossover country-pop, and while that may have been a frustration at one point, at least for those who consider pure country as the only guideline for quality in country, by his sixth album, 2002's *No Shoes, No Shirt, No Problems*, he's landed upon an effortless blend of pop and twang, something that is undeniable in its crossover intentions but rather charming all the same. Perhaps Chesney relies a bit too much on ballads and mid-tempo numbers throughout this album, but even the sprightlier numbers here—the terrific opener "Young," "Big Star"—are not honky tonk ravers, but heartland-styled rockers that gently rock and keep the melody in the forefront. So, all of *No Shoes* flows smoothly, and little of it could be called pure country—the most down-home thing about the entire enterprise is the rounded twang in his voice—but as a mature, even-handed country-pop album, it doesn't get much better than this in 2002, since it's melodic, well produced, strong on solid material, and most of all, very well sung. It's one of the highlights in his catalog.

Stephen Thomas Erlewine

When the Sun Goes Down
February 2004, BNA

Kenny Chesney's stardom snuck up quietly. He had a string of modest successes during the late '90s, but he never made crossover waves until 2002's *No Shoes, No Shirt, No Problems*, when his steady touring and steady shift toward adult pop paid off with his first number one album, but that was nothing compared to the stunning first-week sales of its successor, *When the Sun Goes Down*, which also debuted at number one to the very healthy sales of over 550,000. Chesney had clearly filled a void, one left by the diminished presence of Garth Brooks—a singer who blurred the lines between '70s mainstream pop/rock and contemporary country, a singer who made adult-oriented music about everyday things. At one point Chesney was aligned with neo-traditionalist country singers, but by *When the Sun Goes Down*, he had left that far behind, using country as mere flavoring on an album whose heart and soul is firmly within the tradition of '70s singer/songwriters. Where Garth Brooks merely covered Billy Joel (and a latter-day turn at that), Chesney drops references to Joel, James Taylor, and Steve Miller, while covering Dave Loggins' "Please Come to Boston." So, it's not an entire surprise that he favors ballads, usually the anthemic type designed to fill out arenas, and when he does turn the tempo up, it's still laid-back, in the fashion of Jimmy Buffett, as on the appealing duet with Uncle Kracker on the title track. Chesney often refers to living in the Islands (the Caribbean Islands, that is) in his nice song-by-song liner notes and every one of the many pictures in the disc's booklet features

him on an island, but this is hardly a tropical album—it's a record for middle America, for soccer moms and sentimental NASCAR dads, for those who opted out of the corporate rat race in favor of a loving relationship, as the character in "The Woman With You" did. It's for a generation raised on rock but living on country, people who like to reminiscence but are perfectly happy in their domestic life. If this sounds condescending, it's not meant that way; it's an apt description of an album that captures a time, place, and mindset, the way *Sgt. Pepper* provided the soundtrack to the Summer of Love. Peppered with references to Abercrombie & Fitch, American Express, dogs named Bocephus, old frat brothers, and forgotten sorority sisters, all set to a canny blend of state-of-the-art country, '70s sensibility, and '80s production (check out muted delayed rhythm guitar on "I Go Back"), it's a thoroughly modern mature-pop album. Like Shania Twain's *Come On Over* or *Up!*, this is music that's meant to have universal appeal, but it's far subtler in its approach, not least because it's delivered not by a diva, but a humble guy with a likeable, friendly voice. It may not be country, but that doesn't matter; *When the Sun Goes Down* is winning, sturdy mainstream pop, and after hearing it, it's easy to see why so many listeners now take Chesney to heart—he's writing the soundtrack to their lives.

Stephen Thomas Erlewine

Be as You Are (Songs from an Old Blue Chair)
January 2005, BNA

Conventional wisdom dictates that the Caribbean Islands are where you go to relax, not work, but not for Kenny Chesney. The Tennessee native found his muse on the islands, and it changed his life and work. He started his career as a good, if unremarkable, neo-traditionalist singer, but he slowly built his own identity as a singer and songwriter, largely due to the time he spent in the islands, a love that he celebrated in his music and interviews. Not since Jimmy Buffett has a musician been so thoroughly identified with the life of a beach bum, but there is a big difference between the two. Buffett happily creates a soundtrack to a never-ending party, coasting a combination of good times and easy grooves and while Chesney certainly does indulge in this ingratiatingly lazy vibe, he also finds the islands as a place for introspection, and nowhere is that more evident than on his eighth album, 2005's *Be as You Are (Songs from an Old Blue Chair)*. This is the companion piece to the breezy, bright modern country of 2004's *When the Sun Goes Down*, a relaxed, low-key collection of ballads and easy-rolling pop tunes that strikes precisely the right contemplative note, as if it were designed to be played during a picturesque ocean sunset. Which isn't to say that *Be as You Are* is a confessional album, or even a collection of overly introspective songs. There are autobiographical details threaded throughout the record, particularly on the opener, "Old Blue Chair," but the songs are open-ended, so listeners can identify with the narrator, or they're nice, mellow party tunes like "Key Lime Pie" or slow dance numbers like "Magic." It's a quiet record, but hardly an album that features Chesney alone with his guitar. *Be as You Are* is as polished and professional as *When the Sun Goes Down*, yet it's designed for quiet afternoons, not parties on the weekend. To Chesney's credit, he's as appealing on this set of relaxed tunes as he was on its gleaming, ultramodern predecessor, and taken together, they are strong proof that he's one of best singers and songwriters working in contemporary country music in the mid-2000s.

Stephen Thomas Erlewine

The Road and the Radio
November 2005, BNA

The Road and the Radio arrives at the end of a busy 2005 for Kenny Chesney. As the year opened, he followed up his 2004 blockbuster *When the Sun Goes Down* with the mellow *Be as You Are*. A few months later, he married movie star Renee Zellweger, and four months after that, she filed for divorce. Two months after *that*, Chesney returned with *The Road and the Radio*, the big, splashy proper follow-up to *When the Sun Goes Down*. Given such a tight, hectic schedule, it shouldn't come as a great surprise that *The Road and the Radio* sounds rushed, as if Chesney didn't have the chance to properly decide the right course for this album. He certainly didn't have the chance to write much—only two of the songs here bear his credit, compared to the all-original *Be as You Are* and *When the Sun Goes Down*, which had four original compositions. Since Chesney has always demonstrated a good ear for material, this isn't a great detriment; he picks good tunes here, highlighted by the wry, lazily rocking "Living in Fast Forward." But the haphazard nature of *The Road and the Radio* means not only does the record fail to gel, but that its rough edges are particularly noticeable. "Rough" isn't quite the right word, though, since one thing this album is not is rough: it's a smooth, polished, commercial effort, heavy on anthemic choruses and bright surfaces. In other words, this is the poppiest that Kenny Chesney has ever sounded, from how the atmospheric keyboards on the opening title cut recall U2 to how "Summertime" is driven by a gurgling talk box guitar. This in itself wouldn't be a big problem—it's been a long time since Chesney has pretended to be straight country, and he's very good at country-pop—but the problem with *The Road and the Radio* is that the songs just aren't very memorable. The record is surely pleasant, but apart from the aforementioned cuts, plus the easy-listening Springsteen/Mellencamp tribute "In a Small Town" and the party-hearty "Beer in Mexico," the songs themselves don't rise above background music. And while that's enough to make it an enjoyable enough listen, it's also enough to break the hot streak he began with 2002's *No Shoes, No Shirt, No Problems*.

Stephen Thomas Erlewine

Mark Chesnutt

Too Cold at Home
1990, Universal Special Products

An impressive traditional country debut that often drew on George Jones and Texas swing, *Too Cold at Home* started Chesnutt off strong with the hits "Too Cold at Home," "Brother Jukebox," "Blame It on Texas," and "Your Love Is a Miracle." It also included a version of "Friends in Low Places" that came out at almost exactly the same time Garth Brooks's did.

Brian Mansfield

Longnecks & Short Stories
1992, MCA

Longnecks heralded the emergence of a Texas voice that contained both the knack for humor ("Old Flames Have New Names," "Bubba Shot the Jukebox"), and the depth for heartache ("I'll Think of Something").

Brian Mansfield

Greatest Hits
November 1996, MCA

Mark Chesnutt's *Greatest Hits* does a fair job of summing up the neo-traditionalist's biggest hits, adding two new songs—"It's A Little Too Late" and "Let It Rain"—to the collection. Though his biggest hits are showcased on the album, many of his proper albums offer a better representation of his talent.

Thom Owens

Thank God for Believers
September 1997, MCA

Thank God for Believers continues Mark Chesnutt's streak of winning albums, confirming his status as one of the finest neo-honky tonkers of '90s contemporary country. What sets Chesnutt apart is his passion—he genuinely believes in this music, and he delivers it with conviction. That passion makes the occasional weak song forgivable, but fortunately, there aren't many weak moments on *Thank God for Believers*—it's just strong, thoroughly enjoyable modern country.

Thom Owens

I Don't Want to Miss a Thing
February 1999, MCA

What do we make of Mark Chesnutt's foray into crossover territory? The bulk of *I Don't Want to Miss a Thing* is smooth new country, retaining the elements of neo-traditionalism that characterize the best of Chesnutt's earlier albums. There's a nice mix of material, ranging from the tender "Tonight I'll Let My Memories Take Me Home" to the honky tonk of "That's the Way You Make an Ex," which seems to be an homage to George Strait's "All My Ex's Live in Texas." There's also the witty "My Way Back Home," the tale of a man who returns back to "home sweet mobile home" to find that his woman has left him, literally, homeless, and the vaguely Cajun "Jolie." If *I Don't Want to Miss a Thing* ended there, this would be another good, but not necessarily great, Mark Chesnutt album. But overshadowing the other nine songs on the album is the title track. "I Don't Want to Miss a Thing" was penned by Diane Warren, best known for writing hit adult contemporary ballads for the likes of Cher and Celine Dion. The song's first appearance was on the *Armageddon* movie soundtrack, where it became a major hit for Aerosmith in 1998. While Aerosmith's rendition was over the top, Chesnutt tames the beast, even as the arrangement builds to a dangerously bombastic climax toward the end. On "I Don't Want to Miss a Thing," Chesnutt proves he can sing power ballads with the best of them. But that one of the best honky tonk singers of his generation starts tackling this sort of material says a lot about the state of traditional country in Nashville—none of it good.

Martin Monkman

Savin' the Honky Tonk
September 2004, Vivaton!

There's a lot of truth to the title of Mark Chesnutt's tenth album, 2004's *Savin' the Honky Tonk*. Chenutt began his career as a new traditionalist country singer, indebted to Merle and George and singing straight-ahead honky tonk, but as his star rose and the decade rolled along, he moved further and further into country-pop, culminating in his 1999 crossover hit "I Don't Want to Miss a Thing," a cover of Aerosmith's love theme to Michael Bay's absurd *Armageddon*. It might have been his biggest hit, peaking at 17 on the pop charts, but this wasn't a breakthrough to a new level of success. Shortly afterward, he lost not only that newfound pop, but he had a hard time cracking the country Top 40 as well. He left Decca/MCA Nashville after 2000's *Lost in the Feeling*, releasing a formulaic eponymous album on Columbia in 2002, yet despite a modest hit in its first single, "She Was," the album disappeared quickly and, with it, so did Chesnutt's contract with Columbia. Left without a major, Chesnutt signed with the indie Vivaton and decided to abandon the increasingly poppy, polished material that characterized his albums of the late '90s. So, he turned back to honky tonk as much to save himself as to save it, and the results are by and large pretty terrific. Singing hardcore honky tonk, Chesnutt not only sounds comfortable and relaxed, he's re-energized, both by the straight-ahead setting and the freedom to pick songs without an eye on the airwaves. There are still a couple of ballads that are slightly treacly, but in this unadorned setting, the sentiment doesn't seem so saccharine. Plus, they're primarily used as a change of pace here, since the heart of this record is in twangy, rollicking honky tonk songs. Three songs mention drinking or beer in the title, two others mention honky tonks, one tune is about "Mama's House," and a bunch of others are filled with bad behavior, heartache, and humor. While Chesnutt's band is a bunch of Nashville pros, the music is none too polished—it's clear that they're having a good time, and it's hard for listeners not to have a good time as well. Perhaps *Savin' the Honky Tonk* will be just a one-off for Chesnutt, and he'll return to poppier material after this return to his roots, but hopefully not. This album proves that he's at his best when he sticks to the hard stuff.

Stephen Thomas Erlewine

Terri Clark

Terri Clark
1995, Mercury Nashville

Canadian country singer Terri Clark made her American major-label debut with Mercury Nashville. Co-produced by Keith Stegall and Chris Waters, this solidly assembled set of 12 songs signaled the arrival of a star. Clark wasn't only a pretty face with a voice; she arrived in Nashville a polished, accomplished songwriter who was given the "rare opportunity" (some call it stubbornness, and some call it recalcitrant artistic integrity, but they're both the same thing in this case) to record her own songs on her first recording. In Nash Vegas, that's done rather infrequently—even Vince Gill was only able to contribute two tunes to his MCA debut. Clark wrote 11 of 12 here and scored immediately with her blend

of hard honky tonk-style traditionalism, classic country balladry, and rock & roll aesthetics, and pop savvy. "Better Things to Do" is a fine display of this, as is the swaggering, bluesy "Flowers After the Fact." "Was There a Girl on Your Boy's Night Out" is a lean and mean honky tonk rocker, and of the ballads, "If I Were You" and "The Inside Story" are delivered with conviction and sincerity. *Terri Clark* is an auspicious debut, but hindsight being 20/20, it only hints at what she was really capable of, as displayed on later recordings.

Thom Jurek

Just the Same
November 1996, Mercury Nashville

Terri Clark may be a glamour queen, with lots of high style and flash. But then so is Dwight Yoakam, and he's a hell of a singer and songwriter, right? Clark is a honky angel singer with ambition, taste, looks, and a voice that's as big as a canyon. Oh yeah, and she's a fine songwriter as well. So, bring on the glamour if it brings out the music. Luke Lewis over at Mercury has got to believe in this woman—she gets a producer's credit alongside Keith Stegall! Not every country singer or songwriter gets a production say on her second record. And this one develops the strengths that made her debut so compelling, even if it was flawed. Choosing to cover Warren Zevon's "Poor, Poor Pitiful Me" after the Linda Ronstadt version takes guts. But Clark has more than that; her version is as valid as her predecessor's and as full of rock & roll heart as the songwriter's own version.

Other than this, Clark, Chris Waters, and Tom Shapiro wrote the majority of this album. They're a decent team, though the fullness of Clark's potential as an emotive artist—without sentimentality—is not exploited in these songs. They are solid, they belong here, and they're good listening, but given what she is obviously capable of, they are workmanlike. Other than the aforementioned, the best two tracks on the set are "Something in the Water," where Clark gets her blues growl out into the mix, "Twang Thang," which is as tough as anything Alan Jackson ever wrote and sung with twice the verve and grit, and the ballad "Keeper of the Flame," which Clark wrote on her own. In this song, the protagonist's hope is what keeps a relationship together, and in the grain of her voice one can hear both weariness and determination; when she gets to the top of her contralto time in the refrain, chills run down the listener's spine and recall the fine songs of Lacy J. Dalton, Trisha Yearwood when she was a singer instead of a status symbol, and Loretta Lynn when trying to deliver a countrypolitan song with Kentucky grit. She's not there yet, but so close you can hear the train coming all the way round the bend. Pick it up.

Thom Jurek

How I Feel
May 1998, Mercury Nashville

With *Just the Same*, Terri Clark proved she was going to be around for a while, and that the impression her self-titled debut made was no fluke. And like most acts Luke Lewis oversees, she's been allowed to grow with each release. *How I Feel* opens with one of

the best songs written in the country genre in the preceding decade or so, Kim Richey's testimonial anthem "I'm Alright" from her own *Bitter Sweet* album. In Clark's interpretation, the song is less Americana and more mainstream pop-country, but Clark's voice is no ordinary instrument. She delivers both the humor and the pathos in the tune without forcing the issue. Produced by Keith Stegall, Clark is allowed to let her natural voice more fully into the mix. Her inflections are her own, and the songs are well suited to her forthright style of delivery. To say that Clark is emotive is one thing, to say that her voice is the sound of emotion itself is another, and it is the latter that's true—take a listen to "Everytime I Cry" or Clark's own "Not Getting Over You," a ballad ruled by her throaty contralto, gorgeous pedal steel fills, and synth strings that sound natural. "Till I Get There" displays just how comfortable Clark is with traditional country music. Despite the presence of a B-3 in the mix, the tune itself comes right out of the early '70s. Further, there is Melba Montgomery's classic "Cure for the Common Heartache," a honky tonk pearl handled expertly with the righteous brokenhearted Western swing blues bustin' out all over it. The sum total of these 12 songs is Clark's restlessness as a vocalist and as a songwriter. Her attempt to be true to country's traditions while riding the pop-country wave of the present creates a wonderful tension that never seems resolved. In addition, Clark's songwriting is stronger, more assured, and as recognizable as her voice. A fine effort.

Thom Jurek

Fearless
September 2000, Mercury Nashville

Fearless is the most accurately titled album in Terri Clark's catalog. It's an attempt at breaking out of the bonds of contemporary country without leaving the music entirely behind. She's since distanced herself from it because Nash Vegas—in its typical, screwed-up intolerant way—disowned it as not format friendly. Her label, thanks to visionary Luke Lewis and Keith Stegall, encouraged her to make the record she wanted to make, and promoted the hell out of it. But country radio balked. Nashville critics, and the country music press in general, didn't know what to make of it and consequently it was a commercial failure. The bottom line is her songwriting collaborations with Mary Chapin Carpenter, Beth Nielsen Chapman, Angelo, and Gary Burr are all dead-on. Her own songs, a killer cover of Carlene Carter and Susanna Clark's "Easy from Now On," one from Tammy Rodgers, another from Jann Arden, as well as a Carpenter and Kim Richey collaboration prove one thing: This woman knew how to pick songs that fit around a theme, taking chances and moving toward destiny. The opener, "No Fear," penned with Carpenter and featuring Steuart Smith's trademark electric guitar slashing, is sung with resolve yet without hysteria or false bravado. And along with a statement of purpose like this in life comes one in love as well. "Empty," written with Burr, is the most poetic and naked she's ever written. In the refrain, her voice begins to crack as she sings: "I want to call out for love 'til I can't breathe/I want to stare at the truth until I can't see/I want to pour out my soul 'til I'm empty/Empty, until only the flesh and bones remain. . . ."

On another of their co-writes, "Getting There," Benmont Tench drives the track as Stuart Duncan's fiddle paints the backdrop and Smith's guitars crunch the entire middle into a solid country-rocker. With its mandolin, banjos, and gentle drum loop, "Sometimes Goodbye" is one of the freshest sounding tracks to come out of Music City in 20 years. Listening to it years later, it's so obvious that Clark is not only a bright talent, but an original one. Never has a statement of broken love and a personal decision to end

it sounded so affirmative. Covering "Easy from Now On" after Emmylou Harris' definitive version took guts, but in keeping with the previous track it made sense. And it's an absolutely chilling version with Harris providing the backing vocal. Like the aforementioned, it's a strong statement of determination, of affirmation, and of feminist principle in defining oneself in one's own terms. Certainly one can read plenty of autobiographical interpretations into songs like this and examine Clark's personal life, but it's irrelevant to the work of art in the disc player as it affects the listener. "The Real Thing" is a kicking bit of country-rock with a riff that comes out of Prince's "When You Were Mine." The album closes quietly with Jann Arden's "Good Mother," dedicated to the woman who raised her, and a hymn to personal transformation from the ruin and waste of past mistakes to a future uncertain but supported by the maternal connection to unconditional love. It whispers to a close with acoustic guitars and Jonathan Yudkin's cello, and in the silence, the listener feels empowered, emboldened, and just a bit wiser. Screw Nashville; this record will be regarded as a classic one day. One can only hope that Clark will reconsider one day that what she made here wasn't a mistake, but a real work of popular art. If Shania Twain displayed on her records an ounce of the integrity delivered here in full, she'd be a recording artist instead of a pop star.

Thom Jurek

Pain to Kill
January 2003, Mercury Nashville

Pain to Kill is Terri Clark's pop-country release after the artistic triumph—yet commercial failure—of *Fearless*. There are many things on *Pain to Kill* that are different. For one, like *Fearless*, this is the work of a mature, fully realized artist. She's well aware of her strengths and uses them to her advantage in every song on the set. Secondly, veteran producer Keith Stegall worked on only half this record—the latter half. Byron Gallimore produced the first half, including the first single, "I Just Wanna Be Mad." Thirdly, none of Clark's songwriting contributions to the project appear until the second half of the record. One has to ask why. Clark is a fine songwriter, either alone or in collaboration with others. Gallimore likes country music, he likes lots of guitars (layers and layers of them), and he likes very slick production styles. His drum loops and compression on the guitars squeeze everything so tight that Clark's voice is so far out front she no longer feels as if she's part of the musical accompaniment. It's not bad; it's just very different, jarring even for someone who's been listening to her records for a while. "I Just Wanna Be Mad" was an obvious choice to open the record with a grab-you hook and tough-woman stance. But this is a tough woman who believes in standing by her man even though she's pissed.

The title track is a rock & roll prime mover with Skynyrd-styled slide guitar, with about a million fiddles sawing through the mix. Clark growls her way through the lyric like she's in Black Oak Arkansas—yes, that is a compliment. The Stegall half of the record begins with a Clark and Gary Burr ballad, with a lilting piano, shimmering acoustic, and glistening pedal steel carrying the message about those who love self-destructive people. It's devastatingly real and there's no false solemnity in the body of the tune. "Almost Gone," written with Stephony Smith and Lisa Scott, is an exhortation—prodded by rows of acoustic guitars and a B-3—for a man to get his act together because the woman is on her way. The disc closes with "God and Me," written by Clark and Carol Ann Brown. Once again, here is self-determination, as well as absolute and relative truth, all considered on Sunday morning while watching preachers on television. It's simple affirmation and acknowledgment. Stegall surrounds Clark's vocal with Brent Mason playing Mark Knopfler-styled electric guitar, mandolins, acoustic guitars, and rim shots on top of floor toms. The effect is inspirational without being dogmatic—easy, light, and free with a beautiful coda. As a new chapter in the catalog of an artist who will be with listeners for a long time, it's a fine one.

Thom Jurek

Life Goes On
November 2005, Mercury Nashville

If 2003's *Pain to Kill* was Terri Clark's venture into country-pop, her 2005 follow-up, *Life Goes On*, is her return to straight-ahead hard country. But there's a difference between this and her last hard country effort, 2000's *Fearless*—where that album was devoted primarily to original material, this only has a handful of Clark-penned tunes, all arriving at a cluster toward the end of the record. Since Clark is a strong songwriter, this might initially come as a bit of a disappointment, but she also has a strong ear for material, finding songs that showcase her voice in the best possible light. While the nine professionally written tunes do not stretch the boundaries of neo-traditional contemporary country—they're firmly within their genre and play by its conventions—they're also not run of the mill; they're sturdy, memorable, sharply written songs, and Clark invests them with grit, passion, and an appealing swagger. It also helps that the production—largely by Byron Gallimore, but with a couple of cuts by James Stroud—is lean, clean, and muscular, staying true to the sound of classic country while retaining a bright, fresh sound. The end result may not be as revelatory as *Fearless* or as risky as *Pain to Kill*, but *Life Goes On* is every bit as satisfying as either of those records, acting as further proof that Terri Clark is one of the most reliable country singers of the last decade.

Stephen Thomas Erlewine

Anita Cochran

Back to You
April 1997, Warner Bros.

Anita Cochran's debut album *Back to You* is an audacious statement of purpose, or at least a thrilling display of talent. Cochran wrote or co-wrote all but one of the album's ten songs and played lead guitar, along with contributing banjo, dobro and mandolin on other songs. Those instruments alone give a good idea of what kind of music she makes—it's contemporary country with roots not only in honky tonk, but also in bluegrass. At times, the fusions are a little unfocused—after all, this is a debut—but for most of *Back to You*, Cochran's music is unpredictable and exciting, as her songwriting is inspired and her musicianship is fresh. It's a first-rate debut.

Thom Owens

Tammy Cochran

Tammy Cochran
May 2001, Epic

Tammy Cochran kicked around Nashville for almost a decade before she gained a hearing on Music Row, which says more about the goals of the country music establishment in the 1990s than it does about her. Cochran is a heartthrob singer in the tradition of Loretta Lynn and Tammy Wynette, which is not what Nashville was looking for in the Garth Brooks crossover days of the '90s, and not even what much of Nashville has been looking for in the Faith Hill crossover days of the 2000s. But Sony producer Blake Chancey has been bucking that trend with the Dixie Chicks, among others, and he finally gave Cochran her chance with the May 2000 single "If You Can." Chancey understood that Cochran's strength was ballads, and though "If You Can" wasn't a hit, it displayed her talent well. Her debut album seems to have been delayed several times, until a second single, "So What," released in October 2000, got some traction. It fulfills the promise of those songs by sticking mostly with ballads, on which Cochran emotes most effectively. It's not that she can't handle up-tempo material such as "Better Off Broken" and her own co-composition "When Love Was Enough," it's that she isn't able to put as personal a stamp on those songs, which sound like they could be by any competent female vocalist. But when she gets hold of a slow one with a bitterly romantic edge like "Say Goodbye," she reminds you of generations of great country women. *Tammy Cochran* may be too country for country radio (it always feels funny to say that), but it should attract fans of dyed-in-the-wool country who have been waiting for an artist not so concerned with crossing over to the pop charts.

William Ruhlmann

Life Happened
September 2002, Sony

There's a sadness to Tammy Cochran's music that's hard to put a finger on. Perhaps it's simply in her voice—that delicious Midwestern intonation—or perhaps it's just a direct reflection of the sorrow she's had to overcome in her personal life. Whatever it is, it works with the songs she's chosen for this satisfying sophomore album. "White Lies and Picket Fences," about promising to be together forever and having it go wrong; "I Used to Be That Woman," about a cheating husband; and "If You Can," the first single she ever released about questioning the end of a relationship, all remind listeners about the sometimes gritty realities of existence. Cochran says she tries to keep things real in her music, so she does manage to also give listeners hope in songs like "I'm Getting There," "Life Happened," and "All in How You Look at Things." Cochran's unarguable second effort is a steadfast lesson in determination.

Maria Konicki Dinoia

Mark Collie

Hardin County Line
1990, MCA

This honky tonk rebel's debut evokes the heart of '50s country, with detailed and compassionate songwriting, wildcat vocals, and guitar by James Burton. One song, "Looks Aren't Everything," hit the Top 40, while two others, "Hardin County Line" and "Something with a Ring to It," didn't fare quite so well.

John Floyd & Brian Mansfield

Mark Collie
1993, MCA

At once a move to the mainstream and a return to Collie's West Tennessee rockabilly roots, the album worked fairly well. "Even the Man in the Moon Is Crying" and "Born To Love You" were Collie's first Top Ten hits, and "Shame Shame Shame Shame" rocked as hard as anything he'd done.

Brian Mansfield

Unleashed
1994, MCA

In the same vein as *Mark Collie*, this album is more aggressive. "It Is No Secret" followed in Collie's tradition of midtempo romantic singles, while he rocks it up elsewhere.

Brian Mansfield

Tennessee Plates
July 1995, Giant

Tennessee Plates delivers the edgy rockabilly punch that fans have come to expect from Mark Collie, but not in quite as a consistent fashion as some of his earlier records. Although it has its share of love songs, the album does continue the stripped-down, direct approach of *Unleashed*—it just doesn't have the same amount of high-quality songs. That said, the best songs on the record are very good indeed, and make the album a fun, entertaining listen.

Thom Owens

Confederate Railroad

Notorious
1994, Atlantic

Despite its unkempt, biker image, Confederate Railroad is a country band in the tradition of Alabama. Rooted in traditional country sounds and values, both bands also have the breadth to appeal to those outside the genre (in CR's case,

Southern rockers). The group rocks hardest on the funny stuff ("Elvis and Andy," "Move over Madonna") but gets serious with some impressive ballads ("Daddy Never Was the Cadillac Kind," "Summer in Dixie," "Three Verses").

Brian Mansfield

When and Where
1995, Atlantic

By their third album, Confederate Railroad had established their fusion of Lynyrd Skynyrd and Alabama and knew what worked and what didn't. In other words, *When and Where* offers nothing new from the band, but it is far from a bad record. The group has gotten predictable, but they continue to shine, whether it's on the rowdy rockers or the surprisingly smooth, radio-ready ballads. They do have a problem coming up with a batch of consistent material, but the album is as enjoyable as its predecessor and nearly as solid.

Thom Owens

Unleashed
August 2001, Audium

In some parts of the world, it's always 1974. The deaths of Berry Oakley and Duane Allman still sting, Waylon Jennings and Jerry Jeff Walker are revered, shouts of "Free Bird"!!! at concerts aren't meant ironically, and people still remember who the

Marshall Tucker Band were. It's a simpler, better place, and there, Confederate Railroad are superstars. On their fifth album, the unreconstructed country-rockers plow through songs like the sassy "She Treats Her Body Like a Temple" ("and I treat mine like a honky-tonk," continues lead singer Danny Shirley) and the self-explanatory story-song "White Trash With Money," with all the twangy guitars, honky tonk piano, and keening steel guitar that are required for a good country-rockin' time. David Allan Coe and George Jones drop by to lend a further air of outlaw country badassedness, and the group even throws in an honest to goodness ballad, the touching "Between the Rainbows and the Rain," to prove that it's not just a bunch of retro-macho poseurs. Good stuff.

Stewart Mason

The Essentials
June 2002, Rhino

This edition of Rhino's *Essentials* series does an effective job of chronicling the majority of hits by the modern country/Southern rock band Confederate Railroad from the early to mid-'90s. Among the original hit recordings are "Queen of Memphis," "She Took It Like a Man," "Jesus and Mama," and "Daddy Never Was the Cadillac Kind." For some reason the 1992 hit "She Never Cried" was excluded from this compilation.

Al Campbell

Elizabeth Cook

Balls
May 2007, Thirty Tigers

After a quick listen to *Balls*, it's hard to imagine why Warner Brothers dropped Elizabeth Cook after only one album. Could she have sounded too traditional for country radio? Did they want her to tone down her in-your-face delivery? The mysteries of major labels are many and unfathomable, so suffice it to say that Cook is a major talent and will undoubtedly wind up with another major-label deal. *Balls* has the same power and charm evident on her earlier outings and the bonus of Rodney Crowell's sharp production talents. Every track crackles like a pork fat fueled barbecue fire, full of the spunk and sass that make Cook an artist to watch. "Times Are Tough in Rock 'N Roll" is a sly putdown of the mainstream music industry and a celebration of country roots driven by a traditional track that includes banjo, jew's harp (something you don't hear on many records these days, if ever) and fiddle. When she sings "All my feelings/All my fears/Were confirmed with Britney Spears" you've got to laugh out loud. Cook's been called a cross between Loretta Lynn and Dolly Parton, and a tune like "Sometimes It Takes Balls to Be a Woman" tells you that the comparisons aren't mere hyperbole. It's a honky tonk stomp that delineates the problems facing the fairer sex with good humor and sharp observations of the strength it takes to deal with the male ego. "What Do I Do" is Western swing in the style of Merle Haggard, a weeper that finds the singer torn between giving her heart away and walking away from a bad situation. Some nice Roy Nichols-style electric guitar fills add authenticity to the track. Cook's just as commanding on the album's ballads. "Down Girl" is as dark as anything Gillian Welch has written, "Rest Your Weary Mind," a duet with Bobby Bare, Jr., sounds like a hundred-year-old folk lament, while "Mama's Prayers" is a ringer for Parton's homespun Tennessee tales of tribulation. The most surprising track is "Sunday Morning," the Velvet Underground oldie transformed into a mournful ballad given extra melancholy by Matt Combs' fiddle work. *Balls* is a great album made by people who obviously love the grit and honesty of real music.

j. poet

Bucky Covington

Bucky Covington
April 2007, Hollywood

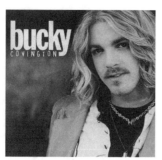

Bucky Covington was one of those charmingly unformed *American Idol* contestants who had plenty of charisma and an interesting voice but couldn't quite pull it together, yet he stayed on the show for a long time in its fifth season because he had a genuine sweetness buried beneath his gruff voice. That sweetness earned him fans, including plenty who saw Carrie Underwood become the first country Idol just the season before, but Carrie always seemed like a pop Idol: smooth, pretty, assured, and well-manicured, just right for Skechers ads. Bucky wasn't so smooth. He sounded and seemed like a good old Southern boy, too rough even for *Nashville Star*, which surely was the core of his appeal, and also made his eventual mid-season dismissal not so surprising; despite all his charm and enormous potential, he was far from the best singer on the show. Nevertheless, he had the raw elements of a true country star, something that led to a record deal with Lyric Street, which had him record his debut album with Mark Miller, best known as the lead singer of Sawyer Brown. Miller helps polish Bucky into a genuine modern country singer, smoothing out the rough edges in his voice and finding just the right blend of rocking country and down-home corn to showcase his gravelly growl and all-American charm. Make no mistake, *Bucky Covington* has been designed to appeal to the middle-American and Southern fans who kept Bucky on *AmIdol* for weeks. It's filled with songs celebrating an "American Friday Night," songs where the country boy is longing for his home back South ("Carolina Blue"), songs where Bucky imagines that heaven would be a lot like his hometown. There's a strange nostalgic undercurrent here, as when Bucky is thinking back to his childhood on "The Bible and the Belt" (his mother taught the former, his father the latter). Such rose-tinted family memories are par for the course in country, but what's a little odd on *Bucky Covington* are the very specific "Different World" and "Back When We Were Gods," where Covington looks back on a childhood that was quite different than today ("We were born to mother, who smoked and drank/Our cribs were covered in lead-based paint") and remembers running around with his high school pals just before Desert Storm in "Back When We Were Gods"—two songs that are designed to sound true to listeners who were adolescents during the first Bush administration. Born in 1977, Bucky is a bit too young to be part of this camp—he would have been 14 when Desert Storm launched, he was in grade school at the peak of the Super Mario Brothers craze—but this cultural carbon-dating reveals exactly what audience *Bucky Covington* is intended to capture: thirtysomethings raised on John Mellencamp and now listening to Kenny Chesney and Alan Jackson. It's country music with anthemic pop hooks and a rock edge, country music that's been crafted with a clear eye on its demographic, which may make it a little crass, but it's still effective commercial country because the songs are melodic, the production crisp, and above all, they're delivered by a singer who is thoroughly likeable. On record, Bucky appears as genuine as he did on the show, but his vocals are stronger than they were on TV: he's not only more confident but his phrasing is more musical and he can now tell a story—perhaps not in an original way, but in an engaging way. This newfound strength is showcased well on this well-made piece of country-pop product. Ultimately, *Bucky Covington* is the sound of a Nashville pro like Mark Miller translating Bucky's TV persona onto record: it may be slick and calculating, but there's pleasure in that professionalism and, thanks to Bucky, there's a ring of truth to the album. After all, Bucky is still enough of a good old Southern boy to be likeable no matter how slick his surroundings are. He may not be driving the car, but he's on the ride of his life and he's enjoying every second of it.

Stephen Thomas Erlewine

Rodney Crowell

Ain't Living Long Like This
1977, Warner Bros.

Rodney Crowell's auspicious 1978 debut, *Ain't Living Long Like This*, not only showcases his songwriting prowess, but also his ability to deliver a song, whether it's one of his own or the work of another writer. Crowell possesses a sort of Everly Brothers, Nashville soul in his strong, emotive tenor, that's equally effective on the country-blues of Dallas Frazier's "Elvira," as it is on the rocking title cut or a country-folk ballad such as the self-penned "Song for the Life." Along with producer Brian Ahern (Emmylou Harris), Crowell employs a who's who of country and rock & roll session players, including James Burton and Glen D. Hardin, both of whom played with Elvis Presley and Gram Parsons, as well as enlisting the aid of artists such as Dr. John, Ry Cooder, Nicolette Larson, Emmylou Harris, Ricky Skaggs and Willie Nelson. As a writer, Crowell, who chose to include three terrific covers over any of his backlog of excellent original material, has the knack for mixing a pop sensibility and rock & roll vitality, with the heart and reverence of a traditionalist. A song such as "California Earthquake (A Whole Lotta Shakin' Goin' On)," sounds as if it could've been written decades before, while "Voila, An American Dream" hit the pop charts the following year for *the Dirt Band*. *Ain't Living Long Like This* became a mining-ground of material for others. Nearly every one of Crowell's tunes from the album was covered within the next few years, spawning at least a couple of major hits. Even "Elvira," which he had resurrected, became an early '80s smash for the Oak Ridge Boys .

Brett Hartenbach

Diamonds & Dirt
1988, Columbia/Legacy

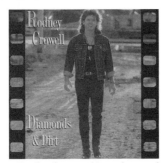

Of the four records Rodney Crowell cut under his name before 1988's *Diamonds & Dirt*, three of them are still regarded as classics of the progressive country genre. The Houston native was well established as a songwriter (Emmylou Harris cut a slew of Crowell songs on her first five records), producer, and performer. Along with then-wife Rosanne Cash, he brought elements of new wave and early rock & roll into the genre, giving it a much needed kick in the rear. But as good as those albums were, *Diamonds & Dirt* put him on the map for good. In the 21st century, Crowell makes his living primarily as a hit songwriter, though he still records independently, cutting one critically acclaimed album after another. Co-produced by Crowell and Tony Brown, *Diamonds & Dirt* yielded five chart-topping singles, including "It's Such a Small World," a duet with Cash (who provided backing vocals throughout the set); a burning rockabilly version of pal Guy Clark's "She's Crazy for Leavin'"; the switchblade swagger of "Crazy Baby" (which sounds like Dave Edmunds and Nick Lowe backing Jerry Lee Lewis); and the stellar ballad "After All This Time." That said, there is something else afoot here,

too. A listen to "I Know You're Married" reveals that Crowell was a real fan of the early Beatles, and, on "I Didn't Know That I Could Lose You," of Roy Orbison. The only other cover on the set is a stellar swaggering honky tonk cum pub rock version of Harlan Howard's "Above and Beyond (The Call of Love)," which could have been recorded by England's Brinsley Schwarz. The remastered Legacy version of the album also includes three previously unreleased demos from the *Diamonds & Dirt* sessions and a wonderfully intimate set of liner notes. For contemporary country fans, this disc is such an important part of the development of modern music that it has virtually influenced everything that's come after it, making it impossible to ignore.

Thom Jurek

Keys to the Highway
1989, Lucky Dog

The success of Rodney Crowell's *Diamonds & Dirt* was a surprise, if only because Crowell had been making records for ten years with only modest sales. It was more country-oriented and less challenging than his previous recordings, but the album threw off a record-setting five number one country hits while remaining in the charts more than two years. *Keys to the Highway*, therefore, should have consolidated Crowell's status as a major country star; instead, it was a commercial disappointment from which he did not recover. Though Crowell had bowed to a traditional approach somewhat on *Diamonds & Dirt*, he remained essentially a stylist as interested in folk, rock, and R&B as he was in country. At the same time, emboldened by his success, Crowell apparently wanted to try to recover some of his critical standing, and he also seems to have been influenced by the death of his father to be true to himself. Momentum pushed the leadoff single, the slow, thoughtful folk-rock ballad "Many a Long and Lonesome Highway," into the country Top Five, but it was not what fans of *Diamonds & Dirt* were expecting, and despite the neo-Nashville sound of second single "If Looks Could Kill," which reached the country Top Ten, *Keys to the Highway* failed to make the country Top Ten or go gold. It's a much better album than that history suggests, however, carefully balanced between exercises in early rock & roll and rockabilly, country-soul, mainstream '60s-style rock, and even dyed-in-the-wool country. *Keys to the Highway* didn't have the songwriting depth of Crowell's early albums, but it was more substantial and more varied than *Diamonds & Dirt*, and if handled well, it might have been even more successful. Instead, it remains an album yet to be really discovered.

William Ruhlmann

Life Is Messy
May 1992, Lucky Dog

After the commercial falloff of *Keys to the Highway*, Rodney Crowell took two and a half years crafting his seventh album, *Life Is Messy*, in the interim going through a divorce from his wife, Rosanne Cash. The most notable characteristic of *Life Is Messy* was that it marked a complete return to his original style. With nary a steel guitar or fiddle to be heard, and featuring top pop session musicians as well as a slew of pop guest stars (Linda Ronstadt, Don Henley, Steve Winwood, etc.), *Life Is Messy* wasn't really a country record at all. A couple of songs had a country-rock, honky tonk feel, but the dominant musical style was a pastiche of late '50s/early '60s pop. The title song was a somewhat abstract meditation on romantic discord and career disappointment that was followed by the equally despairing "I Hardly Know How to

Be Myself," which actually had been co-written with Cash. These songs sounded so pained and deeply felt that some of the more up-tempo songs came off as trivial, even if they made for a change of pace. But other songs came up to their standard without being quite so low in mood. "Alone But Not Alone" found the singer beginning to find his way, and "It's Not for Me to Judge" revealed the noncommittal feelings one can have when emotional certainties are uprooted. Taken together, the songs on *Life Is Messy* made for a fascinating portrait of an artist at a personal and professional crossroad—but it didn't have much to do with commercial country music circa 1992, which is what it was primarily marketed as. After a few months, Columbia Records pulled the plug on promotion and parted ways with Crowell, who moved on to MCA Records.

William Ruhlmann

Let the Picture Paint Itself
1994, MCA

So much of Crowell's best work has been co-produced by MCA executive Tony Brown, it seemed inevitable he would wind up at MCA himself. This, his first release for his new label, emphasizes Crowell, the thoughtful songwriter, over Crowell the neo-honky tonk bandleader. It's a fair trade, but requires repeat listening to fully appreciate.

Dan Cooper

Jewel of the South
1995, MCA

Crowell tries to stretch out a bit too much on *Jewel of the South*, but it remains a fine album, nonetheless. Featuring guest performances by the Mavericks' Raul Malo, Bela Fleck, Vince Gill, Kim Richey, and Billy Joe Walker, Jr., among others, the album tries to do too many thing, but it does enough of them well enough to make it an entertaining listen.

Thom Owens

The Houston Kid
February 2001, Sugar Hill

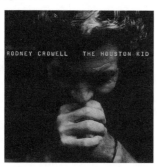

At least impressionistically, this is a soundtrack to a documentary about the life of Rodney Crowell, who grew up in East Houston (the same neighborhood as the Ghetto Boys, but 25 years earlier), a rough and rumble neighborhood lying in the shadows of downtown Houston. It also happens to be the finest record Crowell has recorded since *Diamonds & Dirt*, and it's better than that one by a mile. After being tossed off by the major labels, it took a big-time indie like Sugar Hill—a label founded to showcase bluegrass artists (but also home to many fine singer/songwriters including Crowell's running mate and inspiration Guy Clark)—to release *The Houston Kid*. The album comes off as a song cycle; first, in "Telephone Road," the atmosphere is painted onto a backdrop. Showcasing the dark underbelly's finest sights, smells, sounds, and tastes, it's a country shuffle that moves ahead straightforwardly offering the stage for the creation of a rounder. On "The Rock of

My Soul," Crowell tells all about the boy growing up in such circumstances. Fact and fiction are interwoven in a moving narrative that has plenty of twang and punch. Steel guitars and acoustic Fenders carry the melody along until the story reaches its nadir. "Why Don't We Talk About It" is Crowell's "accept me as I am because this is the real me" narrative. The band sounds like Rockpile playing country music. Truly, the backing vocals and the mix could be pure Dave Edmunds and Nick Lowe. Crowell has always hidden his brashness under a sheen of Nashville style, which is why his songs always sounded truer coming out of other people's mouths. But that's not the case here. It feels raw and immediate, full of something he's never revealed before. "I Wish It Would Rain" is a folk/country song so down and out that it could have been written by deceased writers Townes Van Zandt or Blaze Foley (both Texans and both friends of Crowell). It's a confessional. There is no braggadocio, no posturing. It's a song of regret but not remorse. The guitars are spare, just enough of a skeleton to hang the lyric on, and as he spills his tale of woe, the listener becomes as haunted as the protagonist is hunted. The craziest moment is Crowell's rewiring of Johnny Cash's "I Walk the Line." With an electric country-blues shuffle (à la Merle Haggard), Crowell tells the story of how he first heard the song, and then Cash himself comes in on a completely rewritten narrative and chorus! Cash reportedly told Crowell he had a lot of nerve to rewrite his classic song, to which Crowell brazenly replied, "Yes, sir." Though the record closes two songs later, "Banks of the Old Bandera" is where it could have—and maybe should have—the first song Crowell ever wrote. Author Tom Robbins told him he should write a bunch more songs and tour them in art galleries! Thank God he didn't. *The Houston Kid* offers listeners Rodney Crowell the performer in a way they've never heard before; the songwriter who has been been missing in Nashville for quite some time is back.

Thom Jurek

Fate's Right Hand
July 2003, DMZ/Epic

Fate's Right Hand is one of those albums that couldn't have been written or recorded at any other time in Rodney Crowell's career. Two years after his monumentally acclaimed *The Houston Kid*, Crowell has laid out his autobiography in sight and sound. His track record of hits—written for himself as well as for other artists—could have just gone on untarnished. But *Fate's Right Hand* is the flip side of *The Houston Kid*. Whereas the latter album is about the past, the former is about the present, not only in the artist's life, but in the lives of those around him, and in the question of life itself: why is it worth living and how can suffering be alleviated? While many will think this is blasphemy, *Fate's Right Hand* is the finest record Crowell has issued since *Diamonds & Dirt* and may turn out to be the finest of his entire career—and that's saying a lot. Crowell and Pete Coleman produced this outing and enlisted the help of friends old and new: Steuart Smith, Pat Buchanan, Michael Rhodes, Gillian Welch, David Rawlings, Richard Bennett, Béla Fleck, Carl Jackson, Marcia Ramirez, Charlie McCoy, Kim Richey, and Will Kimbrough, to name a few. Crowell wrote the entire record himself; he digs deep for the ugly stuff in order to uncover what shines beneath it. The opener, "Still Learning How to Fly," is a song about living in the moment because the moment is all you have. Crowell claims he wrote it based on conversations he had with a friend dying of terminal cancer; about what comes in the afterlife. With dobros, electric guitars, and acoustic six-strings wrapping around each other in a big, airy mix painted with a Hammond B-3, it is one of Crowell's transcendent moments. Remember *Diamonds & Dirt*? Yeah—like that. The title track ushers itself in around some warm, rounded bass tones, an organ, and maracas, as Crowell begins a series of seemingly unrelated non sequiturs. It's a pissed-off song that is as close to punk as Crowell will ever write. The notion of the transcendent is again present as it drenches Fleck's banjo riff in "Earthbound." Crowell makes the argument for living day-to-day in a world full of death and cynicism: where surrender is not an option until its time. All of this points to the most naked song Crowell has ever written: "Time to Go Inward," with both spoken word and sung refrains over fingerpicked acoustic guitars and electric dobros. It's a folk song about seeing; a country song about acceptance; a human song about the fear of what you might find when you look so deeply inside yourself. "The Man in Me" is about the negativity found there. It's a country-rock song that looks deeply into the mirror, doesn't like what it sees, and can't escape. Crowell penned "Preaching to the Choir" as an answer to "Time to Go Inward," but it's another mirror he sees: it's a bluesy rock tune touched by country gospel and bluegrass, and it smokes. There are a couple of other thoughtful moments here, cuts where Crowell is trying to make sense rather than preach—which is what this album is all about: making sense of things rather than preaching about them. But it all comes to a head in "This Too Will Pass," a country song with a rockabilly shuffle that expresses the wisdom of those who believe and practice what Buddhism's Four Noble Truths and the 12 Steps of Alcoholics Anonymous teach (no claim is made or intended for Crowell being part of either): impermanence, suffering, and joy—and everything in between—are merely the stages of cyclical existence. Happiness *is* possible. There *is* a way out, but you have it discover it for yourself.

Thom Jurek

But What Will the Neighbors Think/Rodney Crowell
March 2005, Collectables

While his 1978 debut album, *Ain't Livin' Long Like This*, certainly caught the attention of folks in the music business, it was his second album, 1980's *But What Will the Neighbors Think*, that first alerted radio listeners and mainstream country fans to Rodney Crowell's gifts as a songwriter and performer, and while his self-titled 1981 follow-up wasn't the hit *But What Will the Neighbors Think* turned out to be, it confirmed the man was a major talent whose smart, edgy songs were a far cry from what was the norm in Nashville at the time. Collectables has reissued these two albums on a single CD, and decades after it first came out *But What Will the Neighbors Think* still sounds like the work of a talented maverick not afraid to take some chances; Crowell's grim assessment of America at the dawn of the Reagan era, "Here Come the 80's," would have been a gutsy way to open an album in any genre, especially country, and if "It's Only Rock 'n' Roll" takes on a less serious topic (the music business), it's no less venomous, or hits its target with less impact. "Ashes by Now" and "The One About England" showed Crowell was as sure a hand with more personal subjects, and the spare snap of Craig Leon's production allows this to walk a fine line between the rock club and the honky tonk and capture the best of both sides. *Rodney Crowell* was a less immediately striking album, but still has more than its share of great songs (including his original versions of "Shame on the Moon" and "'Til I Gain Control Again"), and Crowell, who also produced, assembled a superb crew of musicians, including Albert Lee, Booker T. Jones, Vince Gill, and Rosanne Cash (who was his wife at the time). These two albums represented Rodney Crowell at the first apex of his career, and after years out of print, it's good to see them available again, and in an affordable format at that.

Mark Deming

The Outsider
August 2005, Columbia

Rodney Crowell's *The Outsider* is a natural extension of his last two offerings: *The Houston Kid* and *Fate's Right Hand*. Where *The Houston Kid* was Crowell's autobiographical confessional and *Fate's Right Hand* was deeply philosophical and influenced by everything from Zen to the working through of anger, *The Outsider* digs deep into social and political consciousness. The album rocks harder than any Crowell record in the past, as evidenced by "Don't Get Me Started," which is an anti-war anthem that takes aim at the war in Iraq. Immediately following is "The Obscenity Prayer," written from the point of view of a hypocritical right-wing pleasure seeker whose positions are not only indefensible, they are, at worst, obscene. Conversely, the Zen-like advice in "Dancin' Circles Round the Sun" is a tough country rocker with killer rockabilly guitar lines by Stewart Smith and Hammond B3 grooves by John Hobbs. It is a testament to personal responsibility and awakening that exhorts and admonishes, but never preaches. There is great tenderness here, as well, such as in the acoustically driven "Ignorance Is the Enemy," with its prayer-like cadence and spoken-word vocals by Emmylou Harris and John Prine. "Glasgow Girl" is as fine a country-rock love song as has been written in recent years. The album closes with "We Can't Turn Back Now," a rousing call for acceptance, forbearance, and perseverance, whose guitars and big bassline is graced by a stellar fiddle line and a beautifully delicate tin whistle winding through it all. Crowell—still writing hits for "Hot 100" country artists to help finance and keep creative control of his recordings—has matured into an artist who has the of hard-won experience that displays itself as poetically wrought wisdom. His work is full of humor, light, poignancy, and killer hooks. He's now written and recorded three big topic records, all of which surpass his early work. The only thing missing here now is a record on the other big topic: Love. Perhaps that's coming. Until then, *The Outsider* is the Rodney Crowell recording to listen to, debate with, and be inspired by.

Thom Jurek

Billy Currington

Doin' Somethin' Right
October 2005, Mercury Nashville

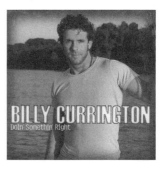

Billy Currington was helped enormously by his duet with Shania Twain on "Party for Two," a new track on her 2004 *Greatest Hits* album. She had two versions of the song on the record—one cut with Sugar Ray's Mark McGrath for the pop audience, the version with Currington for country fans, and it's not entirely a stretch to say that Currington is a country McGrath: good-looking, likeable, entirely comfortable with selling out so he can reach as big of an audience possible, yet kind of ingratiating because he's not only charming, he's good at it. And his second album, *Doin' Something Right* proves this: while it doesn't take any chances, it's a thoroughly entertaining and satisfying contemporary country album. Despite his protestations that he wants to be a hillbilly on the rocking, twangy opening cut, Currington has as strong a foundation in pop as he does in country. He not only gets a nicely mellow, relaxed Californian vibe on the title track, but he collaborates with Michael McDonald on "She's Got a Way with Me," a song that could have fit comfortably onto soft rock stations in the early '80s, when McDonald provided his signature gruff, soulful harmonies on every other track. Currington also covers Kenny Rogers' hit "Lucille," but he does a neat trick with it, one that illustrates why this album is so enjoyable: he does a harder country version than Rogers, proving that he can pull off both lighter pop and straight-ahead country with one performance. The rest of the record goes back and forth between these two extremes—sometimes subtlety, sometimes not—and Currington comes across like a blend of Kenny Chesney, Shania Twain, and Alan Jackson: he has the good looks and frat-boy sensibility of Chesney and the pop sense and common touch of Shania, but it's tempered by a touch of the neo-traditional twang of Jackson. The end is a cheerfully commercial country album, but one with muscle and heart, one that's as enjoyable when it's laid-back as when it rocks out. It's an excellent second album and one that should make Currington a star.

Stephen Thomas Erlewine

Billy Ray Cyrus

Some Gave All
1992, Mercury

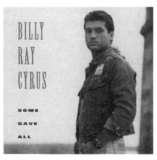

Some Gave All became the first debut album by a country artist to enter the pop charts at number one (it hit number one on the country charts as well). The album's sales were fueled by the breakout single "Achy, Breaky Heart," which offered Southern-fried Rolling Stones rhythms and a goofy chorus with a hook so big it demanded a reaction. Not one to eschew the obvious, Cyrus pumped his songs full of as much rock & roll as the market would bear, so songs like "Could've Been Me" and "Never Thought I'd Fall in Love with You" appealed to young fans who had just discovered the possibilities (both musical and sexual) of country music.

Brian Mansfield

Linda Davis

Some Things Are Meant to Be
January 1996, Arista

Linda Davis is another singer who suffered through struggles to get heard. In her case, however, she tended to release formula-heavy albums empty of much character or

individuality. Always an obvious talent, she bounced between record companies, all of which tried to force her into one ill-fitting trend or another. Davis finally enjoyed some exposure through a hit duet with her co-manager, Reba McEntire. Their song, "Does He Love You," won several awards and gained Davis another record contract, this time with Arista Records. Still, her 1994 album with the company had little impact. This time, she attempted to come across as a steamy chanteuse. She danced through several lame swamp-pop songs, a style that proved as unconvincing as her previous guises. However, on each of her albums, she would display her possibilities when given a chance to sing a grown-up love song. Finally, on her *Some Things Are Meant to Be*, she didn't have to try to sing two-steppers or novelties or country-rock or traditional tear-jerkers. Instead, the strong-voiced singer takes on straight-ahead, middle-of-the-road, pop-country songs, and she lives up to her promise. The songs are about women in their 30s and 40s facing up to the trouble or the joy in their lives. They're about finding strength through acknowledgement, or how sometimes perseverance is the only reward we have. They're good songs, devoid of gimmickry. And Davis brings them to life with a subtle, intelligent power. Perseverance, it seems, indeed has its rewards.

Michael McCall

Billy Dean

Real Man
August 1998, Capitol

Award-winning country singer Billy Dean grew a huge fan base in the early '90s with hit songs like "A Fire in the Dark," "Billy the Kid," and "Somewhere in My Broken Heart," and then he kind of slipped from the spotlight. Then he put his best foot forward again with the release of this emotional and thought-provoking 1998 album, *Real Man*. The acoustic-based tunes on this recording leave a little of the pop flavor behind and lean more comfortably on the simple country he is so good at offering fans. The ballads really let his vocal talents shine. Dean's father was a guitar player and singer and part of a group called the Country Rocks. Working with his band, young Dean grew up under influences like Marty Robbins, Charley Pride, Hank Williams, Jim Reeves, and even Chuck Berry and Elvis. Many of these early influences show on Dean's music. When he started working on this album, Dean took time to rediscover the songwriter within him. The result is that most of the songs on *Real Man* were written by him, or co-written with longtime friend and former frontman of the group Bread, David Gates. Other songwriters lent some talent to this album also, including Richard Leigh. On this album, you'll find great songs like "Voices Singing," which was done with the backing help of the St. Nicholas School Children's Choir of Chattanooga and Dean's son, Eli. Singer Gina Jefferys duets with Dean for the tune "If I Can Find the Heart."

Charlotte Dillon

Derailers

Retrospective: Just One More Time
October 2006, Varese Sarabande

The Derailers were one of those special bands that came out of Austin in the 1990s. Recording for Watermelon, Watermelon/Sire, Freedom, and Pete Anderson's Little Dog labels during their glory years, they blended Bakersfield, California country music, and Fab Four Brit-styled harmonies and backbeats. This 17-cut retrospective covers the years 1995 through 2003 and the six records cut by best friends and musical partners Tony Villanueva and Brian Hofeldt (both originally Oregonians) with whatever rhythm sections suited their fancy—or they could keep together—through endless touring and some seriously slim paychecks. Villaneuva left the group in 2003 to become a pastor. Of these cuts, 13 were written or co-written by both or one or the other songwriters. The rest are covers from people like Wynn Stewart, Harlan Howard, Cindy Walker, and Phil Spector. Of course, the two best-known tracks by this killer little roots country & Liverpool band are "California Angel" and "Can't Stop a Train." The former was performed for Buck Owens at his 70th birthday party. But the band cut some other seamless blends as well, including "Lies Lies Lies," "Jackpot" (which blended Buddy Holly into the mix as well), "One More Time," and "Genuine." There isn't a weak track in the bunch, but this set also makes a case for ten tracks on a country album being plenty. In total, though, if you were or remain a fan, then this is for you.

Thom Jurek

Desert Rose Band

Running
1988, Curb

This is certainly a good representation of the work the Desert Rose Band did in their prime and a project that remains a favorite. With some solid songwriting by Chris Hillman and a cover of Buck Owens' "Hello Trouble," this second release is a definitive work. With hits like "I Still Believe in You," "Summer Wind," and John Hiatt's "She Don't Love Nobody," there is nothing lacking in either performance, production, or material. Like their first release, 1987's *Desert Rose Band*, *Running* was based upon the experience of the bandmembers as musicians, songwriters, and singers who were (and continue to be) an important part of the Bakersfield-Los Angeles music community. Both Hillman and Herb Pedersen have impressive resumés that include working with the Byrds, Gram Parsons, Buck Owens, and Emmylou Harris. As for Steve Duncan, Bill Bryson, Jay Dee Maness, and John Jorgenson, each had equally brilliant backgrounds as California musicians and were recognized as such. Be it Bakersfield honky tonk, love songs, or bluegrass, the Desert Rose Band delivered. This release was followed by *Pages of Love* in 1989 and a greatest-hits package in 1990, *A Dozen Roses/Greatest Hits*. By 1992, members started leaving the band and the last American release was issued in 1993 on Curb, *Life Goes On*. Still, *Running* is the work that listeners will remember with the most affection and longing.

Jana Pendragon

Diamond Rio

Diamond Rio
1991, Arista

One of the most successful debut albums in country music, *Diamond Rio* sparked plenty of hits—"Meet in the Middle," "Mama Don't Forget to Pray for Me," "Nowhere Bound," and "Norma Jean Riley"—by combining bluegrass harmonies, old-fashioned country virtues, and just enough rock to keep things moving.

Brian Mansfield

Greatest Hits
July 1997, Arista

Greatest Hits is a fine collection of the hit singles from Diamond Rio's first four albums, featuring such hits as "Meet in the Middle," "Mirror Mirror," "Norma Jean Riley," "In a Week or Two," "Oh Me, Oh My, Sweet Baby," "Love a Little Stronger," "Night Is Fallin' In My Heart," "Walkin' Away," "That's What I Get for Lovin' You," "Holdin'" and two new songs, inlcuding the single "How Your Love Makes Me Feel."

Thom Owens

Unbelievable
July 1998, Arista

Unbelievable finds Diamond Rio extending the stylistic diversity that marked *IV*, but this time around, they have a better, more memorable set of songs that makes it their best album in a long time. Diamond Rio are professionals, and that's part of their charm. They can deliver any song smoothly, and make their musical eclecticism easy to swallow. Also, Marty Roe's rich, nuanced vocals make the mediocre material (and there are a couple of weak cuts here and there) sound sweet. It's not perfect, but *Unbelievable* nevertheless offers proof that Diamond Rio has found a near-irresistible mix of contemporary country and bluegrass.

Thom Owens

One More Day
February 2001, Arista

The key word with Arista Nashville's Diamond Rio is "consistent." This band is probably one of the finest in the business when it comes to developing a sound all its own and maintaining that sound over time. When the sound is as harmonious as Diamond Rio's, a solid album is a given. *One More Day* remains in the thread of its predecessors; the incredible lead vocals of Marty Roe still float on the breeze of Gene Johnson's mandolin and Jimmy Olander's guitar. The Sunday morning choir harmonies are there too. The title cut, clearly the album's powerhouse cut, has the distinction of occupying the *Billboard* Hot Country Singles chart more than once. "Stuff" is a fun yet insightful tune about how we tend to measure our success in life by how many material things we accumulate. "Sweet Summer" is the epitome of what songwriting is all about. The essence of time is captured here in reminiscences of running home and getting your money before the ice cream man was gone. Chely Wright appears on the CD as well, sharing vocals on the ballad "I'm Trying." If any flaw can be found here it would be the band's choice not to experiment with new sound, but then again, why tamper with a good thing?

Rick Cohoon

Joe Diffie

Regular Joe
January 1992, Epic

Diffie's second album has all the clichés of country music, and all the good stuff, too. If "Ain't That Bad Enough" is a run-of-the-mill song, Diffie rescues it by tearing the melody loose from its mooring. He's also willing to push the line: of all Diffie's country heroes—and you'll be able to name them after one listen—maybe only Merle Haggard would rock out as hard as Diffie does on the title track.

Brian Mansfield

Honky Tonk Attitude
April 1993, Epic

Taking a cue from some of his peers, balladeer Diffie makes a point to get rowdy on this, his most commercially successful album to date. Besides the title track, it includes the hits "Prop Me up Beside the Jukebox (If I Die)" and "John Deere Green."

Dan Cooper

Third Rock from the Sun
July 1994, Epic

Third Rock from the Sun represents a bit of a musical departure for Joe Diffie. Though he keeps his basic honky tonk roots, he experiments more, adding more rock flourishes to his sound. Not all of his attempts are successful, but his ballads are frequently compelling. Nevertheless, it's a little distressing that he has only written one song on the album— there's no reason for his well to dry up by only his fourth record.

Thom Owens

Life's So Funny
December 1995, Epic

Led by the tongue-in-cheek single "Bigger Than the Beatles," Joe Diffie's fifth album *Life's So Funny* delivers the relaxed, funny contemporary country that fans have come to expect from the singer. *Life's So Funny* isn't as consistently engaging as his previous *Third Rock From the Sun*, yet its warm sense of humor and varied collection of ballads and mid-tempo

rockers makes it a worthy follow-up to the most popular record Diffie ever released.

Thom Owens

The Essential Joe Diffie
April 2003, Epic

Epic/Legacy's 2003 collection *The Essential Joe Diffie* weighs in at 14 tracks, just two less than the 2002 collection *16 Biggest Hits*, with which it shares a whopping 12 tracks. Given that considerable overlap, it's not surprising that the two collections are essentially interchangeable, but *16 Biggest Hits* has the edge, not just because it has two more tracks, but because the four songs unique to that collection are stronger than the two unique songs here (for the record, they are the Mary Chapin Carpenter duet "Not Too Much to Ask," which has never appeared on a Joe Diffie album, and the modest hit "This Is Your Brain"). That said, *The Essential Joe Diffie* is hardly a bad album—after, it's pretty much the same album, down to identical sequencing for the first three cuts—and it is also an effective overview of the peak of Diffie's career. *16 Biggest Hits* may be slightly stronger, but that's all it is: a slight difference. On its own terms, *The Essential Joe Diffie* is a first-rate collection.

Stephen Thomas Erlewine

Dixie Chicks

Wide Open Spaces
January 1998, Monument

The Dixie Chicks spent the first half of the '90s toiling away on the independent bluegrass circuit, releasing three albums on small labels, before sisters Martie Seidel and Emily Robison decided to revamp their sound in 1995, adding Natalie Maines as their lead singer and, in the process, moving the group away from bluegrass and toward a major label with Sony/Columbia's revived Monument Records imprint. All of this seems like the blueprint for a big pop crossover move and, to be sure, their 1998 major-label debut *Wide Open Spaces* was a monumental success, selling over ten million copies and turning the group into superstars, but the remarkable thing about the album is that it's most decidedly not a sell-out, or even a consciously country-pop record. To be sure, there are pop melodies here, but this isn't a country-pop album in the vein of Shania Twain, a record that's big on style and glitz, designed for a mass audience. Instead, *Wide Open Spaces* pulls from several different sources—the Chicks' Americana roots, to be sure, but also bits of the alt country from k.d. lang and Lyle Lovett, '70s soft rock (any album that features versions of songs by J.D. Souther and Bonnie Raitt surely fits this bill), even the female neo-folkies emerging on the adult alternative rock stations at the end of the decade. In other words, it hit a sweet spot, appealing to many different audiences because it was eclectic without being elitist but they also had a true star in Natalie Maines, whose powerful, bluesy voice gave these songs a compelling center. Maines was versatile, too, negotiating the twists and turns of these songs without a hitch, easily moving from the vulnerability of "You Were Mine" to the snarl of "Give It Up or Let Me Go." The same goes for the Dixie Chicks and *Wide Open Spaces* as a whole: they are as convincing on the sprightly opener "I Can Love You Better" or the bright, optimistic title song as they are on the breezy "There's Your Trouble" as they are on the honky tonk shuffle of "Tonight the Heartache's on Me" and the rocking swagger of "Let 'Er Rip." It's a remarkably wide range and it's effortlessly eclectic, with the Dixie Chicks bringing it all together with their attitude and understated musicality—as debuts go (and this does count as a debut), they rarely get better than this.

Stephen Thomas Erlewine

Fly
August 1999, Monument

Wide Open Spaces unveiled the new incarnation of the Dixie Chicks, revealing an eclectic, assured group that was simultaneously rootsy and utterly modern, but if that 1998 de facto debut captured the band just leaving the ground, *Fly*—perhaps appropriately, given the title—finds the group in full flight, in full possession of their talents. This time around, the different sounds they draw upon are more fully integrated, which only makes them more distinctive as a group. Even if the whole of the album feels more of a piece, they still take the time to deliver a slice of pure honky tonk on "Hello Mr. Heartache" and a piece of breakneck bluegrass on the rip-roaring, wickedly clever "Sin Wagon," which is also one of the group originals here, a collaboration between Natalie Maines and Emily Robison and outside writer Stephony Smith. It—along with the Maines-cowritten "Without You," the Maines/Robison "Don't Waste Your Heart" and Martie Seidel's co-written "Ready to Run" and "Cowboy Take Me Away"—showcase the trio's increasing craft as writers, which is one of the reasons this album sounds unified. But even the outside-written material *feels* like the group, whether it's the twangy boogie "Some Days You Gotta Dance," Patty Griffin's "Let Him Fly," the melancholy "Cold Day in July" and, especially "Goodbye Earl" where a wife gets revenge on her abusive husband. Like before, the group moves gracefully between these different styles, with Maines providing a powerful, compelling focus with Robison and Seidel offering sensitive support, and this blend makes *Fly* a rich, nuanced album that just gets better with repeated listens.

Stephen Thomas Erlewine

Home
August 2002, Open Wide/Monument/Columbia

Delivering a successor to their breakthrough smash *Wide Open Spaces* was easy—*Fly* followed a year afterward, sounding sleek and satisfying. Following that album turned out to be a little more difficult for the Dixie Chicks, not least because they were involved in an ugly battle with their record company over royalties. While they were away, country radio grew stricter, but there were undercurrents of change, particularly in the grassroots success of the *O Brother, Where Art Thou?* soundtrack. The Dixie Chicks always had deep country roots, but it was entirely conceivable that they could have chosen the pop route, since it's always the safest bet for established stars to follow the mainstream—especially after they have been away for a while. Fortunately, one thing this trio has never been is predictable, and they were emboldened by their successful battle with the label, along with the *O Brother*, leading to the stunner that is *Home*, their sixth album. There may be a Stevie Nicks cover here, but there are no concessions to pop anywhere; there are hardly any electric

guitars, actually. This is a pure country album, loaded with fiddles, acoustic guitars, and close harmonies, but retaining the Chicks' signature flair, sense of humor, and personality. It's a vibrant, quirky, heartfelt record that finds the group investing as much in a funny, rollicking number like "White Trash Wedding" or something as sadly sweet as "Godspeed (Sweet Dreams)." But the key to the album is that, as they so brilliantly put it on the wonderful opener, "Long Time Gone," they recognize many modern country singers "sound tired but they don't sound Haggard" and "have money but they don't have Cash"—and this is a sentiment that doesn't just apply to those riding the charts, but to the po-faced alt-country contenders who are too serious to have fun. They deftly balance modern attitudes with classic instrumentation, all built on terrific songwriting, winding up with an album that feels purer than anything on the charts, yet much livelier and genuine than alt-country. This is what country music in 2002 should sound like. With *Home*, the Dixie Chicks illustrate that country music should be simple but adventurous, sincere but fun. In doing so, they've delivered not just their best album, but what's arguably the best country album yet released in the 2000s. Needless to say, an instant classic.

Stephen Thomas Erlewine

Taking the Long Way
May 2006, Open Wide/Columbia

The road leading away from *Home*, the Dixie Chicks' acclaimed 2002 return to straight-ahead country, proved to be quite rocky for the Texan trio, largely due to anti-George W. Bush and anti-war comments lead singer Natalie Maines made dur-ing the long crawl to the 2003 Iraqi War. Maines' words, initially spoken off the cuff in concert but then repeated in numerous interviews, earned her plenty of enemies within the country community (most notably Toby Keith), but despite the hailstorm of publicity, Maines, Martie Maguire, and Emily Robison did not back down, even as their country audience slowly diminished. But by that point, the Dixie Chicks were bigger than a mere country act anyway: they were international superstars. Their sound and sensibility played to an audience that was much bigger and more self-consciously sophisticated than the country audience, so their shift from country to pop on 2006's *Taking the Long Way* feels natural; even the neo-bluegrass of *Home* felt like a kindred spirit to the alt-country movement and such AAA singer/songwriters as Sheryl Crow, not the pure bluegrass of Ricky Skaggs, or even the progressive Alison Krauss. Given the controversy of 2003, the conscious distancing from country makes sense—and given songs like the defiant "Not Ready to Make Nice" and the redneck-baiting "Lubbock or Live It," the Dixie Chicks don't sound like they're in retreat on *Taking the Long Way*, either; they merely sound like they're being themselves. And *Taking the Long Way* is as genuine a Dixie Chicks album as *Home* or *Wide Open Spaces*, feeling like an accurate reflection of the trio's current life. They are now savvy, sophisticated urbanites—the album cover makes it seem like they've stepped out of *Sex and the City*—and the music reflects that. It's rooted in country—or more specifically country-rock—and it wouldn't sound out of place in Nashville, but sounds more suited for upscale apartments and coffeehouses. The sound might be a little more NPR than hot country, but the trio's harmonies still shine brightly, they still play with conviction, and they still have a strong body of songs here. No doubt reflecting the influence of producer Rick Rubin, the Chicks work with songwriters well outside of the Music Row mainstream: naturally, Sheryl Crow makes an appearance as a co-writer here, but so does acclaimed pop tunesmith Neil Finn, alt-country mainstay Gary Louris, bluesman Keb' Mo', Heartbreaker Mike Campbell, and through much of the album, Semisonic/Trip Shakespeare frontman Dan Wilson. All are accomplished songwriters whose strengths may not seem to lie in country, but they all know how to structure a song, and they help give the group direction and the album focus. Rubin's skill on picking collaborators for the trio makes up for his typically flat production—it's clean and classy, but not colorful, which it begs to be, given that this is a pop album filled with different styles and textures from rollicking rock & roll to soulful laments to sweet ballads. But this lack of zest in the production is forgivable because *Taking the Long Way* is otherwise a strong, confident affair that is far from suggesting the Dixie Chicks are being cowardly for moving away from country. Rather, they're bravely asserting their identity through this varied, successful crossover move.

Stephen Thomas Erlewine

Dusty Drake

Dusty Drake
June 2003, Warner Bros.

Since Dusty Drake has the physique of a body-builder and a neatly trimmed goatee, is seen riding a motorcycle on the back cover of his debut, and sounds a bit like the blustery Toby Keith, it could be easy for some listeners to pass him by, thinking that he's just a trick of macho marketing. That's unfair, because his eponymous debut is a refreshing surprise—a record that navigates the arena rock pomp of contemporary country with a dose of traditional country instrumentation and songwriting smarts. He can succumb to silliness on occasion, such as on the rah-rah radio song "Radio" or any time that he lets the testosterone take over, but his muscular baritone helps sell these songs. Better still, he balances straight-ahead, anthemic modern country songs with some nicely gonzo touches, such as slipping an oversized Van Halen-styled guitar into a rocking country tune. Best of all, he is a strong writer, as evidenced most of all by "Too Wet to Plow," "Not Bad for a Good Ole Boy," "Smaller Pieces," and "Ain't Nobody's Business." A taste for sentiment and silliness may keep this from being continually engaging, but at its best, *Dusty Drake* is tuneful, rocking, memorable modern country, beating Toby Keith at his own game.

Stephen Thomas Erlewine

Steve Earle

Guitar Town
1986, MCA

On Steve Earle's first major American tour following the release of his debut album, *Guitar Town*, Earle found himself sharing a bill with Dwight Yoakam one night and the Replacements another, and one listen to the album explains why—while the music was country through and through, Earle showed off enough swagger and attitude to intimidate

anyone short of Keith Richards. While Earle's songs bore a certain resemblance to the Texas outlaw ethos (think Waylon Jennings in "Lonesome, On'ry and Mean" mode), they displayed a literate anger and street-smart snarl that set him apart from the typical Music Row hack, and no one in Nashville in 1986 was able (or willing) to write anything like the title song, a hilarious and harrowing tale of life on the road ("Well, I gotta keep rockin' while I still can/Got a two-pack habit and motel tan") or the bitterly unsentimental account of small-town life "Someday" ("You go to school, where you learn to read and write/So you can walk into the county bank and sign away your life"), the latter of which may be the best Bruce Springsteen song that Boss didn't write. And even when Earle gets a bit teary-eyed on "My Old Friend the Blues" and "Little Rock 'n' Roller," he showed off a battle-scarred heart that was tougher and harder-edged than most of his competition. *Guitar Town* is slightly flawed by an overly tidy production from Emory Gordy, Jr., and Tony Brown as well as a band that never hit quite as hard as Earle's voice, and he would make many stronger and more ambitious records in the future, but *Guitar Town* was his first shot at showing a major audience what he could do, and he hit a bull's-eye—it's perhaps the strongest and most confident debut album any country act released in the 1980s.

Mark Deming

Exit 0
MCA

Exit 0 essentially follows the same formula as *Guitar Town*, and while it isn't as uniformly excellent as his debut, Steve Earle has come up with a couple of his best songs, including the yearning "I Ain't Ever Satisfied." The major difference between the two albums is the fact that Earle insisted on working with his road band the Dukes, which gives *Exit 0* a tougher sound. If the material had matched the sound of the album, the record would have surpassed *Guitar Town*, but since the songs are uneven, it's just a respectable follow-up.

Thom Owens

The Definitive Collection 1983–1997
July 2006, Hip-O

Steve Earle's tenure at MCA Records has seemingly been anthologized to death by now, with *seven* compilations drawn from his MCA material already on the market at this writing, so one might wonder what the point would be of putting out another one. However,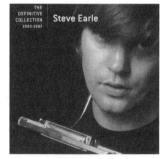
2006's *The Definitive Collection 1983-1997* at least makes an honest effort to live up to its title by also offering a brief look at his work before and after he signed with MCA. While the bulk of this disc concerns itself with Earle's first three albums—and six tracks come from his 1986 debut, *Guitar Town*—the set opens with "Nothin' But You" from his rockabilly-flavored *Pink & Black* EP, first released independently in 1982, and the final six songs document Earle's triumphant comeback from his "vacation in the ghetto" with songs from his underrated acoustic album *Train a Comin'* (1995) and the brilliant, harder-edged *I Feel Alright* (1996) and *El Corazón*

(1997), as well as a live performance of "Valentine's Day" and his superb contribution to the soundtrack of the film *Dead Man Walking*, "Ellis Unit One." During his first 15 years as a recording artist, Steve Earle made far too much good music to fit on one disc (which is one of the reasons to pick up the fine two-disc compilation *Ain't Ever Satisfied: The Steve Earle Collection*), but this set at least manages to match up the cream of his MCA years with some examples of the fine material he recorded elsewhere, and it's a good starter for anyone looking for an introduction to one of America's finest and most fearless songwriters.

Mark Deming

Emerson Drive

Emerson Drive
May 2002, Dreamworks

Emerson Drive, a band of Canadian transplants, eases right into the Music Row pocket with its first effort, a collection of amiable tunes delivered with polish and some degree of drama. What's most refreshing is that the band wrote hardly any of it; with so many non-performing writers in Nashville, it's a blessing to find a self-contained group that doesn't have to inflict its own mediocre material on the world. On the other hand, the gloss and lyrical predictability of these songs doesn't prove that the non-performing writers are necessarily that much more gifted. On balance, with its ebullient spirit, agreeably rough-edged vocal harmonies, and fluid fiddle fills from Pat Allingham, *Emerson Drive* is about as strong a debut as one can expect, given the narrow stylistic rules imposed on the genre.

Robert L. Doerschuk

What If?
June 2004, Dreamworks

Emerson Drive is contemporary country at its poppiest, a band that is country in name only, with a sound and sensibility much closer to the mellow Californian country-rock of the '70s or the slick MOR of the '80s than to Music City. After all, this is a band that, for its second album, 2004's *What If?*, has placed all its chits on producer Richard Marx, who is best known for his post-Eagles adult contemporary hits of the late '80s and is a pop craftsman, not a honky tonker. To country purists, this naturally means that Emerson Drive is not something to be taken seriously, and if you're looking for straight-ahead country, these guys don't deliver. But that doesn't mean they're bad. In fact, they're very, very good, a mainstream pop band with appealing tunefulness and a mild country flair. Marx is a perfect fit as producer, and brings out their strengths, whether it's their endearing everyguy persona or good harmonies, selecting a tight set of 14 songs (including four co-written by Marx) in the process. It's a modest album, yet it's also sturdy and well constructed, growing in stature after several plays. Above all, with *What If?* Emerson Drive proves to be reliable, delivering a record that may not

progress far from the band's debut—it follows the same blueprint, only delving a little deeper into pop—but is certainly its equal in terms of quality, and is a solid second effort.

Stephen Thomas Erlewine

Countrified
August 2006, Montage

Led by the rich-toned lead vocals of Brad Mates, the Canadian-bred band's first two albums on Dreamworks received tons of high-powered accolades from the country music community—including *Billboard*'s Top Country Artist of the Year and Group of the Year for two consecutive years from the Canadian Country Music Association. The sounds were crisp, slick, and fit perfectly into the era's pop-country vibe, but Richard Marx's solid production was a mixed blessing; some felt he made Emerson Drive "too" pop to be legit country artists. That problem is solved on this incredibly infectious, not-a-bad-cut-in-sight collection, not only with a title indicating Emerson Drive's true identity as country artists, but with production by famed genre songwriters and producers Keith Follese and Brad Allen—who also happen to helm the band's new U.S. label, Midas Records Nashville. There's still a rock/pop edge, reflected by the popular, family values-driven first single "A Good Man" and "You Still Own Me." But the richer country elements shine through on the fiddle passages (performed brilliantly by David Pichette) of the raucous, honky tonkin' "Testify" and barnburning "Sweet Natural Girl." Heartfelt, gently twangy ballads like "Moments" and "A Boy Becomes a Man" beautifully balance the feisty tunes. The disc's true masterpiece is saved for the end, when the boys put a crafty rock/soul energy into the classic "Devil Went Down to Georgia," adding to Pichette's fiddle genius with a touch of Latin spice and a few witty, well-placed bars of Led Zeppelin's "Kashmir" by guitarist Danick Dupelle.

Jonathan Widran

Ty England

Ty England
1995, RCA

While his voice hearkens back to classic honky tonk singers like Lefty Frizzell, Ty England's music falls halfway between Garth Brooks and Randy Travis, ranging from up-tempo stomps to heartfelt ballads.

Stephen Thomas Erlewine

Two Ways to Fall
September 1996, RCA

Ty England's second album, *Two Ways To Fall*, is nearly as strong as his debut album, boasting an excellent selection of ballads and honky tonk ravers that establish him as one of the finest mainstream country singers of the mid-'90s.

Thom Owens

Erika Jo

Erika Jo
June 2005, Universal South

Erika Jo is the first female winner of USA Network's *Nashville Star* competition, taking home the crown for the competition that ended April 26, 2005. She's also the youngest winner of the competition, but unlike *American Idol*, where teenagers like Jasmine Trias and Mikalah Gordon struggled to sound adult yet wound up as little girls, country has a tradition of precocious teens sounding wise beyond their years. Erika Jo isn't as gritty as Tanya Tucker was at the age of 13, but she's not dissimilar to how LeAnn Rimes channeled the sound, if not the soul, of Patsy Cline at 13, except Jo's sound is largely based on the bright, friendly feel of Reba McEntire, and how she leans toward crossover pop without ever abandoning county. Erika Jo and her producers pattern her quickly recorded, rush-released eponymous debut album (it hit the streets a little over a month after the show ended) after that sound, usually to quite an appealing end. Despite the quick turnaround on the album, *Erika Jo* doesn't sound hurried or incomplete. It's a glistening, professional Music City production, grounded by a set of sturdy, if generic, songs and crafted with precise, tasteful studio musicians. If it doesn't deliver anything unexpected, it nevertheless works very well within the confines of contemporary country in 2005, not just because it's well made, but because Erika Jo is a good, surprisingly soulful singer and an energetic presence who gives this otherwise conventional music real personality. There aren't as many standout tracks along the lines of the sassy, winning first single, "I Break Things," as there should be, but Erika Jo's infectious spirit and full-throated vocals keep her debut interesting, suggesting that this is a good start to what may be quite an engaging career.

Stephen Thomas Erlewine

Sara Evans

Three Chords and the Truth
July 1997, RCA

Coming on like an up-to-date version of Patsy Cline, Sara Evans tosses her hat into the ring for best new female country artist of 1998. Surprisingly, with *Three Chords and the Truth*, she just may win. This disc rings out with an air of originality helped along by great tunes and solid backup musicianship. Producer Pete Anderson (of Dwight Yoakam fame) helps keep things pared down and centered, giving Evans the opportunity to shine. The title cut is a must for new country fans, while "Imagine That" calls to mind Billie Holiday. All in all, the title of this disc says it all.

James Chrispell

No Place That Far
October 1998, RCA

On the follow-up to her surprise 1997 debut hit, *Three Chords and the Truth*, singer and songwriter Sara Evans shocked many of the fans who embraced it with *No Place That Far*. Where Dwight Yoakam producer and guitarist Pete Anderson helped Evans shape a modern version of hardcore country traditionalism on the first disc, RCA brought in producers Buddy Cannon

and Norro Wilson to protect their investment and take her to the next level by adding plenty of sheen and shine—and a slew of celebrity guests for good measure. It worked: *No Place That Far* firmly established Evans as a bona fide superstar, a down-home singer with the pipes of a diva. Almost immediately, she entered the pantheon reserved for singers like Martina McBride (who appears here) and Trisha Yearwood (who she basically replaced) in the spotlight. Evans co-wrote five of the set's 11 tunes including the title track, which was a smash out of the box. It's not that slick pop completely replaced the torch and twang in Evans' voice and songs; it's more like it was integrated gradually, eventually replacing it. There are still a number of cuts here that show off Evans' roots sound: the opener, "The Great Unknown," co-written with Phil Barnhart and James House; "These Days," written with the great Matraca Berg; and the closer, "There's Only One," penned with Leslie Satcher. But the title track, written with Tony Martin and Tom Shapiro, could have been released in 2007—it bore the adult pop mark of the new contemporary country sound. With backing vocals by heavy hitters like Vince Gill and McBride, it was destined for the Top Five. The soaring emotional euphoria in the refrain (which seemingly underscores the definition of transcendent love) was impossible to resist. Another notable cut is Jamie O'Hara's country pub rock shuffle "The Crying Game." (It sounds like it was written by Hank DeVito and produced like it was a track on an early Rosanne Cash or Rodney Crowell record.) It was a place where Evans' voice was left pretty much untreated and allowed to display its natural range and emotional depth. "Fool, I'm a Woman," with its sprightly mandolins, ringing electric guitars, and crackling snare drum, is another of those crossover tunes that landed as a single. In all, the album scored three, and placed Evans in the multiplatinum category at the top of the charts, where every effort since has landed.

Thom Jurek

Girls' Night Out
March 1999, BMG Special Products

Unlike other country diva collections, no women outshine or overshadow any of the others on this harmless CD, a compilation including three performances each from Sara Evans, Martina McBride, Mindy McCready, and Lorrie Morgan. Morgan's contributions "The Heart That Jack Broke" and "Good as I Was to You" demonstrate the most thigh-slappin' estrogenated chutzpah in this crowd. Martina McBride's selections offer evidence that she is the most accomplished, well-trained vocalist heard here, as she belts out Gretchen Peters' "Independence Day" (the track that established her career) with conviction and the promise-filled "'Til I Can Make It on My Own" with sincerity. Radio-dial darling Mindy McCready ("Ten Thousand Angels," "Over and Over") displays that she has a clear and competent voice but lacks subtlety, yet she readily offers more surprise than the others. Sara Evans is the songwriter of the bunch with "Three Chords and the Truth" (her debut single) and a cover of "Almost New." She possesses the purest "country" voice in the pack.

Becky Byrkit & Thom Jurek

Born to Fly
October 2000, RCA

After the commercial and critical success Sara Evans rightfully garnered for 1998's *No Place That Far* and the extensive tour she undertook to support it, *Born to Fly* emphasizes the more contemporary sounds on the recording, while placing some of the rootsy bluegrass back in the mix. She does this with the confidence and authority of a seasoned veteran who is in control of her work. Sitting in the producer's chair for the first time with Paul Worley, Evans co-wrote six of the set's 11 tracks. The studio players assembled on this date are impressive: Ricky Skaggs, Jerry Douglas, Randy Scruggs, Dan Dugmore, Bruce Hornsby, Biff Watson, Aubrey Haynie, Jonathan Yudkin, and Glenn Worf, to name a few. The stand-out cuts are the playful title track and first single, "Born to Fly," with its fiddles, dobros, and mandolins; the nostalgic ballad "I Learned That from You," with its whinnying pedal steel; and covers of Edwin McCain's "I Could Not Ask for More" and the closer, a reading of Hornsby's gently choogling back-porch love song "Every Little Kiss." Evans moved to the top of the charts again with this one, and was able to go four deep for singles, solidifying her place at the beginning of the 21st century.

Thom Jurek

Restless
August 2003, RCA

Commercial country music has become so slick and predictable that when an artist emerges who conveys even the slightest bit of mold-breaking potential, they're name rolls off of the lips of critics like an answered prayer. Missouri-raised siren Sara Evans has that potential, and uses it sparingly on *Restless*, her fourth record for RCA. The spirited opener, "Rockin' Horse," features fellow crooner Vince Gill on harmony, and impeccable playing from Nashville's finest. "Backseat of a Greyhound Bus" is a lush tale of re-demption that sounds like the musical sister to Train's 2001 smash, "Drops of Jupiter." The Celtic-flavored "Restless," the obvious single, is tailor-made to fit in between the Dixie Chicks and Shania Twain on any FM station. After these three songs, Evans goes on autopilot, exploring the generic world of crossover country like a Shakespeare scholar in remedial English. She sounds bored. Time crawls from ballad to boogie, until finally reaching the tune "Big Cry." This is an outstanding country-soul hybrid recalling early k.d. lang and a direction that Evans would do well to inspect further. Like fellow producer Mutt Lange, Paul Worley knows how to work the machine, and *Restless* plays like a Nashville tutorial on the polished, hit-song assembly line.

James Christopher Monger

Real Fine Place
October 2005, RCA

Three years after the 2000 smash *Born to Fly*, Sara Evans matched its hit status with *Restless*, where singles like "Suds in the Bucket" and "Perfect" balanced her fun-loving country girl sensibilities with a homespun take on true love. She maintains that balance in 2005 with *Real Fine Place*. Evans is unabashed and straightforward about loving her husband and her family, and living her life in the eyes of God. But that doesn't mean she can't paint the town ("Momma's Night Out") or sing one of the best country songs about cheating in a while, the aptly named "Cheatin'." "How do you like that paper plate and those pork 'n' beans you're eatin'?" Evans asks with a perfect blend of spite and hurt. "Maybe you should've thought about that when you were cheatin'." Like on "Momma's Night," where a brassy horn section and backup singers punch up the arrangement, *Real Fine Place* isn't afraid to challenge the conventions of country or even contemporary country. "Coalmine" begins as a typical Dixie Chicks-style traditionalist number, but it's modernized with great lyrics that don't stick to cliché ("Can't wait to get him home/Ain't gonna have nothin' but the supper on . . .") and an ending section that layers Evans' vocal numerous times over the fiddle and rambling percussion. "Roll Me Back in

Time" was written by Sheryl Crow and pop producer John Shanks and it sounds like it, while lead single "Real Fine Place to Start" is a breezy foot-tapper that shows off Evans' throaty vocal over steady pop percussion. While *Real Fine Place* is pretty slick in its production, it's sure to lure traditional country fans with Evans' rich vocal presence and the album's assertion that the simplest things in life are its truest. In that sense, *Real Fine Place* is the nicest part of contemporary country. It looks at both sides of that phrase equally without losing sight of the heart in the center.

Johnny Loftus

Jace Everett

Jace Everett
2005, Epic

On his self-titled 2006 debut, Jace Everett—a native of Indiana who moved to the Lone Star State when he was a kid—swaggers and growls whenever he's not sincerely belting out power ballads, two traits that serve him well. His vocals are assured, and there's a sleek, muscular feel to *Jace Everett* that makes it one of the more testosterone-fueled contemporary country albums in recent memory, yet it often is on the verge of being too sleek. The guitars are big, the drums cavernous, and it's all wrapped up in a glossy production that doesn't have much grit to its sound—so it's to Everett's substantial credit that he makes this album sound tougher than other records of its kind. He pours soul into his performances, which carries him through the songs that are designed for the radio, such as the opening pair of "Everything I Want" and "That's the Kind of Love I'm In." Once those two songs are through, the albums starts to get into Everett originals with the sultry rocka-billy boogie of "Bad Things," which might ape Chris Isaak's "Baby Did a Bad Bad Thing," but turns it into something less menacing and a little rowdier. After that, *Jace Everett* retains its clean, polished sound but the music gets more interest-ing, as he tears through the rollicking barroom anthem "I Gotta Have It" before easing into Bobby Houck and Radney Foster's bittersweet ballad "Half of My Mistakes," which all leads up to a second half comprised of original material. Musically, his tunes—most co-written with Stephany Delray, plus a couple of other collaborators—aren't that far removed from what came on the first half of the record, but they avoid the soaring, deliberate choruses of the professionally written opening pair and have as much earnest soul as his vocals. This is particularly true on the ballads at the end of the record where he decides to show some vulnerability on the sentimental but not saccharine nostalgia of "Nowhere in the Neighborhood" and "Between a Father and Son," where Everett's muscular vocals and direct lyrics keep these songs from seeming drippy. It also helps that Everett balances songs like these with slyly rocking songs like "A Little Less Lonely," since it helps give the record both variety and momentum, illustrating that Everett sounds as comfortable with harder country as he does with the commercial stuff. And what makes this such a thoroughly winning debut is that it walks the line between these two extremes with ease. Some may still wish that *Jace Everett* had a production as varied and soulful as Jace Everett the writer and musician, but there's no denying that this first album showcases a contemporary country singer and songwriter of considerable potential.

Stephen Thomas Erlewine

Shelly Fairchild

Ride
May 2005, Columbia

Shelly Fairchild is young, pretty, and sassy, everything that a mainstream country singer should be in the mid-2000s, at least in marketing terms. If that's all that she was, she'd be the equivalent of the crass Keith Anderson—a good-looking empty space, eager to shill for anybody who looks his way—but Fairchild has a powerful, bluesy voice and a genuine charisma on record that makes her 2005 debut, *Ride*, a pretty cool little record. She's not immune to a lot of the trends of modern country—in fact, she's not a Shania-styled diva, she's a creature of the post-Gretchen Wilson world, where female singers are encouraged to be a little rowdy, have some twang in both their voice and music. And while she indulges in a little bit of name-dropping associations—just like how Wilson knows the words to every Tanya Tucker song on "Redneck Girl," Fairchild listens to B.B. King, Merle, and "Free Bird" on different tracks—she's far removed from Big & Rich's calculated, gonzo hucksterism. Instead, with the assistance of producers Buddy Cannon and Kenny Greenberg, that mildly wild spirit is channeled into a disciplined Nashville production that's canny enough to keep Fairchild loose and lively, and have the music be just as vigorous. It's well-crafted, built upon a strong set of songs, and it pulls off the nifty trick of being classic Nashville product yet fresh and vibrant, due to Fairchild's consistently engaging performances. The result is a fun, infectious first album that, like Miranda Lambert's similar debut, announces the arrival a potentially major star.

Stephen Thomas Erlewine

Foster & Lloyd

Faster & Llouder
1989, RCA

The follow-up to Foster & Lloyd's hit-packed debut only spun off one country Top Ten entry ("Fair Shake"), but don't be fooled—the overall quality of the songs on *Faster & Llouder* is just as good, if not better, than that of the songs on the first album. The relatively low chart placings for follow-up singles "Before the Heartache Rolls In" and the Lloyd-sung "Suzette," therefore, were a bit of a puzzle at the time, and seem even odder in retrospect. The Foster & Lloyd formula of two parts country to one part power pop still works well, and if Foster (who takes most of the lead vocals) tends to dominate a little more of the group's sound than Lloyd, it's still Bill Lloyd's subtle pop/rock touches that end up allowing this record to transcend the duo's origins as Nashville songmill peddlers. Years after its release, *Faster & Llouder* still holds up as a superior example of "new country"—one that just happened to be recorded a few years before the term "new country" was invented.

Rudyard Kennedy

The Essential Foster and Lloyd
April 1996, RCA

The Essential Foster & Lloyd groups together 19 tracks by this influential duo who scored several hits in the 1980s. The two merged Lloyd's melodic pop smarts with Foster's Texas literary soul, giving them catchiness and substance in the same package. They also could rock out, leaning toward a rockabilly energy that didn't carry a trace of the redneck swagger of Southern rock. Instead, this was solid, clean-rocking fun with brains. The duo split in 1990 after three albums, but this collection is a good reminder that they anticipated the country youth movement that followed them.

Michael McCall

Radney Foster

Del Rio, Texas, 1959
1992, Arista

Radney Foster's first album since dissolving the much-missed Foster & Lloyd duo is a tribute to the songwriter's coming of age in small-town Texas and all the musical baggage that stowed aboard for the ride. On many of the tracks, Fos-ter seems a little too conscious of wanting to deliver a pure country effort. The songs are solid, but there's a slight archival feel to the result. I admit that personal biases may be at work here, having been a Foster & Lloyd fan, but it's the more contemporary hybrids that strike me as the disc's best moments. The gutsy "A Fine Line," the infectious "Nobody Wins" (with Mary Chapin Carpenter on background vocals,) and the gospelly country-rocker "Hammer and Nails" are worth the price of admission alone.

Roch Parisien

See What You Want to See
May 1999, Arista

For Radney Foster, country music stopped reaping dividends after his second solo album, *Labor of Love*. Although it had its moments, it sounded a little tired, compared to his work with Bill Lloyd and his debut *Del Rio, Texas, 1959*. Sensing that the time was right for a change, Foster made a pop move with his third record, *See What You Want to See*. Where his former partner decided to return to his power-pop roots, thereby confining himself to a niche audience, Foster decided to shoot for a larger audience, redefining his music as rootsy, adult pop. The presence of Emmylou Harris, Abra Moore, Darius Rucker and Patrice Pike of Sister 7 telegraphs Foster's intentions—he still has a bit of a twang, but this is classy, mature pop music, not contemporary country. By and large, his gambit works. At times, *See What You Want to See* sounds a little bit too mannered and considered, which means the hooks never quite take off, but it all sounds pleasant, and the best moments—"Folding Money," "Angry Heart," and

"I'm In"—showcase him at his best as a songwriter while successfully delivering a fresh, updated sound. It may not feel as weighty as *Del Rio, Texas*, but in its own way, it's every bit as successful and introspective as that album, while occasionally matching Foster & Lloyd at their best.

Stephen Thomas Erlewine

Vince Gill

The Way Back Home
1987, Buddha

This early document by Vince Gill (his second proper solo full-length) on RCA, a couple of years after he left Pure Prairie League, offers solid hints of the storied career to come. Gill is one of the architects of the genre known as contemporary country, and *The Way Back Home* reveals that he was clearly trying something different to break out. But it also tells the story, in a much more subtle manner, that he is deeply steeped in the country music tradition. On *The Way Back Home* he was still trying to gain his footing as a solo artist—his excellent instrumental skills also established him early on as a top-flight session player. Produced by Emory Gordy, Jr., the sessions host a virtual who's who of the session crowd Gill was running with at the time: Rodney Crowell, Rosanne Cash, Emmylou Harris, Bonnie Raitt, Andrew Gold, Sweethearts of the Rodeo, Roy Huskey, Jr., Jay Dee Manness, Lee Sklar, and many others. Gill wrote five of the nine cuts in this set; others were contributed by Guy Clark, Hank DeVito, Reed Nielsen, and Paul Anka! The sound is basically in the laid-back soft rock vein that the latter Pure Prairie League tunes were in, as well as those of the mid-period Eagles. That may not sound like a big deal in the 21st century, but bringing these sounds to country radio at that time was nothing less than revolutionary. Crowell, Cash, and DeVito had helped pave the way with their early songs and recordings, but Gill was clearly trying to cross over, and he was sure to succeed, given his songwriting skill (take a listen to "The Radio" and you'll hear the ballad style that permeated the contemporary genre later on) and his ability to meld and fuse honky tonk, rockabilly, countrypolitan, and bluegrass with pop. The production on this set sounds a bit dated, but the songs endure for the most part, in particular the mournful acoustic ballad that serves as the title cut; the rollicking "Let's Do Something"; and the completely wonderful closer, "Something's Missing."

Thom Jurek

When I Call Your Name
1989, MCA

Vince Gill left RCA after *The Way Back Home* in 1987. Tony Brown signed him to MCA shortly thereafter, and *When I Call Your Name* served as Gill's MCA debut and the beginning of his long association with the label and with Brown as a producer. Gill, already a seasoned pop musician and Nashville session player, brought with him the ability to write terrific songs and play the hell out of a guitar, along with a sweet-looking face and a killer voice. Brown set out to make him a star and pretty much succeeded the first time out, and in the early 21st century Gill is still racking them up on the charts. He served as contemporary country music's first real star and, along with the more traditional George Strait (another longtime survivor and hitmaker), was a true and respectful link to the music's long heritage. The first

track to score on this set was "Oklahoma Swing," a smoking Western swing duet with Reba McEntire written by Tim DuBois, who also wrote an even bigger hit with the title track that paired Gill with Patty Loveless. Gill also did serviceable covers of Guy Clark's (then an RCA staff songwriter) classic "Rita Ballou" and "Sight for Sore Eyes," and Rosanne Cash's "Never Alone," which opened the disc. He also covered the criminally underappreciated Greg Trooper's mid-tempo ballad "We Won't Dance." Gill's own tunes, for perhaps the only time in his career, were used as filler on the album—he wrote three of ten—but he still managed a beauty with the gorgeous romantic stroller "Oh Girl (You Know Where to Find Me)." *When I Call Your Name* serves as the testament to Gill's arrival as a star and an enduring part of the country music legacy.

Thom Jurek

Pocket Full of Gold
1991, MCA

Pocket Full of Gold is one of Vince Gill's straighter country recordings. Produced by Tony Brown, it is steeped in bluegrass, country balladry from the '60s, and smoothed-out honky tonk, all done in Gill's own chameleon-like yet trademark manner. The lineup speaks volumes about what's on the recording: Herb Pedersen, Richard Bennett, Mac McAnally, Barry Beckett, Hargus "Pig" Robbins, Willie Weeks, Patty Loveless, Billy Joe Walker, and Larrie Londin are a few of the names offering this very distinct blend of styles that is all Gill. The opener, "I Quit," is an up-tempo shuffling honky tonk number, with stuttering Telecasters, and it's followed with "Just Look at Us," a gorgeous pedal steel whining love song. Andrea Zonn's fiddle and John Hughey's steel fuel another broken love song, but this one is a late-night barroom two-stepper. "Liza Jane" walks the line between hard country and rockabilly and features some smoking guitar work by Gill, who also provides some of his flatpicking swagger in "A Little Left Over." Gill wrote only about half the tunes on this set, which is unusual, but it was also fairly early in his career. Hit songwriter Max D. Barnes offered another three and maverick Jim Lauderdale provided the burning Cajun-cum-rockabilly closer, "Sparkle." The set was a hit for Gill, and deserved to be, because of its brilliant and sometimes dazzling mix of traditional styles. Records like this are what make him one of the music's most enduring artists.

Thom Jurek

I Still Believe in You
September 1992, MCA

Vince Gill had already enjoyed country success before 1992's *I Still Believe in You*, but it was the album's four number one singles and almost immediate platinum status that assured the honey-voiced performer's fame and staying power. Gill's delivery is as smooth as the glass surface of a secluded mountain swimming hole, shifting from promise and pain to love and loneliness with easy charm and the occasional touch of his high lonesome background ("No Future in the Past," "Say Hello"). The title track fairly glows with slow-cooked soul, while "Don't Let Our Love Slip Away" nods along on a late '70s contemporary country vibe. The whole affair is so gosh darn flawless it's impossible not to like. After all, how can you fault a guy with mainstream marketability who's also a talented session guitar player, songwriter, and the owner of one of Nashville's best voices?

Johnny Loftus

When Love Finds You
1994, MCA

By 1994, Vince Gill was a bona fide country superstar. His recordings had sold into the millions and his tours were sellouts around the globe. He was ubiquitous on the radio as well. Producer Tony Brown took an even heavier hand on Gill's recordings, even though Gill's own songs dominated his records. The tightrope walk between a handsome tender country-pop balladeer and the rootsy rocking honky tonk guitar picker was beginning to fall on the side of the ballads. It was working on the charts, but some of Gill's older fans—those familiar with his multifaceted talent—began to grow weary of him playing it so safe. There are only three up-tempo cuts on *When Love Finds You*: the tough rocka-billy swagger that is at the heart of "South Side of Dixie," the honky tonk shuffle "What the Cowgirls Do," and the mid-tempo country-rocker "You Better Think Twice." The rest are ballads—every last one of them—but there are a few real gems, including the opener, "Whenever You Come Around," and the stunning title track.

Thom Jurek

Souvenirs
November 1995, MCA Nashville

Drawn largely from Vince Gill's first three albums for MCA Records, 1989's *When I Call Your Name*, 1991's *Pocket Full of Gold*, and 1992's *I Still Believe in You*, *Souvenirs* functions as a greatest-hits collection from what is arguably Gill's finest period as a solo artist. Gill's smooth tenor singing is practically the definition of modern slow-burning country sincerity, all done with a touch of that bluegrass "high lone-some" sound, and his ease with ballads frequently obscures the fact that he is one hell of a guitar player when he decides to be. Highlights on this easy to like set are duets with Reba McEntire ("The Heart Won't Lie") and Dolly Parton ("I Will Always Love You"), an interesting cover of the Eagles' "I Can't Tell You Why," and the infectious and upbeat "Liza Jane," which lets Gill rock things out a little. *Souvenirs* isn't the last word on Vince Gill, who continues to record and release quality contemporary country and bluegrass albums, but there isn't a better single-disc introduction to the com-mercial side of his output than this one.

Steve Leggett

High Lonesome Sound
June 1996, MCA

Vince Gill takes off on a tour of American music on *High Lonesome Sound*. The title cut steps back to a time he hasn't visited in a while, drawing on his days as a bluegrass singer and guitarist to create a soaring, harmony-driven sound that applies Appalachian drive to modern country rhythms. Most of the rest of the album's journey treks in new directions. The aggressive guitar riff that opens "One Dance with You" is straight Chicago blues, while the jaunty feel that enlivens "Down to New Orleans" draws on the Windy City's funky rhythms with a deft touch worthy of Little Feat—with Lowell

George, that is. "Tell Me Lover," also bearing the trace print of Little Feat, dances through a swampy groove. The ar-rangements by Gill and producer Tony Brown give tradi-tional sounds a modern sheen while maintaining a distinct regional flavor. Gill gets much more room to show off his impressive guitar prowess than on his past records. A pair of small complaints are that his lyrics don't match the music (they are steeped in the modern country topical schemes) and he can overly sweeten the blues. Elsewhere, he uses the cliché aspects of Cajun music in paying homage to Louisi-ana's musical heritage (R&B and New Orleans second-line rhythms aren't here and should be, because he's musically sophisticated enough to pull them off). Therefore, this album works best when he's not straining for authenticity: "Worlds Apart," "Given More Time," and "Pretty Little Adriana" leaven his tried-and-true formula into arrangements that are more progressively atmospheric than his past hits. Gill owns too many strengths to need to transform himself into Lowell George or Bonnie Raitt at this point in his career; he can leave his own mark on any music he chooses to play and—for the most part—does so here.

Michael McCall & Thom Jurek

The Key
August 1998, MCA

On *The Key*, Vince Gill presents a rather dazzling ar-ray of traditional styles to display his versatile talent. Going back to his Oklahoma country roots for inspira-tion, something he hasn't done in many years, he comes out with a recording so star-tling that even heavy-handed producer Tony Brown left it pretty much alone. Gill is in fine voice throughout, join-ing with a colorful cast of backing singers—including Patty Loveless, Alison Krauss, Sara Evans, Lee Ann Womack, and Faith Hill—to create the type of music that contemporary country radio has not played in over a decade. Over 13 tracks, Gill eases gracefully from one roots country style to another, from a classic hillbilly waltz to the edgy Bakersfield sound. He even skillfully tips his hat to guitar great Roy Nichols on "There's Not Much Love Here Anymore." A duet with Loveless, "My Kind of Woman/My Kind of Man," stands proudly next to the best country duets of George Jones and Tammy Wynette and Merle Haggard and Bonnie Owens. Most impressive is "Kindly Keep It Country," a stone-cold hard country song that details one man's heartbreak and the soothing effects of a jukebox and a bar stool. As heartbreak-ing as any song he's ever written is "Let Her In," told from the perspective of a divorced father who is trying to rebuild his life and still retain his relationship with his daughter. Just as effective is "The Hills of Caroline," a mountain bluegrass tune with a strong melody and narrative enhanced by the beautiful backing vocals of Krauss. The closing title cut is an endearing acoustic country tune, complete with mandolins and banjo, that comes directly from Gill's relationship with his late father. For emotional depth, honesty, and the kind of musical depth and artistry listeners have come to expect from Gill, *The Key* stands among his very finest recordings.

Jana Pendragon & Thom Jurek

Let's Make Sure We Kiss Goodbye
April 2000, MCA

The black-and-white cover photograph and the title of Vince Gill's *Let's Make Sure We Kiss Goodbye* offer a story that unfolds as the recording itself plays. The album was written in the months preceding his marriage to singer Amy Grant, and if there were ever a record drenched in the kind of transformative rush of new love, this is the one. Yes, it is sappy at times, but the songwriting, as usual, is top-notch, and so are the performances here; mostly they're just really mellow and warm. That doesn't mean that sparks don't fly from some tracks: "Baby Please Don't Go" is drenched in choogling rockabilly swagger, "Shoot Straight from Your Heart is solid—if softer—contemporary country, and "Feels Like Love" is a mid-tempo country-pop tune that has that trademark wonderful rousing Gill vocal in the refrain. The rest are mostly love songs but inspired ones. Grant was clearly his muse on this set, and nowhere is it more clear than on the lilting title cut and "When I Look into Your Heart," where Gill and Grant perform a duet. Tony Brown's production is pristine and everywhere, but the craft and arrangements in these songs are all Gill's. This is a beautiful and sincere recording, one that not everyone will taker a shine to because of its tenderness, but that doesn't make it any less of a quality endeavor. You only make a record like this once in a lifetime; Vince Gill should be proud of this one.

Thom Jurek

Next Big Thing
February 2003, MCA

Vince Gill's studio offering following his paean to his new bride, *Let's Make Sure We Kiss When We Say Goodbye*, is one of the strongest recordings in a decade. Perhaps it's the freedom from the usual Nashville production bullsh*t—Gill produced the album himself. His cast of players and singers is a veritable list of stars, including Emmylou Harris, Lee Ann Womack, the Doobie Brothers' Michael McDonald, life partner Amy Grant, Kim Keyes, Andrea Zonn, and Leslie Satcher. Famed producer and engineer Justin Niebank is at the mixing desk, and Gill's regular band propels a mixed bag of pop, boogie, swing, and neo-trad country tunes—and odd for a Nash Vegas album, there are 17 of them, not ten or 12. Standout tracks are the rollicking title with its booming guitars; the mariachi-tinged "We Had It All"; the slow country stroll of "Young Man's Town," despite its sweeping strings and electric violin moan; and the stunning ballad "These Broken Hearts," with McDonald adding a depth of emotion rarely matched on Gill's records. There is also the Merle Haggard tribute "Real Mean Bottle" that features the opening guitar lines to "Mama Tried." But it's far from syrupy—it's a tough song about a tougher, more visionary man than the singer could ever hope to be, sung in an unflinching manner. All of this said, there are the now-requisite Gill saccharine tracks such as "Whippoorwill River," an insufferable homage to his father that drowns in syrup. The hardcore honky tonk rock of "The Sun's Gonna Shine on You" is one of the strongest cuts on any Gill album, full of

shuffling blues and rockabilly swagger. "Old Time Fiddle" is a cross-pollination of Cajun music and bluegrass that works surprisingly well considering how slick it is—perhaps it's the layered accordions and the organic-sounding percussion. The album closes with "In These Last Few Days," another ballad; Gill always makes records that are at least 60/40 ballads to up-tempo tunes, and this track is that forlorn, bittersweet ballad that seems to close every record of his. But lyrically it's so strong and vulnerable that it works, leaving the listener haunted with the notion that something special has occurred, that he or she has born witness to a man becoming aware of the preciousness of his own life. In all, it's a strong effort. It's nice to see established artists reclaim control of their careers—especially when the results are so rewarding.

Thom Jurek

These Days
October 2006, MCA Nashville

As 2006 nears its end, no one can argue that the world of country music isn't, at this moment, the most adventurous in the mainstream pop music industry and that Nash Vegas is taking more chances on its acts as the rest of the biz relies more on narrowing things into smaller and smaller niches that can easily be hyped and digested. Sure, as always, artist's images and many recordings are calculated to score big as in any pop industry. The difference is in approach. The country-listening audience/demographic has widened considerably; therefore, there is a need—as well as an opportunity—for experimentation to see what sticks. This is the most exciting the music's been since Willie and Waylon hit the charts in the '70s, or perhaps to be a bit more fair, when Garth Brooks turned them upside down in the early '90s. Country music's fan base is growing because it still relies largely on radio, and video channels like CMT and GAC, both of which are very supportive of directors and artists taking artistic chances in the way they choose to dramatize, animate, and portray songs—check the work of the brilliant director Trey Fanjoy just for starters. Country's latest audience grew up on rock & roll, MTV (when it still played videos), soul, blues, funk, early rap, and in some cases even punk. And while the marketing approach is still singles-driven, country music artists and producers, as well as the labels that house them, are still concerned with the "album" either as a whole, or as a completely crafted collection of varying singles (in this case meaning "good songs"). What's more, these folks still buy CDs (titles are readily available at the local in mega-marts and department stores) and don't rely on the internet as much as pop and rock fans do for information. Given the long run of the Dixie Chicks' *Taking the Long Way* at number one on the country and *Billboard* charts, one can't simply dismiss the music as being the religious right's stronghold or pop culture front for "traditional family values" anymore, either, though admittedly there's plenty of that around. In the 21st century it's country music and hip hop—not rock—that have been taking on the topics of race, class, basic human dignity and diversity, more than any other popular (chart measured) American music.

This current mindset in both the Nash Vegas offices and in the fan base is what makes Vince Gill's *These Days*, a 43-song, four-disc set, possible. Gill had been planning on making a standard single-disc record in 2006. He wanted it to be musically diverse. Given his long career as songwriter, picker, producer, singer, recording and performing artist, he had a right to expect his label MCA Nashville to go along with his choices. What he didn't count on was recording 31 songs with various groups of musicians and not knowing what to do with them. He approached Luke Lewis, the label's president, with an idea he got from the Beatles multi-release-per-year tactic (the same one everybody used in the '60s), which was to issue three albums approximately three months apart in a single calendar year. Lewis, visionary that he is, went one better. He encouraged Gill to go back into the studio and cut enough quality material for a fourth disc and release them all as a box set. Unlike most boxes on the shelf, this one retails for a fairly modest $29.98—less than eight dollars a disc—an attractive package in time for the holidays.

However, adventurous Nashville music industry or not, it all eventually comes down to the quality of the music after all, right? Yes. These four discs are thematically arranged: there's an acoustic bluegrass-flavored record called "Little Brother" (disc four), a rock record called "Workin' on a Big Chill" (disc one), a trad country & western album called "Some Things Never Get Old" (disc three), and a modern soul and jazz-inflected disc of ballads and more gentle pieces called "The Reason Why" (disc two). What's more, though Gill wrote or co-wrote everything here, he called in numerous guests to help him out. These include Gretchen Wilson, his wife Amy Grant, daugher Jenny Gill, Bonnie Raitt, Rodney Crowell, Sheryl Crow, Diana Krall, pedal steel guitar boss Buddy Emmons, Phil Everly, Rebecca Lynn Howard, the Del McCoury Band, Patty Loveless, Emmylou Harris, John Anderson, Katrina Elam, Lee Ann Womack, LeAnn Rimes, Guy Clark, Trisha Yearwood, Bekka Bramlett, and Michael McDonald. The end result is a magical mystery tour through Gill's own wildly varying aesthetic interests and his uncanny ability to pull off his diverse ideas on tape. *These Days* is not only a showcase of Gill's multidimensional musical persona, but a virtual treatise on the expansive, open-minded, under the umbrella viewpoint that has taken over Nashville in the current era.

"Workin' on a Big Chill" lives up to its name as a rock record as reflected in the tunes, the beats, and the instrumentation. The title track alone, with Gill's own considerable bluesed-out guitar-slinging skills burning down the house, punches a hole in expectations; the track also includes a Wurlitzer, a B-3 and Bramlett's killer backing vocals. "Love's Standin'" was written with co-producer John Hobbs (Justin Niebank and Gill, of course, also inhabit these chairs), and the wonderfully iconoclastic songwriter and producer Joe Henry (it could have been a smash for Fleetwood Mac), and showcases the sheer white soul backing chorus of Bramlett (who was a member of the latter day Fleetwood Mac), Gene Miller, and Gill. Wilson guests on "Cowboy Up," is more an upscale blues tune than a country song and proves Wilson can sing anything she wants and belongs where she is—at the top. While there isn't a weak moment on this set, some of the other standouts include the popping "Sweet Thing," with a full-on horn section, the Jerry Lee Lewis-inspired "Nothin for a Broken Heart," with Crowell, and the utterly sexy and soulful country rocker "The Rhythm of the Pourin' Rain," with Bramlett. The only complaint here is that there isn't more of this material: four CDs of rock & roll tracks would have been welcome, and if rock radio were worth a damn Gill would easily crossover with a couple of these songs.

With its subdued tone, and generally slicker productions that include strings, some muted synthesizers, jazzy arrangements, and pop music stylistic tropes, one might think that "The Reason Why: The Groovy Record" would be the least desirable here. Not so. From the opening cut, "What You Don't Say," with Rimes and a full-on string section with ringing pedal steel, Gill proves he is an American pop songwriter par excellence. If all the music on the charts was done this well, with this much passion and soul and pomp, radio would never have lost its appeal. This is the album in the set that reveals the depth of Gill's craft as a songwriter.

The early rock & roll waltz trappings and vibes, as well as distorted piano on the title cut with Krauss, is a gorgeous love song with some of Gill's finest vocals on tape. Period. "Rock of Your Love" could have been featured on any of Raitt's latter recordings, and that's a compliment. The slow, dirty guitar line and Raitt's R&B slow burning voice carry it home. Where Gill uses guest vocalists—female vocalists have always provided a wise counterpoint to his own husky tenor—the tunes work so well most could be singles. Check "What You Give Away," with Crow, and "The Memory of You," with Yearwood. They're solid; full of honest emotion and pop brilliance. The beautiful love song and gospel tune, "Tell Me One Time About Jesus," with Grant, and "Time To Carry On," with Jenny Gill, are excellent album tracks and give depth, dimension and warmth to this set and are indispensable to it. The duet with Krall is the greatest chance Gill could take. He works in her idiom—and, of course, she plays that wonderful piano of hers—and pulls it off with grace and aplomb in the same way Tom Waits pulled off his duets with Crystal Gayle on the soundtrack for *One from the Heart*.

"Some Things Never Get Old" is subtitled "The Country & Western Record." This is an important distinction because what Gill has assembled here is nothing short of a honky tonk set. Though Gill's voice is a little smooth and high, it hardly matters because he's got the two things that count most on an old-school C&W set: the songs and the band. With Emmons on pedal steel (he's one of the great sonic and stylistic innovators on the instrument) guitarist Billy Joe Walker, Jr., fiddle boss Stuart Duncan, and a slew of backing vocalists who include Dawn Sears, Liana Manis, Jon Randall, Andrea Zonn, and Wes Hightower, as well as his core band, he's in the pocket. The music here collects styles from hardcore honky tonk, countrypolitan, late-night loving and torch songs done as only country singers can, and of course, hillbilly anthems. Some of the top-notch tracks here include "Out of My Mind," with Patty Loveless, the title cut, "Sweet Little Corrina" with Everly (which harks back to those classic Warner Brothers Everly sides), "If I Can Make Mississippi" with Womack, the rowdy good ole boy outlaw anthem, "Take This Country Back," a duet with the truly incomparable John Anderson.

This leaves, finally, "Little Brother, The Acoustic Record." True; some fans of country—especially modern country, may have a harder time with this disc because it is both a bluegrass record full of banjos, dobros, mandolins, white Southern gospel, and mountain music—and simply recorded country ballads. Fans of Gill's shouldn't be surprised; his membership in the *Grand Ole Opry*, his deep reverence for this tradition, and his ability to write, play, and sing in it like an old master—and his previous recordings featuring these qualities—qualify him to indulge that Muse. But Gill's approach, as old-school in thinking as it may be, uses both the music's early reliance on blues and folk styles of the British Isles as a way of expressing the mountain tradition and also the modern scholarship and musical innovations informing it. He is accompanied by the Del McCoury Band on a couple of selections here—"Cold Gray Light of Gone," "A River Like You," with Jenny Gill, "Ace Up Your Pretty Sleeve," co-written with the great and criminally under-noticed Mark Germino, and "Give Me the Highway"—but his own takes on country are actually quite creative in his interpretation on the form. But the chiller here is "Girl" with Rebecca Lynn Howard. Here, the deep, high lonesome sound is informed by all of the early folk musics that came before it, and Gill gives them all free reign as this tune wafts from the Appalachian mountain country to Celtic, Irish, and Scottish meadows and coastlines. And although the set's final cut, "Almost Home," with Guy Clark, has no commercial potential, it's a fitting way to close an album; it's a storyteller's tune, one where

Clark speaks in that age-old wizened rogue manner of his, and helps to create a myth of near-epic proportion.

What it all adds up to is that this is Gill's masterwork. It's an exhaustive, profound, fun and fulfilling set that not only gives fans something to delight in, but goes wide and if given half a chance could and would attract many new ones. It is one of the major recordings not only of 2006, but of the decade so far—in any genre. This is the treatment a seasoned artist like Gill deserves, and along with the benefit and support of being able to indulge in such a project, it lives up to the responsibility of delivering the goods in abundance. This is yet another example that the new media-savvy form of country music introduced by Brooks in the '90s has yielded something far more interesting and exciting than some folks are willing to accept, and yet still others are able to believe.

Thom Jurek

Pat Green

Three Days
October 2001, Republic/Universal

The front cover of Pat Green's *Three Days* shows a weathered cowboy boot hanging on the post of a barbed-wire fence. The picture on the inside of the album sleeve let us know it was Green himself who shed his shoes to walk the southern streets barefoot. It's a fitting metaphor, given the music. The album casts aside the glossy over-production and generic songwriting of pop-country to make a raw, honest album that's not afraid to get its jeans dirty. *Three Days* is a testament to what's right about country music. Some of these tracks could put Green in the neo-folk singer/songwriter class with acts like John Gorka and David Wilcox, but this is a country record from top to bottom. These are songs about the simple life, the call of the road, and sorrows drowned in whiskey, old themes with a contemporary touch. Willie Nelson helps out on "Threadbare Gypsy Soul," adding to Green's credibility and making this album feel even more genuine. *Three Days* may not spark any revolutions in Nashville, but it's sure is a nice breath of fresh air.

Brad Kohlenstein

Lucky Ones
October 2004, Republic/Universal

Lucky Ones is Pat Green's third album for a major label, but it's the first one where he truly seems comfortable gunning for the big time. He enlists producer Don Gehman, who produced a few songs on his previous album, 2003's *Wave on Wave*, for the entire record, and Gehman not only gives *Lucky Ones* a bright roots rock feel similar to the albums he produced for John Mellencamp, he also enlists drummer Kenny Aronoff and violinist Lisa Germano, both Mellencamp vets, for a few tracks. These two, along with a few other session musicians, mix seamlessly with Green's seven-piece backing band, giving the album a consistent sound—and that sound is big and shiny, part contemporary country,

part heartland rock, all polished and designed for a wide audience. The ballads never get too maudlin, the up-tempo numbers never rock too hard. All the songs are about love and good times, whether it's about how it's good to be home or sitting around with Brad Paisley and reminiscing about college. It's all bright and tuneful, closer to the mainstream Midwest rock of the '80s than contemporary country, but that's part of its appeal—it's well-crafted, highly polished, anthemic roots rock that appeals to the heart of America. While it is true that if you listen hard enough it's possible to hear the formula and the calculation behind Green's amalgam of country and MOR rock, there's no denying that at its best it's hard to resist, and there's also no denying that *Lucky Ones* finds the singer at his best.

Stephen Thomas Erlewine

Nanci Griffith

Once in a Very Blue Moon
1984, Philo

Nanci Griffith finds her voice on her third studio album, *Once in a Very Blue Moon*. This is the album where she established her musical identity—she is at home in many genres (which perhaps explains why she never gets played on formatted radio stations), and seamlessly blends folk, bluegrass, and country with a group of stellar musicians, including guitarist Pat Alger and a young banjo player named Béla Fleck. While the music is well-textured with cello, mandolin, Dobro, and fiddle, it is Griffith's lyrics that distinguish her from her peers. Although not a concept album, the main theme explored is travel. She sings about the joys and excitement of the road as well as the longing that comes with extended periods away from home. Nanci Griffith is an excellent storyteller, with detailed, insightful lyrics that vividly portray the hopes and dreams of her characters ("Mary and Omie"). She sprinkles the album with songs of others, as she pays homage to folk veterans such as Bill Staines ("Roseville Fair") and sings a tune by newcomer Lyle Lovett ("If I Were the Woman You Wanted"). This album marks the emergence of a major talent.

Vik Iyengar

The Last of the True Believers
1986, Philo

This is Nanci Griffith's fourth and final release on Rounder Records' folk subsidiary, Philo. At the time Griffith relocated to Nashville, TN, her decidedly Texan sense of musicality had already begun developing subtle hues of Appalachia as well as the cosmopolitan country that would inform her mid-to-late '80s stint on MCA. However, it is the overwhelming strength and conviction in the singer/songwriter's original material on *The Last of the True Believers* that remain indelibly impressed upon enthusiasts and critics alike. As such, Griffith has retained a copious sampling from the disc in her subsequent

live performance repertoire. Griffith's crystalline vocals are well matched to the warm, earthy acoustic instrumentation on the intimate "More Than a Whisper" and "The Wing and the Wheel." At times, the delicate interplay creates a mutual envelopment of the human vocal instrument with that of the stringed nature—most notably on the heartfelt "Love at the Five and Dime." By way of contrast, Griffith defies her somewhat introverted image on the tongue-in-cheek (no pun!) love song "Looking for the Time (Workin' Girl)" and the effervescent waltz "Love's Found a Shoulder." Lying nestled between are spry melodies such as "Banks of the Pontchartrain," featuring some nice picking from Béla Fleck (banjo), and "Goin' Gone," which perfectly captures some of Lloyd Green's finest pedal steel work on the disc. Griffith's pure and otherwise unaffected performance style would continue to carry through her subsequent efforts, most notably *Lone Star State of Mind* (1987), which in many ways is a companion, rather than simply the follow-up, to *The Last of the True Believers*.

Lindsay Planer

Lone Star State of Mind
1987, MCA

Lone Star State of Mind was Nanci Griffith's commercial breakthrough, largely because it was her first step directly toward mainstream contemporary country. Instead of diluting her introspective folk songs, the full-fledged production actually enhances her music, as the steel guitars and dobros add body to her songs. Griffith responds in kind, delivering the most textured and nuanced vocal performance of her career, as evidenced by her version of "From A Distance." Of course, her songwriting is as good as it ever was; "Ford Econoline," "Sing One for Sister," "Beacon Street" and a revamped version of "Mary Margaret" called "There's A Light Beyond These Woods," are all terrific, ranking among her best songs. *Lone Star State of Mind* is one of the rare commercial moves that actually improves and artist's music instead of compromising it.

Thom Owens

Little Love Affairs
February 1988, MCA

Little Love Affairs, Nanci Griffith's second MCA Records album, and sixth album overall, was the crucial release in her attempt to achieve success as a Nashville-based country artist, and in that context it was a failure. But it was also an artistic success, containing 11 well-written and well-performed songs in the reflective style that the singer/songwriter had established previously. Griffith's first MCA album, *Lone Star State of Mind*, had been a moderate seller, reaching the Top 40 and spawning two country chart singles. MCA prefaced *Little Love Affairs* with perhaps its most overtly country song, "Never Mind," written by veteran songwriter Harlan Howard, and prominently featuring a pedal-steel guitar in its arrangement, but the single's failure to crack the country Top 40 suggested trouble, confirmed when the album peaked lower than *Lone Star State of Mind*. "Never Mind" gave a good indication of the album's theme, embodied in its title, of carefully examining the romantic lives of common people. Howard's lovers were itinerant laborers who came out of the Depression, and other songs also looked back at stories of romance past, such as Griffith's compositions "Love Wore a Halo (Back Before the War)," and "So Long Ago." The music, supplied by Griffith's backup band and New Grass Revival, was in her familiar country-folk style, and her vocals, with their ringing, aching tone, conveyed the songs' sense of longing and regret effectively.

Country critics and radio programmers complained that, if anything, she was *too* country, her voice having an off-putting twang and nasality, but that was just an excuse for rejecting her literate lyrics and sophistication. At 33, she wasn't about to become some empty-headed Nashville bimbo willing to mouth romantic clichés, and for that she paid the price of being denied country stardom. Her fans breathed a sigh of relief.

William Ruhlmann

One Fair Summer Evening
November 1988, MCA

This is singer/ songwriter Nanci Griffith's first live album, and it captures the essence of what has endeared Griffith to fans of both folk and cosmopolitan country. Although *One Fair Summer Evening* was not an immediate phenomenon at the cash registers, the revealing

nature of the performance has secured it a place in the hearts of enthusiasts since its release in 1988. In addition to highlights from her six previous long-players, she also adds a few new tracks—including her own composition "I Would Bring You Ireland" as well as "Deadwood, South Dakota" by her ex-husband, Eric Taylor—both of which became standards in her live performance canon. Her backing band, the Blue Moon Orchestra, is known for both its instrumental prowess and its keen knack for subtlety. Examples of this delicate balance range from the intimacy of "More Than a Whisper" and "Love at the Five and Dime" to the boot-scootin' fury of "Spin on a Red Brick Floor" and "Looking for the Time (Workin' Girl)." In between is a sampling of Griffith's organic folky roots ("Trouble in the Fields") as well as her pensive ballads ("Once in a Blue Moon"), which have become standards for the legions of would-be singer/songwriters who followed. Also included are stunning readings of Julie Gold's "From a Distance" and Bill Staines' (whom Griffith rightfully compares to a neo-Woody Guthrie) "Roseville Fair." There is also a 45-minute home video companion to *One Fair Summer Evening* that includes most of the music from this CD; missing are "The Wing and the Wheel," "Trouble in the Fields," and "Roseville Fair," while a whimsical version of "There's a Light Beyond the Woods (Mary Margaret)" has been added.

Lindsay Planer

Storms
August 1989, MCA

Nanci Griffith scored a major crossover hit with *Storms* (1989). After four long-players for the primarily country-intensive MCA Nashville, she switched to their pop division thanks in part to the overwhelming critical and popular acclaim she had gained from her previous studio effort, *Little Love Affairs* (1998). Many purists were critical, but along with legendary producer Glyn Johns Griffith unfurled some of her finest musical stories to date. Joining her backing band, the Blue Moon Orchestra, are the intriguing aggregate of Bernie Leadon (guitars/mando-cello/vocals), Jerry Donahue (guitar), Phil Everly (vocals), and Albert Lee (vocals).

Once again, Griffith's crystalline-toned resonance weaves almost hypnotically through her realistic and acoustic-based neo-folk Americana. Lyrically, her poignant poetry reveals characters that seem wrought with equal measures of vulnerability and fortitude—such as "sister" in "Drive-In Movies and Dashboard Lights" or the semi-autobiographical narrative "backseat driver from America" on the international breakthrough "It's a Hard Life Wherever You Go." Former Amazing Rhythm Ace and Blue Moon Orchestra co-founder James Hooker (keyboards/vocals) co-wrote several tunes with Griffith, including "Radio Fragile"—their upbeat tribute to Phil Ochs. Among the other sides to have gained significant favor as live performance staples are the infectiously melodic "Listen to the Radio" and the more pensive "Brave Companion of the Road." Not to be missed is another Hooker/Griffith collaboration on the stone gem "You Made This Love a Teardrop"—with the aforementioned Everly as co-lead vocals. While curious enthusiasts have speculated that *Storms* was a commentary on the artist's concurrent life offstage, it poised her for the even more pop-oriented follow-up, *Late Night Grande Hotel* (1991).

Lindsay Planer

Other Voices, Other Rooms
1993, Elektra

Nanci Griffith has the kind of beguiling singing voice that's effortless and easily beautiful—like a pretty girl who doesn't ever need makeup to be radiant. Sounding a little bit like Emmylou Harris is never a bad thing, but Griffith doesn't stop there. She duets with Harris and a host of other country and folk notables on *Other Voices, Other Rooms*, her first collection of cover songs. Like Harris, Griffith can climb inside a character-driven song with a simple twist of inflection or a lingering note. This is what she does on Vince Bell's "Woman of the Phoenix," deftly painting images of a winter freeze, cacti, and Michael, the "rock 'n' roll hood from the Odessa plains." Dylan's "Boots of Spanish Leather" rambles like the Texas countryside and features the man himself on harmonica. The guest list for *Other Voices* really is incredible. Alison Krauss, John Gorka, Edgar Meyer, Amy Ray, and Emily Saliers—it's a regular homespun who's who. There's plenty to sigh about here, and occasionally the album can almost be too tasteful for its own good. But raveups like Woody Guthrie's "Do-Re-Mi" let Griffith trade some serenity for dustbowl grit (the addition of John Prine's lascivious gruffness helps a lot, too), and the frustrated anger of "This Old Town" only supports this. What might be most refreshing about *Other Voices, Other Rooms* is its ability to access the warm tones of country, grassroots, 1960s folk, and the '70s songwriting tradition while still sounding more like it comes from Griffith's Texas roots than anywhere else. This is highly recommended for fans of Griffith or any of the like-minded artists who help out here.

Johnny Loftus

Flyer
1994, Elektra

After getting increased exposure with her exquisite cover album *Other Voices, Other Rooms*, Nanci Griffith emerged with an album of originals that demonstrated to her new fans that she was more than just an interpreter of songs. She has always been a gifted and versatile songwriter with a knack for stepping inside her characters in story songs, but she writes from a more personal perspective on this album. With the help of high-profile friends from U2, Dire Straits, Indigo Girls, and Counting Crows, she incorporates more rock & roll instrumentation (electric guitar, piano, drums) into her acoustically based music. In fact, many of the highlights of this album involve collaborations. Mark Knopfler (Dire Straits) adds his usual tasteful guitar work in "Don't Forget About Me," and Adam Duritz of Counting Crows delivers perhaps his best vocal performance in the playful duet "Going Back to Georgia." As in previous releases, she wrestles with issues of love and loss; however, the songs resonate on a deeper level as she writes from the perspective of someone who has seen and done a lot but still longs to connect souls with one special person ("Southbound Train," "On Grafton Street"). Although she falters a bit when choosing to tackle politics ("Time of Inconvenience"), this is her most consistent album of original songs in almost a decade.

Vik Iyengar

Blue Roses from the Moons
March 1997, Elektra

Blue Roses From the Moons expands the smoother sounds of *Flyer* by bringing Nanci Griffith firmly into the adult alternative playing field—not only does Don Gehman, the producer behind Hootie & the Blowfish, produce the record, but Darius Rucker has a vocal cameo, as well. Though the slick sound is a little disarming for longtime fans, Griffith's songwriting remains skilled and assured, and while there aren't as many as standout numbers as before, her graceful melodicism and lyricism and the professional production makes *Blue Roses From the Moons* a very pleasant listen.

Thom Owens

The Complete MCA Studio Recordings
June 2003, MCA

The standard line on Nanci Griffith's five-year sojourn at MCA Records is that Griffith, a Texas-born singer/songwriter, earned a major-label Nashville contract after four independent folkie releases on the basis of Kathy Mattea's Top Ten country recording of her song "Love at the Five and Dime," at a time when country music seemed more open to new sounds and MCA's Tony Brown was also signing such mavericks as Steve Earle and Lyle Lovett. But after two albums, *Lone Star State of Mind* (1987) and *Little Love Affairs* (1988), met resistance, failing to produce a major country hit, Griffith was transferred to the label's pop division, where *Storms* (1989) showed promise but *Late Night Grande Hotel* (1991) turned out to be too much of a pop move and turned off her existing fan base without attracting a new one. Then MCA dropped her. After a sojourn at Elektra Records, Griffith returned to indie status with Rounder in 2002, which oddly landed her back at MCA, since the major had a distribution deal with Rounder. MCA has also reissued Griffith's early albums, which gives the label a considerable stake in her catalog. So, there is a full-priced one-disc compilation of her actual MCA recordings (*From a Distance: The Very Best of Nanci Griffith*), a discount-priced *Millennium Collection* best-of, and now this two-disc package combining all four MCA albums with a few rarities. And when you listen to it from beginning to end, the standard line no longer seems to hold. The first two albums are no more country than Griffith's early "folk"

albums, and the last two are not so "pop." The distinctions have more to do with production approaches, which pale before the dominant aspects of the music—Griffith's sweet and sour voice with its distinctive twang and the terrific songs. Maybe there was something to the notion that Griffith, who delighted in showing listeners what novel she was reading on her album covers, was a bit too erudite for a Nashville thrush, but the result is a set of songs, written by her and some well-chosen others, that stand up well a decade later and are likely to sound just as good many decades hence.

William Ruhlmann

Andy Griggs

Freedom
May 2002, RCA Nashville

Freedom is the follow-up album to Andy Griggs' 1999 *You Won't Ever Be Lonely*, and it proves that the best things in life come with time and nurturing. Griggs has a voice that can adapt itself to ballad and raucous grit alike, interpreting the music with a vocal "soul roll" in the right places. Griggs has been dubbed a follower of outlaw country, which is hinted at on cuts such as "A Hundred Miles of Bad Road" and the title cut, but mostly Griggs gives a variety of cleverly written relationship songs superimposed on vigorous guitar platforms. "How Cool Is That" is, indeed, cool; imagine the irreverence of the tattooed preacher's daughter holding a beer and winking your way. Ok, now picture a couple together on the couch and the man saying "All week I've been your husband; tonight I want to be your man." It's all here, from romantic sweet talk to love 'em and leave 'em in "Brand New Something Going On." This Louisiana native has found a place for himself in Nashville and on the country charts. Let's just hope it doesn't take another three years for album three.

Rick Cohoon

This I Gotta See
August 2004, RCA

Andy Griggs has a voice suited for hard country music: strong and gritty, yet his twangy tenor shows just enough vulnerability to coax out a tear or two. Too bad that he has yet to make an album that lives up to that voice. On his third album, *This I Gotta See*, he delivers a professional, assured contemporary country record that flirts with his harder honky tonk influences, yet it's still the slickest effort he's cut, heavy on sweet ballads and melodic mid-tempo tunes, with a few faster numbers that offer a nice change of pace. These are well-constructed songs and productions, and Griggs sells them well, but they're not particularly memorable; by and large, they're pleasant listening, not captivating, even if his voice demands your attention. At times, he gets a song that gives him a good showcase for his talents—ballads like "Be Still," or ravers like the lean "Hillbilly Band"—but when the album ends with the laid-back, soulful, pure country "No Mississippi" (featuring guest appearances by Bekka Bramlett and Delbert McClinton), it's clear that this loose, down-home feel is right for Griggs. He would prosper on an album that was loose, relaxed, and had its heart in pure country. On *This I Gotta See*, those brief glimpses of straight-ahead country are surrounded by songs that fit the Nashville game plan, and while those are pleasant enough, Griggs is capable of doing something better—as he proves on moments on this solid album, which is enough to make it worth a listen.

Stephen Thomas Erlewine

Hanna-McEuen

Hanna-McEuen
August 2005, MCA Nashville

Jaime Hanna and Jonathan McEuen are the offspring of two founding members of the Nitty Gritty Dirt Band and, in a neat twist of fate that's stranger than fiction, they're also first cousins, since their fathers married twin sisters. They would be noteworthy for their pedigree and their back story, which is at least worth a few column inches, yet that story also throws up some red flags, suggesting that they may only be of interest because of their family tree. Thankfully, their debut, *Hanna-McEuen*, is noteworthy for another reason: it's a hell of a record, one of the best debuts of 2005. It's one of the few contemporary country records that fully integrates the clever classicism of '80s insurgent country (the opening "Fool Around" is a dead ringer for prime Dwight Yoakam) into a bright, accessible mainstream sound. And make no mistake about it, Hanna-McEuen are not an alt-country or Americana act: they may be inspired by the same artists and sounds, from classic country through Gram Parsons and Bruce Springsteen, but this isn't as somber and earnest as much alternative country of the late '90s and early 2000s. Hanna-McEuen have an infectious, friendly vibe that's as warm and appealing as their strong, melodic songs (all 12 tunes are originals), which are hooky enough to be memorable upon the first listen and sturdy enough to get better with each subsequent spin. While they may recall their influences throughout their eponymous debut, there's a freshness to the duo's music that keeps the album from sounding stale or overly reverential. Instead, Hanna-McEuen sound like they're true heirs to a classic American country-rock tradition, making familiar music sound new and vital again. Certainly, it's in their blood, but the wonderful thing about this debut is that it's good enough to make you forget their back-story and just enjoy what this tremendously talented duo has to offer.

Stephen Thomas Erlewine

Ty Herndon

Living in a Moment
August 1996, Epic

Although he is in fine voice throughout the album, Ty Herndon's *Living in a Moment* is bogged down by mediocre material that fails to given him a proper showcase for his talents. Herndon doesn't write his own material, which might not necessarily be a bad thing—after all, hundreds of country singers don't write their own songs—but he doesn't have the best ear for selecting songs. When he does have a strong song—like the title track or "Don't Tell Mama"—he sounds terrific, but otherwise Herndon simply sounds adequate. Furthermore, on the undistinguished numbers, the production sounds generic and canned, which also hurts the record.

Although Herndon still shows promise, it's hard to avoid the fact that *Living in a Moment* sounds like a sophomore slump.

Thom Owens

This Is Ty Herndon: Greatest Hits
March 2002, Epic

Although Epic's 2002 compilation *This Is Ty Herndon: Greatest Hits* is a little short at 13 tracks, it does contain most of the contemporary country crooner's biggest hits, from his debut hit "What Mattered Most" through "Steam." The album isn't sequenced chronologically, which may be a problem for some listeners, but the end result has Herndon at his best, making it a nice summary and introduction.

Stephen Thomas Erlewine

Right About Now
January 2007, Titan Pyramid

Country singer Ty Herndon is back in the studio after a six-year break. Yeah, there was a Christmas record a couple of years back, but this is the first time the Meridian Mississippi wonder has done an honest to goodness modern country record in nearly seven years. Herndon hit the charts and the road in a fury during the mid-'90s, and his demons hit back hard. Right: Herndon had a hellhound on his trail. *Right About Now* is one of those records that a man makes when he feels he has everything to prove. On the Jackson/Titan independent label (which is distributed by Fontana), Herndon lays out 11 new songs with help from songwriters like producer Darrell Brown, Keith Urban, Jess Cates, Beth Nielsen Chapman and others. The opener, written by Brown, Radney Foster, and Urban is a down-tempo modern country rocker turned personal anthem. Herndon's voice is not only unchanged from his missing years, it's stronger, his phrasing is tighter and more expressive, and his manner of handling a song is entirely his own. "You Still Own Me" opens with a fiddle and a banjo and a shuffling snare. It's modern country at its best. This is one of those tracks that if the radio programmers have guts and his label can come up with the cash for a video (Trey Fanjoy should direct it, if there's any justice) it's all but a guaranteed hit. This is the kind of song that Sara Evans can pull off without a lot of trouble, but few male singers can make it seem so easy. Herndon has soul and plenty of it. You can hear the gospel in his voice, his love of the old country songs, but his delivery is thoroughly contemporary. And dig the slippery backbone delivery in John Mallory's and Marcus Hummon's "Love Revival." This is as fine a mid-tempo country love song as there is. It is both prayer and anthem, a statement of purpose, a declaration of commitment and a plea to be met in the middle. "Mercy Line" is a downright soul tune that comes right out of the strut and groove of Memphis in the Stax era-but sung by a true country singer. But hell, Herndon can sing anything he wants. Here is another surefire hit if the label can get down and push radio programmers ears inside it. This is one of those tracks that folks will be turning up and could cross over. If it were Jennifer Nettles singing it, there would be no discussion, but

there are few male vocalists who have the necessary muscle and sensitivity to pull this one off. In sum, *Right About Now* is a monster of a record, period, comeback or no. Herndon re-enters the scene more talented and far more mature than he left it. It's time for Nashville—and the rest country music's faithful—to sit up, listen and take notice that a real master has returned. *Right About Now* is solid, top to bottom. Welcome back Ty.

Thom Jurek

Highway 101

Greatest Hits (1987-90)
1990, Warner Bros.

Country-rock band Highway 101 got off to a great start in the late '80s with several hits featuring the powerful voice of Paulette Carlson. Unfortunately, just as the band was enjoying its greatest success, Carlson and the band parted ways. By that time they had chalked up several number one hits, "Somewhere Tonight," "(Do You Love Me) Just Say Yes," "Who's Lonely Now," and "Cry, Cry, Cry," all of which are included on this recommended *Greatest Hits (1987-90)* package.

Al Campbell

Faith Hill

Take Me as I Am
1994, Warner Bros.

Faith Hill's debut established the willowy singer as the lady-in-waiting to Reba McEntire's throne. Like McEntire, Hill's voice could crackle just as well as it sparkled, and *Take Me as I Am* allowed her to do both. The wide-open abandon of the hit single "Wild One" was immediate and undeniable, and Hill delivered the vocal with sassy, youthful exuberance. But she was just as convincing on the low-key heart-tugger "Just About Now" and the Gary Burr-penned ballad "Just Around the Eyes." She figured out a way to channel Janis Joplin's vocal during a country-fried retelling of "Piece of My Heart," in spite of a canned meat-quality backing track, and handled the Larry Steward duet "I've Got This Friend" with ease. By focusing Hill's vocal and supporting her with unobtrusive instrumentation, producers Burr and Scott Hendricks helped make *Take Me as I Am* that much more effective, and ensured that no one would forget about Hill anytime soon.

Johnny Loftus

It Matters to Me
1995, Warner Bros.

On her second album, Faith Hill confirmed that *Take Me as I Am* was no fluke. Like her debut album, *It Matters to Me* is an ambitious, diverse set of contemporary country that proves Hill can tackle virtually every subgenre of country, singing rockers, ballads, socially-aware stories, and love songs with an equal amount of grace. The singles "Let's Go to Vegas" and "It Matters to Me" aren't the only strong songs here—the entire album is rich with first-rate songs, as well as superb singing from Hill, one of the most promising female vocalist of the mid-'90s.

Stephen Thomas Erlewine

Faith
April 1998, Warner Bros.

On her third album, simply titled *Faith*, Faith Hill put all her chips on a big pop crossover move, picking songs by Diane Warren and Sheryl Crow to sing and giving the entire album a sleek, glossy finish that makes it as comfortable on adult comptemporary radio as it would be on country radio. This may not be country in its sound but it is in its sentiment, as it celebrates love—there are no heartbreak songs here, just love songs—hope and optimism, where "The Secret of Life" is a good cup of coffee, mom's apple pie and a beautiful woman: all things that make it comfortable, mature pop. Unlike Shania Twain, Hill never goes for big, outsized gestures—there's no glamour or glitz here, nor is there much humor, as there is on *The Woman in Me* and *Come on Over*—she goes for cozy and comforting, and while that can make *Faith* a little bit too warm and fuzzy (and despite its sheen, it does feel warm) for some tastes, it nevertheless is an expert middle of the road pop album, one that goes down easy, one that blends into the background, yet is melodic and endearing enough to be listened to closely, and that's due to Hill's strong voice and open personality. This is before she became a diva—it's what gave her that status and while that is a subtle difference, it is nonetheless an important one.

Stephen Thomas Erlewine

Breathe
November 1999, Warner Bros.

"What's in It for Me," the first track on *Breathe*, Faith Hill's follow-up to her starmaking third album *Faith*, is livelier than anything on its predecessor, but that doesn't mean it's country, even if it kicks off with sawing fiddles. This builds upon the pop overtures of *Faith* and turns Hill into a full-fledged diva—something that should be clear from the cover of *Breathe*, where she's moussed and styled like a supermodel. And *Breathe* is as bold and brassy as any big pop album, which only makes sense since this is a country album in marketing only: it's an adult contemporary album, as *Faith* was before it, but where that was a bit of a humble affair, Hill is perfectly comfortable with acting like a star here, belting out songs whether they're rockin' anthems like "I Got My Baby" (which could have been a big hit for Whitney Houston in 1985), effervescent pop like "The Way You Love Me" or a power ballad like "Breathe." She's still celebrating love instead of singing about heartbreak, and while this doesn't have the warm, cozy feel of *Faith*, it has a punchy, rousing feel that makes this an inspirational aspirational record—something to push you forward instead of being happy of

where you are. If Hill still doesn't have the gaudiness or hooks of Shania Twain, or the sense of fun, that's fine—this isn't music for the weekend, it's for getting through the week, and it's as good in an office as it is at home, the defining moment of Faith Hill's superstardom.

Stephen Thomas Erlewine

Cry
October 2002, Warner Bros.

Lavishly produced and packaged, *Cry* marks the continued ascent of Faith Hill from the lowlands of down-home authenticity to the heights of pop superstardom. Though plenty of Nashville A-team players back her up, the sound they churn out has almost nothing to do with country music. Riding a tide of massed synthesizer textures, sweeping orchestral strings, thundering drums, rock guitar licks, and melodramatic dynamics, Hill strives for the biggest possible gestures in her performance. The result is the kind of glitzy fireworks normally associated with *Star Search* or *American Idol*, in which the lyric takes a distant backseat to raw exhibitionism and only the most cursory nod is made toward lyrical convention. (The nod is particularly schizoid in "This Is Me," as Hill proclaims, "I try to love Jesus and myself ... yeah, yeah.") Beyond the general issue of taste, this approach raises twofold problems for Hill in particular, in that her established skills as a song interpreter are lost in all this *sturm und drang* and her voice, while undeniably powerful at its peak, doesn't have the range that allows most singers in this style, from proto-diva Barbra Streisand to flameout icon Mariah Carey, to at least milk the material at some superficial level. With all this in mind, it may be significant that Tim McGraw, a guest on previous Hill albums, makes no appearance here. Perhaps there's no room for country credibility, or even for a spouse, when one's career trajectory is as hot as Hill's.

Robert L. Doerschuk

Fireflies
August 2005, Warner Bros.

It's clear from the cover photo on 2005's *Fireflies* that Faith Hill is beating a retreat from her half-baked, half-successful 2002 pop diva makeover, *Cry*. Not that the album was bad, or even an outright flop—it just failed to do what it was intended to do, which was to make Faith Hill a true rival to Shania Twain, where her pop success was as great as her country following. Big and polished *Cry* may have been, but it just wasn't memorable or hooky enough to be great pop and unlike Shania's very clever everywoman pose, Hill's pop move was too detached, too snooty for her country audience. Since she's no fool, Faith Hill has quickly returned to the country-pop and big ballads that brought her stardom on 1999's *Breathe*, but that doesn't mean she's not playing it smart and savvy. She's recorded several songs by John Rich—best known as half of Big & Rich, but also a professional songwriter who is pretty close to being ubiquitous in 2005, in the wake of his duo's success. Here, he proves to be a sharp professional by bringing his craftsman-like musical skills but not his oversized humor to the table with such songs as the laid-back, breezy "Sunshine and Summertime" and the appealingly slick power ballad "Like We Never Loved at All," delivered with harmonies by Hill's husband, Tim McGraw. Of course, this being a 21st century pop album, he's not the only collaborator or songwriter on board. Longtime Hill producer Byron Gallimore once again produces the great majority of the album, and he's as instrumental in steering Hill back toward the country-pop mainstream as he was in pushing her toward the pop mainstream, helping her deliver a set of strong, professionally crafted songs, highlighted by three selections from acclaimed singer/songwriter Lori McKenna. While it's hard not to wish that Hill had a few more loose, funny numbers like "Dearly Beloved"—a kissing cousin to the Dixie Chicks' "White Trash Wedding" that's not only the purest dose of fun here, it's also the purest dose of country, too—this is a good straight-ahead mainstream country album, aiming squarely at the middle of the road and hitting its target perfectly. The songs are solid and square, sounding comfortably familiar on the first listen and growing more memorable with repeated plays, Hill never oversings, and the entire affair is perfectly likable and pleasant—the kind of thing that will shore up her support after the shaky *Cry*, even if it breaks no new ground.

Stephen Thomas Erlewine

Hot Apple Pie

Hot Apple Pie
June 2005, Dreamworks Nashville

Hot Apple Pie is the latest stop on the long road for country journeyman Brady Seals. A nephew of Jim Seals (the Seals of Seals & Crofts) and country hitmaker Dan Seals, Brady got his first big break in the early '90s as a member of Little Texas, and he shepherded them through some big hits before leaving for a solo career halfway through the decade. After a couple of mainstream country albums, he had a rootsy independent release with *Thompson Street* in 2003, which featured Mark "Sparky" Matejka on lead guitar. Following that, Seals and Matejka hooked up with bassist Keith Horne and Trey Landry for Hot Apple Pie, whose 2005 eponymous debut is the opposite of *Thompson Street*. Released on DreamWorks Nashville and produced by Richard Landis, Hot Apple Pie is a big, slick, knowing contemporary country album that dabbles in a little bit of everything not just because the bandmembers *can*, but because they want to see what sticks. So, the album begins with the goofy novelty of "Hillbillies," which has a bit of the ironic proud-to-be-a-redneck vibe of Big & Rich (it surfaces again toward the end of the album with "Redneck Revolution," a slow bluesy crawl so contrived it makes the opener seem easy), then rolls into the bouncy retro country-pop of Al Anderson's "We're Makin' Up." Soon after that, the group dives into a slick power ballad with "The Good Life," before revamping the Band's classic "The Shape I'm In" as breakneck bluegrass, complete with alternating lead vocals, then hauling out Willie Nelson for a duet on "Slowin' Down the Fall." The latter two moves, along with the Rodney Crowell co-written "Annabelle (Arkansas Is Callin' You)," indicate that Hot Apple Pie have good taste, serious chops, and genuine credentials as pure country musicians, smart enough to know not just what makes for good country music, but smart enough to know what makes it onto country radio. And that's the problem with their album—half of it is really good, smart, fun country, the other half is pandering to the whims of radio, whether it's on the aforementioned "Hillbillies" or such lumbering

mid-tempo numbers as "Everybody Wants to Dance With My Baby." The rest of the album doesn't just prove that Hot Apple Pie are better than those tunes, but that they *know* that they're slumming it with songs like these. Hopefully, one of the stronger songs here will be Hot Apple Pie's breakthrough hit and then, on their next record, they'll loosen up and deliver the loose yet sharp modern country album that this appealing but muddled debut suggests they can make.

Stephen Thomas Erlewine

Alan Jackson

Here in the Real World
1989, Arista

In 1989, country music honky tonk revivalist Alan Jackson scored his first number one hit with "I'd Love You All Over Again"—not bad for being only his fifth single. Interestingly enough, it was a ballad, but a hard country ballad nonetheless. The songs sits somewhere in the no man's land between George Jones and Randy Travis, and floats uneasily seeking an edge. The title track is another hard country ballad, and with its sweet lonesome fiddle it was a more logical choice, but what the hell. The bottom line is that while *Here in the Real World* may not be Jackson's strongest record, it still stands head and shoulders over most of the competition, and that includes Curtain Shirt Brooks, that is, Garth. Producers Keith Stegall and Scott Hendricks understood that Jackson's country sensibilities are a boon, not a bane, in terms of putting his particular brand of new traditionalism onto the charts. Other winners are the honky tonkers such as "Blue Blooded Woman," "Chasin' That Neon Rainbow," and "She Don't Get the Blues," which feels as much like Merle Haggard doing Bob Wills as it does new country. This is a solid effort and established the fact that Jackson was just beginning to come into his own.

Thom Jurek

Don't Rock the Jukebox
1991, Arista

If there was one record that established Alan Jackson as a bona fide star, *Don't Rock the Jukebox* was it. The set featured no less than two number one singles in the title track and "Love's Got a Hold on You," and three more entered the Top Ten. This is Jackson at what he does best, being a modern honky tonk singer not quite as tough as Dwight Yoakam, but with more sex appeal and easier on the ears for those who like their "hard country" smoothed a bit. That's more Keith Stegall's fault than Jackson's, as there is no doubt by his having written or co-written all but one song here that he's the real thing. The truth of the matter is that Jackson's mettle comes in the ballads, like the criminally overlooked "That's All I Need to Know," or in the storysongs like "Dallas." "Midnight in Montgomery" is a stellar song about encountering the ghost of Hank Williams; its Spanish guitar overtones in the intro made it perfect for the radio, but its innovative video far overshadowed the song as a single. But hits aside, *Don't Rock the Jukebox* is solid as a new traditionalist record, meaning that it's a country record with ever-present pedal steel for every synth or glossy fiddle. Jackson's voice is in the groove, down there with Jones and Haggard, tougher than Travis, leaner than Strait, and almost as hillbilly as Yoakam. This is a great record that stands the test of time.

Thom Jurek

A Lot About Livin' (And a Little 'Bout Love)
1992, Arista

Three years after his first number one single, Alan Jackson took his brand of new honky tonk country and pushed it all the way into the mainstream, making it possible for another batch of acts to follow him. Sticking with producer Keith Stegall, Jackson wrote over half the tracks on the set, including a pair of singles, "She's Got the Rhythm (And I Got the Blues)" and "Tonight I Climbed the Wall," as well as "Chattahoochee." The up-tempo numbers with the jukebox kick are what works best with Jackson's restless country-soul voice—check "I Don't Need the Booze (To Get a Buzz On)." The smoking Western swing of "Up to My Ears in Tears" walks a line between Bob Wills and Buck Owens, and could have been covered by Dwight Yoakam. But the set's winner is its closer, the Geddins/Douglas classic "Mercury Blues." Taking the tune back to its country roots and claiming it for the Fender Telecaster's particular brand of pinch and tang, Jackson sings the hell out of it. At this point in his career, Jackson established himself as one of the most consistent talents country had to offer.

Thom Jurek

Who I Am
1994, Arista

By 1994, Alan Jackson may not have scored as many hit singles, but he definitely began to set himself apart from the onslaught of young country hat bands. First, there are 13 tracks on this set—three more than usually appear on country records because labels don't want to pay for more than that. Second, Jackson showed he had cojones by opening his album with Eddie Cochran's rockabilly classic "Summertime Blues," a song as associated with the Who as it is with Cochran. But Jackson shows the 'billy side of the equation while delivering both humor and soul in his reading. "Living on Love," an original, is a mid-tempo honky tonker with killer fiddle, telecasters chopping up the middle, and lyrics that make its sentimental subject matter palatable. "Gone Country," by Bob McDill, is an anti-new country anthem accusing a whole lot of folks of coming into the game for the cash. Jackson is the real hillbilly article, so he can sing that song—and so is the writer, but it's most effective when looking at some of Alan's peers. But it's on Harley Allen's "Who I Am," a mid-tempo two-step barroom love song where the pedal steels whine and the fiddles cascade with their high lonesome song in the bridge, that Jackson's at his best. He sings with a sincerity that turns sarcasm on its head. The same is true on Rodney Crowell's "Song for the Life." In a version that rivals Crowell's own, Jackson's balladry in three-fourths time is heartbreakingly beautiful. And then there's Jackson's own songs like "Job Description," which comes right from the Merle Haggard side of the Bakersfield side of honky tonk, and the same goes for "Let's Get Back to You and Me," which is every bit as tough as Dwight Yoakam with a guitar solo to match. This is where Buck Owens and Ernest Tubb meet Johnny Burnette and George Jones. What a way

to end a record. This is solid from top to bottom and one of Jackson's strongest outings.

Thom Jurek

Everything I Love
October 1996, Arista Nashville

It's hard not to think of the title of Alan Jackson's fifth album, 1996's *Everything I Love*, as a reference to the music he makes, since it is so deeply felt and so deeply rooted in country tradition. *Everything I Love* is no exception to the rule, but there's a wry sardonic streak to the title track here, where everything Jackson loves—"cigarettes, Jack Daniels, and caffeine"—is killing him. It's a classic country sentiment on an album that feels like a classic country album to its bone, from that barroom weeper to the sly novelty of "Buicks to the Moon," the swaggering cheating song "Who's Cheatin' Who," and the terrific cover of Tom T. Hall's "Little Bitty," which tips its hat to the past without being overly reverential. And that's one of the keys to the success of *Everything I Love*. It is surely rooted in the past, and although a bit of post-Garth bombast may be present when Jackson touches on the anthemic sounds of modern country on "Between the Devil and Me," he still gives it true country spin and heart. Plus, that's balanced by the laid-back Bakersfield shuffle of "There Goes," the Western swing of "Must've Had a Ball" (complete with horns and clarinet), and the classic honky tonk ballad "A House with No Curtains"—a co-written original from Jackson that's worthy of early George Jones—all of which gives this album diversity, highlighting several eras of classic country, all the eras that Jackson loves. But the appealing thing about *Everything I Love* is the ease of Jackson's writing and delivery—he makes it all seem natural, and it's an album to savor because of that.

Stephen Thomas Erlewine

High Mileage
September 1998, Arista Nashville

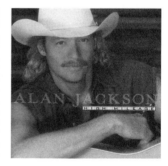

Six albums and nearly a decade into his career, perhaps it could be said that Alan Jackson was beginning to rack up the miles in 1998 when he released *High Mileage*, but he surely doesn't sound ragged or rickety on this typically stellar affair. As always, one of the most impressive things about Jackson is that he never seems forced—he always sounds relaxed and natural, especially on the lazy Western swing of the opener, "Right on the Money," which starts the album off on an appropriately unhurried note. This is a mood that Jackson sustains throughout *High Mileage*, which is by far the most relaxed album he's made to this point, with even the livelier numbers—such as the skipping Bakersfield redux of "Another Good Reason," a particularly funny drinking song—being a little bit subdued, carrying some of the mellow vibe of this ballad-heavy album. This may be long on slow tunes and laid-back melodies, but that doesn't make *High Mileage* dull. There's a certain level of introspection to the songs, a meditative quality, that gives the album depth, but the songs (half of which are originals) are strong and Jackson's delivery, as ever, is warm and compelling, making *High Mileage* a startling, rewarding departure from his previous records and proof of his depth as an artist.

Stephen Thomas Erlewine

Under the Influence
October 1999, Arista Nashville

Anyone who doubts Alan Jackson's roots as a honky tonk singer should turn to *Under the Influences*, his heartfelt salute to his favorite country singers. According to his self-penned liner notes, Jackson has "always wanted to do this album," and that's evident from the songs he chose to cover. There are several hits here, but they're the kind that aren't regularly covered—"Pop a Top," "Kiss an Angel Good Mornin'," "Revenooer Man," "She Just Started Liking Cheatin' Songs," and "Once You've Had the Best." That, along with Jackson's loving reverence, makes this a step above the average covers album. Much of the material dates from the late '70s and early '80s, which makes sense, since he's a fourth-generation honky tonker raised on second and third-generation honky tonk. When he dips into Merle Haggard's catalog, he chose 1979's "My Own Kind of Hat." He picks songs written in the late '70s by Bob McDill. He also pays tribute to Hank Williams—but Junior, not Senior. This all gives Jackson and *Under the Influence* true character. He's not going out of his way to pick historically correct songs, he's just choosing ones he likes. The album is all the better for it—it's relaxed, warm, and entertaining, as he casually shows off his talents with some of his favorite songs. He rarely makes an effort to reinterpret the songs or contemporize the material, although the arrangements can occasionally be a little too clean. It also has to be said that the closer "Margaritaville," performed as a duet with Jimmy Buffett, sticks out like a sore thumb, but these two complaints wind up being nitpicking, since mainstream country didn't produce a better honky tonk album in 1999 than *Under the Influence*.

Stephen Thomas Erlewine

When Somebody Loves You
November 2000, Arista Nashville

Before talking about what a fine country album *When Somebody Loves You* is, there's a disclaimer: If you're a woman, or somebody who wants a great deal of change or evolution in an artist's music, this set won't do much for you. Here are 13 songs about love and being a blue-collar guy who doesn't mind being a redneck, digs the old hillbilly sounds, and hates sushi. Alan Jackson's been at these anthems for an entire career. He's also had the same producer for the whole run. But there has been some change. The truth of the matter is, as close to the line as Jackson has kept his brand of country, it's actually become more so. There are less and less canned sounds on every record, whether it's on a killer love song like the title track with its Spanish guitar overtones that are reminiscent of Marty Robbins or the slamming honky tonk of "The Thrill Is Back" with the rawest sounding fiddle on a country record in a decade. And on the dumbly titled "WWW.Memory," Jackson gets down into a place where the sad lyric fits the tinkling of the upright piano (it's probably synthesized but doesn't feel like it). "Where I Come From" is another redneck anthem, but it rocks a little harder with a ZZ Top-styled guitar. The point is simple: If you like guitars, banjos, pedal steels, and songs about simple things—"I Still Love You" is one of those songs and one of the best Jackson's ever recorded—then *When Somebody Loves You* is your kind of record. This is trad honky tonk country in a country-pop age. Jackson gets a vote not only for holding on to the tradition but because he is able to articulate its heart

in a heartless age. As long as Jackson, Montgomery Gentry, and George Strait are hanging in there on the male side of things, country music won't disappear into the ether of pop music schlock.

Thom Jurek

Drive
January 2002, Arista Nashville

The odd thing about *Drive* is that its centerpiece and its emotional fulcrum is a song that was likely one of the last recorded for the record. That song, of course, is "Where Were You (When the World Stopped Turning)," Alan Jackson's attempt to capture the hurt, pain, confusion, and overwhelming sadness caused by the terrorist attacks on the World Trade Center and Pentagon on September 11, 2001. The song works because Jackson keeps his sights simple as he conveys the bewilderment and sadness of the average American in the days after the attack, sketching the little things that people did to just get through the hours or how time just stopped cold. Given the enormity of the subject—it's simply not something that can be summarized in song—it's a surprisingly effective and moving tune, something that signals that Jackson is indeed in the forefront of the country singers of his time because it plays to his strengths: it's within the tradition of classic country and delivered simply, but with the vernacular and production of the modern day. And that's why even if it was a last-minute addition to the record, it fits so well into a typically strong collection of material from Jackson—musically, it fits perfectly among these heartache ballads and mid-tempo honky tonkers, but it also gives it significant emotional weight. It, in effect, acts as the anchor for the rest of the album, lending songs that are very good genre pieces—whether it's outside material like the excellent, poppy "A Little Bluer Than That" or original material—extra weight. The great thing is that *Drive* doesn't really need it, since it's filled with top-notch songs, including the great George Strait duet "Designated Drinker" and "Drive," a tribute to his dad that's nearly as affecting in its own way as "Where Were You." This is not a total shock, since Jackson's track record is one of the strongest in '90s country, but nevertheless a record this solidly crafted and emotionally resonant is a welcome event all the same.

Stephen Thomas Erlewine

What I Do
September 2004, Arista Nashville

Alan Jackson had been a star for a long time before he released *Drive* in 2002, but that album turned him into a superstar, largely because it had the post-9/11 anthem "Where Were You (When the World Stopped Turning)," a crossover smash that made Jackson a household name. Unlike some of his peers, he didn't embrace this opportunity to become an omnipresent celebrity, he turned out a second greatest-hits album in 2003—complete with another crossover hit in the Jimmy Buffett duet "It's Five O'Clock Somewhere"—before returning with the full-length *What I Do* in September of 2004. Filled with straightforward, unadorned honky tonk and gentle, rolling ballads, *What I Do* makes it clear that Jackson doesn't have the slightest interest in becoming a full-fledged, crossover country-pop star. This is the purest country album he's cut in a long time, but what makes it one of his very best albums isn't its purity, it's how it's delivered with a quiet confidence, a big heart, and a sly sense of humor. Jackson has backed away from any big social statements—there is a song called "USA Today," but far from being a comment on either the state of the world or his celebrity, it merely tells the tale of "the loneliest man in the U.S.A. today"—and sings about love, heartache, churches, fixing cars, and wishing "If French Fries Were Fat Free." As that last song suggests, he's learned from his idol George Jones that even songs about heartbreak can be just as effective if delivered with a sense of humor, but the best joke here is "The Talkin' Song Repair Blues," where Jackson haggles with a mechanic who fancies himself a songwriter. Despite these moments of levity, much of *What I Do* is heavy on ballads. While it's true that the loping drinking song "Strong Enough" and rip-roaring "Burnin' the Honky Tonks Down" are so good it's hard not to wish Jackson threw a few more ravers into the mix, each of these ballads works splendidly, whether it's the sweet "Too Much of a Good Thing," the gently supportive "There Ya Go," or the aching "Rainy Day in June." Given the preponderance of ballads and the laid-back delivery, *What I Do* has an intimate, relaxed feel, the polar opposite of a sequel to a blockbuster like *Drive* usually is. But instead of feeling like a retreat, *What I Do* feels like one of Jackson's most assured and best albums, proof positive that he's the best mainstream country singer of this decade.

Stephen Thomas Erlewine

Like Red on a Rose
September 2006, Arista Nashville

Upon first glance Alan Jackson's devout album of Christian spirituals, *Precious Memories*, seemed like a worthy but curious detour, a step off the hard country path for the best of all modern honky tonk singers, and that the next time around he would be back in familiar territory; after all, he made a career out of being reliable. As it turned out, that studiously quiet collection of traditional gospel tunes kicked off a particularly adventurous 2006 for Jackson, since he followed it up seven months later with *Like Red on a Rose*, a record quite unlike any other he's made. This is a smoky, intimate record; it's romantic, to be sure, but not seductive—instead, it's the sound of longtime love, the sound of happiness. Which is hardly the same thing as a bright, sunny record, since *Like Red on a Rose* is anything but that. This is a record designed for late-night listening, either with the one you love or as you're lost in reflection on your own. In a sense, it's a country variation on Frank Sinatra's classic late-night saloon records. Jackson is certainly not as haunted as Frank was on *In the Wee Small Hours*—if anything, he's the opposite, pleased with where he's at in life—but it has the same sense of introspection, and *Like Red on a Rose* is also at its heart an interpretive work. There is only one Jackson original here, a revival of his 1998 tune "A Woman's Love." The other 12 songs are all penned by other writers, largely songs that aren't well known to the general public (only the closer of Leon Russell's "Bluebird" can qualify as a popular classic). There are plenty of songs about love, but also songs about growing older, having and enjoying a family, yet still sometimes feeling restless. So, it's every bit the concept album that one of Sinatra's albums is, and in its own way, *Like Red on a Rose* is just as effective, thanks to Jackson's supple singing; he's always rightly been acknowledged as one of the great singers in country music, but he's never had a chance to show such a range as he does here. Give some credit to producer Alison Krauss, whom

Jackson originally approached with the idea of recording a bluegrass record. Krauss helped steer Alan in this direction, and he ran with it, winding up with a record that's every bit as surprising as *Precious Memories*, yet greater. On that record, it was possible to hear Jackson work at achieving his goal. Here, he's effortless, and the result is an uncommonly rich and moving album. If 2006 has been this eventful, who knows where Jackson will go in 2007?

Stephen Thomas Erlewine

Shooter Jennings

Electric Rodeo
April 2006, Universal South

In a recent interview, Shooter Jennings claimed that *Electric Rodeo* was actually recorded before *Put the "O" Back in Country*, which was released first. Sonically, *Electric Rodeo* is louder, rawer, more upfront rock & roll than its predecessor, though there are solid, old-school country tunes here as well: the wild fiddle stomp of "Manifesto No. 2," and the broken love song "Aviators," with its spoken word intro and whinnying pedal steel. But as the title suggests, for the most part, *Electric Rodeo* is a hardcore, roaring country-rock record. Jennings' band — Leroy Powell on guitar, Brian Keeling on drums, and Ted Kamp on bass with Robby Turner on steel, and backing vocals by no less than Bonnie Bramlett—are a crack crew. They swagger and slither and stomp, but they know how to whisper, too. On tracks such as the title, "Little White Lines," "Bad Magick," and the jet-propelled swamp funk of "Alligator Chomp"—with a guest vocal by Tony Joe White—Jennings uses angular Texas blues, hard rock/ arena rock dynamics—complete with Mac Truck volume guitars—tight, big whomp drums, and the almighty riff to get his hell-raising message across. There are also some more outlaw country-styled cuts such as "It Ain't Easy," "Goin' to Carolina," "Some Rowdy Women," "The Song Is Still Slipping Away," and "Hair of the Dog." They recall the brand of historic country music Jennings' father helped to pioneer in the 1970s. The term "outlaw" is simply a musically descriptive word now; it's not meant to be a millstone around Shooter's neck—even though he directly references Waylon often (and let's face it, if anyone has a right to do that, it's him). *Electric Rodeo* is solid; it's full of ragged road poetry, defiant rowdyism, and restless, rust-stained, country-soul, with plenty of its own charisma.

Thom Jurek

George Jones

The Cold Hard Truth
June 1999, Elektra

Touted as George Jones' return to hardcore country, *Cold Hard Truth*—the Possum's first record for the revitalized

Asylum Records—certainly does achieve that goal. Under the guidance of producer Keith Stegall, Jones returns to the sound of his classic Mercury and UA recordings, meaning that there's nothing but honky tonk ballads and ravers throughout. Impressively, Stegall made sure that Jones didn't take the easy way out: there are no covers or superstar duets, just strong new songs. And, unlike almost any of Jones' previous albums, there's not a single novelty or throwaway. In short, it's the album hardcore fans have said they've always wanted Jones to make. Like most realized fantasies, *Cold Hard Truth* doesn't quite live up to the imagination, yet it still delivers enough that it isn't a disappointment. Much of the credit must be given to Stegall; his production may be a bit too clean and echo-laden, but he made a wise move in adhering to simple, traditional instrumentation and guiding Jones toward a great set of songs. George sounds terrific, not necessarily better than on his latter-day MCA records, but the strength of the material makes it seem so. For all of its virtues, there's a curious distance on *Cold Hard Truth*, possibly because it's too careful in both its song selection, and there's no grit in the production. Silly songs and rushed performances always gave Jones' albums character, and it's hard not to miss that reckless spirit on *Cold Hard Truth*, no matter how good the music is. But ultimately, such complaints amount to nitpicking. There's little question that *Cold Hard Truth* boasts the finest set of songs Jones has had in nearly two decades, and he delivers the performances they deserve. It's refreshing to finally hear a Jones album that holds up from beginning to end.

Stephen Thomas Erlewine

Wynonna Judd

Wynonna
1992, Curb/MCA

Daughter Wynonna Judd stakes out her own territory with her self-titled debut. It's probably safe to say that she has more in her than most people guessed. From the tender "She Is His Only Need" to the southern rock and soul of "No One Else on Earth," Wynonna sings with a smoldering sensuality that pulsed beneath the surface of the Judds' best records—even "Live with Jesus" sounds sexy. After a few more albums like this, folks may not even remember the Judds. It also includes "I Saw the Light" and "My Strongest Weakness."

Brian Mansfield

Tell Me Why
May 1993, Curb/MCA

Wynonna Judd's second album, *Tell Me Why*, is a more confident and diverse collection than her debut. Drawing from sources as varied as gospel, folk, and blues-rock, Wynonna doesn't necessarily deliver a pure country album, but her blend of roots genres does qualify as a cleverly constructed contemporary country record. The selection of material is first-rate, but what makes *Tell Me Why* her best solo effort is how she ties all of the songs together with her assured—and surprisingly subtle—vocals.

Thom Owens

Revelations
1996, Curb/MCA

Wynonna had no problem with the spotlight; or, as the tabloids regularly revealed, with opening up her private life for all to poke through and ponder. For all of her cultivating of celebrity, her albums continued to turn down the lights and focus on the softer glow of emotional verities her albums. *Revelations* is another worthy solo effort by the younger member of the Judds, the mother-daughter duo through which she first found massive fame. Often somber, and just as often right on the money, she casts a blue tint to several reflective songs that examine spirituality (without sermons) and the quiet discoveries that come with mature relationships. Ballads like "Don't Look Back," "Love By Grace," and "My Angel Is Here"—all album highlights—prove how sympathetic her rich, expressive voice can be when applied to a well-written, sensitive lyric. As in the past, she's equally convincing on up-tempo, R&B-infused strutters, such as Delbert McClinton's "Somebody to Love You" or the gospel rave-up "Dance! Shout!" It's a mystery as to why she would include her version of "Free Bird," which previously was released as part of a Lynyrd Skynyrd tribute album. (Maybe someone should tell her that those people who yelled it out during encores were kidding.) Otherwise, *Revelations* is just that; a revealing next step by a country music star who understands the power of subtlety in an age that tends to prefer overstatement.

Michael McCall

New Day Dawning
February 2000, MCA

Southern gospel and soul, rockers, and ballads all grace Wynonna Judd's fifth release as a solo artist and her first as co-producer. One of the most recognizable voices in country music, the depth and range of her voice can be heard from the first track, the rhythmic "Going Nowhere," to the last, the soulful "I Can't Wait to Meet You." Fans will be delighted to hear Judd put her rock-influenced country-pop spin on Joni Mitchell's "Help Me." And of course, what's a good Wynonna album without her signature growl? As a bonus for Judd fans, *New Day Dawning* includes a special second CD, *Big Bang Boogie*, available in limited quantities with four new tracks from Wynonna and Naomi. The Judds reunion CD, however brief, is an exciting extra to the already electrifying *New Day....*

Maria Konicki Dinoia

What the World Needs Now Is Love
August 2003, Curb

What the World Needs Now Is Love may be titled after a Burt Bacharach and Hal David song, but it as far away from that song musically as one can get and still remain popular music. On her alleged return to her country roots, Wynonna Judd cannot resist the temptation to allow many forms of pop and rock into her sound. But that's fine—just fine. On her first studio outing in three years, Judd turns in a performance that is consistent all the way through, and one that seamlessly blends that astonishing voice of hers with banjos, strings, electric guitars, mandolins, pedal steels, pianos, and lots of drums. In addition to the heartbreakingly beautiful reunion of the singer with her mother Naomi ("Flies on the Butter"), Wynonna also collaborates with überguitarist Jeff Beck on the shimmering country version of the Mick Jones pop classic "I Want to Know What Love Is." This version may replace the original as its emotion is honestly wrought and pouring over the brim of the track's arrangement. Also featured here is her version of "Burning Love," the old Elvis nugget from the film *Lilo & Stitch*, and "You Are," from the *Someone Like You* soundtrack. There are contemporary arrangements galore, but Judd's voice carries them into the realms of history as one can hear voices as diverse as Connie Smith's and Aretha Franklin's in her delivery and phrasing. Tracks such as "Sometimes I Feel Like Elvis," and the rollicking barnburner "(No One's Gonna) Break Me Down," which could have been written by Nick Lowe and Dave Edmunds, deliver intensity, honesty, and theatrics seamlessly. *What the World Needs Now Is Love* is a stellar outing from one of the most singular talents in the country music pantheon. If this doesn't cross over, then radio really *is* dead.

Thom Jurek

The Judds

Wynonna & Naomi
1983, RCA

Though it lacked a strong set of songs, the Judds' eponymous debut album established that the vocals of Wynonna and Naomi played off of each other beautifully, and songs like the hit "Had A Dream (For the Heart)" provide the foundation for their later hit singles. The best moments on *The Judds* have been compiled on their numerous hit compilation, yet it remains a pleasant listen for most dedicated fans.

Thom Owens

Why Not Me
1984, RCA

Despite the promise of their self-titled debut album, Naomi and Wynonna Judd struck pay dirt by issuing the bona fide classic *Why Not Me*, their sophomore outing from 1984. It was produced by Brent Maher and recorded with a small group of  session players who were chosen as carefully as the songs were. From the opening track, the title cut, written by greats Harlan Howard, Sonny Throckmorton, and Maher, it is obvious what a showcase this is for Wynonna Judd's stylized singing. Her big throaty voice rings clear and wide, pulling up every ounce of emotion from the song's root; her phrasing is perfect, and Naomi's harmonies are golden; they soar, float, and lilt in contrast, complement, and counterpoint to her daughter's lead. The elder Judd is also a fine songwriter in that track two, "Mr. Pain," is one of the finest songs on the set, full of beauty and vulnerability but ever present with hope. But it's not until track three, "Drops of Water," that the album breaks wide open. Here Wynonna proves she can sing from the rockabilly side of country as well. From her gritty lead vocal to her sweet swing-style harmony with Naomi and killer dobro runs from Sonny Garrish, the tune is irresistible. "My Baby's Gone" is another such moment, a tough, lean,

bluesy shuffle graced with Andrews Sisters-styled harmonies and country guitar picking from Don Potter that turns this into a stomper. The ballads work too, however, on "Sleeping Heart" or the blues-rooted "By Bye Baby Blues," which is penned by the Howard/Throckmorton/Maher team and is country music from the Patsy Cline fake book. The elements of jazz and early '60s countrypolitan are impossible not to remember. But that's what makes the Judds so special—they can sing it all. All they need is the material, and when they get it—and they do here in spades—they are virtually untouchable. With Wynonna's voice being one of the best in the history of the music, and Naomi's harmonizing being literally the most unconventional, they are wall-to-wall original as an act. With the two closers, "Endless Sleep," a solid rocker in the "Heartbreak Hotel" tradition, and the plaintive "Mama He's Crazy," the duo accomplish the impossible: becoming a longstanding duo who consistently rode the top of the charts until Naomi left for health reasons and who remained a bona fide country music act. Of all their recordings, *Why Not Me* is their best-known, best-selling, and deservedly so. It's perfect.

Thom Jurek

Rockin' with the Rhythm
1985, RCA

On the third album, "Have Mercy" and the title track (among others) kick with a funky glee that makes this the most plainly joyous Judds album.

Mark A. Humphrey

River of Time
1989, RCA

Six years after their debut, the Judds were still cranking out the hits, albeit with a funkier, grittier sound that brought electric pianos and Hammond B-3s into the mix. Using the same basic team that had made their career the monstrously successful thing it was, talent like guitarists like Carl Perkins, Mark Knopfler, and Roy Huskey, Jr. augment *River of Time*. That said, it seems like the funkier and less traditionally "country" the Judds became, the wider their appeal. Album to album, their singles still seemed to resonate with country audiences the most. *River of Time* boasted two number singles, the plaintive country of "Young Love" and the rockabilly shuffle of Perkins' "Let Me Tell You About Love" with Perkins kicking it on guitar. Naomi Judd is also featured here as a prominent songwriter with her partner, John Jarvis, on the title track, "Cadillac Red," and the closer, "Guardian Angel." There is a stunning cover of Boudleaux Bryant's "Sleepless Nights" that equals the Gram Parsons/Emmylou Harris version. And Knopfler's "Water of Love" was stretching it for the Judds, but in its sultry outlaw country feel and the author's guitar snaking around Wynonna's voice, nocturnal and mysterious, it's the most seductive tune on the set. The strutting country boogie of "Cadillac Red" and the shuffling swinging honky tonk of "Do I Dare" are infectious. "Guardian Angel," which Naomi wrote with Jarvis and Don Schlitz, bears the latter's unmistakable imprint. Having written "The Gambler" for Kenny Rogers, Naomi's story is made elegant by a heartbreakingly beautiful melody and refrain. *River of Time* is another ace in the Judds' hands.

Thom Jurek

Love Can Build a Bridge
September 1990, RCA

The last Judds album may not be their strongest but nonetheless featured some killer tracks and is by no means unsuccessful when taken as a whole. There is plenty of merit here. With an opening track like "Born to Be Blue" that begins as an old swinging blues tune à la the 1930s and moves into a hot fusion of country and R&B, the album is off to a good start. There are a handful of Naomi Judd co-writes that feature everything from roots and progressive country to strutting, punchy rock & roll to heartbreaking ballads. The remake of Lawrence Hammond's "John Deere Tractor" may not have be the best move to make, but then, it's not bad either. "Calling in the Wind" sounds like Bruce Springsteen's "Born in the USA" at the beginning, but Wynonna dispels any of that quickly in the verse. "Rompin' Stompin' Bad News Blues" is a ferocious blues rocker with acoustic guitars roiling under the voice of Wynonna, who sings as loud as she growls, and guest star Bonnie Raitt's greasy electric slide doesn't hurt either. Ultimately, *Love Can Build a Bridge* is a fine sendoff for one of the most successful and revolutionary bands in country history. There is much pleasure here, and it is all in the way two voices weave, Wynonna's command of her instrument, and Brent Maher's production that accents all the strengths and leaves just enough weakness in the mix to make the band human.

Thom Jurek

The Essential Judds
October 1995, RCA

The Essential Judds contains a great majority of the duo's biggest hits, as well as a wisely-chosen selection of rarities, making it a definitive compilation.

Stephen Thomas Erlewine

Toby Keith

Toby Keith
1993, Mercury

On the cover of his eponymous 1993 debut, Toby Keith doesn't quite look like the big, swaggering dog that became a superstar roughly seven years later—he's too thin, his shirt too crisp, his mullet too drastic, his smile too eager—but image isn't everything. Underneath that cover, it sure is possible to *hear* the roots of modern Toby Keith on this appealing debut. It is given a production that's a bit too big, clean, glossy and cavernous for Keith's good—it fits the outsized sound of early '90s radio, but not his outsized talent—but beneath that sheen the songs are very strong. He wrote all but two here—the cheerfully swinging "Some Kinda Good Kinda Hold on Me" and the very good "A Little Less Talk and a Lot More Action," which winningly echoes the Georgia Satellites' "Keep Your Hands to Yourself," aren't his—and he's already showing considerable range as a writer, already revealing his wry sense of humor on "Close But No Guitar" and expertly playing of Western mythology on "Should've Been a Cowboy" which was his deserved breakthrough. But if that song, combined with his latter macho stance, suggests that he was always all outlaw, most of *Toby Keith* is surprisingly within poppier territory, as "Ain't No Thang," "He Ain't Worth Missing," and "Wish I Didn't Know Now" all bear influences from Ronnie Milsap. He'd later develop this influence, blending it to a rowdier stance that became his signature, but looking back on this debut it's clear that Keith was a writer and singer of considerable skill even at the outset of his career.

Stephen Thomas Erlewine

Dream Walkin'
June 1997, Mercury

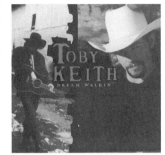

The very title of *Dream Walkin'* has a hazy, laid-back quality, which is rather appropriate since this, Toby Keith's fourth album, comes from the close of his time at Mercury Records, when he was singing more ballads than rockers and when he was cutting nearly as many covers as he was originals. It was all part of an attempt to have Keith fit within the country music machine and he's good enough of a ballad singer to have this work well, although the tunes not written by Keith— "We Were in Love," Sting's "I'm So Happy I Can't Stop Crying"—don't showcase his underrated, understated subtle singing as well as his original ballads, which have a nice sense of grace. Similarly, the wannabe swagger of "Double Wide Paradise" doesn't have the snap of Keith's own livelier material such as the rip-roaring "Jacky Don Tucker (Play by the Rules Miss All the Fun)" and the refurbished Western swing of "I Don't Understand My Girlfriend," both of which go a long way on Keith's outsized humor, or his excellent "She Ran Away with a Rodeo Clown," which plays like a deserved tribute to Moe Bandy. There aren't many of these livelier tunes here—enough to make an impact, enough to make you wish there were more, but even if this is heavy on the smooth stuff, *Dream Walkin'* rides its mellow vibes in an appealing fashion.

Stephen Thomas Erlewine

How Do You Like Me Now?!
November 1999, DreamWorks

Toby Keith jumped from Mercury to DreamWorks after his fourth album, *Dream Walkin'* and *How Do You Like Me Now?!*, his first effort for his new album, finds the singer/songwriter revived and refreshed, shaking loose some of the sleepiness of his two albums for Mercury. Not that he's given up slower tunes—he still has a keen ear for sensitive love songs and heartbreak sagas, manifesting in both the light, sweet "Heart to Heart (Stelen's Song)" and power ballads like "When Love Fades"—but there is a bit of a showy defiance here, best heard on the hit title track, "Die with Your Boots On" and the rocking "Country Comes to Town." When taken together, these two sides present the new Toby Keith persona: the big, bad outlaw who hides a big, soft heart. He would further develop and refine this persona in a series of excellent albums in the 2000s, but this is where he debuted it and if, in retrospect, *How Do You Like Me Now?!* is a little bit ragged compared to what came later—the swagger isn't as gritty, the ballads a little bit syrupy—it nevertheless is a compelling, successful beginning of the second stage of Keith's career, built upon some very fine songs.

Stephen Thomas Erlewine

Pull My Chain
August 2001, DreamWorks

Toby Keith's first DreamWorks album, 1999's *How Do You Like Me Now?!*, unveiled a new persona—one that didn't shy away from the ballads that helped bring him hits in the '90s but put them into the background, emphasizing his humor and his bravado to winning effect. And to success, too, as it became the album that truly turned him into a country star, thereby letting him dig into this new persona on its follow-up, 2001's *Pull My Chain*. In every regard, this is a bigger, better record than its predecessor, possessing a richer musicality and a more confident sense of humor. That humor may be most evident on its weakest track, the mocking macho white-rap "I Wanna Talk About Me" (written by Bobby Braddock, not Keith), but it's better heard on the album opener "I'm Just Talkin' About Tonight," a one-night stand anthem that's wry and clever, not obvious. That sly sense of craft has been evident in Keith's work since his debut but it truly comes to full fruition here, perhaps because of his new co-writer Scotty Emerick, who had only one credit on *How Do You Like Me Now?!* but five here, including "I'm Just Talkin' About Tonight," the mellow soul of "I Can't Take You Anywhere," the power ballad "You Leave Me Weak," the breezy '70s soft rock of "Tryin' to Matter" and the laid-back "Yesterday's Rain." These are the backbone of the record, but they don't dominate it, as Keith's collaborations with Chuck Cannon— "The Sha La La Song," which is the opposite of the bluster of the title track, also written with Cannon—a rocking cover of Dave Loggins' "Pick 'Em Up and Lay 'Em Down" and two collaborations with Elton John's lyricist Bernie Taupin (the ballad "You Didn't Have as Much to Lose" and the bonus track "Gimme Eight Seconds," which is pure arena rock country complete with guitars resurrected from the '80s) are equally as good. All these different co-writers and covers mean that *Pull My Chain* isn't quite coherent, but that's also part of its charm: with his new success, Keith is empowered to try a bit of everything, to sow his wild oats, and he does so in compelling fashion here.

Stephen Thomas Erlewine

Unleashed
August 2002, DreamWorks

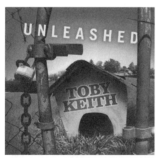

Toby Keith was edging in on superstardom prior to the release of *Unleashed*—he appeared on a national long-distance telephone commercial, after all—but this was the record that made him a household name, thanks to the opening track "Courtesy of the Red, White and Blue (The Angry American)" and the media-created controversy surrounding its release. The rabble-rousing, obstinate flip-side to Alan Jackson's "Where Were You When the World Stopped Turning"—essentially, a 9-11 song for those who thought Jackson's heartbroken confusion was for pansies, but weren't redneck enough to embrace Charlie Daniels' "That Ain't No Rag, It's a Flag" or "The Last Fallen Hero"—"Courtesy of the Red, White and Blue" is, as its subtitle suggests, filled with anger, telling the terrorists (whose "suckerpunch came flying in from somewhere in the back," a rhyme that's tantalizingly close to "somewhere in Iraq," you will yourself to hear it every time it plays) that they'll "get a boot in their ass, it's the American way." Keith was scheduled to sing this on an ABC special on

the fourth of July (not too coincidentally mentioned in the song), when apparently Peter Jennings objected to the tone of the song and asked the network to rescind the singer's invitation, which then lead to reams of print and countless TV appearances that effectively sold *Unleashed* before it hit the stores.

As it turns out, "Courtesy" is a bit misleading of a lead single, as is the title, since most of this album is hardly tough macho posturing. Sure, there's some of it—such as the absurdly anthemic "Beer for My Horses," a duet with Willie Nelson where the two of them hunt down modern day gangsters like cowboys, then drink to their accomplishments—but most of this album is tuneful singer/songwriterism, particularly on the second side, where this album really takes off with a series of rolling, melodic, acoustic-based songs that truly demonstrate that Keith can be a sturdy, memorable songwriter. True, he does descend into cloying cuteness on occasion ("Huckleberry"), but the stretch of songs from "It Works for Me" through "That's Not How It Is" that ends the record is among his finest, and they're balanced by a couple of good moments from the first side (the silly fun of "Good to Go to Mexico," "Losing My Touch") and, of course, "Courtesy of the Red, White and Blue." That song may mischaracterize what's on *Unleashed*, but those who are brought in by that slice of flag-waving jingoism should be pleased by the sweeter fare here since, ultimately, it proves to be more substantive.

Stephen Thomas Erlewine

Shock'n Y'All
November 2003, DreamWorks

Since Toby Keith not only can come across as a loudmouth redneck but seems to *enjoy* being a loudmouth redneck, it's easy for some listeners to dismiss him as a backwoods right-wing crank—particularly when he succumbs to such easy impulses as mocking Dixie Chick Natalie Maines in concert and naming his 2003 album *Shock'n Y'All*, not so cleverly spinning the military catch phrase from the second Iraq war into a bad pun. Those listeners aren't entirely wrong, since he can succumb to reactionary politics, as on swill like "Beer for My Horses," but Keith isn't coming from a didactic right-wing standpoint. He's an old-fashioned, cantankerous outlaw who's eager to be as oversized and larger than life as legends like Waylon Jennings, Merle Haggard, and Willie Nelson, who bucked conventions and spoke their minds. Sure, Keith enjoys pandering to the Fox News Republicans "Courtesy of the Red, White and Blue" won him, and his jingoistic ventures don't have the humanity and humor of Haggard's protest songs (although to Keith's credit they display far more humanity than Sean Hannity and are much more genuine than Steve Earle's post-9/11 songs), but that doesn't mean Keith doesn't have a big, warm heart. In fact, on every album prior to *Shock'n Y'All* he's displayed a taste for mawkish sentiment, but what makes this album work is that he's turned that sentiment into warmth while making the record into the hardest, toughest set of songs he's yet made. *Unleashed* gave him the clout to make any kind of music he wanted, and left to his own devices, he's lonesome, on'ry, and mean, a cheerful advocate of redneck libertarianism with a sly sense of humor. All of which wouldn't mean much if he wasn't a strong songwriter, and more than any of his previous works, *Shock'n Y'All* proves that he's a steady-handed journeyman, crafting songs in the tradition of classic outlaw country. It's a deliberately hard-driving, hard-drinking, gutsy country album, yet it doesn't shy away from modernism, best illustrated on "Sweet," with its funky rhythms and use of "babelicious" (which rhymes with "delicious," btw). Even with these modern flourishes, the album is firmly within the hard country tradition, with lots of barroom humor, propulsive rhythms, hearty humor, and a humanity that contradicts the rabble-rousing of *Unleashed*. And if Keith is more of a party-hearty hound than a profound singer—even when he imagines "If I Was Jesus," it's only so he can turn water into wine at parties—that's now an attribute, not a deficiency, since it gives him focus and sensibility. Keith is happy to be a dirty old SOB, cracking jokes, drinking beer, and flirting with the ladies, and that makes *Shock'n Y'All* a fun, rough, rowdy album that wins you over despite your better impulses. It's not polite, but *Shock'n Y'All* is pure Toby Keith, and the best album he's done to date.

Stephen Thomas Erlewine

Honkytonk University
May 2005, DreamWorks Nashville

Snicker all you want at Toby Keith's shoutout to his "boys in Afghanistan and Baghdad City" in the chorus of "Honkytonk U"— Keith may pander, but that doesn't mean he doesn't deliver the goods. And deliver he does on *Honkytonk University*, his 2005 follow-up to 2003's hit *Shock'n Y'all* and the second album he's released since 2002's *Unleashed* made him into a bonafide superstar thanks to its post-9/11 anthem "Courtesy of the Red, White and Blue (The Angry American)." That song pegged Keith as a right-wing, red-state country singer, but that's not exactly an accurate designation. Not only is he nowhere near as simple as Darryl Worley, but his patriotic posturing was savvy, a good way to endear him to his core audience and broaden his base, all the while being able to keep his country pure, without a trace of pop schmaltz in its arrangements. *Honkytonk University*, as its title suggests, confirms that Keith is the biggest hardcore country singer this side of Alan Jackson, but where Jackson is a strict traditionalist, Keith is a rowdy modern man, building on the outlaw country of Waylon Jennings and the sound of latter-day Merle Haggard, throwing in traces of Dwight Yoakam along with a keen eye for contemporary life. He takes such time-honored themes as love, broken hearts, and drinking and gives them new life through his sharp details and sense of humor—best heard on the wonderfully self-depreciating "As Good as I Once Was" and the absurd, over-the-top "You Ain't Leavin' (Thank God Are Ya)"—and a strong sense of craft. He's been writing good barroom weepers and party tunes for a long time, but here, the love ballads and sad songs are just as good, and there are such nice, breezy changes of pace as "Where You Gonna Go" that recall the best of rolling, folk-influenced country. Indeed, there's a greater variety of sounds and styles on *Honkytonk University* than many Toby Keith records—there's honky tonk, to be sure, but that's only the starting point—and that variety, along with the consistently strong set of original songs (all bearing Keith's writing credits, many co-written by Scotty Emerick), makes this one of his very best records.

Stephen Thomas Erlewine

White Trash with Money
April 2006, Show Dog Nashville/Universal

Toby Keith really is a throwback to a different time, a time when artists came into their own after kicking around for a while, a time when the most popular artists were also restlessly creative. In other words, he hearkens back to the heyday of outlaw country, when Willie and Waylon were making their own way with records that sounded different each time out, a claim that certainly can be made with every record Keith released in the 2000s. With *White Trash with Money*, he tops himself, delivering not only his fifth excellent album in a row, but his riskiest, richest record yet. For this, his tenth studio album, Keith teams up with country renegade singer/songwriter Lari White, an underappreciated country singer/songwriter who made a shift toward country-soul on her 2004 album *Green Eyed Soul*. It's an unusual choice in many respects. First, it's a surprise that Keith has parted ways with producer James Stroud, who has been co-producing his records since 1997's *Dream Walkin'*, but it's also a surprise because White isn't known for her productions, and her albums don't necessarily seem like kindred spirits with the swaggering, macho Keith. But surprises can sometimes be exactly right, and *White Trash with Money* is pretty damn near perfect, a testament to Keith's often underappreciated versatility and his songwriting skill.

White eases Keith into new sonic territory, somewhat related to *Green Eyed Soul* but never far removed from the loose-limbed neo-outlaw country Keith has been mining since the turn of the millennium. By working with White, Keith has added just enough new colors to his palette to let listeners truly appreciate the range in his music. That slight yet significant shift in tone is immediately evident, as the album kicks off with the rowdy, horn-driven "Get Drunk and Be Somebody." With its soulful strut, it recalls White's work, but the album shift gears before it can get pigeonholed, with "A Little Too Late" recalling both lush Nashville country-pop productions and Dwight Yoakam's classicist spin on the same sound, and "Can't Buy You Money" bringing to mind a straight-ahead version of Bobbie Joe Gentry's neo-gothic masterpiece "An Ode to Billie Joe." Soon, the changes in mood settle down, and a spare, muscular version of Keith's country dominates the album, but the music is more robust than it was even on *Honkytonk University*; there are little flourishes, from soulful organs and guitars, that make these songs full-bodied. This variety brings life to what very well may be Keith's best set of songs. Like *Honkytonk University*, *White Trash with Money* lacks the ornery patriotism of the post-9/11 work that brought him fame and it keeps the focus on the basics: love, drinking, heartbreak, forgotten anniversaries, tequila, family, and happiness. Keith's humor is out in full force, and not just on the three new "Bus Session" songs that conclude the record. He's loose and limber, bringing a big heart to these tunes, and to the album as a whole. This is an addictive record, enveloping in its sound and memorable in its songs, and it's proof positive that there has been no other country artist as risky, rich, or consistent as Toby Keith this decade.

Stephen Thomas Erlewine

Big Dog Daddy
June 2007, Show Dog Nashville

After he becoming a bona fide superstar in the wake of "Courtesy of the Red White and Blue," Toby Keith refused to play it safe, blowing up his persona to mythic heights on 2003's *Shock'n Y'All*, stretching his musical legs on

Honkytonk University, and calling off all bets with the Lari White-produced *White Trash with Money*, where he got soulful and soft in equal measures. After that trilogy of exploration, Keith snaps back to the basics on *Big Dog Daddy*, his first self-produced album and his first album of nothing but pure, hardcore country since his star rose in the early years of the new millennium. This isn't a retreat as much as it's a reaffirmation of his strengths as a singer, songwriter, performer, and interpreter. Indeed, two of the highlights here are covers of Craig Wiseman's sighing "Love Me If You Can" and Fred Eaglesmith's "White Rose," a warm, bittersweet slice of nostalgia that highlights how Keith really tells a story when he sings. But if these, along with a handful of Keith originals, highlight his often overlooked sensitive side—love songs rarely come as sweet as "I Know She Hung the Moon," heartbreak songs are rarely as aching as "Walk It Off"— this album swings and swaggers as much as the title boasts. There's the galloping "Get My Drink On," the old-time rock & roll title track (Chuck Berry turned into country-rock via Bob Seger), and the irresistible Bobby Pinson collaboration "Pump Jack," and Keith finds the middle ground between these extremes with the remarkable "Wouldn't Want to Be Ya," which turns a cliché inside out, rendering it remarkably affecting. And that's the real secret to Keith's success: underneath all the bragging he's a songwriter and a damn good one at that, which this lean, sinewy, stripped-to-the-basics record makes clear.

Stephen Thomas Erlewine

The Kentucky Headhunters

Pickin' on Nashville
1989, Mercury

As their album title suggests, The Headhunters aren't entirely comfortable with the country tag, which is appropriate when you hear their guitar-heavy, rambunctious music. The vocals have that twang, but these good old boys are often closer to Lynyrd Skynyrd than they are to Merle Haggard, and all the better for it.

William Ruhlmann

Electric Barnyard
1991, Mercury

The Kentucky Headhunters aren't a remarkable country mutation, just a top-notch Southern rock band with a sense of humor. "The Ballad of Davy Crockett" is the kind of clever novelty that won't work twice; "Big Mexican Dinner" is a novelty that doesn't even work the first time. Once again, the country and bluegrass covers—"Only Daddy That'll Walk the Line," "With Body and Soul"—are the highlights, and most of the originals (the Beatlesque shuffle "Always Makin' Love" aside) are offbeat, adequate filler.

Brian Mansfield

Sammy Kershaw

Haunted Heart
1993, Mercury

The more you know about Sammy Kershaw, the more there is to like about his albums. Though Kershaw doesn't write his songs, he makes some of the most autobiographical albums to come from Music Row. If you know that Kershaw quit performing for a year and a half when it threatened his marriage, "Still Lovin' You" assumes greater significance. Even a song as strange as "Queen of My Double Wide Trailer" makes more sense when you learn that Kershaw still owns a trailer in Louisiana, "in case things don't work out." Sure, he still sounded a lot like George Jones with a south Louisiana accent. But *Haunted Heart* showed that Kershaw was coming into his own as a vocalist. Just as important, he was choosing songs that set him apart from the pack. If some of those were as offbeat as "Double Wide" and "Neon Leon," well, that's just part of what made him distinctive.

Brian Mansfield

The Hits: Chapter 1
September 1995, Mercury Nashville

Sammy Kershaw had only been recording for four years when he released *The Hits, Chapter 1*, but its appearance didn't seem premature. During that time, he had racked up a considerable number of Top Ten country hits, including the number ones "National Working Woman's Holiday" and "She Don't Know She's Beautiful." Both of those songs are included, as well as eight others that prove why he was one of the most popular country singers in the early '90s.

Stephen Thomas Erlewine

I Want My Money Back
March 2003, Audium/Koch

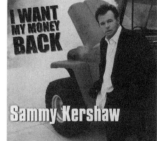

After about a decade, Sammy Kershaw parted ways with Mercury Nashville after his 1999 album *Maybe Not Tonight*, resurfacing four years later on Audium/Koch with *I Want My Money Back*. A switch to an independent at this stage of the game pretty much takes Kershaw out of the running for the charts, but he thanks God in the liner notes "for giving me another chance to do what I love to do so much," so chances are, his eyes aren't on the charts anyway. Kershaw also calls it the best album he's done to date, and he very well might be right, because *I Want My Money Back* boasts a strong set of songs and performances that make it one of his most satisfying efforts. Part of the reason that this works is the fact that he isn't concerned about hits—there are no Leo Sayer covers, in other words—and with producer Richard Landis, he has picked a fine set of songs that highlight Kershaw's country roots. Not that this is an unadulterated honky tonk record; there are plenty of songs that are rock-influenced, neo-traditionalist country, which is now firmly part of contemporary country's tradition. But the difference is, there's not a song that feels pop, not a song with a false performance, not a moment that doesn't feel like Kershaw has made the comeback that he's needed for a long time now. It's easily his best since 1993's *Haunted Heart*.

Stephen Thomas Erlewine

Hal Ketchum

Past the Point of Rescue
1991, Curb

Hal Ketchum writes simple, sometimes moving songs about relationships and/or life's dilemmas, and communicates them in an attractive, unadorned vocal package. But although many of these numbers espouse country themes, Ketchum's delivery, as well as the arrangements and sensibility, lean toward easy-listening pop and light folk. Certainly every country artist isn't a honky-tonking, tough-talking, drinker whining about lost love, but Ketchum comes perilously close on "Past The Point Of Rescue" or his cover of The Vogues' "Five O'Clock World" to the super-smooth "Nashville Sound" of days past.

Ron Wynn

Every Little Word
1994, Curb

Ketchum reconciles the thoughtfulness of his folkie heart with the verve of modern country, tapping into the directness and earthiness that ties them together. His most country album, it's his most consistent.

Michael McCall

Kinleys

II
July 2000, Sony

In 1998, the Kinleys were back in the country Top 20 with "Somebody's Out There Watching," from the *Touched By an Angel* television soundtrack. In the summer of 1999, they put out the single "My Heart Is Still Beating," which was intended to be the curtain raiser on their second album. But it fizzled, dropping off the charts after two weeks. Epic decided to go back to the drawing board, bringing in new producer Radney Foster to replace Tony Haselden and Russ Zavitson, who had shepherded the Kinleys for their entire career. The result, a full year later, is *The Kinleys II*, which is really two half-albums, its first six songs handled by Foster and the next six by Haselden and Zavitson, with "Somebody's Out There Watching" following as the conclusion. Like his own modestly successful solo albums, Foster's half consists of craftsmanlike country-pop with blues tendencies. The tempos are restrained, the material well put together but dull, and the sisters are given a lot of solo singing. Foster seems to conceive of the Kinleys as potential successors to the Judds, but with both singers playing the earthy Wynonna role. Yet anyone who leaves the album playing until the seventh track (the first Haselden/Zavitson track) is in for a surprise—suddenly, the record comes into focus as a lively, driving country disc. Maybe it's just that Epic cherry-picked from a scrapped earlier version of this album, but its second half is a vast improvement over its first. The Haselden/Zavitson numbers are honky tonk harmony performances in which the Kinleys sound much more involved than they do with Foster; it's clear that the Kinleys' first producers have a

much better sense of their real strengths than the hired gun brought in to save the release. You can't help wondering what would have happened if the whole album were as good as the second half—since a successful country album now has the same sales potential as a pop release, the second effort for an act that had good but not great sales the first time around is crucial to its success.

William Ruhlmann

Alison Krauss

Two Highways
1989, Rounder

Two Highways is the first album Alison Krauss recorded with her excellent backing band, Union Station, and, appropriately, it demonstrates that she could lead a band through a number of bluegrass standards, as well as several more contemporary numbers. Of course, her instrumental solo continue to be the most impressive thing about her music on *Two Highways*, but her duets with guitarists Jeff White demonstrate that her vocals are beginning to come into their own.

Thom Owens

I've Got That Old Feeling
1990, Rounder

When *I've Got That Old Feeling* garnered Alison Krauss 1990's Best Bluegrass Recording Grammy, it was an acknowledgement of the talent and poise the former child prodigy had shown through her first three albums. The album's tantalizing blend of tasteful folk and traditional bluegrass certainly deserved the award. But *Old Feeling* was more important as a footbridge to where Krauss would take her music—and bluegrass itself—over the next decade. It blended country and bluegrass with pop elements (the latter being most evident on "Longest Highway") in such an effortless way, the album couldn't possibly be seen as a play for the mainstream. The sentiment behind the gentle sway of "It's Over" and "Wish I Still Had You" was universal; blended into the honeyed voice of Krauss, it was irresistible. At the same time, the playing on "Will You Be Leaving" and "Dark Skies" was not only technically skilled, but startlingly genuine. (Sam Bush's mandolin and the dobro leads of producer Jerry Douglas were particularly impressive.) The record was imbued with the same old feeling that Krauss and her Union Station guitarist Dan Tyminski would later draw upon for *O Brother, Where Art Thou?*—it was a bluegrass album at heart, but it came from a place where emotion and honesty weren't labeled with a genre tag.

Johnny Loftus

Every Time You Say Goodbye
1992, Rounder

Alison Krauss was born to sing bluegrass. Her voice just wouldn't work in a riot grrrl or hip-hop setting. Not even close. The fiddle wouldn't quite fit either. Lucky thing she found her calling. On *Every Time You Say Goodbye*, Krauss is once again teamed with the stellar craftsmen of Union Station, and she sounds as comfortable as a porch swing and lemonade on a warm summer evening. Although Krauss gets the majority of the accolades, this is truly a group effort as the various musicians share the credit as writers and producers. Ron Block, Tim Stafford, Barry Bales, and Adam Steffey also take their turns stepping up to the mic, offering harmony and lead vocals where fitting. The songs range from traditional country fare to unexpected covers like Shawn Colvin's "I Don't Know Why." Their arrangement might seem oddly peppy to those who know the Colvin version. But to those who don't, it works just fine. Other highlights include the title track, "Who Can Blame You," "Last Love Letter," and the Karla Bonoff composition "Lose Again." And you just have to love a record that includes "Cluck Old Hen," which happens to be a fine showcase for Krauss' outstanding fiddle work. She has done a lot to make bluegrass a viable, contemporary genre of music. *Every Time You Say Goodbye* does much to further that cause.

Kelly McCartney

Now That I've Found You: A Collection
February 1995, Rounder

Alison Krauss had been recording a decade before she gained stardom, but she became a star in a big way. *Now That I've Found You: A Collection*, a retrospective of her ten-year recording career for Rounder, became the surprise hit of 1995, rocketing to number two on the country charts and into the Top 15 on the *pop* charts, which is remarkable for a musician who had never captured the attention of a mass audience. It may have been a surprising success, but it also was deserved. Krauss was arguably the leading bluegrass musician of the late '80s and early '90s, pushing the music into new directions without losing sight of its roots. *Now That I've Found You* does a splendid job of chronicling her career, hitting all of the highlights and making a new listener eager to seek out her albums.

Stephen Thomas Erlewine

So Long So Wrong
1997, Rounder

After mainstream success happened for Alison Krauss & Union Station, one would have rightly expected a commercial sweetening of their sound, resulting in diminishing (or even abandoning) the simple but very unique thing that brought them into the public eye—and eventual public acclaim—in the first place. But the group's first new recording in the wake of the surprise success of *Now That I've Found You: A Collection* finds Alison Krauss & Union Station happily keeping their eclectic focus firmly on the prize stretched before them with no silly attempts to court the hat-hunk-of-the-month or the boot-scoot-boogie crowd. Despite the media's singling out of Krauss as country's new bluegrass solo diva, Union Station (with Krauss as simply a featured member of it) remains very much a group, and that's the real refreshing news

here. It is that collective spirit that remains the reoccurring theme and the resounding musical point being made here, and it is the solid anchor that roots this album into place from beginning to end. Krauss' expert evocative way with a ballad is on full display here, with "Deeper Than Crying" and "It Doesn't Matter" featuring her on violas, adding a new voice to Union Station's sound. But the lead vocals are passed around among Krauss, mandolinist Adam Steffey, guitarist Dan Tyminski, and banjoist Ron Block, while Krauss' fiddle work in a backup capacity is an integral part of the sound as well. All in all, this is a totally un-gimmicky album that flies in the face of what usually happens when mainstream success comes calling. And, as a result of that commitment to quality and musical focus, one that makes you want to play it again when it's all over.

Cub Koda

Forget About It
August 1999, Rounder

Alison Krauss gets introspective and personal on her seventh album, one of her solo outings that shoves Union Station in the background while conventional country steps up to the spotlight. But Krauss is a little too sharp for Nashville standard, so *Forget About It* sounds more like an adult pop album with occasional notes of country grace. Unfortunately, the material here isn't very inspired (despite a dip into the Todd Rundgren songbook and the fine title tune), and Krauss herself has a hard time elevating it. Still, her fragile, angelic voice is capable of working wonders, which it often does with even the weakest of songs. A marginal effort.

Michael Gallucci

Lonely Runs Both Ways
November 2004, Rounder

Alison Krauss & Union Station continue their winning streak on the aptly titled *Lonely Runs Both Ways*. While they have in some part grown away from their earthy, rollicking bluegrass roots, they've been able to craft a really polished and honest-sounding brand of mid-American adult contemporary that never dips into the schlockiness of mainstream AC or the formula-driven sound of young country. Instead, Krauss, co-songwriter Dan Tyminski, and the Station dig deep into the classic themes of rural American music, polishing them with terrific production, the finest instrumentation, and two of the best voices around. *Lonely Runs Both Ways* shifts back and forth between Krauss' angelic love songs and Tyminski's earthier tales of rain, roads, and rivers, with one blazing Jerry Douglas-led instrumental entitled "Unionhouse Branch." Banjo player Ron Block takes a vocal turn on his own "I Don't Have to Live This Way," but allows Krauss to take vocal lead on another of his songs (and the album's highlight), "A Living Prayer." This gentle lullaby rocks the album to sleep with its light instrumentation and quietly soaring vocals, appropriately putting the ribbon on the whole tidy package. Although bluegrass purists may long for the days when Krauss rosined up her fiddle with the Cox Family, the pure beauty and craftsmanship of Alison Krauss & Union Station's more commercial sound is undeniable, and somehow they manage to avoid sounding slick and formulaic, still retaining the spark of honesty that seems to be missing from the recordings of so many of their contemporaries. While the group made plenty of longtime fans nervous with its sexed-up 2001 release, *New Favorite*, *Lonely Runs Both Ways* should reinstill their faith in the fact that this band is far and away the best contemporary bluegrass act recording today.

Zac Johnson

Miranda Lambert

Kerosene
March 2005, Epic

It's arguable that Miranda Lambert's debut album, *Kerosene*, is the first true Nashville product produced in the wake of Gretchen Wilson, crafted with an eye on the audience that Wilson's stylized redneck raunch won. Of course, with her golden blonde hair and good looks, Lambert seems like she would be crushed by the rampaging Gretchen, and there's a certain truth that Miranda is a bit fabricated and polished. After all, she started out as an actress, appearing in the long-shelved Piper Perabo teen comedy *Slap Her She's French* (finally released under the lamentably tame title *She Will Have Way*), and only got a foothold in the music industry by participating in USA's countrified *American Idol* knockoff, *Nashville Star*, where she placed in the top three. All this suggests that Lambert will be as slickly packaged as, say, a Southern Diana DeGarmo, but pop music works in mysterious ways: as it turns out, Lambert wrote all of the tunes on her debut, whereas the seemingly more genuine Wilson only wrote about half. That said, *Kerosene* lacks the gonzo humor that Big & Rich brought to *Here for the Party*, and Lambert's sweet girlish voice seems too tame for some of the livelier material. But that's not to say that those tunes don't work as well as the gentler pop tunes (the ballads tend to be a little treacly and nondescript), all of which are sturdily written, delivered with conviction, and given just enough gloss for an appealing sheen. Against all odds, this a rarity in modern mainstream country: a piece of product that's friendly, tuneful, sharper, and more genuine than it initially seems. Maybe Miranda needed a show like to *Nashville Star* to jump-start her career, but the show gave her the opportunity to make this thoroughly winning debut.

Stephen Thomas Erlewine

Crazy Ex-Girlfriend
May 2007, Columbia Nashville

Miranda Lambert didn't win the first *Nashville Star* in 2003, but she sure is the first bona fide star the televised music competition has produced, as her stellar 2007 sophomore album, *Crazy Ex-Girlfriend*, proves beyond a shadow of a doubt. Taking her cue from the vengeful spurned woman of "Kerosene," her hit debut single, Lambert has built her second album around a tough-chick persona, something that may be clear from the very title of the album, but this isn't a one-dimensional record by any stretch. Sure, she plays the crazy ex-girlfriend of the title track—stalking her beau and his new girl to the local bar, which she promptly starts tearing apart—but that's hardly the extent of her hell-raising here. She takes righteous revenge on a guy who slapped her around on the rocking opener, "Gunpowder and Lead" ("he wants a fight, well now he's got one"), she's stranded without booze in a "Dry Town," and she breaks hearts left and right on the surging, hard-edged "Down," while she searches in vain for

a good fling on "Guilty in Here," where she wonders what became of "all the boys that only want one thing." That line reveals that Lambert has a sly sense of humor, but she's not joking around: these are lean, hard-hitting, tuneful country songs, delivered with a classic outlaw strut and a vicious modern punch. If Lambert has a thin, almost girlish voice, she's hardly girly—there's an edge to her delivery that leaves no doubt that she possess nerves of steel. But for as strong as she sounds on the plentiful rockers here, Lambert also lets her guard down on *Crazy Ex-Girlfriend*, as she as she soaks her "Love Letters" with tears, sweetly sighs in "Desperation," and sadly wishes she was "More Like Her" as she looks on as her ex-lover returns to his old love. This last song provides a neat flip side to the rampaging title track, which also hints at this album's complexity. There are songs that are larger than life, songs that are achingly intimate, and they all add up to rich artistic statement of purpose that is also a hell of a lot of fun. Miranda Lambert knows exactly who she is as a musician, and nowhere is that clearer than how the three covers here—Gillian Welch co-wrote "Dry Town," Carlene Carter and Susanna Clark penned "Easy from Now On" (which Emmylou Harris popularized), and Patty Griffin authored "Getting Ready" (also heard on her own 2007 album, *Children Running Through*)—blend seamlessly with Lambert's eight originals. Every one of the 11 songs shares the same spirit and Lambert's is strong enough of a writer to hold her own with such heavy-hitters, possessed with a wry wit and clear eye for little details, mining the unexpected from such familiar subjects as love and loss and jealously and rage. *Crazy Ex-Girlfriend* would have been impressive if it was just a showcase of her strengths as a singer or as a songwriter, but since it is both, it's simply stunning, a breakthrough for Lambert and one of the best albums of 2007, regardless of genre.

Stephen Thomas Erlewine

k.d. lang

Angel with a Lariat
1987, Sire

k.d. lang's first major-label album (and debut American release) was a bit of a switch from the polished retro-country of her best-known work; with Dave Edmunds in the producer's chair, *Angel with a Lariat* often sounds more like rockabilly or roots rock than classic C&W, with a big, snappy drum sound, plenty of guitars mixed upfront, and lots of slapback of lang's vocals (a production decision lang mentioned with little enthusiasm several years after the album came out). "Turn Me Around" and "High Time for a Detour" rock significantly harder than most of lang's body of work, and "Watch Your Step Polka," "Diet of Strange Places," and "Tune Into My Wave" find lang and her band (who are in fine form throughout) indulging her sly sense of humor, which tended to get lost in the shuffle on later albums such as *Ingénue*. While the production and arrangements tend not to focus on the subtleties of lang's voice (with the exception of the weepy closer, "Three Cigarettes in an Ashtray"), she's one heck of a belter on this set, with a set of pipes as big as all outdoors. And the cover of the old Lynn Anderson chestnut "Rose Garden" actually tops the original. Fast, fresh, and funny, *Angel with a Lariat* may not be k.d. lang's best album, but it's probably the best one to put on at a party—it's got a good beat, and you can dance to it.

Mark Deming

Shadowland
1988, Sire

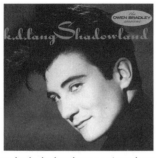

On her first two albums, k.d. lang took a witty and playful approach to the sounds and traditions of classic country music, and while it was obvious she truly loved the music, she also seemed to be having a bit of fun at its expense at the same time. But in 1988, lang proved beyond a doubt that she was serious about country (as well as her own talent) with *Shadowland*, an homage to the polished countrypolitan sounds of the 1950s and '60s that was produced by Owen Bradley, the iconic Nashville producer who was behind the controls for many of Patsy Cline's most memorable recordings. lang herself sought out Bradley to work on the album, and luring him out of retirement proved to be a masterstroke; rather than try to re-create the lush textures and deep atmosphere of Bradley's sides for Cline or Brenda Lee herself, lang went to the source, and Bradley gave her studio settings that referenced his work during Nashville's golden era while adding an ever-so-slight contemporary sheen. Bradley also brought aboard an all-star crew of legendary Nashville studio hands and invited Loretta Lynn, Brenda Lee, and Kitty Wells to sing with lang on the closing "Honky Tonk Angels' Medley." In the hands of many artists, this sort of project might have been an exercise in misplaced, nostalgic fandom, but on *Shadowland*, lang taps into the sound and style of her most vital musical influences while at the same time putting her stamp on the music—this isn't k.d. lang trying to be Patsy Cline, but rather lang demonstrating what she learned from Cline and where those lessons took her. lang's lush, expressive voice has rarely sounded better or more emotionally powerful than it does on *Shadowland*, and it presents her meeting the cream of Nashville's greatest era not as a wide-eyed acolyte, but as a gifted artist collaborating on equal terms. It's a magnificent achievement.

Mark Deming

Absolute Torch and Twang
1989, Sire

Absolute Torch and Twang was the last bona fide country album of k.d. lang's career, and while external circumstances may have forced her hand in exploring other musical avenues, this set suggests she may have already been headed that way. *Absolute Torch and Twang* is the definitive statement of lang's country period; by this time, she'd moved past the slightly kitschy Patsy Cline homages of her earliest work and developed a strong musical personality of her own, using her rich and supple voice to approach material both witty and heartfelt. lang's collaboration with producer and songwriter Ben Mink was reaching its peak as well, with the performances and arrangements hitting a superb grace

note between polish and passion. lang's songwriting had matured, most notably on "Nowhere to Stand," a powerful number about child abuse, and she'd developed a knack for writing about misfits, both defiant and otherwise; as a Canadian lesbian vegetarian performance artist trying to work within mainstream country music, you have to know her heart was with the heroines of "Big Boned Gal" and "Wallflower Waltz." And while lang had embraced vintage countrypolitan sounds on *Shadowland*, *Absolute Torch and Twang* found her bridging a gap between Cline-style balladry and polished lounge styles on "Trail of Broken Hearts" and "Pullin' Back the Reins," and finding a comfortable home in the middle ground. While some fans were disappointed when lang retreated from country music on her next album, *Ingénue*, it's hard to imagine her (or anyone else) topping an album quite as strong as *Absolute Torch and Twang*.

Mark Deming

Blaine Larsen

Off to Join the World
January 2005, BNA

Looking at the cover of Blaine Larsen's 2005 major-label debut *Off to Join the World*—which is a reconfigured version of his first album, *In My High School*, released on an indie about six months before *Off*—it's easy to think that the youthful, clean-cut singer is about 14-years-old, a cloying novelty along the lines of Billy Gilman. First impressions are often misleading, as the music on this lean 11-track album makes clear. Larsen possesses a rich, full baritone reminiscent of his idol George Strait—a sound that sure shouldn't be coming from a kid who looks like he's yet to learn how to shave. Preternaturally gifted youngsters are not uncommon in country music—for instance, LeAnn Rimes came storming on to the scene at the age of 14, sounding like a dead ringer for Patsy Cline, and Tanya Tucker started her career when she was 13—but often the raw talent isn't yet supported by technique. That's not the case with Larsen. He knows how to deliver a song, whether it's ramping up the sentiment or slyly tossing off a punchline, which is something that does not come easily to young singers, as any regular viewer of *American Idol* can attest. Larsen not only has that technique down, but he has excellent taste, sticking to the straight-ahead neo-traditionalist country that made Strait a star, writing and picking hooky, memorable songs. Some of these tunes have more than their fair share of country corn, but they're so unapologetic and spirited, they're quite charming, as is the whole of *Off to Join the World*. Blaine Larsen may not have quite yet broken free of his influences on this debut, but he sounds as if he's absorbed their lessons, beginning to turn what he's learned from Strait, Alan Jackson and Merle Haggard into something of his own, both as a vocalist and a fledgling songwriter (he's penned just over half of the songs here, and there's not a bad tune in the bunch). In the process, he's delivered a terrific debut album, one that qualifies as a totally unexpected and wholly enjoyable surprise.

Stephen Thomas Erlewine

Rockin' You Tonight
June 2006, BNA

Excellent though it may have been, Blaine Larsen's 2005 major-label debut, *Off to Join the World*, didn't sell in the numbers it deserved, so when it came time for Larsen to record a second album, he got a slight makeover to make his surprisingly authentic classic country a little more modern—something that would appeal if not to fans also in their teens, at least to those adults who regularly buy country albums. As such, *Rockin' You Tonight* has a bit more Nashville polish on it, from its production to the song selection, a move that's understandable even if it may be slightly dismaying to fans of the sturdy neo-traditionalism of the debut. That said, Larsen isn't merely a preternaturally gifted country singer/songwriter, he's also enough of a pro to be able to roll through these changes without losing his identity; he makes the concessions to Nashville not seem like concessions. Plus, to the extent that these concessions are noticeable, it's only in comparison: on *Off to Join the World* there were none, so the few that are here stand out all the more. Remove this handful of songs and *Rockin' You Tonight* is as purely country as its predecessor, and just as impressive.

Stephen Thomas Erlewine

Tracy Lawrence

Time Marches On
January 1996, Atlantic

Tracy Lawrence's *Time Marches On*, the singer's fourth album, is another crowd-pleasing set of contemporary country. Like his previous albums, the song selection is a hit-or-miss affair, with about half of the songs failing to make much of an impression. The remainder, however, proves why Lawrence is one of the most popular singers in Nashville.

Stephen Thomas Erlewine

Coast Is Clear
March 1997, Atlantic

The Coast Is Clear again demonstrates that Tracy Lawrence was one of the finest new honky tonkers of the '90s. Lawrence can wring tremendous emotion out of a song, adding nuances that give each line heart-tugging resonance. Unfortunately, his material is not the equal of his talent. Although there are bright spots, such as "Livin' in Black and White," about half of the record is saddled with pedestrian material performed without style. Try as he may, Lawrence cannot bring material of this level to life. Still, *The Coast Is Clear* remains a winning record, since Lawrence sings well no matter what the material, and when he is given a good song, the results are first-rate.

Thom Owens

Strong
March 2004, DreamWorks

Although the album is called *Strong*, Tracy Lawrence sure isn't afraid to show his soft side on his eighth studio album and his first for DreamWorks after spending his career at Atlantic. Lawrence has never been among the most adventurous country singers and of all the post-Garth Brooks new traditionalists, he often avoids honky tonk grit, even though he has a nice twang in his voice that would work well on rowdier material. Nevertheless, *Strong* still ranks among his smoothest albums, a record dominated by ballads and where up-tempo songs are as polished as the slow ones. Not that this is a bad thing, since Lawrence does this kind of music well. There isn't as much musical variety as there is on a Kenny Chesney record, as it is divided between earnest heartache ballads, anthemic mid-tempo numbers, and the occasional mildly rock up-tempo tune. A few of these songs stand out—the sentimental single "Paint Me a Birmingham," the honky tonk dance of "Sawdust on Her Halo," the gently

insistent opener "It's All How You Look at It"—but more than anything, this album is of a piece, a collection of professionally crafted, no-frills modern country with an adult contemporary bent. While it doesn't stand apart from the pack, either from Lawrence's other albums or those of his peers, it's a sturdy record, sure to satisfy anyone who's enjoyed his other albums.

Stephen Thomas Erlewine

The Very Best of Tracy Lawrence
July 2007, Atlantic/Rhino

History may indeed be kinder to Tracy Lawrence than anyone thought. Sure, there are the eight million albums, and seven number one singles in the country charts, but while Garth Brooks and Clint Black are considered legends, Lawrence would seem to be forgotten by all but the most faithful. Truth is, Lawrence is a better—and purer—country singer than both put together. It seems that no less than an authority than Rhino Records, *the* gold standard in reissues, sees that too. This massive 21-cut collection documents his biggest selling years at Atlantic beginning with 1991's *Sticks and Stones*, and continues through his 2003 DreamWorks release *Strong*. The singles are all here, but it goes deeper than that. There are four cuts each from *Sticks and Stones*, *Alibis*, *I See It Now*, and *Time Marches On*. From 1991–1993, Lawrence was always near the top of the charts either with singles or albums. That's an excellent run. That the industry in Nashville moved away from neo-traditionalism and toward pop and rock has no bearing on the quality of his work; indeed, 2007's *For the Love*, released on the tiny Rocky Comfort imprint, stands with his best material. The time is right for this kind of retrospective, where listeners can encounter a modern version of a real country singer. In addition to more than an hour's worth of great music, Melinda Newman's liner notes are exhaustive and engaging, adding to the true definitive nature of this collection.

Thom Jurek

Shannon Lawson

Chase the Sun
June 2002, MCA

Imagine if some mad scientist working for the Nashville office of a major record label created a cross between Marty Stuart and Mark McGrath, and you start to get an idea of what to expect from Shannon Lawson. Lawson shares Stuart's fondness for both traditional country flavors and up-tempo rock & roll, and like McGrath he's a high-attitude bad-boy type with the kind of photogenically unruly hair that's all the rage with marketing departments. Trouble is, judging from Lawson's debut album, *Chase the Sun*, Lawson falls short of Marty Stuart's chops and good taste; while his guitar and mandolin work are pretty good, his rock influences are strictly by-the-numbers, especially on the high-bombast "Who's Your Daddy" (which the overly polished production from Mark Wright only emphasizes), and his honky tonk and bluegrass gestures are neither strong nor original enough to make more than a surface impact (and no matter what Lawson thinks, his acoustic version of Marvin Gaye's "Let's Get It On" is a fun idea, but it sure ain't bluegrass). And while Lawson's pipes are at least as good as Mark McGrath's, he lacks Mr. Sugar Ray's sly humor and easy (if hardly earth-shaking) grasp of musical eclecticism (which, given Lawson's attempted genre-hopping, would help a lot). And as a songwriter, Shannon Lawson suggests he has potential on several tunes here, but never enough to overcome his habit of wandering into clichés. *Chase the Sun* proves that Shannon Lawson has talent, but also suggests he got his record deal because he's easy to market rather than being better than his competition; maybe if this is a hit, listeners will get to hear a stronger and leaner presentation of his style in the future.

Mark Deming

Chris LeDoux

Whatcha Gonna Do with a Cowboy
July 1992, Capitol

Brooks helps out his new friend again by joining him for a duet on the title cut, and LeDoux flashes more of his own personality and gritty charm.

Michael McCall

20 Originals: The Early Years
June 2004, Capitol

Chris LeDoux didn't start having hit singles until the early '90s, 20 years after he began his recording career. Capitol's 2004 compilation *20 Originals: The Early Years* is the best retrospective yet of those pre-hit years, collecting a variety of highlights cut between 1973 and 1986. While LeDoux's aesthetic never changed over the years—he was always devoted to being a modern-day cowboy, loving to celebrate rodeos—the sound of his music changed over the years, melding into production styles of the time. That's why these recordings, largely taken from the outlaw '70s where fuzz guitars battled with twangy Telecasters, are so much fun—they're raw and rowdy, arguably the music that best sums up his attitude. So, while you won't find hits on *20 Originals*, you will find some of LeDoux's best music on a collection that is likely the best overview of his formative years yet assembled.

Stephen Thomas Erlewine

Anthology, Vol. 1
August 2005, EMI

As the title may suggest, 2005's *Anthology, Vol. 1* isn't necessarily a greatest-hits collection—it does have two charting hits from Chris LeDoux, specifically 1992's "Workin' Man's Dollar" and 1999's "Life Is a Highway," but this doesn't have as many hits as Capitol's 1999 collection, *20 Greatest Hits*, nor does it have the great majority of his charting

singles from the '80s and '90s. Instead, *Anthology, Vol. 1* should be considered a sampler of LeDoux's '90s work for Liberty and its parent company, Capitol. There's a rare track in the opener, "Airborne Cowboy," but this is primarily a collection of album tracks, and while it doesn't necessarily contain LeDoux's most familiar work, it does contain a good sampling of his best latter-day work, making it a nice sampler for the curious and casual fan. (Although it has to be said that it would have been nice if there were liner notes explaining why each particularly track was included, nevertheless it's a good, entertaining comp.)

Stephen Thomas Erlewine

Little Big Town

Little Big Town
May 2002, Monument

Little Big Town is a vocal quartet consisting of two men and two women who sing their songs by mixing up lead vocals and harmonies, such that one may start a song only to have another take the second verse, while some other combination sings the choruses. This, of course, is not typical of country music, nor are the song arrangements, which lean heavily to a folk-rock sound with prominent acoustic guitars and rhythm section, but only touches of fiddle and steel guitar; nor, for that matter, are the songs themselves, most of them written by the group members, which tend toward a pop sensibility with their generalized romantic sentiments. In the inevitable game of describing a new act by its antecedents, one must throw out names like Fleetwood Mac rather than any specifically country artists. Actually, Little Big Town does call to mind certain country acts of the past, though not prominent ones. They may remind knowledgeable country fans of such late '80s performers as Foster & Lloyd and Kennedy Rose, duos that earned critical kudos (especially from non-country critics), but struggled to earn a commercial footing and ultimately found greater success behind the scenes as writers. Championed by Monument Records, the same label that changed the parameters of conventional country success with the Dixie Chicks, Little Big Town may succeed by re-writing the Nashville rule book in a similar way. But probably not. The Dixie Chicks had great songs, a powerful image, and an undeniable connection to hardcore country. Little Big Town does not have great songs, their image is diffuse, and they seem ready to cross over to pop at any minute. At least on their first album, the group is more a concept than a fully formed entity, which will make revolutionizing country music a challenge.

William Ruhlmann

The Road to Here
October 2005, Equity Music Group

Little Big Town has undergone adversity since its self-titled debut album, released by Sony's Monument Records, barely reached the country Top 40 in 2002 behind the chart singles "Don't Waste My Time" and "Everything Changes." For one thing, that sales performance was not enough to keep Monument from dropping the group. Then, group member Kimberly Roads' husband passed away, an event marked by the plaintive ballad "Lost." Two other members were divorced. No wonder, then, that it has taken them more than three years to bounce back with their second album, issued by the Nashville independent label Equity Music Group. Whether it's those troubles or just the passage of time, however, Little Big Town has improved significantly since that debut disc.

Before, they seemed more an idea than a band—two male and two female singer/songwriters whose style seemed as much influenced by '70s Southern California soft rock as by any country performers. That influence hasn't changed, really; you can't listen to "Bones," for example, without thinking of Fleetwood Mac's "The Chain." But the group's sound has become tighter, more focused, and more distinctive. Maybe it's experience, maybe it's the absence of the powers-that-were at Monument, and maybe it's the presence of co-producer, co-songwriter, and multi-instrumentalist Wayne Kirkpatrick (the CCM artist who is the co-author of the Grammy-winning Eric Clapton hit "Change the World," among many other songs). Kirkpatrick has taken the group under his wing and overseen a record full of songs arranged to showcase the four lead vocalists in varying solos and harmony parts, backed up by roots-country instrumental tracks dominated by acoustic guitar, mandolin, and Dobro. The initial result was a Top 20 country hit with "Boondocks," which has something of a Montgomery Gentry feel to it. There's more of that sort of thing on the album, particularly in the songs written by the band with Kirkpatrick, but they still have a weakness for stringing clichés together ("This monkey on my back/Has stopped me in my tracks," goes a couplet in "Wounded"). The best songs are actually ones Kirkpatrick wrote with others and brought to the project, particularly "Live with Lonesome" and the novelty "Welcome to the Family." But even when the material is not top-drawer, the performances are, making this the album Little Big Town had in it and didn't manage to get out the first time around.

William Ruhlmann

Little Texas

Kick a Little
1994, Warner Bros.

Super country group Little Texas certainly gives country music a little kick with this 1994 album, *Kick a Little*. There are ten tracks on this recording, and not a dud in the mix. Little Texas seems to be proving good at making big hits. Many of the songs on *Kick a Little* are rowdy and filled with attitude, including the title track, "Kick a Little," "Your Days Are Numbered," and "Red Neck Like Me." There are a couple of kind of sedate numbers here to be had as well, such as "Inside" and "Southern Grace." By the time this album was finished, Little Texas had already landed three number one hits from their second album and earned Vocal Group of the Year honors at the Academy of Country Music Awards. Members of this group are Dwayne O'Brien, Duane Propes, Tim Rushlow, Del Gray, Porter Howell, and Brady Seals.

Charlotte Dillon

Greatest Hits [Warner Bros.]
October 1995, Warner Bros.

At 12 tracks, *Greatest Hits* may be a little brief, but this 1995 collection (later repackaged and reissued by Warner in 2007) contains all of Little Texas' big hits—including "God Blessed Texas," "You and Forever and Me," "Amy's Back in Austin," and "First Time for Everything"—making this a good, accurate overview of the band at its popular peak in the early '90s.

Stephen Thomas Erlewine

Little Texas
April 1997, Warner Bros.

It took Little Texas three years to deliver the follow-up to *Kick a Little*, but it was worth the wait. Entitled *Little Texas*, the album demonstrates the band's continued improvement. Not only is the songwriting stronger and more melodic than before, but the performances are tighter and more effective, making the record one of their best.

Thom Owens

The Little Willies

The Little Willies
March 2006, Milking Bull

The Little Willies could be called a supergroup if they had more than one star in their lineup. Instead, the quintet is a group of five New York musicians—highlighted by pianist/vocalist Norah Jones, but also featuring her regular bassist Lee Alexander, guitarist/vocalist Richard Julian, guitarist Jim Campilongo, and drummer Dan Rieser—who originally came together to play a one-shot gig in 2003 at *the Living Room*, and soon came to play the venue regularly, which eventually led to an eponymous album released in March of 2006. It's a casual, appealing collection of country covers, spiked with four originals from various members of the band. It's so relaxed and low-key that it could be argued that *The Little Willies* wouldn't garner much attention if it weren't for that one star in its midst, Norah Jones, who became a superstar in part because her 2002 debut, *Come Away with Me*, recalled the mellow, burnished vibe of classic singer/songwriter albums from the '70s. A big part of that sound was built on country-rock and both of Jones' albums had an undercurrent of country, so the honky tonk and Western swing stylings of the Little Willies aren't a big stretch for her. In fact, their album has an intimate, relaxed feel reminiscent of the nightclub aura of *Come Away with Me*, but that shouldn't suggest that Jones is the star here. If anything, the Little Willies are led by Richard Julian, an N.Y.C.-based singer/songwriter who has released four albums since 1997. He not only takes lead vocals on just as many songs as Jones, but he has a hand in three of the four originals (the Jones-sung "It's Not You It's Me," "Easy as the Rain," and "Lou Reed"; the other, "Roll On," was written by Alexander, though it's also sung by Jones), all of which fit well among such standards as "Roly Poly," "I'll Never Get Out of This World Alive," "Streets of Baltimore," "Tennessee Stud," and "Night Life." But to suggest that there is a leader to the Little Willies kind of misses the point—this is a group that got together for a good time, and accordingly there's very little ego to be heard in the music itself. But where some jam sessions can veer toward the indulgent and insular, this is warm and friendly, unassuming and unpretentious, even when it gets a little jokey at the end with "Lou Reed." And while the Little Willies don't mess around with the arrangements of these familiar tunes at all—"Roly Poly" begins just like Bob Wills' original, Elvis' "Love Me" gets backing vocals patterned after the Jordanaires (and the vocalists are punningly called the Ordinaires on the back cover)—it doesn't matter, because the band is not only good, but there's a palpable sense of enjoyment in their performances that comes through even though the music is decidedly low-key. Yet that relaxed nature is the very thing that makes *The Little Willies* a gentle surprise—maybe this isn't a major record, but it's thoroughly likeable record that doesn't lose its charm on repeated plays.

Stephen Thomas Erlewine

Lonestar

From There to Here: Greatest Hits
June 2003, BNA

Greatest Hits is the first collection of Lonestar's greatest hits, released after four albums and one holiday record. Not all of their singles are here—the holiday tunes, of course, are left behind, as are smaller singles— but all the big songs are here, highlighted by "Tequila Talking," "Everything's Changed," "What About Now," "Smile," and the big crossover hit "Amazed." These tunes, along with the nine other songs that comprise this record, illustrate that even though Lonestar proudly takes its name from Texas, the band doesn't belong to that state's legacy of musical mavericks. They're a straightforward bunch, whether they're singing ballads or mid-tempo country-rockers, and even when there's plenty of twang in the voice and the guitars, the melodies are firmly in the pop-leaning country mainstream. Still, that twang counts for something—at its best, it made Lonestar's music seem rootsier, more real than many of its peers, and while it wasn't always consistent, the band did make some very good singles that may not have been the best of contemporary country in the late '90s, but captured the sound of the time well. They're all here on this fine retrospective.

Stephen Thomas Erlewine

Let's Be Us Again
May 2004, BNA

Toward the end of the '90s, Lonestar decided to move firmly into the mainstream of contemporary country, leaving behind any hardcore country influences they may have had in favor of sweet anthemic ballads and poppy country-rockers. In essence, they picked up where Alabama left off, so it's little surprise that Alabama's Randy Owen sings on "From There to Here" on the group's fifth album, *Let's Be Us Again*— he's passing the torch to this likeable bunch from Tennessee. Like Alabama, Lonestar are catchy and bright, not as concerned with keeping country as they are with hooks and tunes that keep them on the radio, and after they moved toward contemporary country with 1999's *Lonely Grill*, they have stayed near the top of the country charts. Given that success, perhaps it's inevitable that the group doesn't try much new on *Let's Be Us Again*, but they're savvy enough to pick up on some early 2000s trends, whether it's dedicating "Somebody's Someone" to "the fallen heroes" or cribbing from Kenny Chesney's island obsession on "T.G.I.F." Lonestar are at their best when they keep the tempo and the mood upbeat, and fortunately most of the album is on the faster side, which makes it more entertaining than some of their previous albums. It's also a consistent album, with only a handful of duds—such as the well-intentioned "Let Them Be Little," which sounds disarmingly close to "Let Them Belittle," as if it's an anthem for condescension—which also makes it one of their strongest records. If Lonestar don't quite have the engaging personality to truly make them an

heir to Alabama's throne, they at least are likeable and reliable, a good workingman's band, and they're at their best on *Let's Be Us Again*.

Stephen Thomas Erlewine

Patty Loveless

Honky Tonk Angel
1988, MCA

The song subjects hardly classify Loveless as a honky-tonk angel, at least by Hank Thompson's definition. But this was the album that established Loveless as a major presence, and it includes two of her biggest singles— "Chains," "Timber I'm Falling in Love"—and two of her best—"Blue Side of Town" and "Don't Toss Us Away," a duet with Rodney Crowell.

Brian Mansfield

If My Heart Had Windows
1988, MCA

Patty Loveless' second album didn't set the world on fire when it appeared in 1988, but it did contain a monster single in the title track written by Dallas Frazier. Loveless was a modern singer who sang in a true traditionalist twang. She had a mountain voice that was suited particularly well to the new wave in "neo-traditionalist country," and her producer/husband, Emory Gordy, Jr., knew exactly how to combine the two. A prime example is her reading of Steve Earle's "A Little Bit in Love," which walks the line between rockabilly and jump boogie. This is one of those great Connie Smith-styled strutters on which a honky tonk piano, steel guitar whining around the acoustic six-strings, and thumping upright bass work like a charm. Loveless has enough growl in her voice to not only get the tune across but make it her own. The tight and unobtrusive string arrangement, acoustic guitars, and bassline on an uplifting tune like "You Saved Me" offer Loveless everything she needs to dig in and wrench every ounce of gratitude out of the lyric. There are other notables here in Eric Kaz's "Once in a Lifetime" and Pat Bunch's swaggering "Baby's Gone Blues." In sum, this, like virtually every record Loveless has ever made, is worth owning if you can find it. Her integrity, down-home sincerity, and utterly stunning voice have helped to create a streak of fine recordings and chart success that continues to this day.

Thom Jurek

On Down the Line
May 1990, Universal Special Products

Patty Loveless entered the 1990s with *On Down the Line*, an excellent album that contained such major hits as "The Night's Too Long," the gutsy "Blue Memories," and the infectiously rockin' "I'm That Kind of Girl." Despite all the talk about Loveless being part of a neo-traditionalist movement in country, this isn't an album for purists—there's plenty of pop and rock influence here, and a 33-year-old Loveless is undeniably folky on the haunting ballad "Some Morning Soon." Loveless still found herself being compared frequently to Patsy Cline, who was no stranger to pop and rock elements either. Not that Loveless excludes more hard-core country—"I've Got to Stop Loving You (And Start Living Again)" is a honky tonk gem. Unpredictable and consistently inspired, *On Down the Line* remains one of Loveless' finest albums.

Alex Henderson

Only What I Feel
April 1993, Epic

Loveless underwent throat surgery and switched labels before creating this album, and both helped. She sounds stronger and more impassioned than she had in years, and her artistic drive seemed more confident and determined. "Nothin' but the Wheel" ranks with her best ballads.

Michael McCall

When Fallen Angels Fly
1994, Epic

Patty Loveless expanded on the success of her comeback album, *Only What I Feel*, on its successor, *When Fallen Angels Fly*, which made the country Top Ten, went gold, spawned four Top Ten singles, and was named the Country Music Association's Album of the Year. Songs like the feisty hit "Halfway Down" had a bouncy rockabilly feel, and Loveless rode the rhythms well, while on the ballad "Here I Am," another hit, she sounded like a country Stevie Nicks. And then there was "I Try To Think About Elvis," a comic rocker that was one of the best pieces of material to turn up in Nashville that year, and that Loveless performed with just enough tongue in her cheek. Of course, there were a couple of those hopelessly hokey Gretchen Peters ballads, but even one of those, "You Don't Even Know Who I Am," was a hit.

William Ruhlmann

Trouble with the Truth
January 1996, Epic

Having broken through at the tail-end of the neo-traditionalist trend in country in the 1980s, Patty Loveless was one of the few established artists to navigate the transition into the post-Garth pop-country trend of the '90s. *Trouble with the Truth*, her third album and the follow-up to the CMA Album of the Year *When Fallen Angels Fly*, found her again relying on her steady stable of writers—Gary Nicholson, Jim Lauderdale, Tony Arata, Matraca Berg—for another series of songs that acknowledged the country tradition of twang, yet kept to a sharp beat, and that maintained the female country sensibility of faithful loving, while avoiding victimization. "You Can Feel Bad," the album's first single and a number one hit, was a breakup song with a twist or two, while the second single, "A Thousand Times a Day," treated love as a 12-step addiction, and "I Miss Who I Was (With You)," caught a sense of regret tempered with acceptance. Some of the writing was a bit abstract, notably the title track, and there didn't seem much reason to cover Richard Thompson's up-tempo, Cajun-flavored "Tear-Stained Letter," which Jo-El Sonnier took into the Top Ten in 1988 (except, of course, that it's a great song). But *Trouble with the Truth* was a consistent collection that consolidated Loveless' prominent place in the country music scene of the mid-'90s.

William Ruhlmann

Long Stretch of Lonesome
September 1997, Epic

Patty Loveless has created one of the most consistent bodies of work within contemporary country, and *Long Stretch of Lonesome* does nothing to erase the notion that she is one of the finest singers of the '90s. Stylistically, there isn't much difference between *Long Stretch of Lonesome* and her other records, but the key to its success is Loveless' unerring knack for picking the right material. Usually, contemporary country albums have a few hit singles surrounded by filler, but with any Loveless album, you can expect consistently excellent material, and this is no exception.

Thom Owens

Classics
March 1999, Epic

As expected, Patty Loveless's second hits compilation, covering her first five years on Epic Records, was even better than her earlier *Greatest Hits* on MCA, showing off a more confident singer who rocked out convincingly and was comfortable on weepy ballads, even if the latter tended not to be the best compositions she got to sing. Typical of country hits collections, this one was on the skimpy side, containing only 12 tracks, and typical of nearly all contemporary hits collections, it failed to contain all the hits while tossing in a few new songs. The most serious omission was "Halfway Down." But Loveless's biggest hits of the era, "You Can Feel Bad," "Lonely Too Long," and "Blame It On Your Heart" were included, and there was enough here to justify all those Female Vocalist of the Year awards she won during the half-decade. At the same time, the selection reflected the recent downturn in the singer's fortunes, containing nothing from the commercially disappointing 1997 album *Long Stretch of Lonesome*. As so many hits collections do, this one seemed a summing up that confirmed the artist's past triumphs, while she herself stood at a crossroads.

William Ruhlmann

Strong Heart
August 2000, Epic

"I tell you what, we're in a rut," Patty Loveless sang in "That's the Kind of Mood I'm In," the single released in May 2000 in advance of her tenth album, *Strong Heart*, which followed in August. The song, a plea from one lover to another to shake up a stale romance, also worked as an unintended metaphor for Loveless' career, as the 43-year-old, who had enjoyed widespread success in country music from the late '80s to the mid-'90s, struggled to stand up to a newly pop-oriented Nashville. "That's the Kind of Mood I'm In" bowed somewhat to Faith Hill's approach, though (to its credit) it ended up sounding more Cajun than crossover, but by the time *Strong Heart* was released it had only gotten into the lower reaches of the country Top 40, not boding well for the album's commercial prospects. Even so, it turns out to be another well-balanced set of songs from a singer who can give effective performances in a variety of styles and tempos. The most impressive harder-rocking tunes are "You Don't Get No More," which sounds like a ZZ Top song, and the bluesy "The Key of Love," songs you can imagine Loveless singing in a roadhouse on a Saturday night. The chaste ballads "My Heart Will Never Break This Way Again" and "Thirsty" (the latter featuring Travis Tritt on harmony vocals) sound like singles, but the song that cries out to be a country hit is "She Never Stopped Loving Him," one of those big, sentimental, string-filled country ballads that ends in the cemetery. True to form, Loveless and Gordy somewhat underplay it, when this kind of tearjerker should be done all out or not at all. At any rate, *Strong Heart* is a worthy addition to her catalog.

William Ruhlmann

Mountain Soul
June 2001, Epic

A 180-degree departure from contemporary commercial country music, album number six from the always dynamic Loveless is like a breath of fresh air on a steamy summer afternoon. *Mountain Soul* is a rare and brilliant acoustic 14-track album of bluegrass mountain music. Amidst the mandolins, fiddles, and banjos is Loveless' harking alto voice, singing from her soul to the music she grew up with. Just when you thought the days of Lester Flatt, Earl Scruggs, Bill Monroe, and the Stanley Brothers were gone, Loveless brings them back with new life and staggering grace. Rounding out this ubiquitous collection are soft-singing collaborators Travis Tritt, Ricky Skaggs, and Rebecca Lynn Howard.

Maria Konicki Dinoia

On Your Way Home
September 2003, Epic

Who says country music is dead? Patty Loveless and her producer, husband Emory Gordy, Jr. obviously don't give a damn about what's popular in the morally reprehensible and artistically bankrupt world of Nash Vegas (anti)culture this week. *On Your Way Home* picks up where the rootsy heart of Loveless' awesome *Mountain Soul* left off—with a solid, emotionally moving, honestly delivered set of honest-to-God country songs written by fine contemporary songwriters. These 11 songs lend a glimmering hope that the major labels in the heart of the beast of modern country haven't been totally swallowed by aesthetic greedy blindness. The album opens with "Draggin' My Heart Around," by Paul Kennerley and Marty Stuart, full of guitars—both acoustic and electric, caressed by a lonesome fiddle and pedal steel, and a honky tonk two-step

rhythm. The tale is classic, about a man doing his woman wrong and the woman in near despair, but the delivery is up-tempo and defiant. The old folksy mountain groan that opens "Nothin' but the Lonely," a seemingly transformed old fiddle tune, takes the listener back to a time out of space, a color out of time, a place where the song revealed someone's truth. Not their production values. And then there's that sheen of country boogie and rockabilly in the Al Anderson/Gary Nicholson/Jessie Alexander-penned "I Wanna Believe," driven as much by a pair of fiddles as an electric guitar and a subtle double-time beat. As for ballads, like the title track, leave it to Matraca Berg and whomever she happens to be writing with—in this case the wonderful Ronnie Samoset—to deliver the consummate broken yet determined break-up song every time. In Loveless' voice, this song is an issue of profound truth for the protagonist; she is the one waiting up for the lies and excuses. In fact, in each of these songs Loveless offers everyday life as episodic revelation and epiphany. Her voice is a full million miles deep, full of mystery, pathos, and a hard-won tenderness. Nowhere is this more evident than in Roger Brown's Celtic-flavored country waltz "Born Again Fool." Here Loveless is the storyteller, offering both empathy and plainspoken wisdom about a man who actually believes a woman can save him from himself. There is no "I told you so" doublespeak here, and both people in the tale contain elements of victimization and perpetration. The shuffling honky tonk of "Lookin' for a Heartache"—written by Jim Lauderdale with Buddy and Julie Miller—swings with pure Texas aplomb. Likewise, Rodney Crowell's "Lovin' All Night" is shuffling, scuffling rootsy rock & roll disguised as up-tempo honky tonk. The final song on the disc, "The Grandpa I Know," is caressed by a dobro and mandolins and falls like a prayer from Loveless' mouth. Turning away from the shell left by a recently departed loved one is disregarded in favor of vibrant, reverent memory. In a lesser singer's voice, this cut might seem corny or superficial; in that loose, untamable grain in Loveless' instrument, it is an epitaph that holds the story of an entire life. Ultimately, *On Your Way Home* is further proof that in her mid-40s, Loveless is a singer who has just reached the pinnacle of musical and artistic greatness she has worked so hard for and has become a vocalist entitled to a legacy in the rich lineage of historic country music. It's alive and well in her care.

Thom Jurek

The Definitive Collection
June 2005, MCA Nashville

MCA's 2005 release *The Definitive Collection* runs a generous 22 tracks, mostly taken from Patty Loveless' time at the label in the second half of the '80s, although there are a couple of mid-'90s hits she had on Epic tacked on to the end for good measure ("You Can Feel Bad," "Lonely Too Long"). While this misses many of her biggest hits from the early '90s—they were all recorded for Epic and fall outside of the licensing restrictions—this nevertheless is the most generous and thorough Loveless compilation yet assembled, containing the great majority of her big hits for MCA and enough of a teaser with her '90s work to suggest the arc of her carer. Until there's a collection that balances the two labels in equal measure, *The Definitive Collection* will stand as the best Loveless overview.

Stephen Thomas Erlewine

Dreamin' My Dreams
August 2005, Epic

Patty Loveless breaks the Nash Vegas mold. She's living proof that talent—God-given and well-tended—is enough to keep listeners' attention over the years. Loveless worked hard to get where she is by consistently offering solid records, full of fine material and passionate, true performances. *Dreamin' My Dreams* is no exception, in fact;, it may be a crowning achievement in a career full of them. Produced by husband Emory Gordy and Justin Niebank, the set features 12 tracks by writers as diverse as Richard Thompson (the stunning, rocking opener "Keep Your Distance"), Steve Earle (a fine reading of "My Old Friend the Blues"), Allen Reynolds (the wonderful title track), Delaney Bramlett ("Never Ending Song of Love" with Dwight Yoakam as a duet partner), and Gordy (who wrote "Big Chance" with Loveless and "When I Reach the Place I'm Going" with Joe Henry), just to mention a few. Players include guitar slinger Albert Lee and fiddle ace Stuart Duncan. This is an adventurous outing for the likes of Music City. But Loveless has a track record that demands she get to take chances. Her voice (which gets better with age) never strays from the heart and soul of country music's grand tradition. The ballads here (such as "Nobody Here by That Name" or "When Being Who You Are Is Not Enough," by Jim Lauderdale and Leslie Satcher) are otherworldly; the rockers, such as Delbert McClinton's "Same Kind of Crazy" and Thompson's tune, strut, swagger, and dig deep into the basics of love and loss. Ultimately, the sheer range of sounds, emotions, and the integrity of Loveless' voice make *Dreamin' My Dreams* a candidate for country album of the year.

Thom Jurek

Lyle Lovett

Lyle Lovett
1986, Curb

While Lyle Lovett's debut album is easily the closest he's ever come to making a straight country disc, right out of the box Lovett made it clear he was an eccentric in the great Texas tradition, and rather than sounding like the new boy in Nashville, he presented himself as the odd but likable distant relative of Guy Clark and Jesse Winchester. While "This Old Porch" and "If I Were the Man You Wanted" proved he could write a sincere and affecting song as well as anyone, they also made clear that he wasn't cut out for Nashville-style radio-ready singles, while the ironic "Cowboy Man" and the wickedly cynical cheating song "God Will" proved Lovett possessed a genius for taking traditional formulas and giving them a hard twist. The jazzy sway of "An Acceptable Level of Ecstasy (The Wedding Song)" offers a witty and engaging preview of the blues-flavored sound Lovett would hone on later album, and in this context the tunefully obsessive "You Can't Resist It" sounds like the great pop hit he never had. While under Tony Brown's production (and with a team of Nashville session vets backing him up) some of the sharper edges of Lovett's musical personality were smoothed down, Lovett's reedy but soulful voice shines through, and a casual listen confirms that Lovett's music was just as strong as his lyrics. Along with Steve Earle's *Guitar Town*, *Lyle Lovett* was one of the most

promising and exciting debut albums to come out of Nashville in the 1980s, and like Earle's album, this set a high bar for what would become an exciting and idiosyncratic career, proving first-rank singer/songwriters didn't just come from New York or Los Angeles.

Mark Deming

Pontiac
1987, Curb

While Lyle Lovett's self-titled debut album made it clear he was one the most gifted and idiosyncratic talents to emerge in country music in the 1980s, his follow-up, 1987's *Pontiac*, took the strengths of his first disc and refined them, and the result was a set whose sound and feel more accurately reflected Lovett's musical personality. While much of *Pontiac* favors the country side of Lovett's musical personality, the bouncy swing of "Give Back My Heart" and the weepy stroll of "Walk Through the Bottomland" have a lighter touch that suits them noticeably better than the stiffer production and arrangements of the first album, while the breezy snap of "L.A. County" serves as a perfect contrast to the tune's violent dénouement. The second half of the album gives Lovett a chance to indulge his fondness for jazz and blues flavors on the cynical "She's No Lady," "M-O-N-E-Y," and "She's Hot to Go," and if Lovett would follow this path with great musical success on his next few albums, he was already traveling in the right direction and the songs and the arrangements are aces. And it's all but impossible to imagine anyone being given a big push by a major label in Nashville who could get away with the fanciful whimsy of "If I Had a Boat" and the stark and unsettling character sketch of "Pontiac" on the same album. If *Lyle Lovett* left any doubts at all about this man's gifts as a performer and songwriter, *Pontiac* proved that he had even more tricks up his sleeve than he'd let on first time out, and it's the first of several masterpieces in Lovett's career.

Mark Deming

Lyle Lovett and His Large Band
1989, Curb

While from the outset Lyle Lovett sounded like a hard artist to pigeonhole, his sponsors at Curb Records and MCA Records seemed determined to sell him as a country artist, though the blues and retro-jazz leanings of Lovett's second album, *Pontiac*, suggested that strategy would only be practical for so long. With his third album, 1989's *Lyle Lovett and His Large Band*, Lovett seemingly sidelined any career aspirations as a mainstream country act he or his handlers may have held. The album kicks off with a lively cover of Clifford Brown's "The Blues Walk," and the next five tunes all bear the smoky, late-night vibe of a low-key jazz joint, with top marks going to the hilariously off-kilter "Here I Am," the witty scenario of potential infidelity "What Do You Do/The Glory of Love," and the marvelously sly "Good Intentions." The second half of the album is steeped in twang, but it was hardly more comforting for country radio programmers; "I Married Her Just Because She Looks Like You" is a "sweet on the outside and sick on the inside" tale of romantic obsession, "Nobody Knows Me" bears a punchline that makes "God Will" sound generous, and Lovett's straight-faced cover of "Stand By Your Man" stubbornly refuses to either announce itself as a joke or suggest another interpretation. Wherever you choose to file it, *Lyle Lovett and His Large Band* made it clear that Lovett was only getting better with each album; the songs are uniformly well-crafted, Lovett's vocals are full of subtle nuance, and his band is in brilliant form throughout (with special kudos to Lovett's frequent vocal foil, Francine Reed).

If you're going to burn your bridges, you could hardly find a better way to do it than this.

Mark Deming

Joshua Judges Ruth
March 1992, Curb

While *Lyle Lovett and his Large Band* wasn't a massive chart hit, it was successful enough to establish an audience for Lovett outside the boundaries of the country market, and 1992's *Joshua Judges Ruth* found Lovett seemingly free to follow his muse wherever it cared to go. *Joshua Judges Ruth* only bore the faintest glimmers of Lovett's country leanings (notable exception: "She's Leaving Me Because She Really Wants To"), and more surprisingly it suggested he was also moving away from the broad-shouldered jazz and blues accidents that dominated much of *Pontiac* and *Large Band*. Compared to his previous work, *Joshua Judges Ruth* sounds startlingly spare—producer and engineer George Massenburg brings a clear and keenly detailed sound to these sessions that allows all the details of the low-key arrangements to be heard, and "She's Already Made Up Her Mind," "Baltimore," and "Family Reserve" seem to have been recorded with this in mind. The songs also reflect a shift toward more serious and introspective themes for Lovett; outside of the gospel-influenced "Church" and the easygoing "She Makes Me Feel Good," his trademark humor is conspicuous in its absence, and loss, loneliness, and heartbreak dominate the lyrics. While the craft of *Joshua Judges Ruth* ranks with the finest work of Lovett's career, its spare and sober surfaces aren't especially engaging, and it's the sort of album fans are more likely to admire than embrace with pleasure.

Mark Deming

I Love Everybody
September 1994, Curb

Lyle Lovett's 1992 album, *Joshua Judges Ruth*, was a highly ambitious project for the Texas-born singer/songwriter—perhaps too ambitious, since despite the album's beautiful surfaces, the results simply weren't especially absorbing. Released in 1994, *I Love Everybody* seemed to find Lovett taking a step back—it consists of 18 tunes Lovett had written prior to the recording of his first album—but for the most part it succeeds where *Joshua Judges Ruth* disappoints, largely because the songs offer enough changeups to keep the listener engaged at all times. Also, for a set of tunes that were apparent leftovers, the writing on *I Love Everybody* is startlingly strong, from the saucy "Hello Grandma" and "Record Lady" to the stark and edgy storytelling of "I Think You Know What I Mean" and "The Fat Girl." The album also offers up plenty of Lovett's trademark dour humor and playfully sinister undertones; the title song was originally intended to be "Creeps Like Me," and it's hard to decide if one should laugh or frown in disgust while listening to it. And like *Joshua Judges Ruth*, *I Love Everybody* is dominated by clean, stripped-down arrangements and transparent production, but the players bring a lot more spirit and swing to these sessions (top honors go to bassist John Leftwich and drummer Russ Kunkel, a superb and soulful acoustic rhythm section), and the dynamics bring more drama to the performances rather than weighing them down. *I Love Everybody* is just eccentric enough to be best recommended to folks already familiar with Lovett's work, but anyone attuned to his sensibility will find plenty to enjoy here—and a little to make you a shade uncomfortable.

Mark Deming

The Road to Ensenada
June 1996, Curb

Since *Pontiac*, Lyle Lovett has been experimenting with different sounds, whether it was the big band posturing of *Lyle Lovett and His Large Band*, the gospel overtones of *Joshua Judges Ruth*, or the '70s singer/ songwriter flourishes of *I Love Everybody*. With *The Road to Ensenada*, he hunkers down and produces his most straightforward album since *Pontiac*. As it happens, it is also his best record since that breakthrough album. Lovett strips the sound of the album down to the bare country essentials, allowing it to drift into Western swing, country-rock, folk, and honky tonk when necessary. He also decides to balance his weightier material ("Private Conversation," "Who Loves You Better," "It Ought to Be Easier," "I Can't Love You Anymore," "Christmas Morning") with fun, lighthearted numbers like "Don't Touch My Hat," "Fiona," and "That's Right (You're Not From Texas)," which are funny without being silly. In fact, *The Road to Ensenada* is the lightest album Lyle Lovett has ever made—the darkness that hung around the fringes of *Pontiac*, *Joshua Judges Ruth*, and *I Love Everybody* has drifted away, leaving his wry sense of humor and a newly found empathetic sentimentality. The combination of straightforward instrumentation and lean, catchy, and incisive songwriting results in one of the best albums of his career—he's just as eclectic and off-handedly brilliant as he has always been, but on *The Road to Ensenada* he's more focused and less flashy about his own talent than he's ever been.

Stephen Thomas Erlewine

My Baby Don't Tolerate
September 2003, Lost Highway/Curb

Lyle Lovett is many things, but prolific is not one of them. Yes, at the outset of his career, he released an album every year or two, but by the time he became a star in the early '90s, he slowed down quite a bit. Between 1992's *Joshua Judges Ruth* and 2003's *My Baby Don't Tolerate*, his first release on Lost Highway, he only released one album of new original material: *The Road to Ensenada*, in 1996, which followed 1994's *I Love Everybody*, a clearing-house of songs he wrote *before* his first album. So, *My Baby Don't Tolerate* is his first album of new songs in seven years, and two of its 14 songs—"The Truck Song" and "San Antonio Girl"—were previously released on 2001's *Anthology, Vol. 1* (which is bound to frustrate fans that bought that uneven collection just for the new tunes), leaving this as a collection of 12 new songs. Given the long wait between albums and since the record is so firmly in the tradition of *The Road to Ensenada* that it could be branded a sequel, there may be an initial feeling of anticlimax, since there's not that many songs and they all feel familiar. Such is the complication of a long wait—it invariably raises expectations—but judged as a collection of songs against Lovett's other albums, *My Baby Don't Tolerate* holds its own very well. As mentioned above, it is very similar to *The Road to Ensenada*, sharing that album's clean, unadorned production, directness, and preponderance of straight-ahead country songs. And it's not just that the album is country; it's that many of his eccentricities are toned down, to the point that when Lovett ends the album with two gospel numbers, they sound like shtick. Even the handful of ballads are lighter, lacking the somber introspection of *Joshua Judges Ruth* or the subtleness of *I Love Everybody*. Everything here is out in the open, and it's the better for it; musically, it may offer no surprises, but its directness is appealing, particularly because Lovett simply sounds good singing country songs. And that's what *My Baby Don't Tolerate* offers—Lovett singing good country songs and sounding good. It's not a complicated pleasure, but it doesn't need to be, and after a long dry spell, it sure is nice to have a new collection of songs from this reliable songwriter.

Stephen Thomas Erlewine

Rockie Lynne

Rockie Lynne
May 2006, Universal/Universal South

On the cover of his eponymous 2006 debut, Rockie Lynne looks a little like a little brother of Australian country hunk Keith Urban and his blend of contemporary country, melodic pop, and anthemic rock is not all that dissimilar to Urban, either. And like Urban, who can never quite escape his roots in New Zealand and Australia, Lynne is most certainly the product of his homeland, but Rockie is from the American South, so his modern country feels a little more genuinely country than Urban's. Even when Lynne's music seems a little calculated—and there are plenty of times where it does, especially on the ridiculous watered-down Big & Rich of "Super Country Cowboy," the sappy "That's Where Songs Come From," and the well-intentioned we're-all-American clichés of "Red, White and Blue" ("The black man, the white man, and the Sioux/The middle class, the poor, and the well to do/They're red, white, and blue")—it is a calculation that's purely American, and feels genuine. Plus, even if these songs pander a little, they do illustrate that Lynne knows how to craft songs that push the right buttons to get him heard and get him on the charts, and that hits at the heart of what makes *Rockie Lynne* an appealing debut: behind his good-looks image, Lynne is a solid songwriter and singer, turning out friendly, sturdy modern country, whether it's on lightly rocking tunes like "Big Time in a Small Town," surging country-pop like "Lipstick," or sentimental ballads like "More." He may not push the boundaries of the genre much, but he works well within its confines, hitting the mark more often than not. Not every cut here works, but the ones that do are quite good and add up to a mainstream country debut that's both satisfying and promising.

Stephen Thomas Erlewine

Shelby Lynne

Tough All Over
August 1990, Epic

Before Shelby Lynne reinvented herself at the end of the 1990s and began recording for Mercury, she made a number of fine recordings that were unfortunately lost in the heap of "new traditionalist" and female superstar recordings that were popping out of Nash Vegas like zits. This 1990 effort,

produced by the great Bob Montgomery, is a case in point. Not only does this hold up to her best work, it's at the very least on a par with Kathy Mattea, Trisha Yearwood, Martina McBride, etc. It just isn't a strictly country outing, but it's a truly fine pop-country record. Interestingly, it also has the range of her later records. While there are songs here from the then-current crop of Nash Vegas song churners, like the opener, "I'll Lie Myself to Sleep," there are also cuts like the gorgeous gentle Western swing of "Don't Mind if I Do," by the legendary Skip Ewing. The tune borrows as much from Billie Holiday's "Ain't Nobody's Business" as it does from early Bonnie Raitt and Maria Muldaur.

And then there's a burning, hard-rocking cover of Charlie Rich's early hit "Lonely Weekends." It's more Dixie-fried than Rich's version, but it comes across as a thoroughly contemporary country-rock song with ringing guitars à la the Doobie Brothers' *Toulouse Street*, an Elvis-styled delivery, and a piano shuffle in the background that keeps the lyric from sinking under the weight of a cooking band. Wayne Carson's "Dog Day Afternoon" sounds like a latter-day Rich number, or one Tom Waits wrote for Crystal Gayle on the *One from the Heart* soundtrack; it's all jazzy, warm, and sensual. If there were any doubts about Lynne's country pedigree, it vanishes when her radical working of "I Walk the Line" comes through the speakers. Bluesy, shuffling, and the slightest bit funky, her sense of Cash's melody remains untouched. The set ends with another Western swing-influenced nugget, but this one comes from Duke Ellington, "Don't Get Around Much Anymore," before it breaks out into a full-blown Patsy Cline country-jazz tune. She saved the best moment for last here, and it is so original in its swinging elegance that listeners can only wonder if she might have taken the Diana Krall route, in that she not only has the pipes and the chops, but the feel for this material. *Tough All Over* is wonderful from start to finish.

Thom Jurek

Temptation
July 1993, Morgan Creek/Mercury

Shelby Lynne is nobody's fool. Since 1990's *I Am Shelby Lynne*, this artist has defiantly resisted any attempt to pigeonhole her, and has fought record labels tooth and nail to make the kind of records she wanted to—even if they weren't commercially viable. *Temptation* is a case in point. While *I Am Shelby Lynne*—a contemporary country groundbreaker and a classic record in anybody's book—scored big and *Soft Talk* netted a couple of mid-level hit singles, nothing could have prepared fans of her first three records for 1993's *Temptation*. Produced by Brent Maher, whose work with the Judds earned him recognition, the album was Lynne's first for Morgan Creek/Mercury, after leaving Epic a year earlier. What is so utterly startling about the disc is that, while the cover photo features a short-haired, sultry-looking Lynne, who appeared as if straight from a Vogue photo shoot, the music is hardcore jacked-up Western swing and big-band country, featuring a full-on orchestra of the size Bob Wills hired at his zenith—this one contains an eight-piece horn section, pedal steel, fiddle (of course), guitars galore, bass, and drums. With arrangements by Buddy Skipper, the disc is equally balanced between up-tempo finger-popping Western swing and hillbilly boogie and killer jazzed-up country ballads that Patsy Cline would have been hungry to sing in her transition years. What's more, Maher and Lynne (separately) wrote the lion's share of the album, with one track each from John Jarvis and Rory Michael Bourke. The title track opens the set and it roars out of the gate swaggering, with killer male chorus backing vocals done in call-and-response style, a fiddle solo, and burning horns. The mid-tempo strut of "Feelin' Kind of Lonely Tonight," with its honky tonk piano, waves of horns, and Lynne's upfront sassy vocal, is the kind of jazzy "good girl about to go bad" number that will get the punters on the dancefloor as well. But in the ballads, with their blues roots (like in "Tell Me I'm Crazy" and the closer, "Where Do We Go from Here"), one can hear traces of Peggy Lee in front of a polished Ray Charles Orchestra orchestrated and produced by Owen Bradley. Jarvis' "I Need a Heart to Come Home To" is a country song that feels a little like Eric Kaz's "Love Has No Pride," and Lynne's big throaty contralto digs right into the blues in the tune even as the fiddle and pedal steel whine. The jump and swing tunes work best, though, like the title cut, "Don't Cry for Me," and Lynne's "Some of That True Love," all of which are memorable burners. This is a sadly overlooked recording that deserves reexamination in light of the wide berth of styles that contemporary country welcomes within its ranks—it's hip, sassy, and tough.

Thom Jurek

Kathy Mattea

Walk the Way the Wind Blows
1986, Mercury

Oh yeah, 1986, when Kathy Mattea was still a country singer, she was one of them, the "new traditionalists" at that point in time, before she became such an awesome pop singer. *Walk the Way the Wind Blows* is the rootsiest (in the American sense of the word) album Mattea had recorded up to that time. With a cast of players that included progressive bluegrass upstart Béla Fleck, country legend Don Williams, Wendy Waldman, Buddy Spicher, up and comer Vince Gill, bass king Bob Wray, and a slew of others, Mattea took honky tonk songs, shimmied them up against bluegrass energy and funky horns ("Train of Memories"), and came up with something entirely different. And while it's erratic in places, *Walk the Way the Wind Blows* is a fine outing overall. It's on the funky, rocked-up or old-timey down swing jazzers like "Evenin'" where the disc works the best. Her ballad singing hadn't gotten to the place it did just three years later; on "Reason to Live" it falls a tad flat, and the stirring conviction of her later singing is not yet in place here. The one exception is her cover of Nanci Griffith's "Love at the Five and Dime." Its pacing and restraint—courtesy of expert production by Allen Reynolds and Don Williams' harmony vocal—make the song a mind movie. Mattea's vocal tells the story as if she is looking back on her own life instead of being a reportorial account of fictional characters. The refrain with Williams is chillingly beautiful, as if, now old and gray, they are singing to one another in the moonlight. The stellar dobro and Cajun accordion carry the lyric into the stratosphere on "Back Up Grinnin' Again." Mattea found a formula; restless as she is, changing direction and producers so often, she didn't stick with it long. Nonetheless, *Walk the Way the Wind Blows* is one of her better efforts.

Thom Jurek

Untasted Honey
September 1987, Mercury

In many ways, Kathy Mattea's *Untasted Honey* is about as close as she's ever come to recording a bluegrass album. Of course, it's not bluegrass; it's more like Nash Vegas grass. The appearance of players and singers like Tim O'Brien, David Schnaufer, Ray Flynn, Ray Flacke, and a host of others suggests Mattea is sticking close to the roots formula. Her reliance on songs by O'Brien, Fred Koller, Don Henry, and Pat Alger also directs the mix in a certain direction. With producer Allen Reynolds and backing vocals by O'Brien, Beth Nielsen Chapman, and John Thompson, this set is consistently fine. All of the songs seem to segue into one another, creating a tapestry, or a series of snapshots placed together in an album. "Untold Stories," a flashy stomp & roller with the influence of Bill Monroe haunting the background, is a hell of an opener—especially with the mandolin and guitar solos. The Nelson Brothers' "Eighteen Wheels and a Dozen Roses" is a song Rodney Crowell wishes he would have written, and as storyteller here, Mattea is so deep inside the story it's difficult to tell if she's recording a story or giving the listener a recounting of something that happened to her. "Late in the Day" is another O'Brien winner, full of rambling pedal steel and entwined acoustic guitars. Other standouts include the title track, with a virtual choir of backing vocalists and the punch of Bob Ray's voice. This is the most '80s neo-trad country track on the set, and it works. The funky country blues of Pat Alger and Mark D. Sanders' "Like a Hurricane" has that high lonesome ring to it, and Mattea's voice—which is so large you can hear it echo within itself—was created to sing a tune like this. In all, this is solid for such a young effort; the selection of tunes, particularly near the end of the record, falls apart, but there's plenty here to engage even the most casual of listeners.

Thom Jurek

Willow in the Wind
1989, Mercury

The year 1989 was awesome for Kathy Mattea. Her brand of country-pop music began to evolve toward folk and Celtic-oriented influences, which were actually encouraged by her label—changes like this in Nash Vegas are few and far between—and what's more, it all translated in terms of chart success and record sales. A strong and indeed the first completely realized project of her career, *Willow in the Wind* boasted three hits, "Burnin' Old Memories," "Where've You Been," and "Come from the Heart." The hard honky tonk/West Texas swing of "Burnin' Old Memories," with its slightly rocked-up tempo, is more than just catchy; it's infectious. "Hills of Alabam'" is one of those gorgeous songs where the weary traveler—with a lonesome harmonica in the background—romanticizes home as contrasted with the harsh questions of the present and the uncertain future. Mattea's phrasing is impeccable in that she becomes an itinerant musician riding endless hours on some forsaken urban freeway in the predawn light.

But the true stunner on *Willow in the Wind* is, of course,

a love song. Written by Zen bluegrass queen Laurie Lewis, it's the most springlike testament to new love and is free of sentimentality or emotional manipulation, and Mattea's voice is perfect for its utterance. Slippery acoustic guitars, a piano, and a strolling bass anchored by a small drum kit are what frame the verses, with a shimmering pedal steel on the refrains. It's simply orchestrated, with an old-timey feel, and when Mattea takes the last verse she lays all cheesy, false, and clichéd love songs to waste: "Love cuts like a torch to a heart behind steel/And though you may hide it, love knows how you feel/And though you may trespass on the laws of the land/Your heart has to follow when love takes your hand/And it seems we're two people/Within the same circle/It's drawn tighter and tighter/'Till you're all I can see/I'm full and I'm empty and you're pouring through me/Like the warm rain fallin' through the leaves on a tree/Tell me now if I'm wrong are you feeling the same/Are your feet on the ground/Are you callin' my name/Do you lie awake nights/Please say you do/You can't choose who you love/Love chooses you." The record closes two tracks later, but it hardly matters—the case has been made.

Thom Jurek

Time Passes By
1991, Mercury

On her most ambitious album, Mattea gets impeccably chosen songs (as usual) and strong supporting performances (from Emmylou Harris, Dougie MacLean, and the Roches). She doesn't write her own stuff, so she may not be the romantic dreamer of "Asking Us to Dance," but she sure sounds like it. Songs like "Time Passes By," co-written by husband Jon Vezner, suggest there's more honesty here than image. She can even make the half-baked "From a Distance" convincing.

Brian Mansfield

Lonesome Standard Time
1992, Mercury

Mattea had vocal-cord surgery that threatened to end her career before she made *Lonesome Standard Time*, but you couldn't prove it by listening: her voice hasn't lost a bit of its deep alto warmth. *Lonesome Standard Time* isn't as ambitious as *Time Passes By*, but it's filled with lovely performances from Mattea's favorite sources: bluegrass ("Lonesome Standard Time"), gospel-influenced country ("Standing Knee Deep in a River (Dying of Thirst)") and Nanci Griffith ("Listen to the Radio").

Brian Mansfield

Good News
1993, Mercury

Kathy Mattea's album for the Christmas season is unlike any country Christmas record ever released. For starters, she and producer Brent Maher commissioned original songs rather than taking them from the canon, or adapted obscure songs from the ages. Secondly, the band was formed around what served each song to make it feel as organic as possible. Strange instruments appear, such as the marimbas on "New Kid in Town," recorders and a high string guitar and recorders on "Christ Child Lullaby" (courtesy of Dougie MacLean and Jim Horn), and a full choir on the closing title track. This doesn't feel like any Christmas record you've ever heard before, either. It sounds like a well-crafted, gorgeously wrought folk/country/Celtic-flavored Kathy Mattea record. Give a listen to any of the above, or especially the haunted traditional song "Brightest and Best," completely reworked by Mattea and Maher. The guitars caress the open

space between themselves and Mattea's voice, as the pipes and recorders float within. Likewise, listen to "Mary Did You Know," which is one of the most stunningly beautiful Christian folk songs written in decades (by Mark Lowry and Buddy Greene). But then, while songs can be many things, they cannot be given life without a singer, and on *Good News*, in Mattea's instrument, the grains of truth add up to something incalculable: high art.

Thom Jurek

Walking Away a Winner
October 1993, Mercury

Walking Away a Winner is the rocked-up/pop side of Kathy Mattea. With records by Mary Chapin Carpenter gathering steam as well as those of Beth Nielsen Chapman, Lucinda Williams getting some notice, and Bonnie Raitt riding the very top of the charts over the previous two years, Mattea took a listen and apparently liked what she heard. There are layers and layers of guitars on the album, and nowhere are they borne out more than on the title track that opens the album. With producer Josh Leo and a deck of tough songs, Mattea showed a side her country audience hadn't yet seen, and one that the adult contemporary and emerging AAA formats could embrace. In other words, the album, with its tightly knit group of astonishingly well-written pop songs done in a slight country manner by a crack group of players, was a winning formula. It's a record that stands the test of time. What makes Mattea such a great singer—besides her gift of a voice—is her empathy. She finds herself in every song she records. On tape, there is no separation between her and her characters, whether it's the woman finally walking away from a dead relationship and seeing herself not as beaten but as free in the title track, the rambling woman relentlessly seeking that lost love no matter where the search takes her in the rollicking "Streets of Your Town," or the overworked, underappreciated wife and mother who breaks down in "Maybe She's Human." From "Clown in Your Rodeo," with its ringing electric 12-strings and hard-swinging refrain, through the final track, the haunting jazzy ballad "Who's Gonna Know," conviction and commitment are fully on display, along with an elegance that is both accessible and sophisticated. This is a winner indeed.

Thom Jurek

The Innocent Years
May 2000, MCA

A brisk song with tempo and lyrical substance, "Trouble With Angels" is one of only two songs on this 11th studio release from Mattea that isn't a ballad. Written and recorded during a time when she was facing the declining health of her father, much of the music on *The Innocent Years* is about the tender mercies of life: love, family relationships, faith in God, perseverance, commitment, and growing old. Most notably poignant is "That's the Deal," a tribute to her father and the health struggles he's recently faced. The album gets high marks for vocal collaborations with the likes of Suzy Bogguss, Alison Krauss, and pop singer Graham Nash. And the album's bonus track, "BFD," a crowd favorite in her live shows, ends the album on a playful note.

Maria Konicki Dinoia

The Mavericks

What a Crying Shame
1994, MCA

The Mavericks fully hit their stride with their third album, 1994's *What a Crying Shame*, in which the band's blend of rootsy country and vintage pop sounds finally found the balance they'd been searching for. While producer Don Cook gave the band a significantly glossier sound than that of their first two albums, with a hefty number of guest musicians (and guest songwriters) on board, remarkably enough the Mavericks' personality wasn't subsumed in the process; if anything, the high-priced help seemed to have prodded the boys into playing at the top of their game. Raul Malo's keening tenor gets a superb workout on "I Should Have Been True" and the title cut (the latter of which boasts a guitar hook Roger McGuinn would have been proud to come up with), while "Pretend" and "There Goes My Heart" are honky tonk floor-fillers of the first order. Robert Reynolds and Paul Deakin are a rhythm section who can give these songs the nervy drive of a rock band without betraying the Mavericks' country leanings, and they give the covers of "All That Heaven Will Allow" and "O What a Thrill" a taut foundation most contemporary Nashville acts lack. Truth to tell, *What a Crying Shame* doesn't have a single dud track, and offers encouraging proof that it's still possible to make an engaging and idiosyncratic country album while signed to the Nashville division of a major label . . . and the best news is, the band managed to turn that accomplishment into a hat trick over the next few years.

Mark Deming

Music for All Occasions
October 1995, MCA

With their third album, The Mavericks added slick country-pop to their arsenal of retro-country styles. The result straddles the line between affection and camp, since the band never goes completely overboard by drenching their songs with strings, and Raul Malo retains his aching Orbisonesque voice. However, that doesn't mean their songwriting has slipped, as all 11 originals are first-rate, updated honky tonk ravers or countrypolitan numbers. And the closing cover of "Somethin' Stupid," recorded with Trisha Yearwood, is a fun, kitschy delight.

Stephen Thomas Erlewine

Trampoline
March 1998, MCA

As their career progresses, the Mavericks are becoming more of a showcase for vocalist/frontman Raul Malo, both for

better and for worse. They may be losing their band identity, but that may have been inevitable, considering that Malo is such a gifted, powerful musician. He is the driving force behind all of the group's stylistic fusions, their blend of honky tonk with country-rock, classic rock & roll, pop, and Latin. On *Music for All Occasions*, the stylistic blends sounded a little gimmicky, but the band sounds revitalized on *Trampoline*—even the vaudevillian "Dolores" rings as true as the shuffling, cha-cha "I Should Know." If anything, the album is the least "country" album the Mavericks have ever done, but that's primarily because all of their influences have blended seamlessly together, creating an original, altogether intoxicating sound. Furthermore, they're not simply surface—Malo's songs are clever constructions, ranking among the most imaginative roots songwriting of the '90s. His writing, combined with his band's musical panache, makes *Trampoline* a ride worth taking.

Thom Owens

Martina McBride

The Time Has Come
1992, RCA

Rest assured, it's highly unlikely that Martina McBride will ever issue another record that sounds like *The Time Has Come*. With co-producers Paul Worley and Ed Seay (who also worked with her on her breakthrough, *The Way That I Am*), McBride delivers a set of neo-traditionalist country and progressive country-inflected folk songs that showcase her ability to get to the heart of a song and turn it into something communicative and thought provoking. With a host of Nashville superpickers and backing vocalists from Garth Brooks and Carl Jackson to Kathy Chiavola, McBride turns in intense performances of the Emory Gordy/Jim Rushing classic "Cheap Whiskey" for a neo-honky tonk feel, as well as the stompin' nightclub country of the Longacre/Wilson-penned title track and the Lonnie Wilson/Charlotte Wilson/Herbert Wilson weeper "Losing You Feels Good." The album ends with Gretchen Peters' "When You're Old," a meditative love song delivered with the empathy, grace, and elegance that have become McBride's trademark. This is a very solid debut, even if it resembles none of her other work.

Thom Jurek

The Way That I Am
1993, RCA

While Martina McBride's blend of traditional country and progressive folk styles—along with her powerful, remarkable voice—got country audiences to sit up and take notice in 1992, it was *The Way That I Am*, and most notably its Gretchen Peters-penned single "Independence Day," that blew minds. While the song itself—told from the point of view of a surviving daughter of an alcoholic wife-beater and an abused, long-suffering wife and mother—ends in a tragedy of suicide and death, it is nonetheless a redemptive song that makes no moral judgments yet asks real questions about what "independence" actually means. Set on the Fourth of July, it pointedly asks, Does Independence Day mean independence for everyone or does it mean making the choice to free yourself from your bonds, no matter how horrific the consequences? Is it a choice made independent of society, morals, and cultural and religious mores because of the depth of one's convictions? McBride delivers the story with a tough, matter-of-fact, barely concealed rage, and yet that gives way to a transcendence in the refrain so stirring and shatteringly moving it was used in the aftermath of September 11th (even if it was taken out of context in the same way that Bruce Springsteen's "Born in the USA" was). It was an instant classic and remains one over a decade later. It's the kind of troubling song you cannot immediately—or perhaps ever—fathom. The listener is carried into the heart of the contradiction of a day of celebration and raw horror inside a tune so seductive and catchy it feels at odds with its lyric, yet comes together on the refrain only to split again into more fragments than can be counted. When McBride declares, "Now I ain't sayin' it's right or it's wrong/Maybe it's the only way/Talk about your revolution/It's independence day," the entire world inside the song comes apart, and you are left wondering who the right, wrong, and guilty are in the refrain, and you have to make out your own point of consideration regarding a "day of reckoning." There are no answers, just facts, questions, and ciphers. The single could have sold the album alone, but the other nine tracks here are quality as well. From the opener, "Heart Trouble," to "She Ain't Seen Nothing Yet," to the closer, "Ashes," the feel on the album, set by the completely modern country-pop sound of the single, is up-tempo, glossier, and more streamlined in its focus than her debut, but that's fine because McBride proves herself capable of delivering any kind of song in the end. There isn't a weak track in the bunch, and despite the more modern, less traditional sound, it makes little difference because McBride is a singer's singer: tough, true, and in full control of her gift.

Thom Jurek

Wild Angels
September 1995, RCA

Coming two years after her smash *The Way That I Am* and her mind-bogglingly successful single, "Independence Day," Martina McBride had nothing to prove—except to the folks in accounting at her record company. *Wild Angels* continues her exploration of melding classic country influences and modern pop—long before Shania Twain dreamed it—in the same way (albeit in a radically different time and context) that Patsy Cline did 30 years earlier. Using the same production team of Ed Seay, Paul Worley, and herself—with a literal boatload of engineers—McBride and company assembled a fine collection of songs and performers, including the Band's Levon Helm and Ashley Cleveland on backing vocals, to deliver a powerful set that is her most consistent yet despite not having a single as memorable as "Independence Day" (but you only get those once or twice in a lifetime anyway, right?). Here there are many standout tracks, not the least among them being a rocking & rolling country version of Delbert McClinton's classic "Two More Bottles of Wine" that blows away Emmylou Harris' version and rivals McClinton's. In addition, there are a couple of Matraca Berg cuts, including the modern country title track and the soulful weeper "Cry on the Shoulder of the Road." The Bunch/Stinson-penned "You've Been Driving All the Time" has that irresistible lead-in of acoustic guitars that gives way to compressed ringing electrics that underscore her voice so well and make the track a winner. But there aren't any weak moments here, and

McBride proves for the third time that she not only is for real, but that she has the ability a lot of her peers don't to make consistently engaging, moving, and memorable music from album to album. That's an achievement.

Thom Jurek

Evolution
August 1997, RCA

Evolution is an appropriate title; it's clear that Martina McBride has grown—evolved—between *Wild Angels* and this terrific follow-up. That's not to say *Wild Angels* wasn't wonderful in its own right—its blend of rootsy country and contemporary production was clever, and her singing and songs were spot-on—but *Evolution* is different and special in its own way. It is true that it's smoother than its predecessor, especially with polished duets like "Valentine" (with Jim Brickman) and "Still Holding On" (Clint Black). What makes *Evolution* work is the purity and power of McBride's voice—she is one of the few contemporary country singers who can pull off this kind of country-pop. And that's not all she can do, as the rocking "Keeping My Distance" or the gospel-inflected "A Broken Wing" prove. Furthermore, McBride's songs remain staunchly independent and strong-willed, with clear feminist overtones, which helps make *Evolution* a rarity among contemporary country albums—it's catchy and it has a heart.

Thom Owens

Emotion
September 1999, RCA

Emotion is the fifth installment in a series of platinum albums from one of the most underrated voices in country music. After two years since the release of her double platinum *Evolution*, Martina McBride tears into these tracks showcasing the range and power of her incomparable voice. *Evolution* was a big-sounding record with lots of overdubbing and production. *Emotion* scales back musically using a very small band and the result is fresh and authentic, allowing McBride to captivate us with her resounding vocals. Aptly titled, *Emotion*, with lyrics like "anything's better than feelin' the blues" and "love's the only house big enough for all the pain in the world," tugs at the heart strings at times. But it's in "Do What You Do" that McBride lets us know that she's just doing what she does: "If you want to give them something different—something to sink their teeth into—well baby, you just do what you do."

Maria Konicki Dinoia

Martina
September 2003, RCA

One of the greatest voices in country music today and reigning CMA female vocalist of the year shines on this, her sixth album. McBride's previous catalog of music has always been intelligent and full of emotion, and these 12 tracks are decidedly no different. True to womanhood, *Martina* embodies the spirit of being female in every role. McBride sings about a bride-to-be in the guitar-strumming "Wearing White," as a daughter in the gospel-infused bluegrass "Reluctant Daughter," as a mom in the affecting ballad "In My Daughter's Eyes," as a confident lover in the smooth and gentle "When You Love Me," and as a friend in the soft, mid-tempo "She's a Butterfly." Other standouts include a delicious reinterpretation of "Over the Rainbow" as only McBride could sing it and the dramatic "How Far" in the style of her 1997 hit, "Whatever You Say." In a lush career that now spans ten years, Martina McBride always has something new to offer with immeasurable artistry.

Maria Konicki Dinoia

Timeless
October 2005, RCA

Timeless refers to the 18 songs Martina McBride covers on her seventh studio albums, classic country tunes every one. Most of the songs date from the '60s and '70s—the oldest songs here are the opening pair of Hank Williams' "You Win Again" and Ray Price's "I'll Be There," both dating from the '50s, along with Hank Snow's "I Don't Hurt Anymore" and another Price perennial, "Heartaches by the Number"—and the great majority of these songs are quite familiar. "I Can't Stop Loving You," "(I Never Promised You A) Rose Garden," "Today I Started Loving You Again," "Satin Sheets," "I Still Miss Someone," "Love's Gonna Live Here," "Make the World Go Away," and "Help Me Make It Through the Night" have all been covered regularly and remain radio staples to this day, and even such comparatively obscure choices as Harlan Howard's terrific "Pick Me Up on Your Way Down" (made into a hit by Charlie Walker) are well-known to hardcore country fans. Instead of being a detriment, the familiarity is a blessing, since these well-known songs illustrate McBride's range, power, and subtlety as a vocalist, as well as her skill as an interpreter. *Timeless* strikes a tricky and effective balance of being traditional—the thoroughly annotated, well-detailed liner notes reveal that this extended down to the recording, where mostly vintage equipment, with no digital plug-ins, were used—and contemporary. The songs and sounds are familiar, and even when McBride does an unexpected arrangement—the mellow, introspective acoustic-based "I Still Miss Someone"—they're not wildly unexpected, yet this all feels fresh, due to the excellence of the band, McBride's sterling taste in material, and, best of all, her extraordinary voice. She has always been one of the greatest vocalists in contemporary country, but *Timeless* is the first time that she's recorded a full-fledged singer's album, one where she not only has the material to showcase her range, but also a sympathetic band, arrangements, and production to highlight her remarkable voice. The result isn't just one of the best country albums of 2005 but her best album since *The Way That I Am.*

Stephen Thomas Erlewine

Waking Up Laughing
April 2007, RCA/BMG/Sony Nashville

Martina McBride scored big with *Timeless,* her collection of classic country tunes in 2005. It was yet another feather in the singer's cap. McBride's reign near the top of country music's pantheon has been near constant. She's picky about the songs she chooses to sing, she works with sympathetic producers, and her voice is, well, timeless. She's got the Southern twang, but its timbre carries within it a vast scope of American music. Check "Anyway," the first single and video from 2007's *Waking Up Laughing,* and one of two tunes on the set McBride had a hand in writing (and she produced the set

herself—she's earned the right). It's subject is to pray regardless, take the action and leave the result in the hands of Divine Providence: "God is great, but sometimes life ain't good/ When I pray it doesn't always turn out like I think it should/ But I do it anyway/I do it anyway." It's anthem to the beauty of failure, the courage in tenacity, and a testament to the willingness to do the right thing no matter how it turns out. It's got a massive string section, a slow, pronounced piano. The guitars crash against the strings in the refrain and the entire thing nearly lifts off the ground. The only thing holding it steady is McBride's big contralto. This kind of drama is her stock-in-trade. Celine Dion has nothing on her. Song itself is where McBride's quest as an artist resides. In the opener, "If I Had Your Name," rocking guitars, fiddles, mandolins, and big bad drums underscore McBride's scathing indictment of another's character flaws: "If I had your name/I'd be changin' it by now." A popping bassline and twin lead guitars fill the middle with menace and rage. "Everybody Does" feels like a flip side for "Anyway," with the subject of failure in love. "Loveland" and "House of a Thousand Dreams" have less of that large, theater-sounding dynamic. They are more traditionally "country" songs, a term that in the 21st century can mean almost anything—and yes, that's good: it simply stands for American music these days. *Waking Up Laughing* is another brick in Martina McBride's astonishingly consistent catalog. Her continual affirmation for Christian faith may alienate some but will no doubt register with many country fans. Any way you look at it, *Waking Up Laughing* is a winner.

Thom Jurek

Mindy McCready

Ten Thousand Angels
April 1996, BNA

Mindy McCready's debut *Ten Thousand Angels* is an appealing debut album, despite a handful of flaws. The songwriting on the album is occasionally a little weak, but throughout the record McCready turns in a powerhouse performance that elevates her to the front ranks of young female contemporary country singers.

Thom Owens

If I Don't Stay the Night
November 1997, BNA

If I Don't Stay the Night fulfills the promise of Mindy McCready's debut album *Ten Thousand Angels,* finding the singer developing a stronger voice, both as a singer and a storyteller. Although McCready doesn't write any original songs, she has selected a set of songs—ranging from the title track to a cover of Linda Ronstadt's "Long Long Time"—that establish her as a strong, independent female voice in country music. Furthermore, her voice is growing stronger, turning even the mediocre songs into something special. It's a record that confirms that she is one of the strongest singers in the post-Shania world.

Thom Owens

I'm Not So Tough
August 1999, BNA

Taking a bit of a cue from Faith Hill and Shania Twain, Mindy McCready shoots for the crossover adult contemporary audience with her third album, *I'm Not So Tough*. She doesn't take things quite as far as either Faith or Shania, retaining a distinct country twang to the music (if not the voice) throughout the album, but it's clear that the album has a smoother, brighter sheen, all the better for pop radio, plus ballads and mid-tempo pop cuts that are designed for wider plays. This may dismay some longtime fans, but McCready pulls it off because she sings with conviction and she has true charisma. That said, the music itself isn't as appealing as that on her first two albums and the material is a bit more uneven, but it is often entertaining and is ultimately at least a musically successful bid at a crossover adult pop record.

Stephen Thomas Erlewine

Reba McEntire

Out of a Dream
1979, Mercury

Reba McEntire's 1978 album *Out of a Dream*, reissued in its entirety on this budget-line CD, steps away from the hard country leanings of her first album and toward the more pop-oriented direction she would subsequently explore. Five of the songs on this album made the country Top 40, including "Last Night, Ev'ry Night," "Sweet Dreams," "(I Still Long to Hold You) Now and Then," "That Makes Two of Us" (a duet with Jacky Ward), and, perhaps the best of the bunch, "Runaway Heart." Other highlights are the biographical "Daddy" and "It's Gotta Be Love," both of which are stronger than some of the Top 40 singles.

Greg Adams

My Kind of Country
October 1984, MCA

When Reba McEntire switched from Mercury Records, the label that had developed her from being a 19-year-old singing the national anthem at a rodeo in 1974 to back-to-back number-one country hits in 1983, and moved to MCA as of October 1 of that year, the idea was that the new company was going to take her to the next level, outright superstardom in country music. Instead, her career hit a speed bump with her first MCA LP, *Just a Little Love*, produced by Norro Wilson, who, like Jerry Kennedy, her Mercury producer, wanted to take advantage of her vocal range by having her sing a wide variety of material, but succeeded only in giving her a fuzzy image with record buyers. MCA next brought in Harold Shedd, the hot producer of Alabama, for the follow-up to *Just a Little Love*, but McEntire was dissatisfied with the songs he brought her and with the pop sweetening he applied to the tracks initially, and she went to the new company president Jimmy Bowen, who told her to go ahead and find her own songs and cut them her own way. (Shedd retains his producer credit, no doubt for contractual reasons, but it's in name only.) That might have been a daunting prospect to another country singer, but McEntire was paying attention to the charts, and she realized that the country-pop of the urban cowboy era in country music of the early '80s had given way to the new traditionalism of Ricky Skaggs and George Strait, and she shrewdly decided to jump on the bandwagon. She got a new song from country legend Harlan Howard ("Somebody Should Leave," co-written with Chick Raines), but instead of making the rounds of the Nashville publishers, she rooted around in her record collection and came up with songs from old LPs previously recorded by the likes of Ray Price ("Don't You Believe Her," "I Want to Hear It from You"), Carl Smith ("Before I Met You"), Connie Smith ("You've Got Me [Right Where You Want Me]"), and Faron Young ("He's Only Everything"). In the studio, she and Bowen banished the strings that had played a big part on *Just a Little Love* and her Mercury recordings in favor of hard country arrangements dominated by the fiddles of Johnny Gimble and Mark O'Connor and the steel guitars of Sonny Garrish and Doyle Grisham, with Jerry Douglas' dobro also having a pride of place. Then she sang this collection of country shuffles as if she were Patsy Cline back from the grave. The result was the breakthrough she was looking for. "How Blue," the leadoff single, went to number one, followed by the irresistible "Somebody Should Leave," a characteristically direct Howard story song about an impending divorce a couple was studiously avoiding, as the female narrator put it, because "He needs the kids, and they need me." McEntire, who grew up on a ranch in Oklahoma and spent her summers traveling to rodeos with her father, a professional cowboy, had no trouble investing this material with a sense of authenticity, and the old songs were simultaneously familiar-sounding and yet not actually well known. *My Kind of Country* vaulted her into the ranks of the hottest performers in country music, circa 1984.

William Ruhlmann

Have I Got a Deal for You
1985, MCA

During its first decade, Reba McEntire's career had a "two steps forward, one step back" quality to it, even though she kept doggedly progressing, year by year. In 1984, her two big steps forward came with her surprise win as Female Vocalist of the Year at the Country Music Association (CMA) awards and the release of her bid to join the new traditionalist movement, *My Kind of Country*. Her next album, *Have I Got a Deal for You*, released nine months later, constituted another step back, if only a slight one. On *My Kind of Country*, McEntire had eschewed the Nashville publishing houses for the most part to pick old songs previously recorded as LP tracks by the likes of Connie Smith and Faron Young, which she then sang as if she were Patsy Cline reincarnated. The topping on the cake was Harlan Howard's newly written song of divorce-in-the-making, "Somebody Should Leave." On *Have I Got a Deal for You*, McEntire, who co-produced the album with MCA label president Jimmy Bowen, went back to the publishers for new songs. She stuck to the traditional country arrangements, but with a bit more variation; leadoff track "I'm in Love All Over" was an up-tempo number in the style of the Bakersfield sound, for example, while "I Don't Need Nothin' You Ain't Got" was given a Western swing treatment. The trouble was that even a newly minted CMA recipient couldn't find strong songs. The title tune and first single was one of those metaphors taken too far in which Nashville songwriters specialized, and elsewhere McEntire was reduced to mouthing overused clichés in songs like "Red Roses (Won't Work Now)." Another mistake was that she dared to do some writing herself, although her "Only in My Mind," which actually got to number five in the country charts, demonstrated that she had absorbed the lesson of "Somebody Should Leave" in trying to come up with songs that addressed the viewpoint of contemporary women. It was also disheartening that, just after having staked her claim as the leading female new traditionalist, she was already backsliding. There were no strings on *Have I Got a Deal for You* and Johnny Gimble's fiddle was still prominent, along with Weldon Myrick's steel guitar. But the closing track, "Don't Forget Your Way Home," still sounded like an adult contemporary pop ballad, albeit one sung with McEntire's distinctive Oklahoma twang. *Have I Got a Deal for You* was hardly a disaster, but it was not the album to consolidate the advance McEntire had made with *My Kind of Country*, much less push her career further.

William Ruhlmann

What Am I Gonna Do About You
1986, MCA

Since most country artists do not write their own songs, they can have more trouble maintaining the quality of their records than keeping a string of hits going. Reba McEntire broke through to massive success—recognized by the Country Music Association with its 1986 Entertainer of the Year Award—with the chart-topping *Whoever's in New England*, featuring the career-making title song. The album represented the perfection of an approach she and producer Jimmy Bowen had been taking for a couple of years, and one they only tinkered with on McEntire's next album, *What Am I Gonna Do About You*. But, even with Nashville tunesmiths burning the midnight oil to write songs tailor-made for her, she was unable to come up with material that matched. Not that these ten songs were bad. In fact, the title song had something of the feel of "Whoever's in New England" in its portrayal of a woman trying to recover from a painfully ended love affair. That track hit number one, as did "One Promise Too Late," in which a woman lamented a suitor who had come along after she'd already said her wedding vows with another. And "I Heard Her Cryin'," reflecting on the impact of marital squabbling on an uncomprehending child, was another strong ballad. But McEntire and Bowen seemed to feel that perhaps *Whoever's in New England* had been a bit too heavy on slow songs, and they tried for a more stylistic variety here, including a playful, '50s-style rocker, "Take Me Back," and giving an equally light Tex-Mex feel to "Till It Snows in Mexico." "Let the Music Lift You Up," a tribute to music itself, managed to struggle as high as number four on the singles chart despite being an unsuitable piece of material for McEntire, who would have been better advised to release the cleverly constructed barroom saga "My Mind

Is on You" on 45 instead. Still, the album replicated its predecessor in going to number one itself, thus consolidating McEntire's position as country's top female singer. A listener might wish that she would have come up with another "Whoever's in New England," but then such works are called signature songs because they only come along once or twice in a whole career.

William Ruhlmann

Whoever's in New England
1986, MCA

In the field of country music, where most artists are not also songwriters, there is a constant search among the Nashville publishing houses for that one song that will not only catapult a singer to the top of the charts, but also define a career. After a slow build lasting nearly a decade, Reba McEntire became an established country star in the mid-'80s, winning the Female Vocalist of the Year award from the Country Music Association in 1984 and again in 1985. But she had never had even a Top Ten LP on the country charts, and her successes seemed to vie with her failures in a back-and-forth pattern. She had turned to the new traditionalist style with her 1984 album *My Kind of Country*, and seemed to have hit on a theme of embodying the emotional conflicts of women with "Somebody Should Leave," a song from that disc that went to number one. But *Have I Got a Deal for You* in 1985 missed the mark. *Whoever's in New England*, which followed in early 1986, was a bull's-eye. The first reason was, of course, the title song, written by Kendal Franceschi and Quentin Powers, and sung by McEntire with the clenched emotion that the lyrics required. Against a stately ballad setting, the singer embodies the character of a Southern wife whose husband is, it seems to her, taking more business trips to Boston than he really needs to. Her surprising response is to tell him she thinks he's cheating on her, but that "when whoever's in New England's through with you," she will be waiting for him. The singer's sense of martyrdom is both unbearable and irresistible, and Franceschi and Powers achieve the added effect of casting the story in a South vs. North context. A mere 121 years since the end of the Civil War, that's a subtext that remained compelling to Southerners. "Whoever's in New England," which quickly soared to number one on the country singles charts (and later won McEntire her first Grammy for Best Female Country Vocal Performance), was reason enough for the album named after it to be considered a triumph. But producers McEntire and Jimmy Bowen surrounded it with other material of a similar ilk, female-oriented ballads like "You Can Take the Wings Off Me," "I'll Believe It When I Feel It," "I've Seen Better Days," "If You Only Knew," and "Don't Touch Me There" that explored women's emotional turmoil as they tried to navigate the troubled seas of romance. In "If You Only Knew," for example, a single woman counseled a married one that, however rocky things might get, having a husband was infinitely better than being alone as she was. And in "You Can Take the Wings Off Me," a woman submitted to seduction rather than continue to be a chaste angel, but not without a somewhat solemn and mournful feeling about it. (Either of these songs could have been a chart hit on its own if released as a single.) McEntire and Bowen threw in some up-tempo material for contrast, beginning with the frisky honky tonk number "I Can't Stop Now"; leading off the LP's side two with the cheery cheating song "Little Rock" (another number-one hit); and providing the requisite Western swing romp with "One Thin Dime." But it was the big ballads that were at the heart of *Whoever's in New England*, and they sold Reba McEntire to her female country constituency once and for all. The singer who'd never had a Top Ten album before went straight to number one with this one.

William Ruhlmann

Reba
April 1988, MCA

In 1984, when she first achieved notable commercial success, Reba McEntire declared herself part of the new traditionalist movement in country music, claiming that the pop-oriented recordings she had made in the '70s and early '80s did not reflect her real taste and that, as an album title put it, *My Kind of Country* was the sound of steel guitars and fiddles. In 1988, however, McEntire and her longtime co-producer Jimmy Bowen demonstrated that she was more interested in hits, in whatever style, than in country music orthodoxy. *Reba*, her 13th regular studio album, featured no steel guitars or fiddles; the most prominent instruments were the keyboards—piano and a DX-7 synthesizer—played by John Jarvis. Rock drummer Russ Kunkel, known for his association with James Taylor, pounded out the crisp beats, and Wayne Nelson popped his bass strings as if he were doing a funk session on the leadoff track, "So, So, So Long," which could have fit in snugly on adult contemporary radio, but certainly didn't sound very country. It was followed by McEntire's cover of the '40s song "Sunday Kind of Love," the album's first single, done in a lazy jazz style. Bowen and McEntire had not forgotten the singer's core audience of women wanting to hear heartbreaking ballads about regret and love gone wrong, and after "Sunday Kind of Love" peaked at a disappointing number five, the more characteristic "New Fool at an Old Game" and "I Know How He Feels" extended McEntire's string of number-one hits. But the song that really set Nashville back on its heels was a cover of Otis Redding's "Respect" in an arrangement very similar to Aretha Franklin's. The makeover worked commercially; *Reba* spent eight weeks at number one on the country charts, more than any previous McEntire album. But the country singer of a few years back, decked out in blue jeans held up by her a belt commemorating her father's rodeo championship, a singer who said she cared about her roots, had been replaced by a much more fashion-conscious performer who clearly wanted to go toe-to-toe with pop acts.

William Ruhlmann

Sweet Sixteen
1989, MCA

Reba McEntire's 13th regular studio album *Reba* shocked some fans and critics by taking a distinct pop crossover direction after several years during which she maintained that she was a neo-traditionalist country artist. On *Reba*, the fiddles and steel guitars were banned from the studio as McEntire made like Aretha Franklin singing "Respect." The album topped the *Billboard* country charts for eight weeks, but McEntire seems to have felt that she should reassure her country base, and so *Sweet Sixteen* (which is her 16th album only if you count her *Greatest Hits* and *Merry Christmas to You*) welcomes the fiddles and steel guitars back as she returns to the neo-traditionalist fold. This is an album on which McEntire doubles back to a formula that worked for her in the past. Kendal Franceschi and Quentin Powers wrote her 1986 career song "Whoever's in New England," and they are back for two selections here, both of which have some of the melancholy of that ballad, but aren't as good. "It Always Rains on Saturday," for which McEntire claims a co-writing credit, takes too long to get to the point of its story, that the narrator is a divorced mother made lonely

when her young son goes off to spend the weekends with his father. "Little Girl" (which became the LP's third country Top Ten hit) has the singer confessing to being overanxious and to having failed at love again. McEntire once coaxed a major hit, "Somebody Should Leave," from legendary country songwriter Harlan Howard. She hasn't obtained another one from him, but she has crossed pens with another heavyweight tunesmith, Don Schlitz, co-writing "Am I the Only One Who Cares," a too-cute story song about a fight between a mother and her teenager daughter that is mediated by a talking moon, and "You Must Really Love Me," a bluegrass workout in the style of Emmylou Harris. Another genre exercise is "'Til Love Comes Again" (the record's second country Top Ten), which leans heavily on fiddle and steel guitar and sounds like it was written for Patsy Cline, whom McEntire successfully impersonates still another familiar country style, honky tonk. The album's pop elements are either muted or more closely tied to country than those on *Reba*. The track list begins with a cover of the Everly Brothers hit "Cathy's Clown" on which McEntire has altered the pronouns to add a third character to the story, another woman, the narrator, who observes the man she loves being Cathy's clown. It doesn't quite work, but that didn't keep the single from going to number one in the country charts when it was released in advance of the album. Another not-exactly-country-but-not-far-removed selection is "Somebody Up There Likes Me," an up-tempo CCM number that sounds like it might have been written with Amy Grant in mind. Perhaps the greatest indication that McEntire hasn't entirely given up on crossover is the recurrent sound of a saxophone in the album's arrangements. Its wail reminds the listener that, while the singer may be harking back to her country roots on *Sweet Sixteen*, her loyalty to tradition may be only temporary.

William Ruhlmann

Rumor Has It
1990, MCA

Reba McEntire's break of 16 months between the May 1989 release of her 14th regular studio album, *Sweet Sixteen*, and her 15th, *Rumor Has It*, in September 1990 was unusually long for a country artist and the longest for her since Mercury Records, her label at the time, waited over two years after the release of her debut LP, *Reba*, in August 1977 to issue her second, *Out of a Dream*, in September 1979. Back then, she was struggling for recognition; by the late '80s, she was country music's biggest female star. In the interim between *Sweet Sixteen* and *Rumor Has It*, she married her manager, Narvel Blackstock, released a live album, and had a baby. Meanwhile, the stream of country Top Ten singles from *Sweet Sixteen* kept her on the radio steadily, and she only took five months off from the road for maternity leave. The break between studio sessions seems to have given her an opportunity to take a fresh look at her recording career. She replaced her regular producer, Jimmy Bowen (who had left his job as president of her label, MCA Records), with Tony Brown, a well-known Nashville figure with a taste for crossover. And, abandoning the move back toward neo-traditionalist country she had undertaken on *Sweet Sixteen*, she made an album closer to its predecessor, *Reba*, a contemporary country crossover effort. Once again, the fiddle was gone, and while steel guitar and mandolin were listed in the credits, they were de-emphasized in favor of synthesizers. Musically, *Rumor Has It* was more of an adult contemporary pop record than a country record, except that McEntire's singing voice retained some of its Oklahoma twang, although even that seemed to have been softened deliberately. The leadoff single, "You Lie," which became McEntire's 15th country number one, sounded like a '50s doo wop ballad, even if the lyrics were typical ones for McEntire in their emphasis on a troubled relationship. Love was also in trouble in the title song, a Top Five country hit, in which the singer suspected infidelity; "Waitin' for the Deal to Go Down," about an impatient bride-to-be ("The ring's still sittin' in a store downtown"); "Now You Tell Me," which repeated the theme of an earlier McEntire song, "One Promise Too Late," a lover waiting too long to declare himself; the self-explanatory "Fallin' Out of Love" (another Top Five country hit); "This Picture"; and "That's All She Wrote." Country fans love to read their favorites' personal lives into the songs they sing, which can be dodgy since country artists so rarely write their own songs, and attempting to do so here would tend to emphasize McEntire's 1987 divorce over her remarriage and motherhood. But some songs did seem to have autobiographical elements. As she had twice on *Sweet Sixteen*, McEntire co-wrote a song with Don Schlitz, this time coming up with the driving leadoff tune, "Climb That Mountain High," which, while not specific, was full of the language of self-assertion. This sounded like the McEntire who had left her first husband and her Oklahoma home for Nashville. Even more interesting were the two covers of old songs. McEntire reserved her most impassioned singing for her version of Bobbie Gentry's 1969 song "Fancy" (a country Top Ten in this new reading, which it was not when Gentry sang it), a song about a "white trash" woman whose mother, well, pimps her out as an escape from poverty. It was a curious choice for revival from a singer who had suffered accusations of having abandoned her roots personally and professionally, and there was a feisty defensiveness in McEntire's performance. Then there was her version of Jesse Winchester's gently cutting "You Remember Me," in which a musician on the road barges in on an old flame who has become more upper class after dumping him long before. Singing it allowed McEntire to turn the tables on the charges of gettin' above her raisin' and throw the accusation at someone else. Doubtless, she herself would say she simply found a couple of good old songs and recorded them, and that's true, too. But *Rumor Has It*, like many of its predecessors, was an album that showed Reba McEntire restlessly in transition, never able to forget her past, but never letting that stop her from grasping at the future.

William Ruhlmann

For My Broken Heart
1991, MCA

Only the quietly moving "If I Had Only Known" might be considered a tribute to the members of McEntire's band who died in a 1990 plane crash, but the tragedy creeps into McEntire's voice and her song selection. Throughout the album, McEntire dwells on regrets, unvoiced feelings, and missed chances. The best songs aren't the hits "For My Broken Heart" and "Is There Life out There" but a group of evocative story-songs which unfold slowly, leaving loose threads and developing complex emotional undercurrents. *For My Broken Heart* may be the strongest album of McEntire's career; it's certainly her most heartbreaking.

Brian Mansfield

Read My Mind
April 1994, MCA

This 1994 album, *Read My Mind*, is another wonderful offering of songs performed by the gifted country singer Reba McEntire. Half of the tunes on this album became hits. Many carry a deep emotional impact, with themes that move from a wife confronting a cheating husband in "I Won't Stand in Line" to lost love in "And Still" to a young woman dealing with AIDS while her friends and family face her nearing death in "She Thinks His Name Was John." There are also a couple of good everyday love ballads on this offering, and the fun and fast-paced song "Why Haven't I Heard From You." Mixed in with the expected country styling on this album you'll find a little soul, a little swing, and some pop, too. This is one of the few albums music lovers will find out there where almost every song is a good one, and worth repeated listening.

Charlotte Dillon

So Good Together
November 1999, MCA Nashville

It hasn't been hard to notice that Reba McEntire's usually reliable stream of number one hits has slowed lately. But *So Good Together* re-examines McEntire's artistry and puts fans back in touch with the Reba we know and love. No one sings emotion better than McEntire, and the relaxed warmth of her voice produces one of the finest vocal performances she's bestowed on listeners since before *Starting Over*. *So Good Together*'s first release, the introspective "What Do You Say," has been making its way up the charts in glowing Reba style.

Maria Konicki Dinoia

Room to Breathe
November 2003, MCA Nashville

Four years seems to have done Reba McEntire some good. On her first studio album in four years, she resurrects her passion for country music that seemed to have been missing on her previous album. She sings all 12 tracks like she's happy to be home in country music. From the longing of "My Sister" to the soulfulness of the title track, McEntire reminds listeners why they missed her. She's always good for the affecting story-songs and doesn't disappoint with "Moving Oleta" and "Somebody." And what's a Reba album without the lovely Linda Davis on background harmony vocals or a duet with country music faithful Vince Gill? (Think 1992's "The Heart Won't Lie.") You'll find many of the old staples here, but you'll also get a revitalized and cool-sounding Reba.

Maria Konicki Dinoia

Reba #1's
November 2005, MCA Nashville

It's hard to believe, but 2005's double-disc *#1's* is the first multi-disc retrospective of Reba McEntire's career, which has had several single-disc sets prior to this. While this, like many similarly titled collections, does not strictly follow the rules set up in its title—not counting the two new songs that open up each page here, there are 11 songs among these 35 tracks that did not hit number one in *Billboard*'s country charts—it's hard to complain about this. After all, *#1's* includes all of her number one singles, and those 11 hit singles that did not make it to the top spot all were Top Five singles and rank among her best work. Taken together, they make for the best overview of and introduction to McEntire's lengthy, consistent career.

Stephen Thomas Erlewine

Tim McGraw

Tim McGraw
1993, Curb

Three songs—"Welcome to the Club," "Memory Lane," and "Two Steppin' Mind"—appeared on the bottom half of the *Billboard* singles chart, which suggested that Tim McGraw had some talent but wasn't anything special . . . yet. In a year that introduced Clay Walker and Doug Supernaw, hardly anybody noticed this young-hat act at the time (but they would), while his contemporaries have already become has-beens. Signed to Curb Records, McGraw, a Louisiana native, would quickly establish himself, becoming a superstar and a modern-day legend of contemporary country music who has yet to rest on his laurels. Produced by Byron Gallimore, this debut is memorable if only for those three singles, and the trademark voice that harked back to the tradition begat by Merle Haggard and George Jones, though McGraw is also deeply stylistically indebted to singers like Randy Travis and George Strait. And even though McGraw's sound at the time was a bit generic, he would soon delve deeply—with his own crack band, the Dancehall Doctors—into country-rock, blues, and even hip-hop for inspiration. Not only would he find them, he would turn the country world on its ear in doing so. Of all his peers, McGraw is the real thing, and the roots of that individuality are heard on this set; it contains the grain of that now instantly identifiable voice.

Brian Mansfield & Thom Jurek

Not a Moment Too Soon
March 1994, Curb

"Indian Outlaw," with its controversy and its resemblance to the Raiders' "Indian Reservation," made Tim McGraw a star and earned him the nickname "Outlaw McGraw." The ballad "Don't Take the Girl" reinforced the image. *Not a Moment Too Soon* contained better hooks than its predecessor, but it also belabored the obvious with songs like "It Don't Get Any Countrier Than This" and "Give It to Me Strait." That said, McGraw's identity as a singer and as a bandleader was being forged bit by bit. Taken as an album, *Not a Moment Too Soon* is actually a solid listen, containing the first real hints of the influence of Southern rock on his sound, one that would endure. While producer Byron Gallimore seems to get credit for this, it was actually inherent in McGraw's sound

from the beginning and Nashville tried to take it out—until they figured out how to sell it. And while it's true that Hank Williams, Jr. had used the authentic members of that rock subgenre many years before on his *Hank Williams, Jr. & Friends* album, the mantle hadn't really been picked up since. McGraw not only began to use it, but because of his success beginning with this album—proving the adage that no publicity is bad publicity—he spawned countless imitators, making rock & roll a steady part of contemporary country music.

Brian Mansfield & Thom Jurek

All I Want
September 1995, Curb

Tim McGraw's early albums always suffered from uneven material, but *All I Want* is a surprisingly consistent record that consolidates his strengths while allowing him to expand into new territory. He didn't abandoned the honky tonk and jokey country-rock that made him famous, but he made it rock harder and hired songwriters who would help him make it more believable—just check the track "Renegade" for an example. Similarly, his ballads, such as "I Didn't Ask and She Didn't Say," and "Can't Be Really Gone," are heartfelt; they're delivered with convincing sincerity. In other words, he has grown musically and developed into a thoroughly entertaining vocalist. And that growth is what makes *All I Want* the best of his early records. It is still somewhat uneven, with several weaker songs, but McGraw learned on his first couple of efforts how to disguise the flaws in the material with his singing and lessen them considerably from here on in.

Stephen Thomas Erlewine & Thom Jurek

Everywhere
June 1997, Curb

Everywhere, Tim McGraw's fourth album, finds the vocalist in a bit of a rut, following the same formula of slick ballads and measured rockers that made his second record, *Not a Moment Too Soon*, a blockbuster success. That's not necessarily a bad thing, since he remains an appealing singer when he has the right material, such as on the single "It's Your Love." In fact, it's the ballads that work better here; they prove truly outstanding and even moving: "You Just Get Better All the Time," the title track, and "I Do But I Don't." When he has a lesser tune, however, the results are bland and uneventful "Hard on the Ticker" is an example. Those songs don't prevent *Everywhere* from being a pleasant listen, and it satisfied his legions of fans well enough, but it did suggest that he should break free from these constraints and move toward the excellence he was capable of and eventually delivered.

Stephen Thomas Erlewine & Thom Jurek

Place in the Sun
May 1999, Curb

Everywhere may have continued Tim McGraw's streak of hit albums, but it also suggested that he was falling into a bit of a rut. That doesn't seem to have bothered McGraw, since *Everywhere*'s sequel, *A Place in the Sun*, is much like its predecessor in its balance of polished ballads, country-pop and up-tempo ravers, which are supposed to sound like honky-tonk but are closer to country-rock. Since he's a professional and works with professionals, *A Place in the Sun* sounds good and has a number of highlights, from ballads like "My Best Friend" and the Patty Loveless duet "Please Remember Me" to harder numbers like "Something Like That," "My Next Thirty Years," and "She'll Have You Back." The problem is, there's nothing new here—not only is the music in the same vein as his previous efforts, it has nearly the same ratio of hits to misses. Since the moments that do work are very good, and since it is a stronger overall record than its predecessor, it will be worthwhile for fans, but it doesn't help erase the impression that McGraw won't deliver a truly satisfying album until a greatest-hits compilation comes along.

Stephen Thomas Erlewine

Set This Circus Down
April 2001, Curb

Tim McGraw's first studio album on Curb Records after the multi-platinum success of *A Place in the Sun* delivers a more diverse selection in its 14 tunes with longtime producers Byron Gallimore and James Stroud. From the energetic honky tonk sound of "Forget About Us," to the upbeat tempo of "Telluride" to the Latin-laced "Let Me Love You," McGraw masterfully and consistently flows from one sound style to the next. Yet his familiar country-pop sound remains evident throughout, especially on the title track, a song about a fast-paced couple yearning to kick back and relax in the country (no one said the themes would be original). Sung with such confidence, one might believe it's a self-imposed goal set by McGraw. Just as convincing are the heartfelt ballads of "The Cowboy in Me" and "You Get Used to Somebody," and "Angel Boy." McGraw's wife, Faith Hill, contributes subtle harmonic vocals on the emotionally compelling "Angry All the Time," written by maverick Americana outsider Bruce Robison. It portrays a relationship gone sour; a tune that was added to the set list no doubt to digress from his usual slate of love songs. Although the sentimental "Grown Men Don't Cry," written by Steve Seskin and Tommy Douglas, was the first official release from the album, McGraw's uplifting performance of "Things Change" at the Country Music Awards mysteriously found its way onto Napster first. Subsequently, the album track hit the country radio airwaves, where it received not only airplay, but enthusiastic response form listeners and helped to push the sales of the album even higher. McGraw's aggressive approach to *Set This Circus Down* makes it one of his finest efforts.

Deborah Wong & Thom Jurek

Tim McGraw and the Dancehall Doctors
November 2002, Curb

Tim "Outlaw" McGraw has been one of the most consistent of the late '90s country superstars. Never content to reply on his reputation, he continually pushed at the pillars of the hall that created him, namely Nash Vegas. McGraw's particular gift as an interpreter of other songwriters' works is almost singular among his generation of singers. Not relying solely on production, McGraw uses numerous voices to get to the heart of a song. On this album, McGraw convinced his label and co-producers, Byron Gallimore and Darran Smith, to use his road band, the Dancehall Doctors, to make a more organic and immediate sounding record. It worked. From the stunning opener, "Comfort Me," by Craig Wiseman and Don Poythress, an ancient military sounding snare drum and a bleeding guitar note usher in a tune that is the only non-cloying patriotic song that was recorded after September 11, 2001. It's a hymn equal parts country and Celtic that is an homage to all of those who entered this country by going past the Statue of Liberty and entered the American experience. When he reaches the end, "I am the tired, I am your poor in spirit/yearnin' to breathe, breathe free . . . ," the listener is caught up in the "us" of the song; it's inclusive,

and captures in McGraw's prayer for comfort, for deliverance not from something else but to the space that freedom is—defined both individually and collectively—is unique among the country songs that came up after the disaster struck. Interestingly enough, it sets the tone for a record full of romantic archetypes, not only the icon of Lady Liberty, but family ("Home"); the reliving of experience unconsciously ("Red Ragtop"); escape and recreation of oneself ("That's Why God Made Mexico"); the idealization of love as a force in and of itself ("Watch the Wind Blow By", a killer soul-oriented track by Anders Osborne, and McGraw sings the hell out of it); dislocation and the realization that home isn't such a bad place to be ("Sing Me Home"); and others. McGraw closes the record with Elton John's and Bernie Taupin's "Tiny Dancer," and for a verse or so, you'd swear it was the same recording. It's frightening how close to the original it is. Why would anyone try to recreate a song so close to its original version; simple, because they love it. And McGraw's version is gorgeous, soulful, and deep like the rest of *And the Dance Hall Kings*.

Thom Jurek

Live Like You Were Dying
August 2004, Curb

There's good reason for Tim McGraw's endurance at the top of contemporary country: he's a restless visionary who's worked hard to improve as an interpretive singer. In 2002, McGraw bucked the trend and convinced his label, and producers Byron Galli-  more and Darran Smith, to let him use his road band in the studio. The rough and tumble intimacy of the set put it over the top and appealed to music fans outside his circle. On *Live Like You Were Dying*, McGraw ups the ante. Using the same production team and his Dancehall Doctors, McGraw cut a whopping 16 tracks and helped in the mixing of the record, as well as co-producing. The song selection runs the gamut. There's the blues-rock energy of the opener, "How Bad Do You Want It," where he evokes the ghost of the Mississippi Delta as well as the hard country-rock sounds of Marshall Tucker and Lynyrd Skynyrd. Then there's the shimmering Americana of "My Old Friend" that would not be out of place performed by Pierce Pettis, and the fantastic "Old Town New," by renegade songwriters Bruce Robison and Darrell Scott. The monster single from this record, "Live Like You Were Dying," by Craig Wiseman and Tim Nichols, is the very best kind of modern country song; the emotion in McGraw's delivery is honest, not saccharine. In anyone else's voice, a song like "Drugs or Jesus" would be just plain bad. The tune itself is solid and beautifully constructed, a perfect marriage of melody, hook, and direct, simple lyrics. But the temptation to over-perform such a song is irresistible to most of the hit factory's mainstays. Not for McGraw though: his understatement underscores the lyric's seriousness. The tenderness in Rodney Crowell and James T. Slater's "Open Season on My Heart" is vulnerable in all the right ways. The moody poignancy of "Walk Like a Man," is a fine and haunting centerpiece for this fine album. "Kill Myself" has to be experienced—it's a miracle and a testament to McGraw's clout that this tune made it on to the record. "We Carry On" is a soulful anthem, gritty, true, and beautiful. It's a fitting close to McGraw's finest moment yet. The young hell-raiser has grown to be one of modern country's most compelling and multidimensional artists.

Thom Jurek

Let It Go
June 2007, Curb

Tim McGraw stayed out of recording studios for nearly three years after his smash single and album *Live Like You Were Dying*. McGraw is a road dog and a husband to Faith Hill. The pair had a child and McGraw comes back to a style of country music he helped form in the early '90s. His backing band, the Dance Hall Doctors, is the E Street Band of country music in the 21st century. McGraw—who, with help from Byron Gallimore and Darran Smith, produced *Let It Go*— is once more willing to push the sonic formulaic envelope with a wonderfully textural array of sounds and the moods they help to underscore. (Think, if you will, Mitch Easter as a country music producer with a big road band to rein in.) In fact, the sound of the record, its varied richness, and its pluralities illustrate that this is an era in countrymusic when creatively almost anything is possible. It still comes down to songs, though, and the 13 here are all winners. The honky tonk songs are more so ("Shotgun Rider," "Whiskey and You"), the pop tunes are more on the rock & roll side of pop ("Last Dollar [Fly Away]"), and the romantic and story-songs ("I'm Workin'") are so utterly, unabashedly plainspoken, they hit the listener straight in the gut. But the real shock is the psychedelic country-rock of the title cut, written by William C. Luther, Aimee Mayo, and Tom Douglas. There are multi-layered pedal steels, baroquely jangled electric guitars, and McGraw's singular vocals riding above the wall of multivalent yet melodic noise to offer a message of threadbare hope in the face of adversity. In the grain of his voice, you can hear the determination to talk and walk from the place of redemption rather than the terrain of suffering. He's singing to convince himself as much as he is the listener. "Put Your Lovin' on Me" is another one, but this one is an anthem, albeit one that pleads for relief and sustenance. There is an amazing spirituality at work in the songs that McGraw chooses here. A Hammond B-3, spiky guitars, and booming snares and cymbals play at the distortion point in this tune by Hillary Lindsey and Luke Laird, but no matter how loud and proud the music is, McGraw's insistence on delivering an unfettered, albeit desperately sincere, melody is what makes him stand apart. When he sings "Put your lovin' on me/Take this weight off me/Put your lovin' on me," he's way beyond the ledge of asking, "There's nothing here to catch me now/ I'm gonna fall anyway." He has nothing to lose and expresses that. The haunting guitars and mandolin lines that introduce "Between the River and Me" offer a story-song that is tough, overblown, and full of anger, regret, and the voice of a man haunted by his anger. The other great rocker is the obligatory country train song called "Train #10." The sound here evokes the arid desert landscapes, where frontier and train tracks meet one another. It's a leaving song that's offered with a vengeance. And, of course, there is the beautiful love song duet between McGraw and Hill in "I Need You," with its provocative line "I need you/Like a needle needs a vein." Hill answers from the loneliest space in her full-throated alto: "I want to dance to the static of an AM radio/I want to wrap the moon around us/Lay beside you, skin on skin/Make love till the sun comes up/Till the sun goes down again/'Cause I need

you." It's the equation of death, addiction, love, and redemption all rolled into a four-minute tune. While this set of songs doesn't have the same unabashed optimism that *Live Like You Were Dying* does, it is no less so in its own gruff, rock & roll way. That said, this is one of the best interpretations of the country tradition by McGraw yet, and while he no longer has the wild edge of his earlier records, McGraw has something deeper: he can look at the dark side without flinching and bring it up to the light, always looking to find his way home. *Let It Go* was well worth the wait and McGraw is still at the top of the heap.

Thom Jurek

Jo Dee Messina

Jo Dee Messina
March 1996, Curb

Country singer Jo Dee Messina has been voted top new female vocalist by the Academy of County Music, and walked away with the Country Music Association's Horizon Award. Before then she made her full-length debut into the music world with this 1996 self-titled album. Producers Byron Gallimore and well-known singer Tim McGraw oversaw the recording. The resulting album was an impressive outing for Messina. On this recording, music lovers can enjoy country ballads like "He'd Never Seen Julie Cry," "On a Wing and a Prayer," and "Every Little Girl's Dream," as well as upbeat, energetic pop-flavored numbers such as "Do You Wanna Make Something of It" and "Heads Carolina, Tails California." The latter is an early favorite of many Messina fans. After such a great first effort, it wasn't surprising that her next album, *I'm Alright*, released two years later, went double platinum.

Charlotte Dillon

I'm Alright
March 1998, Curb

On the follow-up to her self-titled breakout debut, Jo Dee Messina and her production team of Tim McGraw and Byron Gallimore don't mess with what's not broke. Messina took two years to get *I'm Alright* to the fans, quite frankly because she was so busy touring in support of her hit record. Certainly a fencepost in the foundation blueprint for contemporary country records in the 21st century, *I'm Alright* contains ten cuts that either walk the line between country and straight-up radio-friendly pop or fall just to the country side of that fence. Messina has an enormous voice. While she doesn't have to stretch her contralto range much, her sense of dynamics is a near trademark, learned from the very best in the business. For proof, all one needs to do is go to the ballads, such as the Kostas and John Sherrill-penned "Because You Love Me," with its sense of restraint until the key moment in the refrain when caution is tossed to the wind and the singer delivers the proof in her conviction. The other tune Sherrill contributed to the set is the poignant "Even God Must Get the Blues," co-authored with Dene Anton. Messina's real musical companion in the tune is a lost and lonely Hammond B-3 organ—which seems to have become a standard in contemporary country just as the upright piano was to the countrypolitan sound of the '60s—and she walks with it, strolls with it, and dances with it through this socially conscious heartbreaker. But Messina can deliver party tunes, love songs, and break-up songs as well as anyone, as evidenced by the title cut that opens the disc. Driven by banjo, mandolin, pedal steel, and acoustic guitars, this one rolls with a backwoods back-porch vibe, and all is well with the world. Certainly the record is clean, perhaps a bit too clean, but the song selection is close to impeccable. Gallimore and McGraw were still finding their way with Messina here, and they hit pay dirt with her next record, 2000's *Burn*, where they found the perfect balance between country, pop, and '70s soft rock to dress Messina's voice in.

Thom Jurek

Burn
August 2000, Curb

Co-producers Tim McGraw and Byron Gallimore struck gold on *Burn*, Jo Dee Messina's third offering for Curb, and her last for five solid years. The formula on her first two offerings, her self-titled debut (1996) and *I'm Alright* (1998), seemed to work, and the pair didn't tinker with it all that much, except for the fact that the pair could see the bend in the road where the fork between contemporary country and slick adult pop came together and they met it head on. Given the monster set of contralto pipes that Messina possesses, it didn't matter; she crossed over into the pop mainstream anyway. The hits here include the awesome "These Are the Days," written by Holly Lamar and Stephanie Bentley, which wound layers of acoustic guitars, pedal steel, and a soaring harmonica that filled the center as fiddles and mandolins colored the backdrop. Messina expressed the "never say die" philosophy in the song with hunger and verve, putting it across with conviction and even a little mischievous delight. The title track is a love song like no other she'd recorded before. Its ringing guitars and nearly urban R&B bassline carried the monochromatic melody line into deep emotional territory, and once more Messina put the song across as if she'd lived it all, asking the question "Do you want to be a soldier, for love?" with all the authority necessary to communicate it to fans. "Dare to Dream" is such a straight-up pop/rocker it's a wonder it wasn't on every Top 40 station simultaneously. The album opens with the killer single "Downtime," which defines the heart of contemporary country: its themes of determination in the face of adversity, the belief in true love as a redemptive force, and a musical backdrop that is equal parts pop, country, and the light rock that powered the 1970s. There's even a more convincing argument for rock on the set in the Roy Hurd and Templeton Thompson tune "Nothing I Can Do," which has a near thundering guitar riff in the verse. *Burn* is a kind of small masterpiece that never dates, despite its occasionally sugary sound and very slick production; it's

a testament to the vocal prowess of Messina, who is able to convey even the most ordinary lyrics with authority. Of the recordings she issued between her debut and 2005's *Delicious Surprise*, *Burn* remains her finest moment.

Thom Jurek

Greatest Hits
May 2003, Curb

A greatest-hits album appearing after just three studio albums and following a Christmas album by months can only mean one thing—an artist is reaching the end of her contract, and she's riding it out. So appears to be the case with Jo Dee Messina, whose *Greatest Hits* was released in May of 2003, seven years after her first album. During those seven years, she amassed quite a number of hits, including five chart-toppers. All of them are here on this generous 15-track collection, along with four new tracks, highlighted by the opening track and lead single "Was That My Life." Only two of her charting singles for Curb are missing—the first, "Do You Wanna Make Something of It," and the last, "Dare to Dream"—which makes this an excellent summary and introduction to an artist who may not have blazed trails, but delivered consistently enjoyable mainstream and fairly traditional country, as this fine collection proves.

Stephen Thomas Erlewine

Delicious Surprise
April 2005, Curb

Not counting a Christmas album and a greatest-hits compilation, Jo Dee Messina didn't release an album between 2000's *Burn* and 2005's *Delicious Surprise*. Five years is a long, long wait between records, and Messina does what any smart artist should and pretends that the gap doesn't exist by patterning her new album after the prevailing trends in current country music. At the midpoint of the 2000s, the hottest thing around is the Muzik Mafia spearheaded by gonzo country-poppers Big & Rich, whose protégée Gretchen Wilson is the biggest new female country singer of the mid-'90s. Messina uses Wilson, or at least Wilson's rowdy redneck image, as the foundation of her comeback on *Delicious Surprise*, which is filled with sexy pictures of Messina, starting with her toned stomach on the back cover to a shot of her topless on a white piano in the liner notes (for those interested in such things, the poster promised on the back cover is nothing more than the large picture on the fold-out booklet, meaning that if you tack this up on your wall, your CD no longer has a booklet). Wilson's attitude is also apparent on the sassy first single, "My Give a Damn's Busted," which sports not only the funniest lyric here, but also the leanest, liveliest arrangement. That's because, for all of the exterior makeover, Messina pretty much remains the same as she was in 2000: a dynamic, charismatic singer who's good enough to make her professionally crafted Nashville country-pop sound less formulaic than it is, but that doesn't disguise the fact that it's often standard Music City fare. And it's not the songwriting that's a problem—she gets some of the best professional tunes on the market and her original material here (four songs, which is a grand total of a quarter of the album) is assured, confessional, and among the best material here—but it's the production and presentation, which are too safe, predictable, and radio-ready. True, *Delicious Surprise* is well done, sounding as good as anything in mainstream contemporary country, but as "My Give a Damn's Busted" proves, Messina's already appealing vocals sound better in arrangements that don't rely on soaring choruses and aren't polished til they shine. Not that she sounds bad—it's just that she doesn't sound as distinctive as she could or should, given that great voice of hers. All things considered, *Delicious Surprise* is a solid comeback—after a five-year hiatus, it's simply good to have Jo Dee Messina back—but the best moments here, whether the aforementioned single or her searching ballad "It Gets Better," are good enough to hold out hope that she releases an album of songs that consistently strong the next time around.

Stephen Thomas Erlewine

Ronnie Milsap

My Life
June 2006, RCA

Prior to 2006's *My Life*, Ronnie Milsap had not made an album of new material for a major label in years. The last was *True Believer*, recorded for Liberty in 1993, which followed *Back to the Grindstone*, his parting of ways with RCA Records, by two years. Over that decade-and-a-half, Milsap wasn't exactly inactive—he continued to play shows and record, including re-recording his biggest songs for Capitol in 1996, and a collection of standards in 2004, but *My Life* qualifies as a genuine comeback, as it finds Milsap returning to RCA and recording songs that are not only new, but addresses American life in the early 2000s. This, of course, is most explicit on "A Day in the Life of America," a chronicling of mundane everyday events that borders on the depressing, but *My Life* finds Milsap reminiscing about his life in a manner appropriate only for a singer in his sixties. This provides *My Life* with slightly nostalgic undertones at times, but the album never feels melancholy: it's as bright and tuneful and relaxed as the best of his early-'80s crossover albums. In fact, if it wasn't for Keith Stegall's crisp, thoroughly modern production, it would be easy to mistake *My Life* as an unearthed lost album from Milsap's early '80s peak, and that's what makes it such a good comeback: song for song, this stays true to Milsap's strengths as a country-pop hitmaker, yet recasts it in a manner that's fresh without pandering to the charts. If he doesn't make another record, *My Life* will stand as a worthy coda to his career, but hopefully, this excellent album will be the start of a third act in a career that's been quite remarkable.

Stephen Thomas Erlewine

The Essential Ronnie Milsap [Double Disc]
August 2006, RCA Nashville

To get an idea of exactly how many Ronnie Milsap collections are on the market, just turn to the back page of the booklet for RCA/Legacy's 2006 double-disc set *The Essential Ronnie Milsap*, where it lists other Ronnie albums you might also enjoy. There are ten listed, all but one of them a compilation (that would be his very, very good 2006 comeback, *My Life*). Which begs the natural question, is *The Essential Ronnie Milsap* needed? Especially since there is already *another* compilation called *The Essential Ronnie Milsap* (dating from 1995), and there already was an excellent double-disc set called *40 #1 Hits* released six years earlier? The answer

is, yes it is, particularly since *40 #1 Hits* has fallen out of print. Of course, it also helps that *Essential* is an expertly chosen and sequenced collection of Milsap's best work, from 1973's "(All Together Now) Let's Fall Apart" and running all the way to 1989's "A Woman in Love." Most of this material was on *40 #1 Hits*, so if you already own that, there's not much need for this, but this has a slight edge over the previous comp because it has a greater concentration of his prime material and is very listenable; its non-chronological sequencing works for it, since it emphasizes the consistently high quality of his hits singles. So, even if there is a surplus of Milsap collections out on the market, this superb set indeed proves that there's always room for another good one.

Stephen Thomas Erlewine

Montgomery Gentry

Tattoos & Scars
April 1999, Columbia

With all of the comparisons to Southern rock legends Lynyrd Skynyrd, Marshall Tucker, Charlie Daniels, the Outlaws, and so forth, this solid, hardcore rockin' honky tonk duo and their amazing band is an entity unto themselves. Eddie Montgomery (brother of John Michael) and Troy Gentry are equal parts country music that comes from Merle Haggard, George Jones, Wynn Stewart, Dwight Yoakam, and even Hank Williams. At the same time, they play a scorching brand of rock & roll that has everything to do with the aforementioned heroes of the 1970s and the Allmans too because the blues are at the root of everything they do. This is an auspicious debut album, one that not only shows promise, but delivers the goods in the form of great songs written by a host of Nash Vegas' and Texas' finest—if unknown new breed—and absolutely tremendous performances. Check the hard rocking opener, "Hillbilly Shoes," with its flatpicking guitar intro supplanted by overdriven fiddles and screaming dual lead guitars. And "Trying to Survive" with its guitar, pedal steel, and piano fills is reminiscent of the feel, not sound, of Tucker's "Can't You See." It's easy to embrace Tim McGraw and a host of others who use rock & roll as way of framing their country music, but Montgomery Gentry don't use rock; they are a rock band who make country music, real country music. Check the gorgeous chorus on "Lonely and Gone" that is commenced with a heavy metal guitar intro only to become a gorgeous mid-tempo ballad. Other tracks, like "Self-Made Man," are pure modern honky tonk. Vocally, the harmonies between this pair are a perfect balance of beer and fine whiskey. Montgomery's rough hewn baritone and Gentry's almost unreal range and trademark phrasing make something highly original in the face of so much cookie-cutter Nash Vegas big-hatted crap. The funky blues on "Daddy Won't Sell the Farm" with those fiddles and pedal steels wrapping around a greasy keyboard line lead into a rebel Southern son's admiration for a man and a way of life that is quickly disappearing. The drums propel the tune forward, and the guitars fill what little space there is with rollin' and tumblin' blues. The Bakerfield honky tonk of "I've Loved a Lot More Than I've Hurt" is as traditional as it gets, and Jones or Yoakam could have cut it. The title track is a great morality tale, and "Trouble Is" is a Gentry showcase with his singing tenor in the hillbilly groove that is equal parts blues, tonkin' stride, and arena rock. Montgomery Gentry should be nothing less than amazing in a few years if they keep this up, because this is solid, ass-kickin' country-rock. This is one of the best pop records of the year. Period.

Thom Jurek

My Town
August 2002, Columbia

The core of Montgomery Gentry's musical appeal lies in the duo's vocal contrast, alternating lead singing between the gruff low tenor of Eddie Montgomery and the sweeter high tenor of Troy Gentry. The core of their cultural appeal lies in another dichotomy, between the hell-raising and church-going aspects of stereotypical Southern rural life. "My Town," the leadoff track, title song, and advance single from their third album, concerns itself with the latter, depicting a small community in which you have to get up early on Sunday morning to be able to find a seat in church. But by the fifth track, the singers are having trouble keeping to the straight and narrow, deciding that they'll be "Bad for Good," and that song is a good candidate for a single, too. To a country fan, of course, there isn't that much of a conflict between the duo's rowdy Saturday night and reverent Sunday morning postures. In fact, they're two sides of the same coin. Similarly, to Montgomery Gentry, as to many fans, contemporary country music isn't just acoustic instruments and cheating songs, it's also the legacy of 1970s Southern rock. The session musicians number Allman Brothers Band alumni Chuck Leavell and Johnny Neel, and the album, which rocks harder as it goes along, concludes with a cover of "Good Clean Fun" from the Allmans' 1990 album, *Seven Turns*. Just as their image, with Montgomery decked out in a black jacket with tails and a big, flat-brimmed hat and Gentry in excessively casual wear, is calculated, so their musical approach is tempered. But the contradictions are the same ones their listeners live with every day. You may want to jump on the bar and yell "Hell Yeah," but "Montgomery Gentry supports responsible drinking," as a sleeve note discloses. And be early for church.

William Ruhlmann

You Do Your Thing
May 2004, Columbia

On album number four, Troy and Eddie make no major breaks with the tried and true formula that weds solid modern country music to the long raucous tradition of redneck rock. But then again, they don't need to. It's true, they streamline it, rock it up, and bring in some more rock & roll, but essentially, these cats lay down 12 very solid tracks written by a slew of Nash Vegas songwriters, most notably Rivers Rutherford, Jeffrey Steele, and Bob DiPiero, who wrote the lion's share of the set. Steele and Rutherford also produced various tracks, as did Blake Chancey and Joe Scaife. But it all comes down to the performances, and Montgomery Gentry sing these songs like they were their own. And in a sense, now they are. The album opens with "Something To Be Proud Of," a reflective country song that looks at the past as a way of informing the present. It's got the anthemic chorus, but for the most part it digs deep into the heart of country music. The red, white, and blue individualism of the title cut may be hard for some fans to swallow—but unlike many others who sing anthems to jingoistic patriotism or make self-righteous accusatory judgments in the name of political correctness

(the other censorship), these good ol' boys offer tolerance at the heart of their message and insist on it in return. (And the roaring refrain is on a wailing par with that of "My Town.") The album's first single, "If You Ever Stop Loving Me," with its crunching guitars in the refrain, popping banjo in the verse, and even hip-hop scratching in the backdrop, is the summertime country-rock anthem for 2004. Rebel rock granddaddy Hank Williams, Jr. shows up on "I Ain't Got It All That Bad," a rootsy, moving statement of gratitude and acceptance that is the most resonant track on the set. There is also the sheer rock & roll roar of cuts like "If It's the Last Thing I Do" and "Gone," and the hillbilly craziness of "I Got Drunk," written by one of this album's guitarists, David Grissom. Grissom, who spent many years with Joe Ely and later starred with the John Mellencamp band, outshines virtually everyone here with his searing tone, in-the-pocket licks, and soulful fills—and he never overplays. There are even a couple of old-school love songs here in "She Loved Me" and the mid-tempo ballad "All I Know About Mexico." Ultimately, this is easily the finest outing by modern country's most relevant duo; it rocks, it's soulful, and it's memorable.

Thom Jurek

Something to Be Proud Of: The Best of 1999–2005
November 2005, Columbia

Montgomery Gentry's first compilation, *Something to Be Proud Of: The Best of 1999–2005* is an excellent, concise collection of highlights from the duo's first four albums. For some, it may be a little too concise, since its tight 13-track running length means that there are a handful of charting singles that didn't make the cut—four to be precise, with three of them dating from 2000 and 2001 ("All Night Long," "Self Made Man," and "Cold One Comin' On," with 2004's "You Do Your Thing" being the other charting single from 1999-2005 that's missing). While there may be a few fans that will lament the absence of these tunes, it's otherwise hard to find fault with this fine compilation, since it not only contains the duo's biggest hits—including "Daddy Won't Sell the Farm," "Lonely and Gone," "She Couldn't Change Me," "My Town," "Speed," "Gone," "Hell Yeah," "If You Ever Stop Loving Me," and "Something to Be Proud Of"—but the new song "She Don't Tell Me To" is solid, helping to make this hits collection an entertaining listen in its own right.

Stephen Thomas Erlewine

Some People Change
October 2006, Columbia

Since the release of *Tattoos & Scars* in 1999, Eddie Montgomery and Troy Gentry have been making consistently fine country-rock records and videos (the latter thanks in large part to the wonderful director Trey Fanjoy). While their albums translate to CMT and GAC—and of course to the *Billboard* charts—the duo has never been comfortable making one kind of recording. They dig deep with their producers—in this case Mark Wright is primary—to find the best songs and let them rip. Guitars roar, wail, and whisper, and Montgomery Gentry's wonderfully contrasting voices and passionate, down-home delivery tie them to the great traditions of both rock and country. They've consistently sent out a message of tolerance—but they demanded to be tolerated as well. (Do we ever need that message in a nation as deeply divided as the United States in 2006.) Each successive album has been a hit, and deservedly so. *Some People Change*, however, is a step above.

These two fellas have a way with a song. Kenny Chesney was the first to record the wonderful "Some People Change" by Michael Dulaney/Jason Sellers/Neil Thrasher. Given that it's a great song, nobody could do a bad job with it, and Chesney's was better than decent. But it simply turns to gray in lieu of the treatment given it by Montgomery Gentry, with a blend of acoustic and electric guitars that wind together before Montgomery's deep baritone lays out the contrast in the lyric: "His ole man was a rebel yeller/Bad boy to the bone, he'd say/Can't trust that feller/He'd judge 'em by the tone/Of their skin. . . ." A wah-wah peddle floats atmospherically and a synth slips in gently and Montgomery continues: "He was raised to think like his dad/Narrow mind, fulla hate/On the road to nowhere fast/Until the grace of God got in the way/And he saw the light and hit his knees and cried and said a prayer/Rose up a brand new man and left the old one right there. . . ." The guitars build to an almost unbearable tension and finally break with a B-3 announcing Gentry's arrival on the refrain, which is an anthem: "Here's to the strong/Thanks to the brave/Don't give up hope/Some people change/Against all odds/Against the grain/Love finds a way/Some people change. . . ." Simply put, the song addresses race, class, religion, and (later) addiction, as well as hope, tolerance, and the willingness to believe redemption is possible in any situation. When was the last time a country recording addressed topics like this in a single tune that opened an album? When a gospel choir enters near the end to join the pair on the refrain with soloing guitars and tight, clipped drums, it becomes transcendent. It's one of those tunes that define something that lies at the heart of what is good about Americans. True to form, however, Montgomery Gentry aren't about to have their music co-opted by anybody—left or right—and the very next cut, "Hey Country," quotes from Lynyrd Skynyrd, Hank Jr., Marshall Tucker, funk, and hip-hop, and is a true redneck rabble-rouser. Killer metal guitars, banjos, funky basslines, and chanted choruses all war with each other and finally come to an equal level to make this the best tune that's never been on rock & roll radio. "Lucky Man" is a pure country song, and it updates "I Ain't Got It All That Bad" from *You Do Your Thing*. Its protagonist—Montgomery in this case—is older, wiser, and even more grateful. Here again, it's a message tune, but one that is poignant no matter what color collar you wear, whether or not you support the President of the United States, and whatever religion you choose—including none at all. The steel guitar whines ring above the impeccably recorded vocals while the electric guitars and tom-toms pop and jump to underscore the lyric. That's how the album goes, without a filler cut in the bunch. Other notables include a woolly country-rocker "It Takes All Kinds"—it would be a great second single—that also celebrates American difference. These guys know how to use a B-3, electric guitars, and drums as a basic function of carrying song lyrics, not as merely accompaniment. There are broken love songs ("Your Tears Are Comin'") and faithful ones ("If You Wanna Keep an Angel," a rock & roll country song with an amazing chorus of backing vocalists). There are paeans to lost fathers from stubborn—and newly wizened—sons ("20 Years Ago"), and a gorgeous ballad written by Montgomery called "Clouds." A piano carries his voice, cracking, breaking, and utterly sincere in its sadness and tenderness. When synths shimmer in the background,

they don't intrude, just color. This is an elegy that, one more time, offers a portrait of the sheer diversity and range of this band's ability to deliver songs with conviction, sass, grit, and softness whenever necessary.

Some People Change is one of the many things that's right with mainstream country music in the new millennium. It's brave and it looks for commonality, not to define people but to celebrate them. Its tone is balanced and even and wild and raucous, all at the same time. Country taught rock & roll plenty in the past and there is no doubt that rock & roll is influencing modern country presently—and this album is a showcase of that. Both are the better for it. *Some People Change* is a new pinnacle for the duo. It feels like it was conceived as an album, not merely as a collection of songs or singles, and to the credit of Montgomery Gentry, they execute it like one. It's a masterpiece; listeners need more records that aspire to this kind of excellence.

Thom Jurek

John Michael Montgomery

The Very Best of John Michael Montgomery
August 2003, Warner Bros.

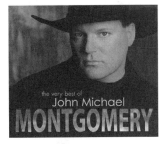

For the millions of fans who have made John Michael Montgomery a major country music star, and who probably already own most (if not all) of the eight albums from which this best-of is drawn, the main appeal of this album will be functional: it pulls together a disproportionate number of the power ballads for which he is justly famous, making this a heartland makeout record of considerable utility. (It also features two previously unreleased power ballads, "Cool" and "One Day Less.") Not every song here is a heart-tugging love song, but most of them are, and those are the best ones. Lyrically, this stuff is exquisitely predictable: she's strong, life goes on, she thinks he's wonderful even though he's just a regular guy, she's his best friend, they've been through some tough times and now he loves her more than ever, love can move a mountain, etc. But to complain about that would be to miss the point; mainstream country music is about meeting expectations, not confounding them, and there's absolutely nothing wrong with that. That said, there are one or two mild surprises, such as the unusually complex and soulful "Angel in My Eyes" and the Alison Krauss/Dan Tyminski cameo on the tearjerking "Little Girl." They're not surprising enough to be a problem, though. Recommended.

Rick Anderson

Allison Moorer

Alabama Song
September 1998, MCA

Alabama Song is country singer and songwriter Allison Moorer's debut album. She attracted the attention of the general public when her song "A Soft Place to Fall" was one of the tracks picked for airplay from the *Horse Whisperer* soundtrack; it struck a chord with country radio listeners. That cut, along with ten others (nine of them self-penned), along with "The One That Got Away" were written with cigar chomping, chart-topping songwriter Kostas. As a first offering on a major label, writing virtually all of your own material is no mean feat. Producer Kenny Greenberg and executive producer and label boss of MCA Nash Vegas Tony Brown were firm believers in Moorer's promise. What's more compelling is that the set is a near perfect balance between classically styled country tunes and modern Nashville's more pop-oriented approach. With elder statesmen like Glen D. Hardin as arranger, and Justin Niebank as engineer, Greenberg brought in a slew of performers not normally associated with country chart success including Ashley Cleveland, Buddy Miller, Russ Taff and Louise Red. They perform alongside studio aces like guitarist Richard Bennett, Dan Dugmore, Larry Marrs, and Greg Morrow and, of course, Greenberg, a stellar guitarist. While the aforementioned cuts scored the airplay making the album a modest success, other tracks, such as the rootsy folk of "Call My Name," and the high lonesome honky tonk in the title song, "I Found a Letter," "Easier to Forget," and the late night Patsy Cline-esque swing of "Set Me Free," resonate well the alt country crowd who made her a minor patron saint. Either way, it was an auspicious beginning, but MCA cut her loose to Island after just one record. That's no reflection on the album, but on the fact that Moorer was just a little bit ahead of her time. *Alabama Song* has dated well and continues to be a signpost for contemporary country producers, artists and fans.

Thom Jurek

Craig Morgan

I Love It
March 2003, Broken Bow

In 2000, Craig Morgan dipped his toes into the current of country music with a self-titled album on a dying Nashville label. That album yielded "Something to Write Home About," which introduced Morgan to a CMT video audience and modest radio airplay. Now backed by Broken Bow Records, Morgan's first single, "Almost Home," from the new *I Love It* disc, is a mere sampling of a pleasingly diverse CD. On the fun side, Morgan sings about the almighty dollar in "Money," a real toe-tapper. "Look at Us," with its plucky string riffs, has a rolling melody fit for head bopping, as does "Where Has My Hometown Gone," about revisiting a strange and now unfamiliar stomping ground with a mini-mall where squirrel hunters used to stalk their prey. The subject matter may not always be weighty, but the writing (Morgan co-wrote most the cuts) is believable and well-crafted. Especially noteworthy are ballads like "Every Friday Afternoon," which may well be the album's prime cut. Morgan captures the heart-wrenching duplicity of two stories about letting go: one about the girl leaving the boy seamlessly interwoven with the story of a father and child. Because of his tenure in the United States Army, it is no surprise that Morgan includes "God, Family and Country." In the post 9/11 world, a token patriotic cut graces almost every album, but the singer's experiences justify the patriotism. It is obvious that Craig Morgan's career is taking on new meaning and direction with the release of *I Love It*. The material is solid, the performance is quality, and the collection is worthy of attention.

Rick Cohoon

Lorrie Morgan

Leave the Light On
1989, RCA

Lorrie Morgan's debut album for RCA Records, *Leave the Light On*, is a skilled and assured blend of traditional country, honky tonk, country-rock and modern pop sensibilities that pointed the direction toward the sound, style and musical eclecticism of '90s contemporary country. Boasting a clean production and uncluttered arrangements, the record shifts between straightforward country rockers and ballads, to soul-inflected numbers, all of which help showcase Morgan's exceptional voice.

Thom Owens

Watch Me
October 1992, RCA

Morgan's second and third albums each improved on the last. *Watch Me* contains more good songs than the first two combined, including "I Guess You Had to Be There" and "From Our House to Yours" but not "What Part of No" or the remake of Bonnie Tyler's 1978 hit "It's a Heartache."

Brian Mansfield

Secret Love
September 1998, BNA

This 1998 Lorrie Morgan offering, *Secret Love*, is dedicated to her late father. The songs you'll find on this album aren't the normal country fare fans might expect from Morgan. That doesn't mean it's not worth a listen, or maybe a number of them.  As always, her voice and emotional delivery are up to the test, even for old ballads and standards. It helps that she had the backing of some top instrumental artists, along with the Nashville String Machine. *Secret Love* was a career risk for Lorrie Morgan. It meant moving out of the comfort zone that country fans held her in and taking a step away from all of the success she had in one genre to try a new one. It seems she gambled and won. This album is filled with classic romantic numbers, many from the '50s and earlier, including such songs as "Fly Me to the Moon," "Good Morning Heartache," "Once Upon a Time," "I've Got the World on a String," and "My Foolish Heart." *Secret Love* makes a great accompaniment to candlelight and dinner for two.

Charlotte Dillon

The Color of Roses
March 2002, Image Music Group

Lorrie Morgan says that she has always wanted to do a live album, but it wasn't until 2001 until the opportunity "arose," no pun intended. *The Color of Roses*, released in March 2002, encapsulates Morgan's remarkable career while celebrating her ability to move live audiences with her music. Most of the singer's hits are bundled in the package, including an emotional performance of "Something in Red," the uplifting "I Didn't Know My Own Strength," and the sassy "Watch Me." One hit that would have perfectly rounded the collection, "Heart Over Mind," is conspicuously absent, however. Still, the album offers enough nostalgia to satisfy longtime Lorrie Morgan fans, yet opens the door to build new bridges with songs such as the title cut and a classy version of "My Favorite Things." No one can deny that Lorrie Morgan is one of the foundations of modern country music. It is one thing to be top-notch recording artist, but quite another to be able to connect with an audience. Morgan can do both. It's high time people stop the chatter about Morgan's personal life and put an ear to the music.

Rick Cohoon

Show Me How
January 2004, Image Music Group

It would be unkind to point out that Lorrie Morgan looks a little the worse for wear on the cover of *Show Me How*—if she didn't do a song on that very subject on the album ("Now my idea of letting it all hang out/Sure has changed with time/And that's hard on a bombshell"), and if she didn't have a perfect right. So it's doubly a pleasure to find that Morgan sounds, at an age that usually takes its toll on the tight throats of female country vocalists, better than ever. Check out the perfectly controlled descent into baritone territory in "I Can Count on You," one of four songs here in which songwriter Angela Kaset, the creator of Morgan's mega-hit "Something in Red," had a hand. In other ways, too, *Show Me How* feels like a reunion of the forces who created Morgan's long string of smart country-pop hits in the 1990s. Morgan rejoins with producer Richard Landis, who once again mixes classic keyboard-based sounds that put Morgan front and center with fun, funky electronic experiments. The songs he and Morgan select range from good to superb, with "Used" (Bekka Bramlett and James House) a particular standout; they showcase Morgan's sense of humor and play to her usual strengths in the genres of the breakup ballad and everywoman barroom encounter song. And it's especially good, in this era of Nashville smugness, to hear a song ("Rocks") that takes swipes at both racism and anti-gay bigotry. How much of a hearing Morgan will get for this independent-label release remains to be seen, but her longtime fans will be well satisfied, and so will anyone else who happens upon it or seeks it out.

James M. Manheim

Willie Nelson

Across the Borderline
1993, Columbia

If ever there were doubts about the breadth and depth of Willie Nelson's ambitions and talents, *Across the Borderline* should put them to rest. Nelson surveys roughly two decades of popular music, tackling songs by writers as varied as Paul Simon, Bob Dylan, Willie Dixon, and Lyle Lovett. That Nelson covers such a variety shouldn't really come as such a surprise:

the songs on *Across the Borderline* simply consolidate the range of material he's covered previously, from the Bing Crosby-inspired pop standards albums *Stardust* to the folk-rock of "City of New Orleans." Nelson, along with producer Don Was, assembled a stellar cast of musicians for the album. Paul Simon, Bonnie Raitt, and Mose Allison all guest, and a rock band is Nelson's backup unit for most of the tracks. Of course, country music is at the center of Nelson's vast repertoire, and the two Lyle Lovett compositions he chose to cover for *Across the Borderline* are wonderfully done, with the accompaniment of Nelson's regular backing band. There are also Nelson's own songs, both new ("Valentine") and old (the rather gloomy "She's Not for You"), as well as a writing and singing collaboration with Bob Dylan ("Heartland"). For all the strengths of the other 13 tracks, the most stunning song on the album is Peter Gabriel's "Don't Give Up." The parts originally sung by Kate Bush on Gabriel's *So* album are sung here by Sinead O'Connor, a brilliant piece of casting. Nelson and O'Connor's rendition is quietly triumphant and every bit as powerful as Gabriel and Bush's original. The result of the apparently scattershot song selection and numerous musicians is an album that possesses a quiet majesty, further establishing Willie Nelson as one of the most important writers and interpreters of the last half of the 20th century.

Martin Monkman

Spirit
June 1996, Island

Of all the records Willie Nelson made in the 1990s and since that time, none is more misunderstood or ignored than *Spirit*. Coming as it did so quietly and unobtrusively in 1996, a year and a half before the celebrated *Teatro*, *Spirit* is Willie's most focused album of that decade. Self-produced and featuring the sparest of instrumental settings—Willie and Jody Payne play guitars, Bobbie Nelson plays piano, and Johnny Gimble plays fiddle on certain tracks—Nelson weaves a tapestry, a song cycle about brokenness, loneliness, heartbreak, spiritual destitution, and emerging on the other side. The set begins with the instrumental "Matador," which seems to usher in the atmospheric texture for this album. "She's Gone" tells its heartbreak story with as much lilt and pastoral grace as is possible without being sentimental. Willie's guitar soloing is gorgeous; he's deep in the groove of the washes of Bobbie's chords. Hearing a steel-string guitar play rhythm and a nylon-string guitar play lead is an interesting twist as well. But Nelson digs the notion of "She's Gone" deeper into the listener's consciousness with "Your Memory Won't Die in My Grave": "Been feelin' kinda free/But I'd rather feel your arms around me/Because you're takin' away/Everything I ever wanted. . . . /It's a memory today, it'll be a memory tomorrow/I hope you're happy someday/Your memory won't die in my grave. . . ." And when Nelson moves to the full acceptance issue as he does on "I'm Not Trying to Forget You," the music is slightly off-kilter in the intro, as if the singer cannot come to grips with the song. Payne plays just behind Willie, stretching time, making it slip and shimmer all the way into "Too Sick to Pray," the most devastating country waltz to be recorded since Johnny Paycheck's Little Darlin' albums.

On "I'm Waiting Forever" and "We Don't Run," the sun begins to rise out of the heart's bleak night and comes to the dawn of a new day in the life of love and spiritual connection. This is Nelson writing conceptually as he did early on with *Phases and Stages* and *Red Headed Stranger*, but he is at his understated best here, moving deeply into the skeleton of the song itself and what it chooses to reveal through the singer. And while *Spirit* is quiet, it's a tough, big record that makes you confront the roar of silence in your own heart.

Thom Jurek

Songbird
October 2006, Lost Highway

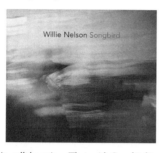

Willie Nelson Songbird

The pairing of Ryan Adams and his band the Cardinals with Willie Nelson may seem a tad odd, but Nelson has always had a penchant for the unusual and extraordinary; from Placido Domingo to Leon Russell, Nelson enjoys working with others in collaboration. That said, *Songbird* is a collaboration of a different sort, and it most resembles—in feel, not sound—the work Nelson did with Daniel Lanois on *Teatro*: loose, relaxed, adventuresome. In essence, Nelson allowed Adams to produce him using the Cardinals, and a couple of Nelson's sidemen, harmonica player Mickey Raphael and Glenn Patscha on Hammond B-3. This is Nelson singing electric rock and blues. While that may read like it would be a travesty, it actually accounts for Nelson's best record since *Teatro*. His easy delivery, contrasted with Adams wiry production, creates an emotionally honest, deeply moving recording with the best traits of both men shining forth. Nelson wrote four tracks on this set, Adams wrote two, and the selection of covers—"Songbird" by Christine McVie, Leonard Cohen's "Hallelujah," Jerry Garcia and Robert Hunter's "Stella Blue," Gram Parsons' "$1,000 Wedding," and Harlan Howard's "Yours, Love"—is stellar.

Opening with Nelson's "Rainy Day Blues," featuring Raphael and Adams in deep blues counterpoint, Willie seems to take energy from the ban; finding a slippery sense of time in the verses, he walks between the instrumentalists. It's an unlikely opener but a fine one. Christine McVie's classic title track, originally appearing on Fleetwood Mac's *Rumours*, has been utterly reinvented here. The band, in full jangle mood, Nelson sounding decades younger than his 73 years, make this a hungry song, one that pledges to the beloved in absentia, writing a letter and pouring out his heart to the woman he desires. The guitars sting and slither in the breaks. Adams' "Blue Hotel" follows and is the mirror image of the title cut. This is the road-weary, lonesome protagonist strolling aimlessly and forlornly; he's raw and confused and the song is the only outlet for expressing his desolation. A chorus of backing vocalists enters the tune on the final refrains and takes it over the top. It's devastatingly beautiful. Turning Leonard Cohen's "Hallelujah," into a country waltz is no mean feat, but Nelson and Adams strip away all the overblown intensity the song has been imbued with in the past by others and states it matter of factly. There are some wonderfully understated sound effects and again a choir picking up the refrains and a pedal steel guitar leading the changes as the band helps the singer through the tune. Adams and band had

to adjust to Nelson's rollicking style of performance-oriented songwriting on his "We Don't Run," that spits and struts and glides by like a tour bus on the highway in the night. The haunting reading of "Amazing Grace" that closes the set is almost an Adams' nod to Lanois' liberal interpretations of traditional songs. The band all centers around the B-3, and Nelson sings in counterpoint, reinventing the melody. His protagonist is standing on the verge of the abyss between life and death and has the sobering enlightenment that grace comes only when it is granted unexpectedly. Ultimately, Nelson is at a peak here; he's had many and hopefully there will be many more—God knows we need him—and Adams' understated, true-to-the-song production leads us to hope for more of this from him. *Songbird* is a late-year surprise, and a stunner from top to bottom.

Thom Jurek

Joe Nichols
III
October 2005, Universal South

Joe Nichols gets a little loose on his third major-label album, appropriately titled *III*, as evidenced by the very title of its first single, "Tequila Makes Her Clothes Fall Off." It's a silly name and would seem like a throwaway novelty, but it's not only genuinely funny, Nichols delivers it with sly humor and a low-key swagger that shows more character, as a vocalist, than he did on his previous albums. And that's the key to this album—it's the first time that Nichols displays some genuine on-record personality that sets him apart from the Music City machine. While he still has a couple of generic numbers here, by and large the material is much stronger, bearing a harder country edge than the songs on his previous album, *Revelation*. Since Nichols has always had an appealing twang to his baritone, this harder country bent suits him well, particularly because it's not only present on straight-ahead country numbers like the two-step "Honky Tonk Girl" or Steve Earle's mournful "My Old Friend the Blues," Nichols also gives such softer, '70s-styled numbers like "Talk Me out of Tampa" a touch of grit, which is something he couldn't do on his previous albums. He's managed to steer away from the suburban country tract he was on and head back toward the country, which has made his music livelier and quite entertaining. Nichols still isn't a traditionalist on the level of his clear idol Alan Jackson—the subjects, sound, and feel are more modern than traditional—but he manages to strike a good balance of classic and contemporary here on *III*, which not only makes it his best album to date, but the first to suggest that he's carved out a distinctive niche for himself.

Stephen Thomas Erlewine

The Notorious Cherry Bombs
The Notorious Cherry Bombs
July 2004, Universal South

The Notorious Cherry Bombs are the country music equivalent of a supergroup. Most of the members of this band—Rodney Crowell, Vince Gill, Tony Brown, and Hank DeVito—all met while playing together in Emmylou Harris' Hot Band. The original Cherry Bombs were Crowell's recording and touring band after he left Harris' group. Guitarist Richard Bennett stepped into the Cherry Bombs when Albert Lee left to tour with Eric Clapton. The late drummer Larrie London was also a member of that band, as was Emory Gordy. While London makes an appearance by the magic of tape, Gordy had no interest in the reunion. Also present on this set are Nashville session hotshots Eddie Bayers, John Hobbs, and Michael Rhodes. Jenny Gill, Vince's daughter, sings backup on one track as well. Sonically, the music is loose good-time country-rock, and the gorgeous harmonies between Gill and Crowell are a high point. The songs are mostly spread out between the pair; they co-wrote three, and each contributed a pair of solo tracks with a smattering of others carefully chosen for full relaxed effect. All the collaborations—the rollicking opener, "Let It Roll, Let It Ride," which is a modern-day version of country boogie, the single "It's Hard to Kiss the Lips at Night That Chew Your Ass Out All Day Long," and the mid-tempo torch song "Dangerous Curves"—are clear standouts, as is a studio version of Gill's live rockabilly standard "Oklahoma Dust." DeVito's classic "Sweet Little Lisa," immortalized by Dave Edmunds, is another watermark. Given the inclusion of this track and DeVito's link to Edmunds, the Notorious Cherry Bombs have a metaphorical relationship as the country music cousin of Rockpile, the Edmunds and Nick Lowe-fronted multi-talented group that issued the classic *Seconds of Pleasure* in the early '80s—while the original Cherry Bombs were performing and recording together here and in England. As reunions go, this is as solid and wonderfully played a set of tunes—with a boatload of guitar players—as one could assemble. There's "destiny" inscribed in all these grooves. If listeners connect, this seeming one-off may turn into something else. Let's hope they do.

Thom Jurek

K.T. Oslin

80's Ladies
1987, RCA

With her breakthrough album *80's Ladies*, K.T. Oslin established a new voice in country music—that of an upscale, middle-aged divorcee, trying to cope with the turmoils with life. The subject matter basically remained the same, but it was given a new viewpoint—Oslin sounded like no other singer, in terms of viewpoint, in the late '80s. *80's Ladies* suffered from a few weak tracks, but on the whole, it was an exciting, fresh change.

Rodney Batdorf

Love in a Small Town
1990, RCA

Oslin built this loosely defined concept album from ten years of song, including the first one she wrote. Oslin sings of the guises romance wears in the small-town South: Nelda Jean Prudie waxes nostalgic about weekend dances of her Texas youth; a young girl enthuses about a pick-up-driving Romeo named Cornell Crawford; and people searching for perfect partner wind up lonely. *Love in a Small Town* also contains a low-key version of the 1946 standard "You Call Everybody Darling" and a cover of Mickey And Sylvia's "Love Is Strange." Oslin's coyness isn't always flattering, and the arrangements sometimes border on a new countrypolitan, but those moments are rare. On most of *Small Town*, Oslin displays her best assets: her worldly sensibility and complex maturity.

Brian Mansfield

Greatest Hits: Songs From an Aging Sex Bomb
April 1993, RCA

You'll find K.T. Oslin in the country section, but don't be fooled. This music is to country as Kenny G is to jazz—a slicker, poppier variation on a familiar formula. And Kenny G's example to the contrary notwithstanding, there's nothing necessarily wrong with that. Oslin's reedy alto doesn't have much of that mountain twang to it (her singing owes much more to Phoebe Snow than to Loretta Lynn, whether she knows it or not) and you're not going to hear any tearjerking steel guitar on this collection. But you will certainly hear lots of snappy pop music with good melodies and slick production. Country radio listeners will recognize staples like "Hold Me" and "80s Ladies," but if no one told you that "You Can't Do That" was a country song, you'd never guess. And who cares? This is great pop music, no matter what bin you find it in.

Rick Anderson

RCA Country Legends
September 2002, RCA

When K.T. Oslin came along in the mid-'80s, she was a true original. She broke the mold of young, cute singers doing cookie-cutter songs and injected some much-needed spunk and maturity to pop country. This collection rounds up tracks from her tenure at RCA in the '80s and her stay at BNA in the '90s. The 16 tracks include ten Top 40 hits, including the number ones "Do Ya'," "I'll Always Come Back," "Hold Me," and "Come Next Monday." This collection is recommended to anyone who loves women who sing real country music, like Patsy Cline or Loretta Lynn or k.d. lang. Be sure to add K.T. Oslin to that list.

Tim Sendra

Brad Paisley

Who Needs Pictures
May 1999, Arista Nashville

It's easy to glance at Brad Paisley and assume that he's another in a long line of contemporary country artists that get by on their good looks instead of their talent, but his debut album *Who Needs Pictures* suggests otherwise. Paisley follows the pattern set by such neo-traditionalists as George Strait, Randy Travis, and Alan Jackson, yet he adds a bit of a pop sheen—never as much as John Michael Montgomery, but similar to Tim McGraw. Although it boasts a shiny, clean production, *Who Needs Pictures* keeps itself firmly within country territory, even if it doesn't feel like its roots dig that deep. Similarly, Paisley's voice is a little thin, lacking the resonance of a Travis, but it is appealing, as are his songs, all of which he co-wrote with a host of collaborators (most notably Chris DuBois and Kelley Lovelace). His material may be a little cutesy, but it's catchy, particularly on the faster numbers. Those tunes are surprisingly diverse, ranging from the Western swing-styled "It Never Woulda Worked Out Anyway" and the breezy "I've Been Better" to the skittering Bakersfield instrumental "The Nervous Breakdown," the rocking contemporary country opener "Long Sermon," and the winning honky tonk of "Sleepin' on the Foldout." And even if his ballads tend to drag, "He Didn't Have to Be" is strikingly autobiographical and heartfelt, showcasing his potential in that area, as well. So, even if *Who Needs Pictures* is a little uneven, it hits considerably more than it misses, and those hits suggest Brad Paisley is an artist worth following.

Stephen Thomas Erlewine

Part II
May 2001, Arista Nashville

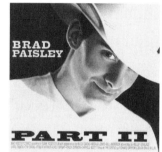

Like many sopho-more efforts called *Part II*, Brad Paisley's second album is indeed a continuation of the debut, but the singer/songwriter and guitarist hard-ly sounds like he's repeating himself the second time around. Instead, it sounds as if he's digging in deeper as both a writer and performer, which for the most part means that he's digging deeper into classic country, specifically the Bakersfield and honky tonk of the '60s and '70s. Ironically, one of the exceptions to the rule is the title track, a slow heartbreak ballad that sounds crafted with the radio in mind (even more ironically, it didn't turn into a hit), but apart from this song and a couple other left turns, like the too bombastic power ballad "I Wish You'd Stay," Paisley manages to make *Part II* sound simultaneously classic and contemporary. This is as true on lean, lively, guitar-heavy tunes like "Two Feet of Topsoil" and the rampaging instrumental "Munster Rag" as it is on the lazy, jazzy "You Have That Effect on Me," the haunting, folky "You'll Never Leave Harlan Alive," and his spare reading of the gospel standard "The Old Rugged Cross." And it's not just that Paisley is faithful to the sound and feel of classic country; he's a sucker for classic country corn, which surfaces as humor— "All You Really Need Is Love," where all the hidden costs of a wedding are ticked off, or "I'm Gonna Miss Her," where he's enjoying a day fishing so his old girlfriend is slipping his mind—and sentiment, as on the unapologetically sappy "Too Country," where George Jones, Buck Owens, and Bill Anderson are all hauled out to celebrate country clichés. It's this embrace of Nashville schtick that separates Paisley from other neo-traditionalists—he values the music and he values the pageantry in equal measure, and he's excellent at both, as this thoroughly entertaining second album proves.

Stephen Thomas Erlewine

Mud on the Tires
July 2003, Arista Nashville

Ever since 1999, Brad Paisley has been touted by some critics and fans as new traditionalist country's great hope. Blessed with good looks, good taste, and a nice twang in his voice, Paisley could have gone pure country-pop but decided to stick fairly close to his roots and play a nice amalgam of honky tonk, Western swing, and pop. It was straight out of the George Strait handbook, but it was nicely done on his first two records, particularly compared to a crop of new artists who seemed anxious to gun for the big hit. Paisley never seemed that desperate for chart success; he took it easy, so any sales seemed to be the side effect of his easygoing charm. That, along with his exceptional taste, garnered critical favor and a nice, dedicated base of fans, but his third album, 2003's *Mud on the Tires*, is where some cracks in the facade are revealed. It's not that it's a bad album, because it isn't. Far from it, actually—it's a really good record, boasting a set of songs that are arguably his most consistent and illustrating Paisley's capable grasp on a wide variety of styles and sounds, from honky tonk and Western swing to plaintive bluegrass, country-folk, and even country-pop novelties. These are all the things that have made Paisley such hot commodity among those listeners who prize traditionalism in country music (which, let's face it, most country fans *do*).

With his crackerjack band, featuring guitarist Redd Volkaert and bassist Kevin "Swine" Grantt, he sounds good, reverent, and muscular, recalling classic country in a way that will be appealing to most listeners, whether they prefer George Jones or George Strait. No, the cracks in the facade do not lie in the sound of the music—it's in the feel and flavor of the music. Brad Paisley suffers from a near-terminal cutesiness that undercuts his music, making even good moments seem a little affected. And this cutesiness just flows from every other song on the record. There's the hit single "Celebrity," where he "skewers" celebrity hijinks in a way that suggests nothing but the "wacky" video that's sure to accompany it. There's "Ain't Nothin' Like," a paean to simple pleasures boasting one of the shrillest kid's chorus ever committed to tape. Then, there's "Spaghetti Western Swing," primarily a showcase for Volkaert, but burdened with an awful mock radio play written by Paisley and performed by George Jones, Little Jimmy Dickens, and Bill Anderson. There are the homespun "truths" on "That's Love" (as in, "That ain't a lie/ That's love") that operate on the same level as Tracy Byrd's "The Truth About Men," only without the conviction to be truly silly. The Byrd comparison is a good one—Paisley has more musical muscle and a better band than Byrd, but he lacks the spirit; he seems to be putting on a show, and that affectation keeps his music from digging as deep as it should. On the surface, *Mud on the Tires* is a fine, satisfying listen, but to truly live up to the mantle that's been bestowed upon him, Paisley had better start adding substance to his admittedly fetching style.

Stephen Thomas Erlewine

Time Well Wasted
August 2005, Arista Nashville

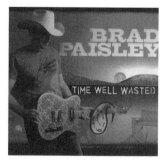

As anybody who follows country music knows, Brad Paisley is acknowl-edged among audiences and critics alike as the new traditionalist standard-bearer for the 2000s—the new guy that not only keeps the fire burning, but also rakes in the cash, having number one hits along with good reviews. He's not big and brassy like Toby Keith; he's the heir to George Strait,

Randy Travis, and Alan Jackson, the guy who hails back to George Jones, Merle Haggard, and Buck Owens but is savvy enough not to play to overly serious Americana fans, the listeners who like their country music somber. That's not Paisley—he may take his music seriously and will sing a serious ballad or two, but he also likes to crack wise and have a little fun. Although that's certainly preferable to colorless alt-country singers, Paisley has been known to overdose on fun, favoring a cute turn of phrase or a knowing wink to his audience. Of course, humor has always played a big part in country—George Jones, one of Paisley's heroes, made novelties his stock-in-trade—but there was a terminal cutesiness that threatened to overwhelm his otherwise excellent third album, *Mud on the Tires*. Thankfully, Paisley has reigned in this trait on its superb follow-up, 2005's *Time Well Wasted*.

Paisley hasn't suddenly become a humorless bore—how could he be when he persists on reviving the Grand Ole Opry's old-fashioned cornpone radio plays, heard here on "Cornology," which, like "Spaghetti Western Swing" before it, features George Jones, Little Jimmy Dickens, and Bill Anderson and adds Dolly Parton for good measure (which naturally results in some silly boob jokes: "he turned around to see two huge 38s pointed right into his face"). The difference is, Paisley no longer leans hard on either his silly or sentimental streak, preferring to lay back and let everything flow naturally. That gives his already attractive music a greater appeal, since his humor is now sly and lived-in, a perfect match for his faithful but not dogmatic country. As should be expected by any deliberately traditionalist musician, there are no surprises, no left turns here—Paisley remains indebted not only to George, Merle, and Buck, but to how George Strait fused this holy trinity into a fresh yet familiar sound that encompassed the best of Bakersfield, Texas, and Nashville. Change can be overrated, particularly in regard to traditionalist music, and Paisley benefits from mining the same musical vein each time around. He's turned into a genuine craftsman, both as a songwriter and musician, and now with four albums to his credit, he's hitting his stride. His band sounds looser, warmer than it did on *Mud on the Tires*—and they're given another dazzling showcase for their prowess on the frenzied "Time Warp," which is as delirious as prime Speedy West & Jimmy Bryant—and Paisley's singing is relaxed and assured. These are welcome subtle improvements, but what makes *Time Well Wasted* Paisley's best record yet is the writing. Song for song, this is his best set of tunes, whether it's one of his ten originals or the sharply selected professionally written numbers that round out the album (these are highlighted by the sentimental but not saccharine ballad "Waitin' on a Woman" and a duet with Alan Jackson on Guy Clark's "Out in the Parkin' Lot"). Although Paisley hasn't abandoned goofy humor—indeed, "I'll Take You Back" has mock crying built into its chorus, and a pivotal line in "Alcohol" concerns how it makes "white people dance"—this tendency is balanced by wittier jokes and his knack for keenly observed human nature, best heard in the savvy "Alcohol," but not isolated to that, either. It's not just that the words are stronger, but the music is weathered and sturdy, sounding familiar on the first spin and getting stronger with each play. Each of Paisley's prior albums gained stature with repetition, but *Time Well Wasted* is not only richer than his first three records, it's more gripping upon its first play. Paradoxically, it demands attention partially because Paisley isn't trying too hard to deliver a classic, nor is he working overtime to please his fans. Instead, he lays back and delivers his songs with the ease of an old pro, which means for the first time, he's made a record that can hold its own next to his idols.

Stephen Thomas Erlewine

5th Gear
June 2007, Arista Nashville

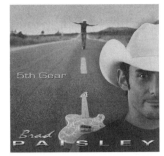

Brad Paisley is in a strangely nostalgic mood on *5th Gear*, its title both a reference to its status as Paisley's fifth studio album and to the numerous car songs scattered across this album. Those car songs aren't mere celebrations of magic machinery; they're infused with nostalgia—he holds to a very teenage interpretation of the power of the car, meaning that the automobile is the embodiment of freedom, and this isn't his only gaze back to adolescence, either. He's even writing letters back to his 17-year-old self, consoling him that things are gonna turn out OK after all is said and done, which gets to the core of *5th Gear*: Paisley is happy about how things have turned out but he still can't help but look back just a little wistfully. He may be a little melancholy about his teenage wildlife, but he acknowledges that things don't get any better than this in not one, but *two* songs—in "It Did," where a storybook romance just grows stronger, and "Better Than This," where he says the only way the party could improve is if there were a 1,000 gallon keg and Merle and Willie provided a live soundtrack. It's a curious mix of acceptance and regret, but it's appropriate for somebody who is starting to realize that he's settling into his mid-thirties, recognizing that things are changing, sometimes not always in comfortable ways. Case in point: he snipes at Internet nerds sequestered in their basements, lying about themselves on MySpace in "Online," an obvious joke that comes just a bit too close to bullying, but he saves himself with his smarts—not just verbal (obvious they may be, the jokes are cutting) but musical, as he ends it with a marching band that delivers an aural punchline set up by the words. This isn't the only time that he tells jokes (and that's outside of his traditional cornpone down-home *Grand Ole Opry* shtick that closes his records): there's the wonderful "Ticks," which has the best pickup line in many a moon, and he pulls off a great musical joke on "Mr. Policeman," where he captures a getaway with a torrid instrumental break that slows down into a very funny quote of "In the Jailhouse Now," capped off by a bizarre, unexpected, yet fitting allusion to *South Park*'s Cartman. That fleeting joke, along with "Online" and a duet with *American Idol* winner Carrie Underwood, is one of the clearest indications that Paisley is a modern guy, but as always his greatest trick is that he's modern while being proudly traditionalist, never copping to the arena rock bombast of Garth Brooks, never going for a boot-scooting shuck-and-jive crossover, and never succumbing to the goofy Big & Rich cabal. Paisley just lies back and turns out songs that flow naturally, then pumps them up with hot-wired guitar. Even if he's from West Virginia, this is the sound of modern-day Bakersfield and he proves that this lean country sound never grows old provided it's executed right and with good songs, which is what Paisley always does. This is a form that's flexible—depending on the attitude, it can sound old, it can sound contemporary, and Paisley is both a classicist and a modern guy, at once sounding like his idols but sounding like nobody else in 2007. He distinguishes himself on *5th Gear* by deepening his attitude with that longing look back at his own past, which combined with his reliable sharp wit, strong songs, and blazing guitar, gives this album some considerable weight.

Stephen Thomas Erlewine

Lee Roy Parnell

Hits and Highways Ahead
August 1999, Arista

Hits and Highways Ahead compiles the majority of Lee Roy Parnell's hits from his first five albums, adding two new songs ("She Won't Be Lonely Long," "Long Way to Fall") plus "John the Revelator," taken fro, the various-artists album *Peace in the Valley: A Country Music Journey Through Gospel.* It isn't quite definitive—not only are there a handful of hits missing, there are also some good album tracks absent, and nothing is taken from his fine debut—but it's nevertheless a strong, entertaining hits collection, blessed with two strong new entries and such highlights as "Tender Moments," "Love Without Mercy," "On the Road," "I'm Holding My Own," and "What Kind of Fool Do You Think I Am." For casual fans and the curious, this is the ideal choice.

Stephen Thomas Erlewine

Gretchen Peters

The Secret of Life
1996, Imprint

Although this record is stylistically more folk and pop than country, Gretchen Peters' songs are similar to Mary Chapin Carpenter's work in that they contain thoughtful and intelligent lyrics that are at times highly introspective. Ten of the 11 tracks on the album were written or co-written by Peters, and she turns in a credible cover of Steve Earle's "I Ain't Ever Satisfied," with Earle and Emmylou Harris providing harmony vocals. Other guests include Raul Malo singing background on the beautiful "Border Town" and James House on "A Room with a View," a song written from the perspective of a cab driver. Another highlight is the opening track, "Waiting for the Light to Turn Green," co-written with Suzy Bogguss. Overall an impressive first outing for this talented singer/songwriter, whose songs have been hits for Trisha Yearwood, George Strait, Patty Loveless, and Martina McBride.

Jack Leaver

Gretchen Peters
February 2001, Valley

Chart-topping country songwriter Gretchen Peters filled her own debut album, *The Secret of Life*, with guest performances by friends in high places such as Steve Earle, Emmylou Harris, and Raul Malo. While the songs were strong, the performances

only served to overshadow Peters' true strength: it lay in her own voice singing her songs. On her self-titled sophomore effort, she and producer Green Daniel play it closer to the vest in terms of personnel, while offering a far more adventurous sampling of Peters' wares. Bryan Adams makes a backing vocal appearance, but his is the only name that folks outside the Nash Vegas studio system would be familiar with. Peters stacks her band with veterans, such as longtime keyboard ace Barry Walsh, organist Steve Conn, and guitarist Michael Severs, and she and Daniel handle most of the rest aside from horns and strings. The songs range from the stellar opener, "Souvenirs," with its laid-back hand percussion and Caribbean feel, to rootsy alterna-country like "In a Better World," moody ballads like "Love and Texaco," the truly beautiful and moving "Amelia and Me," the mid-tempo, lushly orchestrated "Like Water into Wine," and the truly enigmatic "Picasso and Me," which could have been covered by Rickie Lee Jones in her beat days. This is a musical autobiography, a concept recording about coming of age, bittersweet memories, and the haunting of a life with old ghosts. While it didn't even grace the country Top 100, it doesn't matter. Peters, simply because of her songwriting skill (just ask Martina McBride, Patty Loveless, and Trisha Yearwood, to name three artists who've scored number ones with Peters' tunes), deserves to be taken seriously as an artist, one who helped to shape contemporary country while playing both sides of the studio system fence without making any sort of artistic compromise. Her 2007 record *Burnt Toast & Offerings* was the delivery of the promise on her earlier records, of which this one particularly stands out as a work of real art.

Thom Jurek

Kellie Pickler

Small Town Girl
October 2006, BNA

The first 2006 *American Idol* contestant out of the gates with an album is not winner Taylor Hicks or runner-up Katharine McPhee or even Web favorite Chris Daughtry: it's Kellie Pickler, the Carrie Underwood wannabe with an "aw shucks" grin and a down-home charm. Kellie certainly didn't have the greatest voice among the 2006 contestants, but she sure did have the most personality—who else could have held their own against Wolfgang Puck in a sketch comedy, as she did on the show's season finale?—which made her an excellent candidate to be polished and packaged into a pop star. Or, more accurately, a country-pop star, since there was no hiding the twang in Pickler's voice (something that hindered her rendition of Queen's "Bohemian Rhapsody," or made it more exquisite, depending on your perspective), nor was there any denying that her strongest base of support was the South, which was only natural for this North Carolina girl. Pickler always played up her country girl persona on the show, and while her antics sometimes bordered on shtick—there's no other word for her trademark apology, "I'm saw-ree!," which was equal parts Gomer Pyle and *Hee-Haw*—it did give her an identity that could be transferred to record, as it is on *Small Town Girl.* That title makes it crystal clear what Kellie's persona is: she's the girl next door made good, and while she may be on her way in the big city, her heart belongs back home, where she can eat cheeseburgers, not calamari, where girls like her can act like one of the guys, where wild ponies run, and where grandmothers are saints. Some of this does bear the trace of biography—Pickler indeed is a small-town girl turned into a celebrity, her grandmother was indeed her "angel," raising the young Kellie, whose mother had run off and whose dad was in jail—but it all plays a bit like a story invented for those fans who loved Pickler's act on *AmIdol*, and frankly the record is better for it. It's more fun to listen to *Small Town Girl* knowing the bits and pieces of Pickler's past and present, since it gives some meaning to songs that otherwise are rather formulaic. There are songs of empowerment ("Gotta Keep Moving," "I'm on My Way," "Small Town Girl"), songs that are sassy but not sexy ("One of the Guys," "Red High Heels," which rewrites Miranda Lambert's "Kerosene" by leaving out all the threats and energy), songs that are nothing more than corny jokes ("Things That Never Cross a Man's Mind"), songs that are pure sugary sentiment ("Didn't You Know How Much I Loved You," "I Wonder," "My Angel"), all fitting some aspect of Kellie's personality as seen on TV. Without that context, these songs range from moderately catchy to pleasantly forgettable, but with that outside knowledge, this is a thoroughly likeable record, almost as likeable as Kellie herself. Oh, and as for Kellie the singer? She sure makes for a great TV star, that's for sure.

Stephen Thomas Erlewine

Bobby Pinson

Man Like Me
May 2005, RCA

Bobby Pinson isn't quite a roughneck rebel, isn't quite a contemporary country crooner. He falls between those two extremes on *Man Like Me*, his 2005 debut for RCA Nashville, and the results are, perhaps not surprisingly, a little confused, alternating between ragged but right confessionals and cloying, calculated sap. This is a record that begins with heavy, distorted guitars on the fist-pumping "I'm Fine Either Way" and ends with an unlisted bonus track of a plaintive acoustic reading of the schoolhouse standard "Jesus Loves Me," complete with a group of kids murmuring along on the fadeout. Throughout *Man Like Me*, Pinson yo-yos between these two extremes, at times writing good, restless numbers like "Nothin' Happens in This Town" or the carefully observed "Ford Fairlane," but just as often penning cloying ditties like the born-again anthem "One More Believer" or the string of clichés on "Don't Ask Me How I Know," where he passes on such wisdom as "Sell your truck while it's still running" and "Don't drink the water in Mexico." To his credit, Pinson co-writes all of the 11 songs on his debut, and these songs have the seeds of an interesting persona: he has an appealingly ragged voice that fits the rougher side of his material, and with producer Joe Sciafe, he can make some lean, vigorous music. The problem is, he sounds like he's trying to cover too many bases on *Man Like Me*, to try to be a rowdy outlaw while preserving a church-going image. Plenty of artists have partied on Saturday night and repented Sunday morning, but Pinson has the tendency on *Man Like Me* to sound too studied on good-time tunes like "Started a Band" and on his sentimental songs. At his best, he dispenses with that kind of commercial condescension and reveals himself to be an observant songwriter and a captivating singer. He doesn't hit the mark enough on *Man Like Me* to make it a success, but he hits it often enough to make you wonder where he's going to go next.

Stephen Thomas Erlewine

Jon Randall

Walking Among the Living
September 2005, Epic

Walking Among the Living is Jon Randall's first record in six years, his first since the independent 1999 release *Willin'* failed to earn an audience. That followed two major-label LPs—his 1995 debut, *What You Don't Know*, for RCA and his 1998 effort for Asylum, *Cold Coffee Morning*—that also didn't make many waves, and after three strikes, he turned to a career as a professional musician and songwriter, playing with Sam Bush, Lyle Lovett, and Patty Loveless. Then, in 2004, Brad Paisley and Alison Krauss had a Top Ten country hit with his original song "Whiskey Lullaby," and Randall suddenly became a hot commodity. He wound up signing with Epic, releasing *Walking Among the Living* in the fall of 2005. While this LP marks his third shot at the big time, there is a big difference between this album and *What You Don't Know* and *Cold Coffee Morning*. On those two records, he had to play the Nashville game, recording songs by other writers. Here, he sings nothing but his own material, and the result is revelatory. This is first and foremost a writer's record: it's quiet and gentle, spare and unadorned, with the minimal, acoustic-based arrangements emphasizing not just Randall's words, but his lean, tightly constructed compositions. This makes *Walking Among the Living* an album that rewards close attention, yet unlike some songwriters who place the lyrics above the music, Randall also has a way with a sweet melody, and has an appealingly laid-back performing style. This is such a relaxed album that some listeners may take it for granted, since Randall makes it sound so easy, but what makes *Walking Among the Living* a small gem is that it's ideal for either relaxation or introspection, and repeated listens reveal what a strong, subtle writer Randall is. Surely, there are plenty of songs here that other performers could poach and have a hit with, but what makes *Walking Among the Living* a success is that it showcases Jon Randall's strengths as both a writer and a musician. It may have taken him a decade to finally make a record worthy of his talents, but fortunately "Whiskey Lullaby" gave him the opportunity to cut this fine, understated album.

Stephen Thomas Erlewine

Rascal Flatts

Rascal Flatts
June 2000, Lyric Street

Rascal Flatts are three average, nice guys. They make contemporary country-pop that's nice, but ever so slightly and satisfyingly a cut above average. Nothing on their eponymous debut deviates from the norm—it's squarely down the center of the mainstream, edging closer to pop than it does to real country—but it's sweetly endearing and unassuming. Take the lead song and single, "Prayin' for Daylight," for example. It's almost defiantly square, but the trio doesn't ever realize that it's not hip to be square—the very quality that makes it so much fun. They revel in their warm harmonies, bright production, catchy mid-tempo pop tunes, and ballads of heartbreak and love that always seem happy. Rascal Flatts never really changes their approach at any point during the album—many of the zippier songs sound a lot like "Prayin' for Daylight" and the slower numbers are just slower variations of that tune—but that doesn't matter, since this is an amiable, well-crafted, professional record. Are there some slow moments? Well, yes, but they pass by easily, thanks to the surface gloss and the boys' cheerful attitude. *Rascal Flatts* may not be weighty, but it's not supposed to be. It's designed to be a sunny, pleasing modern country-pop album, and that's exactly what it is.

Stephen Thomas Erlewine

Melt
October 2002, Lyric Street

Gary LeVox has amazing vocal ability unsurpassed by any other male country singer heard on the charts today. That's why the best songs from *Melt* are the ballads—he sings them with such a fiery zeal that you can't help but be transfixed by the titanic sound coming out of the speakers. But that certainly doesn't mean that the up-tempo and quicker songs aren't worth listening to. In fact, the whole 11-song collection is worth listening to over and over. A platinum-selling debut album with a follow-up sophomore album that's as brilliant as the first—if not more so—doesn't happen all that often in an industry subject to dozens of newcomers a minute. Their harmonies are musically superior and their songwriting efforts continue to be original and fresh. Rascal Flatts is a band that deserves more than its due.

Maria Konicki Dinoia

Feels Like Today
September 2004, Lyric Street

Rascal Flatts are such nice guys that it's hard not to find their music rather endearing, even if it's drifting ever further toward the middle of the road. On their debut—highlighted by their breakthrough hit single "Prayin' for Daylight," a cheerful, infectiously low-key country-pop tune that remains their best moment—there was a hint of a looseness to their performances, a suggestion that for as tasteful as the band was, they weren't too reserved. Bit by bit, that looseness has been refined, and the group has unapologetically wound up in the middle of the road by the time of their third album, 2004's *Feels Like Today*. Since they always traveled close to the center, this isn't a huge change, but it is noticeable one, because the tempos don't change as much, the dynamics are muted, and the album consists almost entirely of ballads. There isn't anything as effervescent as "Prayin' for Daylight," then, nor is there anything that's truly memorable as a single, but the guys sure are likeable, even when they're singing unabashedly formulaic adult pop music that has only a hint

of country to it. And that likability goes a long way, making *Feels Like Today* a good, relaxing listen, even if it's a shade closer to background music than it needs to be.

Stephen Thomas Erlewine

Me and My Gang
April 2006, Lyric Street

Ever since their eponymous 2000 debut there has been more pop than country in Rascal Flatts' contemporary country-pop, but with each subsequent record the trio has been drifting slowly, steadily toward outright adult pop, which is where they arrive on their fourth album, 2006's *Me and My Gang*. Discounting the steel guitar that's used occasionally as tonal coloring, the most country song here is the jokey "Backwards," which blatantly (and proudly) recycles the old joke of "what happens when you play a country record backwards?" (the punch line is "Ya get your house back/Ya get your dog back," etc.—although it is a little strange that in this version ya get your best friend Jack back before your wife). This isn't a complaint, just a matter of fact: while some country-pop does place equal emphasis on country, Rascal Flatts makes pop music for mature audiences under the guise of country, partially because pop music doesn't have much room for adults anymore. Not that Rascal Flatts are always serious—there's the aforementioned "Backwards," but also the silly title track where the boys try to domesticate Big & Rich's outsized swagger by simplifying it, singing "la la la" on the bridge and throwing in a talk box guitar stolen from Bon Jovi's "Livin' on a Prayer"—but they do not make any concessions to sounding young, which does make them kind of unique among mainstream groups of any kind in 2006. Furthermore, Rascal Flatts are good at this kind of thing: they choose their material well, pick the right musicians and producers, and turn out appealing slick music that sounds good even when the songs themselves are kind of forgettable. And there are some forgettable tunes here, too— there are also those that are memorable in their mawkishness, like "Ellsworth," which attempts to create a portrait a grandma losing her mind but is undone by its clunky heavy-handedness ("Grandma burned the biscuits/Nearly took the house down with it/Now she's in assisted livin'/We all knew that day would come")—but as a whole, *Me and My Gang* holds together well, since the slower moments glide by on the same smooth, glistening surface as the tunes that catch hold, like the single "What Hurts Most." There are no great surprises here—well, apart from the vague reggae rhythm that fuels "Yes I Do"—but there are no disappointments, either. Rascal Flatts continue to deliver exactly what their fans have come to love and expect, and that's a virtue, since it is hard for pop groups of any stripe to be both consistent and reliable, which is exactly what the trio proves they are with this solid-as-a-rock fourth album.

Stephen Thomas Erlewine

Collin Raye

In This Life
August 1992, Epic

The soft-focus yet rugged album art helps establish Collin Raye as the heartthrob his silky smooth tenor makes him out to be. Inside, it's an even smoother mix than *All I Can Be*, with Raye indulging his tendencies at every turn, including a revival of the Everly Brothers' make-out classic "Let It Be Me." The hit "I Want You Bad (And That Ain't Good)" put some sweat and muscle into Raye's image, but even the trucker song, "Latter Day Cowboy," sounds like it was written for the women back home. The album also includes "In This Life," a number one hit; "Somebody Else's Moon," and "That Was a River."

Brian Mansfield

Extremes
1994, Epic

Tired of the balladeer image "Love, Me" and "In This Life" had tagged him with, Raye set out to show that he was made of stronger material. The first single, the rollicking "That's My Story," was a Lee Roy Parnell tune that Raye roared through. *Extremes*, as its title suggested, caromed recklessly from that type of song to, of course, ballads—but "Little Rock," about a recovering alcoholic, and "Dreaming My Dreams with You," earlier cut by Waylon Jennings, were two of the most powerful recordings of Raye's career.

Brian Mansfield

I Think About You
1995, Epic

After attempting a somewhat rougher approach with *Extremes*, Collin Raye returned to his smooth ballad stylings on *I Think About You*. Though he still sings the occasional honky tonk raver, the high points on his fourth album come when he slows the pace down. *I Think About You* does suffer from a few bland tracks, but the album does demonstrate why Raye was one of the most popular country singers of the mid-'90s.

Stephen Thomas Erlewine

The Best of Collin Raye: Direct Hits
March 1997, Epic

The Best of Collin Raye contains all of the contemporary country singer's biggest hits and best-known songs—including "Every Second," "That Was a River," "Little Rock," "One Boy, One Girl," "Not That Different," and the number one singles "Love, Me," "In This Life," and "My Kind of Girl"—making it an excellent introduction to the popular vocalist.

Thom Owens

LeAnn Rimes

Blue
1996, Curb

With this fabulous record that brought joy and fun to all avid listeners of country music, LeAnn Rimes arrived just in the nick of time, when country needed it most, amidst all the regulars of the scene such as Garth Brooks, Holly Dunn, etc. The record is a delightful free-for-all of sassy pick-me-up country that spells GOLD in many sorts of ways. Of course, the sleeper hit is "Blue," Rimes' radio-friendly airplay single

that landed her a Grammy at the tender young age of 15. "Blue"—both the song and the record as a whole—certainly should and does affect listeners in a charismatic and light-hearted way. At the time, since she was still a teen herself, this collection of songs meant so much to Rimes and her adoring fans; it inspired thousands of teens then and continues to inspire them through to this day. Perhaps people of any age or style of interest will feel youthful again after a good listen and a half. This record of songs written by the best songwriters in country music served as a stepping stone for Rimes, and was deservedly a breakthrough album for the country music scene.

Shawn M. Haney

LeAnn Rimes
October 1999, Curb

Essentially, *LeAnn Rimes* is a covers album, with one new song ("Big Deal") tacked onto the end, which makes it a return to her roots—which, in turn, means that it's sort of a salute to her main influence, Patsy Cline. Rimes tackles no less than five songs from Cline's *12 Greatest Hits*, plus "Lovesick Blues," which Cline also recorded. It's a tricky situation for a singer pegged as a Cline soundalike with her first hit single, "Blue." If those comparisons bother Rimes, it's impossible to tell from her performance, since she sings these six songs *exactly* like Cline does. As it turns out, imitation is a crutch Rimes uses quite often, since she mimics Janis Joplin on "Me and Bobby McGee" and pretty much uses Marty Robbins as a guide vocal on "Don't Worry." Since she has a good voice and these are, by and large, great songs, it's hard to complain—given the best set of songs of her career, she delivers good, professional performances, stumbling only on "Me and Bobby McGee" with Joplin-like histrionics. So, *LeAnn Rimes* winds up being one of her better efforts, even if her vocals are fairly mannered and the arrangements are fairly predictable. But the most curious thing about this covers album is that Rimes turns in her best performance on the lone new track. She sounds loose, confident and exciting on "Big Deal," and even more importantly, she never sounds like one of her idols—she sounds like herself. And since it comes at the end of the record, you can't help but wish she'd recorded an album of new, pure country songs as good as "Big Deal" instead of a collection of covers, no matter how well she sang those covers.

Stephen Thomas Erlewine

This Woman
January 2005, Curb

LeAnn Rimes has taken so many twists and turns in her career that it's hard to know what to expect whenever she delivers a new record. Is she returning to the neo-traditional country that made her a star at 14? Is she singing country-pop, or trying to be a straight-up mainstream pop singer? Since she's dabbled in all of these styles since her 1996 debut, *Blue*, suffering upheavals in her management and label in the process, it's hard to tell exactly where Rimes fits into either country or pop music in 2005, nearly a full decade after her commercial breakthrough. It's even harder to tell if Rimes has a clear musical identity outside of her powerhouse voice and a desire to keep selling records. As long as she kept making solid records, this vagueness didn't really matter, but her 2002 stab at dance-pop and adult contemporary pop arrived too late and was too awkward to succeed, which was quite a surprise after her lithe crossover with the *Coyote Ugly* soundtrack. Its successor, 2005's *This Woman*, is a corrective measure, stripping away the sexiness and post-Britney pretensions of *Twisted Angel* and steering toward the middle ground between adult contemporary and contemporary country. This is territory that Shania Twain and Faith Hill abandoned as they became slick, sexy superstars, and it suits Rimes well. The tunes on *This Woman* are on a smaller, friendlier scale than those on *Come On Over* or *Breathe*, but their modesty is appealing, particularly because the melodies are sturdy and the production is polished without being too glossy. There are no knockouts here, but on a song-for-song basis, *This Woman* is her strongest album yet, not least because it's the record where Rimes sounds the most comfortable, where she's not yearning for pop hits or aping her idols. This is a sound and format that fits LeAnn Rimes, and with any luck she'll continue in this vein for a while—but given her track record, it's reasonable to doubt that she will, so enjoy *This Woman* while it rides the country and adult pop charts.

Stephen Thomas Erlewine

Julie Roberts

Julie Roberts
May 2004, Mercury

It would have been a snap for Luke Lewis and the Mercury braintrust to craft Julie Roberts into a contemporary country songbird and smother her in gooey, soulless gloss. Instead, Roberts' eponymous debut never overdoes anything, relying on an easygoing ramble instead of running the Music City hat race. Roberts is beautiful, to be clear about it. But in her choice of song and style of singing, the South Carolina native keeps things gorgeously simple. "Aw, this old thing?" her bluesy phrasing says. But there's also a wink, like she knows just how good she is. Opener "You Ain't Down Home" takes a flashy city boy to task, and showcases Roberts' Bonnie Raitt sass. It also establishes guitarist Brent Rowan's even-handed production, which allows for a marketable studio sheen, but lets the grit get through, too. The snare is crisp, the guitars ride shotgun, and the background vocals of Wes Hightower (and Vince Gill on a couple of tracks) are full of warmth. Delbert McClinton stops by as a supporting vocalist, too, riffing on the nothin' but each other story line in the fun country rocker "No Way Out." Roberts is great on the single "Break Down Here"—she moves the track along with a mixture of anger and hope, and sells its desperation better than Trace Adkins did on his *Comin' on Strong* record. Her twangy vocals set the songs' scenes throughout the album, with support from whatever instruments are needed to make the mood work. In "Pot of Gold," an accordion lends a cheery storybook lilt to Roberts' romantic contentment. However, a few songs later she's sleeping in her makeup and talking to the bottle, hooking up with a stranger and waking up older, missing the one she really loves. There's a little of Shelby Lynne's achy resignation layered into Julie Roberts' music, even if the surface is accessible as Faith Hill. The melancholy ballad "Rain on a Tin Roof" could've exploded with keening strings and enormous, fluttering-hand singing.

It never does. Rowan's quiet soloing supports Roberts and Hightower's harmony as an introspective piano mirrors the song's downpour patter—the song's self-control is admirable, and emblematic of the offhanded determination of Julie Roberts' wonderful debut.

Johnny Loftus

Men & Mascara
June 2006, Mercury

Although country stars generally do not write their own songs, the songs they choose from the Nashville publishing houses reveal something about the musical personas they are trying to project, even if all they say is, "I want to have a hit." Julie Roberts actually participated in the writing of four of the songs on her second album, not having had any creative input into its predecessor. But whether she is picking from the available demos or forging her own efforts with the help of others, it's clear what she is trying to project: heartbreak. She is the first to admit this, noting in the press biography accompanying advance copies of *Men & Mascara*, "I enjoy writing sad songs. If somebody brings in a happy idea, I like them if they are not too, too happy. Sometimes I'll say, 'That is just too happy for me.'" Roberts' tendency toward the dark side jibes well with her vocal quality, which has a torn, ragged, emotional edge that underscores the unhappiness in the lyrics. Her affinity for emotional turmoil is what causes the comparisons to Bonnie Raitt and Shelby Lynne instead of the sweet Faith Hill or the rowdy Gretchen Wilson, and gives her appeal beyond Nashville. And she plays to that affinity over and over on *Men & Mascara*, which certainly doesn't contain any songs that are too, too happy. Even when something positive is being described, as in "Smile" and "Too Damn Young," there is more than a suggestion of trouble. And the rest of the time, trouble is the main topic of conversation, as Roberts sings—in the voices of women who are romantically obsessed—to and about men who aren't worthy of them. "Men and mascara always run," she notes in the title song, and that's pretty much the way that the male sex is portrayed in song after song; "She was looking for love, he was looking for fun" is the song's other key line. Even realizing this, Roberts' women can't help themselves. The best they can do is to try to resist taking up with married men until they're sure they've left their wives ("A Bridge That's Burning") or try to escape a bad relationship by leaving town for parts unknown ("First to Never Know"). The only apparently worthy lover is the absent one in the heartrending album closer, "All I Want Is You," and the conditional verb tense ("Everyone says, 'Move on'/That is what you would want") suggests that he may have left the singer a widow. If all of this sounds like old-fashioned female victim music, Roberts invests these women with dignity amidst their troubles and, forced to sing powerfully over producer Byron Gallimore's aggressive arrangements and loud music mix, she gives them a toughness, no matter how dire their circumstances. The result is a Nashville country album that transcends the usual clichés to a remarkable extent.

William Ruhlmann

Kenny Rogers

Eyes That See in the Dark
1983, RCA

This is a masterpiece of a pop recording from Kenny Rogers. It is clear that Barry Gibb, Maurice Gibb, and co-producers Karl Richardson and Albhy Galuten remembered Rogers' pop roots with the First Edition and, despite the country twang of "Buried Treasure," the slick musicianship and modulation are not your typical country & western. There are four tracks written by Barry and Maurice and five more by Barry, Maurice, and brother Robin Gibb, including the stunning number one hit from September 1983, "Islands in the Stream." It hit number one across the board on adult contemporary, country, and the Top 40, and deservedly so—the melody is infectious, impeccable, and perfectly recorded. Keep in mind this was five years after they created Frankie Valli's biggest-selling solo record, "Grease"—the pairing of Dolly Parton with Rogers makes for an amazing vocal sound to carry the melody. "Living With You" features the Bee Gees—it is Rogers fronting the Bee Gees, and why they didn't seek out more artists, new as well as established, to work their magic on is a pity. It's a lush setting for the country superstar, and as Barbara Streisand and Dionne Warwick enjoyed success thanks to this creative team, Eyes That See in the Dark stands as an important piece of the Rogers catalog and a really timeless recording. The Gatlin Brothers add their magic to "Evening Star" and "Buried Treasure," and these elements bring the Barry Gibb/Richardson/Galuten thousand-tracks production down to earth. "Evening Star" doesn't have the complexities of Samantha Sang's "Emotion," the producers being very careful to keep it simple, something they just weren't doing on all their other records. There are only ten tracks on Eyes That See in the Dark, Jimmie Haskell's strings the major instrument next to Rogers' sympathetic vocal performance. "Midsummer Nights" is co-authored by Barry Gibb and Galuten, making Barry the catalyst and driving force, as he is the only person with a hand in every tune. "Midsummer Nights" brings things back up after "Hold Me," and it is more adult contemporary than country. It would have made a great single but, as it was, the opening track, "This Woman," went Top 25 in early 1984, and by the end of that year Rogers would post his 27th Top 40 hit, ending a string started 16 years earlier in 1968. It isn't clear why they didn't, but the pretty Barry and Maurice Gibb tune "I Will Always Love You" (not to be confused with Parton's hit of the same name) and the title track certainly should have found some chart action as well. Eyes That See in the Dark is not the definitive Kenny Rogers album but, outside of greatest-hits packages, it is absolutely one of his most consistent and one of his best.

Joe Viglione

Sawyer Brown

Cafe on the Corner
1992, Curb

By *Cafe on the Corner*, the members of Sawyer Brown had essentially (i.e., for recording purposes at least) given up on being rock 'n' rollers and revealed themselves to be a pretty decent country band. "Cafe on the Corner" paints a graphic picture of small-town desolation, but these guys are smart enough to avoid preaching: most of the album reflects the marvels of love. The rock & roll sneaks back in on the last two cuts, but by then it's too late to matter. A album filled with good songs, it also includes a great one (Mac McAnally's "All These Years").

Brian Mansfield

The Dirt Road
January 1992, Curb

The band's robust work ethic makes it into these songs about simple life and small-town values, and Mark Miller controls a tendency to over-sing them, maybe because he believes them. Miller's heart is still filled with cliches like "Burning Bridges (On a Rocky Road)," but the sleaze in his voice is convincing on "Ruby Red Shoes," which has to be a song of lust for Judy Garland.

Brian Mansfield

Greatest Hits 1990–1995
1995, Curb

Greatest Hits 1990–1995 collects ten Sawyer Brown charttoppers recorded for Capitol Records, and yes, it does include the slick country-pop band's biggest singles from those years: "Some Girls Do," "Dirt Road," and "Cafe on the Corner." Unfortunately, several key tracks recorded prior to 1990 are missing. So, if you're looking for "Step That Step," "Shakin'," "Betty's Being Bad," "Leona," or "This Missing You Heart of Mine," you won't find them here.

Al Campbell

Six Days on the Road
April 1997, Curb

Sawyer Brown's records are frequently hampered by undistinguished material, which is what makes the live album *Six Days on the Road* such a treat. By featuring the cream of the band's repertoire and capturing the group in its natural live setting, the album is more exciting and engaging than the majority of Sawyer Brown's releases, making it a live album that's not just for the dedicated—it's for all of their fans.

Thom Owens

Mission Temple Fireworks Stand
August 2005, Curb

If the cover depicting Sawyer Brown as a bunch of tough yet well-groomed carnies wasn't an indication that their 2005 effort *Mission Temple Fireworks Stand* captures a rougher, rowdier version of the veteran country-pop band, the opening title cut confirms it. A galloping bluesy rocker, patterned on a gospel-tent singalong but sounding like pure Southern rock, it's a welcome change from the cautious crossover pop of 2002's *Can You Hear Me Now* and it's a good indication of what the overriding character of the album is. Throughout much of the rest of the album, Sawyer Brown favor loose, lean, humorous country-rockers, whether it's spiking Steven Curtis Chapman's "Tarzan and Jane" with "ooga-chakas" lifted from Jonathan King's take on B.J. Thomas' "Hooked on a Feeling" or doing a spirited cover of the Georgia Satellites' "Keep Your Hands to Yourself." It's as if the group heard the raunchy sounds of Big & Rich and Gretchen Wilson and decided the way to compete was going for straight-ahead Southern rock. Of course, this is Sawyer Brown, the group that first came to fame on *Star Search*, so they haven't abandoned their taste for big sentiment, and they have two of their most unbearably mawkish numbers to date here: "With You Daddy," a tale of a father dying from lung cancer, and its flip side, "One Little Heartbeat at a Time," a tale about a newborn baby. These are syrupy, drippy tunes, but they don't slow down the album too much, since most of the record moves along briskly—the hooks are plentiful, the band sounds tight, and the production is uncluttered, making for their best record in over a decade.

Stephen Thomas Erlewine

Brady Seals

The Truth
February 1997, Warner Bros.

Brady Seals comes from a family of musical stars, including Dan and Jim Seals. When Brady followed the same path, he got used to being in the music spotlight himself as singer, keyboardist, and songwriter for the popular contemporary country group Little Texas. Around 1995 he left the band to take a chance at a solo career. This album, *The Truth*, is the result—his first solo offering. Many fans knew his work as part of Little Texas, but weren't sure how Seals would do on his own. The songs on this debut, all of which he wrote or co-wrote, prove that his talents can stand him alone successfully. A few of the best cuts are "Still Standing Tall," "Natural Born Lovers," "Another You, Another Me," "She Doesn't Love Here Anymore," and the title track, "The Truth." The music is what one expects from Brady Seals: country full of pop and rock. Some of these songs could easily cross over on the pop charts if given the chance.

Charlotte Dillon

Brady Seals
August 1998, Warner Bros.

Seals' traditional-country roots come through loud and clear on such tracks as "Country as a Boy Can Be," "I Fell" and "Whole Lotta Hurt." The addition of talents like Ricky Skaggs, Vince Gill and the Eagles' Timothy B. Schmit add a bit of spice to the proceedings.

John Bush

SHeDAISY

The Whole Shebang
May 1999, Hollywood

SHeDAISY is one of those contemporary country acts who are country in name only. Using the work of Faith Hill, Shania Twain, and the Dixie Chicks as a starting point, the three Osborn sisters—Kristyn, Kelsi, and Kassidy—have created an appealingly polished collection of modern country-pop, which means it sounds as much (if not more) like mainstream, radio-ready adult contemporary pop as it does contemporary country. For purists, that will be a problem, but

the fact of the matter is, SHeDAISY does this music very well and their debut, *The Whole Shebang*, is every bit as winning as Hill's *Faith* and Twain's *Come on Over*, even if it doesn't quite match the Dixie Chicks' *Wide Open Spaces*. The key to the record's success is not only the sisters' harmonies, which are very good, but Kristyn Osborn's fine songwriting skills. She wrote or co-wrote every song on the album, and while there are a few tunes that feel like filler, most of them are well-crafted, melodic, memorable songs which are distinctive enough to give the group their own identity. *The Whole Shebang* may not be pure country, but its glossy pop sheen and big hooks, along with SHeDAISY's charismatic vocals, are enough to make it a winning debut.

Stephen Thomas Erlewine

Knock on the Sky
June 2002, Hollywood

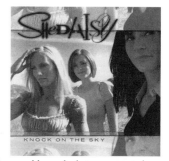

The exuberance of SHeDAISY practically leaps off this disc, thanks to a dream marriage of savvy, catchy writing, crisp instrumental backup, and inspired solo and harmony singing. There's a sense that the session veterans called in for this one went above and beyond what was expected; on "Man Goin' Down" and the vamp at the end of "Get Over Yourself," for instance, Steve Brewster is all over the drums, never losing the beat yet never lapsing into formulaic patterns. There's imagination in the production too, with a very effective switch to an old-timey radio episode on the bridge of "I'm Lit," and a canny decision to record the vocals, like the fiddle accompaniment, with minimal sweetening on the power ballad "Rush." Which, of course, points to the fact that SHeDAISY has achieved such a fusion of stadium gesture and reference to tradition that they can put a power ballad into a country framework and make it work. In fact, cinematic touches—muffled voices, a touch of thunder before the melodramatic "Repent," the "I Am the Walrus" strings that gliss from hoedown to hi-tech effect on "Everybody Wants You"—turn *Knock on the Sky* into a concept album; despite essentially mundane lyrics, the music and vision is enough to spirit the listener far from the farm toward more visionary places.

Robert L. Doerschuk

Sweet Right Here
June 2004, Hollywood

SHeDAISY's third official full-length is a product crafted finer than Waterford crystal. Like anything at the macro end of the gleaming Hat City sweatband, there's a heapin' helping of puffy filler. However, the harmonizing Osborn sisters have quite a bit of charm, and *Sweet Right Here* does showcase some fine songwriting from Kristyn. Led by the strong first single "Passenger Seat" (full of evocative lines like "Vinyl seat soft from the heat of the sun"), the album is a seamless mixture of themes and tempos familiar to the pop-country audience. Throughout, the sisters are a little bit of Dixie Chick sass, a lot of womanly Shania confidence ("360 of You" could be an outtake from *Come On Over*), and quite cognizant of Nashville's success with the lite rock crossover, as the piano ballad "Without a Sound" proves. (Is that Kristyn Osborn or Vanessa Williams singing?) Collaborations with songwriting pros like Connie Harrington for the aforementioned "Seat" and "360" and John Shanks (the blah missing-you number "Come Home Soon") are nice enough, but it's Kristyn's work with Jason Deere that's the most resonant, retaining that stage-glitter sheen but gaining some purchase with lyrical bite and an adequate appropriation of time for the contributions of Kassidy and Kelsi Osborn. In this contempo country world, it's the details that matter, since the gaggle of studio cats backing you up ain't going to sound that much different on the next songbird's record. Proving that, the Osborns sound great when their harmonies *do* find a way to the top, and those little lyrical specifics make a whole barrel of difference. "Heard you're moving to Denver," Osborn sings in "Love Goes On," while the slick honky tonk of "Good Together (Bucket and Chicken)" references dancing outlaw and Appalachian fringe celebrity Jessco White. (The latter track also features some nice fiddle work from Jonathan Yudkin.) *Sweet Right Here*'s best moment might be "Don't Worry 'Bout a Thing." A sonic cousin to Tim McGraw's "Something Like That," SHeDAISY takes the song's message to heart, loosening up and having a good time instead of sticking mightily to Music City convention. "Ever found your last record in the bargain bin?" they sing, before "blah blah"ing their way through a pre-chorus (seriously!) and admitting that, behind closed doors, everyone has a little junk in the trunk. Though it settles SHeDAISY even more comfortably in their pillowy Disney (via Lyric Street) niche, *Sweet Right Here* does have enough genuine moments to make it the Osborns' own.

Johnny Loftus

Fortuneteller's Melody
March 2006, Lyric Street

More than ever, SHeDAISY occupies the middle ground between contemporary country and rootsy adult pop on *Fortuneteller's Melody*, walking the fine line that separates Shania Twain and Sheryl Crow. As a matter of fact, Crow co-wrote two of the songs on *Fortuneteller's Melody*, which gives a good indication of where the hearts of the Osborn sisters lie on their fourth album. This is music that's country in marketing and name; if judged by sound, it's much closer to the bright, sunny pop of Crow's *C'Mon, C'Mon* than it is to Gretchen Wilson, Miranda Lambert, or even Shania at her poppiest. What's nice about this album is that SHeDAISY doesn't try to run away from their pop inclinations—they embrace them, from the hard rock guitars that push "Kickin' In" along to the sweet, surging pop of the opening pair of "23 Days" and "Whatever It Takes." Although this record is not without its missteps, most egregiously on Jann Arden's "God Bless the American Housewife," which is too cute and calculating, there's no denying that this is not only the most comfortable and confident the trio has been on record, but it's also their most consistent set of songs. This is due to Kristyn Osborn, who co-writes all but one of the album's 12 songs with a variety of professional writers (the aforementioned "God Bless" is the only one she didn't pen), and she's wound up with a set that's both varied and solid, and SHeDAISY's best record yet. It may be too pop for some country fans, but for those who found Sheryl Crow's *Wildflower* a tad too subdued, this might be the follow-up to *C'Mon, C'Mon* they longed to hear.

Stephen Thomas Erlewine

Blake Shelton

Blake Shelton
July 2001, Warner Bros.

This impressive ten-song compilation is an earnest debut full of lots of promise and originality. Shelton delivers a wealth of traditional country music in its most honest-to-goodness form, with his young, delightful cowboy-esque charm. The Oklahoma-bred Shelton sure can fire off a tune with the sincerest tenacity. Notables include "Austin," a tremendously imaginative song about getting back together with someone by leaving messages for one another on their answering machines; "I Thought There Was Time" about neglecting a relationship; and "Same Old Song" about an artist looking for some originality in country music today. Producer Bobby Braddock ("He Stopped Loving Her Today" and "D-I-V-O-R-C-E") and Shelton's "all-time musical hero" writer Earle Thomas Conley round out the cast on an album all too destined for musical greatness.

Maria Konicki Dinoia

The Dreamer
Warner Bros.

Rough, rawboned energy drives Blake Shelton's sophomore release, but it's not quite enough to distract from its brevity or the fact that the young singer would benefit from a little more seasoning. His vocal technique is fine, and his willingness to tackle a lyric is admirable; the problem lies more with the material, which represents the doldrum state of songwriting in music city. The story told by "The Baby," for instance, has been told more than a few times: basically it's "My mom is dead." But whether presented tongue-in-cheek, as in the Commander Cody trucker lament "Mama Hated Diesels," or as poetry, which Merle Haggard achieves in "Mama Tried," there's something less formulaic in the older tunes. The same applies throughout *The Dreamer*, which explains why Shelton is at his strongest on the least-ambitious material, such as "Playboys of the Southwestern World," a rowdy collision of "Brown Eyed Girl" and "American Pie," sung with a mischievous twist that suggests, at times, Bruce Springsteen with a corn liquor hangover. None of the drawbacks of *The Dreamer* suggest any reason for pessimism about Shelton's prospects; there's nothing here that an escape from music row wouldn't cure.

Robert L. Doerschuk

Blake Shelton's Barn & Grill
October 2004, Warner Bros.

Although he's delivered two promising albums, country singer Blake Shelton has had a bit of problem finding his own voice. On his first record, he was a hardcore country singer and on his second, 2003's *The Dreamer*, he tempered his country with anthemic heartland rock and contemporary Nashville songcraft. His third album, 2004's *Blake Shelton's Barn & Grill*, finds a happy medium between the two extremes. While he can still delve a little too deeply into country corn—especially on the ballads—he finds a happy balance between Nashville craft and pure country, throwing a bit of everyman charm and a little of Kenny Chesney's Jimmy Buffett fixation into the mix as well. All of this makes Shelton a bit of an all-purpose contemporary country singer—he can do it all from the honky tonk ("Cotton Pickin' Time") to the beach ("Some Beach") and everywhere in between—but since most of *Barn & Grill* has its heart in hardcore country, it winds up as his best, most assured album to date.

Stephen Thomas Erlewine

Pure BS
May 2007, Warner Bros.

With *Pure BS* Blake Shelton proves he is one of the country music artists who are in it for the long haul and cannot rest on his laurels. From the cover photo to the last track the listener can easily be startled by what is on offer here. As his first three albums showcased, Shelton has always had a powerful baritone range and can write and sing drinking, heartbreak and driving songs all night. Working with producer Bobby Braddock, Shelton forged a sound that showcased him as a country music hell raiser who had a tender side, but he did it all with one voice. On *Pure BS* (a great double entendre), Shelton worked not only with Braddock, but with producers Paul Worley and Brent Rowan as well. What the sum total of these 11 songs reveals is that Shelton is really and truly a *singer* of modern country music. The opener is a Southern rocker with napalm guitars called "This Can't Be Good" (a tale with a humorous twist). It's the Shelton everyone knows, but he reaches for notes he hasn't hit before. "The More I Drink" is one of the first sobriety songs since Ray Wylie Hubbard's classic "Hey, That's Alright" to actually make sense even as it makes the listener laugh. (It's interesting that they are both from small towns in Oklahoma.) Then there's the bittersweet "I Don't Care," with steel guitars and strings, where Shelton digs deep into the heart of his voice where searing honesty, even as it begins in lying to oneself, comes to the fore as he digs deeper into the lyric than he ever has before, and yes, that's saying something. "Back There Again" is the most haunting and moving loving and leaving songs Shelton's ever recorded. Written by Tom Douglas, it's on a par with "By the Time I Get to Phoenix." Transformations, turnarounds, realizations and reflection are at the heart of *Pure BS*. That's not to say that there aren't the trademark Shelton rollicking country-rock tunes here; there are, in the aforementioned "This Can't Be Good," "The More I Drink," and to a slightly lesser degree "I Have Been Lonely," with its acoustic and electric guitar shuffles and popping snare drums. But even in these songs, Shelton's ability as a singer (with help from Rachel Proctor on harmony vocals) to get the message across over the music is rather startling. His previous three recordings offered him a solid ground to get this one across. To build on what he's accomplished as an artist he's reached inside himself to pull these songs off so convincingly. The album ends with "The Last Country Song,"

written by Shelton and Braddock. It's a stellar, hard-driving country-rock song that offers a very insightful view of how music itself is changing as the landscape changes as corporate interests swallow up the land the music got made on, with help from John Anderson and George Jones quoting from their own songs "Swingin'" and "He Stopped Loving Her Today." *Pure BS* is the album Shelton's been waiting to make his entire career and gives us an absolutely stunning new view of an established artist who is here to stay.

Thom Jurek

Shenandoah

Greatest Hits
March 1992, Columbia

Shenandoah's *Greatest Hits* collects ten chart-toppers recorded for Columbia Records, and yes, it does include the slick country-pop band's biggest singles from those early years: "The Church on Cumberland Road," "Sunday in the South," and "Two Dozen Roses." Unfortunately, a few key tracks recorded after 1990—"I Want to Be Loved Like That" and "If Bubba Can Dance (I Can Too)"—are missing, making this less than perfect for most fans.

Al Campbell

Daryle Singletary

All Because of You
October 1996, Giant

Daryle Singletary's debut album was a fine slice of neo-traditional country, but his followup, *All Because of You* is even better, boasting a stronger set of songs—such as the single "Amen Kinda Love"—and a more confident performance by Singletary. There are still a couple of weak tracks, which suffer from underdeveloped songs or slick production, yet *All Because of You* remains a solid neo-traditional modern country record.

Thom Owens

Ain't It the Truth
February 1998, Giant

Although it doesn't quite match the peaks of *All Because of You*, Daryle Singletary's third album, *Ain't It the Truth*, is a solid neo-traditional country album. Singletary's performances are becoming more assured all the time, as is his songwriting. Nevertheless, he relies more on outside writers than his own songs. As a result, the record is arguably his most consistent yet, even if it doesn't quite have the spark of his earlier records.

Thom Owens

That's Why I Sing This Way
April 2002, Audium

What do names like Buck Owens, George Jones, Conway Twitty, and Johnny Paycheck have in common besides being the rulers of traditional country music? They all have songs they originally recorded included on this exciting mix of country lore from the expressive baritone Daryle Singletary. Singletary's first album in two years brings tradition back into the spotlight with an album of mostly covers by such classic artists as Owens, Jones, Lefty Frizzell, and Merle Haggard. But what gives the album its appeal are the harmony and background vocal guests—Dwight Yoakam, bluegrass queen Rhonda Vincent, and Jones himself on his 1967 hit, "Walk Through This World With Me." The 12-track collection is like an ode to the '60s when the Bakersfield sound dominated country music.

Maria Konicki Dinoia

Todd Snider
That Was Me: The Best of Todd Snider 1994–1998
August 2005, Hip-O

Affable maverick singer/songwriter Todd Snider celebrates his MCA years with *That Was Me: The Best of Todd Snider 1994–1998* by pulling the best bits and pieces from *Songs for the Daily Planet*, *Step Right Up*, and *Viva Satellite*. This is a great introduction to the humble wit and easy frat-boy charm that's earned the Nashville-by-way-of-Portland, OR, tunesmith a devoted fan base over a decade's time. Whether he's crooning a twilight ballad like "You Think You Knows Somebody," taking advantage of last call on the barroom rockers "Hey Hey," "Late Last Night," and "Moondog's Tavern," or dabbling in Dylan-esque talking blues on live staples like "Tension" and "Talking Seattle Grunge Rock Blues," he's in complete control of the situation. His often acerbic Randy Newman-style social commentary always comes off as charming rather than prickly, a trait that gives each song's eventual lyrical zinger a soft—but still penetrating—barb. That said, fans hoping for a "lost track" or anything remotely new will be disappointed. However, they may want to pick this up solely for Snider's play-by-play liner notes, in which he closes with "By the way, none of this is true. Come on out and see me sometime and I'll tell you the real story."

James Christopher Monger

Doug Stone
Super Hits
March 1997, Columbia

Super Hits is a brief but strong compilation of Doug Stone's biggest hits, including "These Lips Don't Know How to Say Goodbye," "Faith in Me, Faith in You," "Fourteen Minutes Old," "I'd Be Better Off (In a Pine Box)," "Come in Out of the Pain," "More Love," "In a Different Light," and "Why Didn't I Think of That."

Stephen Thomas Erlewine

George Strait
Strait Country
1981, MCA

Given George Strait's stature and his enduring popularity, it's easy to forget just how startling his debut *Strait Country* was in 1981. At the time, country music was given over to lush country-pop crossovers, aging outlaws, urban cowboy swagger and the emergence of Alabama-styled country-rock, all sounds that evoked the dawn of the Reagan era (and still do to this day), but Strait flew in the face of all of these trends, drawing deep on honky tonk tradition, undeniably rooted in Texas but willing to wander outside of the Lone Star State's borders. This restlessness manifested itself most notably on Strait's clear love of Merle Haggard, evident on the warm, breezy "Blame It on Mexico" whose verses could have been lifted from Hag's early '70s efforts, but this wasn't a tune that was stuck in the past: this, along with the Top Ten hit "If You're Wanting a Stranger (There's One Coming Home)," was given enough of a light production sheen so it could fit alongside urban cowboy, but Strait's delivery and attitude made these slight forays into poppier material sound as pure country as the harder stuff here. And that's the genius of *Strait Country*—it showed how it was possible to be planted firmly in traditional country yet flexible enough to play softer stuff without losing that hardcore stance. As the years rolled on, Strait moved away from the softer stuff here—and something like "I Get Along with You" now sound close to early '80s soft rock in tone and feel—but by blending the hardcore honky tonk, Western swing and Bakersfield country with a few melodic ballads that weren't designed for the barroom, he set the template for years and years of modern country. So, *Strait Country* is influential, but it's also flat-out great, the beginning of a remarkable streak of continually satisfying albums from George Strait. He does sound younger here—a little thinner, a little twangier, than he did later, when his voice deepened and softened—but he negotiates the turns on barroom anthems like "Unwound" and "Down and Out" or the Western swing of "She's Playing Hell Trying to Get Me to Heaven" like an old pro, and he has a great set of tunes here, from those tunes to the clever "Every Time You Throw Dirt on Her (You Lose a Little Ground)." It's what makes *Strait Country* not just influential, but still satisfying after many years of great albums from Strait.

Stephen Thomas Erlewine

Strait from the Heart
1982, MCA

George Strait may have landed his first number one in 1982, making him an "overnight sensation," but he'd been working for it since 1976. *Strait From the Heart* boasts "Fool-Hearted Memory," a perfect slow two-step that raged in all the dancehalls in America for half a year and sent folks to the bins in droves seeking out Strait's records. What they found was a singer of uncommon vitality who could sing honky tonk, countrypolitan, and the new traditional sounds that were just beginning to assert themselves after the first wave of "new country." The new Strait fans were interested in the ballads such as "Marina del Rey" and "A Fire I Can't Put Out," but they are hardly the best cuts on the set. In fact, when Strait lets it get on the raw side is when he is at his best. Tracks such as "Honky Tonk Crazy," his cover of Guy Clark's "Heartbroke," the Western swing of his original "I Can't See Texas From Here," and the strutting barroom anthem "The Steal of the Night" offer a portrait of Strait as a man who can do it all. His work is not over-produced, and his voice rings clear and true, offering only what the song needs to reveal itself to the listener. *Strait From the Heart* may not be the exact beginning of the story, but it is the first part of the legend.

Thom Jurek

Right or Wrong
1983, MCA

The electric pianos that kick off "You Look So Good in Love," the opening song on George Strait's third album *Right or Wrong*, may suggest that Strait is softening a bit, but that first impression is a bit misleading. As soon as that ballad is over, he launches into the Bob Wills standard that gives this album its title and he's as dexterous and as pure country as ever, and the rest of the album follows the lead of its title song, not the opening cut. To be sure, there are other ballads and slightly slicker material here, but the heart of this record is in the pure country of the Bakersfield love tune "A Little Heaven's Rubbing Off on Me," the light, funny "80 Proof Bottle of Tear Stopper," the Merle Haggard cover "Our Paths May Never Cross" and the barroom weeper "Let's Fall to Pieces Together." The overall tone of *Right or Wrong* is a little bit lighter than his first two albums—the Western swing skips, it doesn't ride the beat hard, the honky tonk numbers don't hit at the gut, they hit at the heart—but that only emphasizes how natural Strait's delivery is, and how he makes it all sound easy, and all sound good. It's another fine album from a singer who was already notching up a lot of them.

Stephen Thomas Erlewine

Does Fort Worth Ever Cross Your Mind
1984, MCA

Two years after his breakthrough album, *Strait From the Heart*, George Strait was riding the charts again with perhaps his finest recorded moment. *Does Fort Worth Ever Cross Your Mind*, both the album and the song, were, along with Dwight Yoakam's *Guitars, Cadillacs, Etc., Etc.*, the only real traditional country records on the radio in 1984. And Strait is not a "new traditionalist." He came out of Texas a country singer, and album after album he proved that he was a traditional country singer. The title cut, written by Sanger and Darlene Shafer is one of four they placed on the album, and another, "Honky Tonk Saturday Night," charted as the disc's second single. Jimmy Bowen staggered the tunes here to reflect all of Strait's considerable strengths—there are hot and jumpy Western swing numbers such as "Any Old Time" and ballads like "You're Dancin' This Dance All Wrong," along with honky tonk weepers such as "I Should Have Watched

That First Step." But there are a few barroom ravers as well as the swinging honky tonk of "Love Comes From the Other Side of Town" and the smoking closer "The Fireman." This is the tightest selection of tracks, perfectly sequenced and gorgeously sung by an earthy country singer who was at the very top of his powers. *Does Fort Worth Ever Cross Your Mind* is an enduring classic two decades later and is timeless in its appeal.

Thom Jurek

Something Special
1985, MCA

George Strait's 1984 album *Does Fort Worth Ever Cross Your Mind* is widely regarded as his greatest album but its 1985 successor, *Something Special*, doesn't pale in comparison, even if it doesn't quite offer something special or different from what Strait has done before. Far from being a departure, if anything *Something Special* digs even deeper into traditional country, rooted heavily on Western swing and pure honky tonk, from the shuffles to the barroom ballads that pop up regularly. Only the side openers—the Top Five hit "You're Something Special to Me" and "You Sure Got This Ol' Redneck Feelin' Blue"—and the number one single "The Chair" have a bit of radio-ready gloss—gloss that may be slick, but not too pop—and the rest of the album is lean classic country, typified by the excellent tribute "Lefty's Gone" and the giddy "Dance Time in Texas." It's a no-fuss, straight-ahead record, and while it may be no different than Strait's other records, it doesn't make *Something Special* any less special.

Stephen Thomas Erlewine

#7
1986, MCA

While the title of George Strait's 1986 album *#7* may be slightly misleading—it suggests that this is his seventh album of new material when it's only his sixth, but it is his seventh release, following a greatest-hits album released the previous year—there's no question that Strait hardly leads you astray with the music here. Again, Strait sticks to the basics, reviving Bob Wills' lazy "Deep Water," ratcheting up the Western swing on "You Still Get to Me," kicking up energy for the truck-driving "Rhythm of the Road," laying back for the great Texas shuffles "Stranger Things Have Happened" and "Why'd You Go and Break My Heart," and then slowing it down for a couple of radio hits, the number ones "It Ain't Cool to Be Crazy About You" and "Nobody in His Right Mind Would've Left Her." As usual, those singles are the slickest things here, designed to be radio hits without compromising Strait's country credibility, while the rest of the album would seem to spill over with hard country riches if it weren't so trim, weighing in at less than 27 minutes. That's one lean album, but without an ounce of fat it winds up being every bit as tremendously entertaining as the other five Strait albums to date.

Stephen Thomas Erlewine

Ocean Front Property
1987, MCA

This excellent album went triple platinum for country-singing great George Strait. It was a sure success with songs like "Am I Blue," "All My Ex's Live in Texas," "Burning Flames," "My Heart Won't Wander," and the fun title track, "Ocean Front Property"—which hit the *Billboard* music charts with a firm number one debut holding spot. In today's country music world, Strait, a native Texan and one-time rancher, has served as a strong role model for many young artists hoping to follow in his impressive footsteps. His music seems able to reach both critics and fans, either with emotion or simple toe-tapping swing rhythm, offering modern country that doesn't forget its roots. *Ocean Front Property* is one of those albums that you'll want to keep close at hand, since it's a perfect replayer, and great if you like to sing along.

Charlotte Dillon

If You Ain't Lovin' (You Ain't Livin')
1988, MCA

George Strait revived the classic Faron Young anthem "If You Ain't Lovin' (You Ain't Livin')" for his eighth album, 1988's *If You Ain't Lovin' (You Ain't Livin')*. By this time, it was no great surprise to have Strait draw directly from classic country and while there are no great left turns here, it does pack one surprise: the album isn't quite as rip-roaring as its hell-raising title would suggest. Instead of being packed with barroom ravers, this is a pretty laid-back affair, which is part of its appeal. Again, a few of the singles are a bit glossier than the rest—"Baby Blue," "Famous Last Words of a Fool," both chart toppers, both very good—but the rest of the material has an appealingly lazy vibe, from the jazzy textures of "Don't Mind If I Do" and "Is It That Time Again," to the hazy, cheerfully resigned closer "Back to Bein' Me." Even the faster tunes here—and there are really only two, the galloping 2-step "Let's Get Down to It" and the happy Bakersfield shuffle of "Bigger Man Than Me," both echoing classic Haggard moments—aren't as energetic as companion pieces from earlier Strait albums, and while some may miss that, this slight change of pace makes it a neat little gem within a wonderfully consistent catalog.

Stephen Thomas Erlewine

Beyond the Blue Neon
February 1989, MCA

It could easily be argued that George Strait never made a bad album and they were all hits, but even among that remarkably consistent catalog, 1989's *Beyond the Blue Neon* stands apart from the pack, with half of its ten tracks reaching the country charts. Three of these topped the charts—"Baby's Gotten Good at Goodbye," "What's Going on in Your World," and "Ace in the Hole"—with "Overnight Success" peaking at eight and "Hollywood Squares," a novelty so sly and understated that it never cracks a smile, scraping the bottom reaches of the charts. An easy nature is one of Strait's signatures—he never makes anything look difficult—and he's never made music that seems as easy as this. That casual virtuosity can disguise just how virtuosic this album is. Strait hits the same touchstones as always—Western swing, barroom ballads, honky tonk shuffles, laments, and two-steps—but what's missing is that slight coat of gloss that always distinguished his singles on the albums after he turned into a superstar. Instead, this is all pure country—lean and clean, punchy enough to be modern but never making concessions to the radio, without being slavishly faithful to the past—and that vibe alone is enough to make this different. But what

makes *Beyond the Blue Neon* exceptional, one of his very best records, is that every one of the ten songs is irresistible, whether galloping along like "Angel, Angelina" and "Oh Me, Oh My Sweet Baby" or wallowing in its misery like "Too Much of Too Little." This diversity makes *Beyond the Blue Neon* a classic barroom album, playing equally well as party music or music to drown your sorrows. In a career filled with good music, this is one of the truly essential records.

Stephen Thomas Erlewine

Holding My Own
1992, MCA

By the time he released his twelfth album *Holding My Own* in 1992, George Strait had been having hits for over a decade, a long time in any kind of pop music, so it should come as no surprise that when this hit the market it was surrounded by albums cut by singers inspired by Strait. As such, the title itself can be read as a little bit defensive, proving that Strait was indeed comparing well to such new stars as Garth Brooks, and there are other slight signs of Strait and producer Jimmy Bowen reacting to the shifting times. There's the return of a coat of gloss on such slow singles as "So Much Like My Dad," a slight tempering of Western swing, a brightening of the Telecasters and beat on the up-tempo tunes, which does result in the delightful modern rockabilly of "It's Alright with Me," reminiscent of nothing less than an updated Ricky Nelson tune. All these changes are incorporated within the framework of Strait's traditional country, sitting alongside the shuffles and barroom ballads that are familiar but have hardly worn out their welcome at this point. It's a sound as comfortable as a pair of slippers and Strait is appealing as ever here; appealing enough to disguise that for as likeable as many of these songs are, they're not among his best. That may be true, but even average George Strait is quite enjoyable, and, in retrospect, this not only held its own against the new guys, it's aged better than many of their LPs—it only pales in comparison to other records by Strait himself.

Stephen Thomas Erlewine

Easy Come, Easy Go
1993, MCA

Popular country singer George Strait once again does what he does so well on this late-1993 album, *Easy Come, Easy Go*. He mixes the standards of traditional country, a bit of good ol' honky tonk, along with just a tiny little taste of pop and Texas swing to offer up some really worth-a-listen tunes, including "Stay out of My Arms," "I'd Like to Have That One Back," "Without Me Around," and "That's Where My Baby Feels at Home." He also adds in his own take on an old George Jones cover, "Lovebug." The songs on this recording cover the basics: heartbreak, loving, drinking, and cheating. A fantastic addition to any country collection, especially a George Strait one.

Charlotte Dillon

Lead On
November 1994, MCA

Award-winning singer George Strait's 1994 album, *Lead On*, went double platinum—and for good reason. The songs on this superb country recording showcase the artist's smooth Texas baritone along with the expected honky tonk fiddle cries and steel guitar twangs. Though *Lead On* doesn't have an enormous runaway hit in its tracks, many of the songs found their way onto the music charts. Some of the offerings on this release include "I'll Always Be Loving You," "What Am I Waiting For," and "You Can't Make a Heart Love

Somebody." The album's liner notes carry the lyrics for those who can't resist the urge to sing along but need a little help with the words.

Charlotte Dillon

Strait Out of the Box
September 1995, MCA

A truly comprehensive four-CD compilation covering the years 1976-1995, including all 31 of his number one hits, 11 more chart singles of great musical significance, 19 LP tracks, and 11 more rare tracks, plus a brace of unreleased songs that are anything but leftovers. The opening three tracks, all written by Strait and dating from 1976-1979, show a lot of potential on his part as a singer fronting a competent band. 1981's "Unwound" was where his career lifted off, and his singing takes on serious depth and range. Beyond "Unwound," there's a lot here that could've done well as singles, displaying his early sound as a mix of traditional country and country-pop. Strait ultimately rebelled against the latter, but the songs off of his first two LPs show a prodigious talent in any milieu he'd have chosen to work. Disc two opens with the Bob Wills number "Right or Wrong," which became central to Strait's sound and image and, in the early '80s, was a reminder that as smooth as those early MCA songs had been, Strait had a genuine commitment to Western swing and traditional country music. Disc three divides its space between ballads and honky tonk numbers, with some comedy and some bracing Western swing. Disc four is all '90s material, right up through 1995. The cut that helped sell this set is Strait's never-issued 1993 duet with Frank Sinatra on "Fly Me to the Moon," which never should have been left off the *Duets* album—the two singers' voices sound right together, and the song works as is. The producers have provided a booklet with an extensive biographical essay, a full sessionography, and comments from Strait himself on each of the songs included.

Bruce Eder

Blue Clear Sky
April 1996, MCA

Country's most consistent traditionalist, George Strait, scores again with *Blue Clear Sky*, one of the best albums of his 15-year career. *Blue Clear Sky* shows off Strait's range with a well-chosen sweep of material. "Rockin' in the Arms of Your Memory" and "I'd Just as Soon Go" prove that well-written, mainstream adult ballads can carry an insinuating strength when performed with the subtle grace of a master. On "Need I Say More," Strait reveals again that he's also a wonderful jazz-tinged crooner. "I Ain't Never Seen No One Like You" swings with the joyful ease of a youngster on a backyard set, and "Do the Right Thing" gives Strait the chance to show casually that he can navigate an eccentric meter, masking how difficult the inventive arrangement might have been for a lesser vocalist. Strait, an experienced calf-roping competitor, also includes "I Can Still Make Cheyenne." Instead of creating a deadly, dramatic situation or

joking about the macho manner of the lifestyle, the song uses a telephone call between a struggling rider and his lover to convey the dreams, the fears, the financial hardships, and the difficulties of life on the road that surround the sport. Just like the singer, the song relies on quietly reserved emotion to convey enormously important sentiments.

Michael McCall

One Step at a Time
April 1998, MCA Nashville

One Step at a Time continues the hot streak George Strait began with *Blue Clear Sky*. It's not on par with that latter-day masterpiece, yet equals its follow-up, *Carrying Your Love with Me*, by offering a uniformly excellent set of songs that are all delivered with conviction from Strait. If anything, Strait is getting better with age, as he's able to give even mediocre material nuanced, impassioned performances, which is a trick younger country artists need to learn if they're ever going to have a catalog as rich and consistently rewarding as his.

Thom Owens

Always Never the Same
March 1999, MCA Nashville

The problem with George Strait is this: His albums are so consistently good that a fine effort like *Always Never the Same* runs the risk of getting overlooked simply because it's not a masterwork like 1996's *Blue Clear Sky* (to pick but one). Of course, we should wish that all artists could have such a problem. With his smooth, emotive voice, George Strait continues to show the rest of the pack how country music can (and should) be done. *Always Never the Same*, like the rest of his albums, never panders to the latest trend that happens to be sweeping Nashville at the time. Strait has always remained true to his country roots, and here they are in evidence once again. Songs like "Meanwhile," "What Do You Say to That," "That's the Truth," and the title track are classic Strait songs, building on the 20 years of success he's had as a pure neo-traditionalist. *Always Never the Same* doesn't offer anything new from George Strait, just the same great voice put to work singing solid songs in a pure country style.

Martin Monkman

George Strait
September 2000, MCA Nashville

George Strait continues his foray into the neo-traditionalist country style that he helped to pioneer on his 24th album, the simply titled *George Strait*. His voice has deepened over the years but he sounds just as alive as he did on his 1981 debut, and his songs hold just as much pain. The stark "If It's Gonna Rain" and the rich "She Took the Wind From His Sails" are testaments to the years that Strait has put into his craft and his unique ability to infuse a song with honest heart and soul. While some fans of "young country" might wonder where the screaming guitar solos and distorted fiddles are, fans of traditional country will no doubt be able to tell them where to go.

Zac Johnson

Honkytonkville
June 2003, MCA Nashville

The release of *Honkytonkville* should make anyone who harbored insane thoughts about George Strait having his best years behind him certifiable. While it may be his 27th album—not counting greatest-hits and Christmas records—Strait sounds hungrier than ever here. Produced by Strait and Tony Brown, the tough barroom ballads and breakneck dance tracks are back with a vengeance, and the material, written by the more imaginative tunesmiths in Nash Vegas, is his strongest in a decade. A quick for-instance is the jukebox-breaking opener, "She Used to Say That to Me," penned by Jim Lauderdale and John Scott Sherrill. Done is a slick 4/4 with a Wynn Stewart-esque melody line and a lyric that's as tender as it is tough, Strait wraps that voice of his around all the pain in it and comes out still standing. The title track, written by Buddy Brock, Dean Dillon (who is well represented here), and Kim Williams, is a fiddle-laden traditionalist anthem to the ghosts of people and places gone yet ever present. "Look Who's Back in Town," with its gorgeous piano lines (reminiscent of a Billy Sherrill production) sounds like a country version of Johnny Rivers' "Poor Side of Town," while everybody had better watch it because "Cowboys Like Us" could signal a return to outlaw country. The weepers work too, such as "Tell Me Something Bad About Tulsa," the Guy Clark-inspired "Desperately" by Bruce Robison and Monte Warden, and the soul-country of "Heaven Is Missing an Angel." But the barnburner on this one is "I Found Jesus on the Jailhouse Floor." It may be a gospel song, but it'll have the honky tonky line dancers pounding the beer before sweating it out on the dancefloor on the Saturday night before Sunday morning. It is completely conceivable to hear this song being done by Merle Haggard's Strangers in 1967 or by Buck Owens in 1969. "Honk if You Honky Tonk," another Dillon joint, is harder rocking than anybody but Montgomery Gentry—and they will kick themselves for not recording it first. If the DJs at country radio can hear, they'll be playing the hell out of this one—it's got five or six singles if it has one. Not that Strait was ever anything but country; this is the first hard country album of 2003, and he's got the torch burning bright for the tradition while not giving up an inch of his modernity.

Thom Jurek

50 Number Ones
October 2004, MCA Nashville

There have been plenty of George Strait compilations, and most of have been very good, but none have been as good as 2004's *50 Number Ones*. While the 1995 box set *Strait Out of the Box* illustrated the range and depth of Strait's musical achievement, it may have been too lengthy for some listeners, and shorter compilations like the two-volume *The Very Best of Strait* left too many hits behind—and by 2004, all those compilations were out-dated, since Strait continued to top the charts until the release of *50 Number Ones*. This double-disc contains all the big hits that he's had since *Strait Out of the Box*, along with all of his classics from the '80s and early '90s. The title might bend the truth a little bit—at least according to the *Billboard* charts, such latter-day singles as "True" and "Run" only peaked at number two, not number one—but it doesn't matter, since this contains all of his major singles in one convenient package. And it's not noteworthy just because it's one-stop shopping, it's also noteworthy because it proves exactly how consistent George Strait's body of work has been over the last 20-some years. From start to finish, there's not a slow spot here—it's a thoroughly entertaining collection that belongs in the ranks of country's greatest-hits albums.

Stephen Thomas Erlewine

Somewhere Down in Texas
June 2005, MCA Nashville

George Strait has been so good for so long that it's easy to take him for granted, and *Somewhere Down in Texas*—his 28th album, if you're keeping score—is the kind of *album* that's easy to take for granted, since its scope and scale are so modest. Which isn't to say that it's dull: it's just that it's such a low-key, assured album, it's easy to overlook the craft and skill involved in its production, particularly because Strait always makes his music sound so effortless. He never changes, always staying within the confines of pure country, but part of his genius is that he has an excellent ear for material, picking songs that uphold the hardcore country traditions of George Jones and Merle Haggard yet feel fresh and contemporary. He also knows how to group these songs together, sustaining a mood throughout a full album. If 2003's *Honkytonkville* was a lean, tough honky tonk record, this 2005 sequel is its more sedate, introspective flip side. There are still moments that are pure honky tonk—from the mid-tempo anthem "If the Whole World Was a Honky Tonk" to the quick two-step "High Tone Woman"—but this is a gentle, nostalgic, ballad-heavy affair that takes its tone from Strait's terrific cover of Hag's sweet, lazy (and often overlooked) "The Seashores of Old Mexico." It's a warm, occasionally bittersweet, often soothing collection of perfectly pitched, reflective tunes, ranging from the clever breakup tale "She Let Herself Go" and the Lone Star valentine "Texas" to the excellent slow duet with Lee Ann Womack, "Good News, Bad News." Again, there's nothing new or surprising here, but it's a completely satisfying listen thanks to the strong material, sustained mood, and Strait's unhurried, confident performance. These have been hallmarks of Strait's work throughout the decades, and they haven't let him down yet, nearly 30 years and 30 albums into his career, as *Somewhere Down in Texas* proves.

Stephen Thomas Erlewine

It Just Comes Natural
October 2006, MCA Nashville

It's just too easy to say that *It Just Comes Natural*, the title of George Strait's 29th album, applies to the man himself, but that doesn't mean that it isn't true. Few singers have ever sounded as natural as George Strait. Throughout his long career, it  has never seemed like he's had to work hard at his music—not in its performance, not in the songs he chooses to sing, nor in the records he makes. Over the course of 25 years he's not released one bad album and 2006's *It Just Comes Natural* keeps country music's longest winning streak rolling. It holds no surprises apart from its sheer strength: at 15 songs, it's a little longer than some of his recent records, yet it feels lean, largely because there isn't a bad song here. As usual, he has an expert ear for material—whether it's reviving Guy Clark's classic "Texas Cookin'," finding Trent Tomlinson's slow heartbroken blues "Why Can't I Leave Her Alone," or recording the absolutely terrific, slyly funny breakup song "Give It Away," which kicks off the album and gave Strait his annual number one country hit—and while he may not stretch himself too much, it's hard to think of another singer who knows his strengths so well, it never seems like he's trying. It doesn't seem like he finds songs; it seems like the songs come to him. He and his band have a similarly assured performance, mining the heartbreak in ballads like "I Ain't Her Cowboy Anymore" while kicking into gear on up-tempo numbers like "One Foot in Front of the Other." But what might be most impressive about Strait and his band is how they come across as compelling even when they seem relaxed and off-the-cuff as they do many times on *It Just Comes Natural*, including on the lazy, Tex-Mex-tinged "Come on Joe," the laid-back "Wrapped," or the title track itself, where they do indeed sound natural. After all this time and all these good records, it's hard to see another good George Strait album as an event, but in a way it is: few other artists have been as good for as long as he has, and that's something to celebrate, particularly when the records are as good as this one is.

Stephen Thomas Erlewine

Marty Stuart

Hillbilly Rock
1989, MCA

Hillbilly Rock is the epitome of what the adult Marty Stuart is all about. With a new groove that runs just left of center, while still retaining a classic country & western-bluegrass flair, *Hillbilly Rock* is a wild ride to what surely must be honky tonk heaven. On par with Dwight Yoakam's debut, *Hillbilly Rock* sets the tone for a whole new faction of neo-traditionalists. Opening with the title cut, an infectious romp that demands your attention, and ending on a high note with a love song, "Since I Don't Have You," crafted by Stuart and another tragically overlooked supernova, Mark Collie, this is one heck of an album. "Western Girls," a favorite of the numerous cowgirls who follow his career, and the Merle Kilgore-Tillman Franks tune "The Wild One" all demonstrate how effective Marty Stuart is. "Cry, Cry, Cry," a Johnny Cash hit, is made new again. While this release displays more of Stuart's own songwriting skills, it also displays how deeply involved he is with the music he plays.

Jana Pendragon

Tempted
1991, MCA

Equal in scope and purpose to Dwight Yoakam's sophomore release, *Hillbilly Deluxe*, *Tempted* is still a wild and wonderful adventure into hillbilly territory. With a slight tempering of Marty Stuart's sharp edge and abandon, there is still plenty here to rave about. Stuart kicks country-pop in its well-defined hindquarters with his take on the always popular Hank Sr.-Bill Monroe number "I'm Blue, I'm Lonesome." More than just infectious, this is one song you can't get enough of. "Little Things," "Burn Me Down," and "Paint the Town Tonight" all capture the spirit of honky tonk. But Stuart is just

as deadly when he slows things down and does a ballad. "Till I Found You" and "I Want a Woman," written with Montana's most notable resident, Kostas, are a delight. Another winner from the man who said, "You can't really be in country music unless you've spent a few nights in the parking lot of the Palomino" (use your imagination). An experienced night owl, Stuart brings all those nights at the Pal and many other bars, dives, and dancehalls to good use here. Very authentic.

Jana Pendragon

This One's Gonna Hurt You
1992, MCA

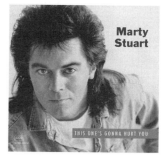

When Marty Stuart cut *This One's Gonna Hurt You* in 1991 with producers Richard Bennett and Tony Brown, he opened it with a modern country equivalent of what is now *de rigueur* in the hip-hop community: a skit that became a song. The disembodied voice of Hank Williams comes out of the ether before Stuart's does; a trippy synthesizer plays in the foreground; and clapping, cheering audiences are heard between the two. But this isn't the skit; it's the track. "Me & Hank & Jumpin' Jack Flash" offers a weird, acid cowboy tale of the two meeting in outer space and having a conversation about everything from the lineage of country to rock & roll—Marty happens to dig both and was sure Hank would've dug the Rolling Stones as well. It's a bizarre way to open a contemporary country record, but given Stuart's maverick nature, it's utterly understandable and even charming the first three or four times you hear it. After that it's best to start on track two, "High on a Mountain Top," a tough, rockin', high lonesome honky tonk tune with blazing guitars, whining fiddles (courtesy of Stuart Duncan), and a chorus of backing vocalists including Ashley Cleveland and Pam Tillis. The set gets even better from here, as evidenced by the title track, a wonderful mid-tempo ballad done in duet with Travis Tritt, and by Jimmie Skinner's "Doin' My Time," with a guest appearance by then father-in-law Johnny Cash. The rest walks from the very traditional reading of Cowboy Jack Clement's beer weeper "Just Between You and Me" to rockabilly on "Down Home" and jangling Rickenbacker country-pop on "Hey Baby" (both written by Paul Kennerley), another straight rocking tribute to Williams on a cover of Allen Shamblin's "The King of Dixie," and Stuart's own spunky, hard country "Honky Tonk Crowd," which closes the set. Of his early records, *This One's Gonna Hurt You* is truly inspired and hungry; it's the very best from the period. Even in the 21st century, it endures as a watermark for the music at the time and as one of Stuart's finest moments in a career full of great ones.

Thom Jurek

Let There Be Country
August 1992, Columbia

This early recording gives a clear idea of just who Marty Stuart is. Without all the hype and over production of many of the MCA recordings, *Let There Be Country* displays Stuart's traditional hillbilly bent. Only his 1982 Sugar Hill debut, *Busy Bee Cafe*, defines him better. Self-produced, it is obvious that the artist knows what he is doing in terms of material and performance. With the inclusion of only two original songs, the rest of the tunes are strong statements by Stuart concerning country music. Merle Haggard's "Mirrors Don't Lie" is strong evidence of Stuart's affiliations. Also good is Bill Monroe's "Get Down on Your Knees and Pray." Stuart's version of the Johnny Horton hit "One Woman Man" is priceless and the sincere sweetness he reflects on the Harlan Howard-Max D. Barnes number "I'll Love You Forever (If You Want Me To)" is stunning. A worthy addition to any Stuart collection.

Jana Pendragon

Love and Luck
1994, MCA

On *Love and Luck*, Marty Stuart's fourth album for MCA, he balances some of the requisite country pop/rock cuts with more traditional honky tonk numbers. Stuart himself either wrote or co-wrote seven of the 11 tracks, and with the exception of "That's What Love's About," where the schmaltz factor unfortunately cancels out some of the interesting harmonic moments of the composition, they are uniformly strong. The rock-influenced title track and the haunting "Oh, What a Silent Night" are some of his strongest efforts, but they pale in comparison to the centerpiece of the record, a moving version of the excellent Billy Joe Shaver song "If I Give My Soul." Also particularly nice is Stuart's version of the Byrds' "Wheels," which perfectly captures the song's bittersweet feel. Stuart is one of that rarest of all commodities: a superstar country vocalist who also has enough instrumental chops to make the services of even Nashville's cadre of virtuosos unnecessary. He demonstrates this on the instrumental "Marty Stuart Visits the Moon," where the singer gets to flash his mandolin chops on a catchy, up-tempo track. This is not to say that the studio band isn't top-notch, because they are, and they include such notables as Randy Scruggs, John Jorgenson, John Barlow Jarvis, Paul Franklin, and Bela Fleck. There are some clunkers on *Love and Luck*, like the repetitive and boring "Shake Your Hips," but overall this is a fine effort from Stuart, and shows his range nicely.

Daniel Gioffre

The Marty Party Hit Pack
1995, MCA

This is a hits package that shows off Marty Stuart's hard-earned success with tongue firmly planted in cheek. The man is a precious commodity and the songs presented here include his contribution to the Mercury tribute album to Elvis, *It's Now or Never*. "Don't Be Cruel" is handled expertly and given a little panache by the Don Was Band and the Jordanaires. The Staple Singers join Stuart for a gospel version of "The Weight," produced by Was. As for the known hits, they are all here, including the Tritt-Stuart duet that appeared on Tritt's album of the same name, "This One's Gonna Hurt You (For a Long, Long Time)," another classic from the man who also penned "The Whiskey Ain't Workin'" with Ronny Scaife. "Western Girls," "Hillbilly Rock," and two previously unreleased cuts, "If I Ain't Got You" and "The

Likes of Me," round things out. Hoopin' it up Marty style is whole lot of fun.

Jana Pendragon

Honky Tonkin's What I Do Best
June 1996, MCA

Honky Tonkin's What I Do Best is a rather strange record for Marty Stuart, while remaining unquestionably something that reflects his character as a songwriter. Produced by Tony Brown (a producer who unquestionably gets most of the credit—as well as the criticism—for the contemporary country sound), the album was recorded in 1996. Stuart wrote or co-wrote virtually all the cuts on the set, some with friends, others with members of Brown's ready stable of go-tos at the time, like Kostas. The title cut, a duet with Travis Tritt, is stellar; it's classic rockin' rowdy honky tonkin' Stuart at his best. Then there's "The Mississippi Mud Cat and Sister Sheryl Crow," a song he wrote specifically for the pop diva, where though he is stretching to the point of near novelty, he and his killer band of crack sidemen manage to pull this tune—with its clunky title—off. That said, this is a rather low-energy effort for Stuart. The production is oftentimes over the top, blunting his delivery as a singer and as a guitar and mandolin picker; at others times it is too soft, detracting from what could have been a better way to present Stuart in a mellow mood. Stuart wrote or co-wrote all the tunes, and he and Kostas came up with a fine ballad in "You Can't Stop Love." But "Country Girls" is a rehash of an earlier tune of his called "Western Girls"—it worked, but this one doesn't. Overall, the album falls kind of flat. It doesn't deliver on the promise of earlier albums, nor does it capture the wide-ranging ambition of those he cut after 2000. This is one spot in a long career where Stuart, who has always stood apart from this crowd, fits right in—to his detriment. If *Honky Tonkin's What I Do Best* proves anything, it's that Stuart—not Brown (or any other Nash Vegas producer)—knows best when it comes to cutting his own records.

Jana Pendragon & Thom Jurek

Country Music
July 2003, Columbia

Marty Stuart's *Country Music* is not, as some have said, a radical departure from his already eclectic body of work. As to whether it's "the album of his life," is also up for debate, since he doesn't sound here like he's slowing down. Stuart has given us one of the most consistent catalogues in the country genre since 1980, and has few peers in terms of quality—George Strait, Dwight Yoakam, and a few others are in his league. But *Country Music* is different and may be the finest recording he's ever issued. This is his first full-on country-rock record and, teamed with grand master engineer/producer Justin Niebank (Widespread Panic, the Subdudes, etc.), Stuart and His Fabulous Superlatives turn old nuggets such as "A Satisfied Mind" and Johnny Cash's "Walls of a Prison" (the tracks which open and close the album, respectively) into wooly country-rockers with killer three- and four-part harmonies and burning guitars, Hammond B3s, mandolins, pedal-steel guitars, and rocking drums. On the other hand, newer songs by the performer and a handful of others are already revved up and cut to fly. This is a rock & roll record cut from the man vein of honky tonk country, and the country that it comes from is pure. Listen to "Farmer's Blues," a sweet, slow, two-step drenched in pedal steel with a duet vocal by Merle Haggard, or the burning-down blues-rock with dobro and banjo of "Tip Your Hat" with Uncle Josh Graves and Earl Scruggs. But even straight-up rockers such as "Sundown in Nashville," "By George" (which has dumb lyrics but still kicks ass), "Wishful Thinkin'," and "Too Much Month" feel as if they could have been played by a rowdier version of Rockpile, while the mid-tempo tracks ("Fool for Love," "Here I Am," "If You Wanted Me Around") only serve to underscore the influences of Dave Edmunds and Nick Lowe. Ultimately, this album is relentless in both its attack and in the pleasure it provides to the listener. There are hot licks everywhere, with great songs, vocals, and a tapestry of moods, textures, and shades that serve to leave one impression: Stuart's radical experimentation of the last ten years has resulted in his finest moment thus far. He offers a prolonged look at how inseparable country and rock & roll are from one another.

Thom Jurek

Live at the Ryman
February 2006, Superlatone/Universal South

After two killer, groundbreaking studio recordings in 2005—*Souls' Chapel* and *Badlands*— about the last thing one would expect from Marty Stuart and his Fabulous Superlatives was a live bluegrass LP recorded at the historic *Ryman Auditorium*. To be accurate, *Live at the Ryman* was recorded in July of 2003. In addition to his regular band—which includes guitarist Kenny Vaughan, Harry Stinson on snare drum, and Brian Glenn on bass (all of whom sing)—guests that night are in the stratospheric category: fiddler Stuart Duncan, banjo master Charlie Cushman, and pioneering dobro boss Uncle Josh Graves. According to Stuart's liner notes, there was a 20-minute rehearsal before the gig to agree on tunes to play. That was it. If he's not jiving, this is an even more astonishing record than its sound and contents give up. The set opens with a rollicking "Orange Blossom Special," with Duncan literally tearing up the middle, improvising on the theme with reckless abandon. Stuart then throws a curveball, letting his mandolin dig deep into the blues and Chuck Berry's "Johnny B. Goode" riff on "No Hard Times." It slows down a bit for the wonderful old hillbilly blues tune "Homesick," with killer vocal harmonies. "Shuckin' the Corn" is a vehicle for Charlie Cushman, who tears it up from the inside and quotes "Foggy Mountain Breakdown" as Duncan kicks into high gear with a solo and Cushman comes back right at him turning the mode inside out. There is no stopping this band, who follow the twists and turns of the tune like jazzmen. Honky Tonk gets a nod here as well with "The Whiskey Ain't Workin' Anymore," though done in proper bluegrass fashion—Jimmy Martin would be proud of the treatment of this tune. The read of "Train 45" has Josh Graves' signature technique all over it, and his sense of humor, as well. When it all comes to a romping close with Stuart's own "Hillbilly Rock, done in hardcore bluegrass fashion that unearths the true roots of the savage rockabilly played by Johnny Burnette, Gene Vincent, and Elvis in his earliest incarnation. Something special has happened in that these musicians have brought everything from the Mississippi Delta to the Carter Family to the Monroe Brothers and the Stanley Brothers to rock & roll out in rough-and-tumble display from the heart of mountain music. This one smokes.

Thom Jurek

Sugarland

Twice the Speed of Life
October 2004, Mercury

Sugarland is a shot at the big-time for a trio of singer/songwriters who have languished on the outskirts of country

and folk for the better part of a decade. Kristen Hall had a career of her own as a recording artist, Kristian Bush was in Billy Pilgrim, and Jennifer Nettles is the new discovery, previously fronting Soul Miner's Daughter, who never had recorded. With her powerful, soulful voice sounding a bit like a mainstream, country-oriented Shelby Lynne, Nettles is the frontwoman in Sugarland, and she gives the trio sex and commercial appeal, turning the professionally crafted songs on the group's debut, *Twice the Speed of Life*, into something that's charmingly mainstream. Hall may have been stuck playing in the folk circuit and Bush may have had little more than a cult following, but both have considerable skills as writers, crafting sturdy, melodic songs reminiscent of a streamlined, pop-ready, less quirky Dixie Chicks. If there's any flaw with *Twice the Speed of Life*, it's that it plays it a little too safe, fitting too comfortably into the confines of contemporary country radio, but it does its job so well, it's hard to complain. Besides, once Sugarland finds an audience with this debut, the group will be able to stretch out on the second record. Based on how solid *Twice the Speed of Life* is, they'll likely find fans who will be eager to hear how they grow.

Stephen Thomas Erlewine

Enjoy the Ride
November 2006, Mercury Nashville

There is a lot at stake for Sugarland on their sophomore outing, *Enjoy the Ride*. First, there's the fact that their first release, *Twice the Speed of Life*, was a multi-platinum success. Its singles and videos drove the record outside country music's audience to appeal to a degree to mainstream rock & roll listeners who didn't mind at all when vocalist/songwriter Jennifer Nettles appeared in a duet with Jon Bon Jovi on a video of Bon Jovi's "Who Says You Can't Go Home." Secondly, there is the "sophomore jinx," which tends to plague many celebrated acts whose debut albums are successful—especially beyond expectations. Thirdly, Sugarland were formed by songwriters Kristen Hall and Kristian Bush, who heard Nettles and asked her to join the band. Hall wrote or co-wrote everything on the band's debut—though Bush and Nettles are serious songwriters in their own right (see below). Hall left the band suddenly and somewhat mysteriously at the beginning of 2006, issuing a gentle yet terse statement that the life of the road and high visibility weren't for her and she wished to concentrate on being a songwriter. She wished Bush and Nettles well and graciously thanked them. Her name only appears on one track on *Enjoy the Ride*, the album's final cut, "Sugarland," and is nowhere mentioned in the voluminous "thank-yous" on the credits page. Hmmm. . . .

The real question is whether or not the band delivers on *Enjoy the Ride*. Bush and Nettles co-wrote most everything on the set, which was produced by the pair with Byron Gallimore. Third parties Lisa Carver (underappreciated but gloriously talented), Tim Owens, Bobby Pinson, and Jeff Cohen joined forces to round out the various tracks here. Nettles wrote the brilliant liberation story "Stay" on her own, and Bush worked with Hall and Vanessa Olivarez on "Sugarland." Musically, *Enjoy the Ride* is a likely but more chancy part two of the Sugarland story. The songs are tough, lean, direct, and in their way poignant. Gallimore's production hand is brighter and tighter than that of Garth Fundis, who worked on the band's debut. The mix is brighter and a bit more rocked up, and that's a good thing. So it all comes down to the songs themselves, and the way they come across.

The keyboard lines that open "Settlin'," along with the big anthemic guitars, B-3, and drums are a shock to the system, but then Nettles drops right into the center of the groove with "Fifteen minutes to get me together/For Mr. Right Now, not Mr. Forever/Don't even know why I even try when I know how it ends/Lookin' like another 'Maybe we can be friends'/I've been leaving it up to fate/It's my life so it's mine to make/I ain't settlin'/For just getting by/I've had enough so-so/For the rest of my life/Tired of shooting too low/So raise the bar high/Just enough ain't enough this time/I ain't settlin' for anything less than everything. . . ." The guitars careen off one another and Nettles—arguably (along with Gretchen Wilson) the finest singer in country music today—soars above the fray in her gritty R&B-tinged voice. This is a terrain familiar to rock audiences. John Mellencamp has been laying this down for 30 years and it becomes even more pronounced on "County Line," the next cut. With crunchy six-strings, popping snares and kick drums, and mandolins and fiddles—with an ornate B-3 to fill in the spaces—rock & roll meets the folksiness of country music.

This is more rock & roll than anything that's come down that pipe in a decade. Mellencamp, Bob Seger, and even Bruce Springsteen could get away with this song. But Nettles is firmly in her own voice here. In the grain of her throaty wail, and in the anthemic refrains she and Bush sing, is the sound of American experience, the sound of life in process. It's not a movie floating by, but the grit and grist of the mill flowing through the marrow of listeners and musicians alike. This is the music of an inclusive experience known to working people, those whose difficulties are borne in the moment. When the first single, "Want To," busts into the mix, all bets are off. As a Dobro, a mandolin, and those shimmering guitars offer Nettles a shelf, she walks out on the ledge, a step at a time. The Dobro signifies the distance she's willing to go. By the time the drums and electrics rock themselves into the middle, she's going for it: "The whole world could change in a minute/Just one kiss could stop it spinning/We could think it through/But I don't want to, if you don't want to. . . ." This is the sound of desire, ready to be thwarted again if necessary, but dancing out on the wire of chance. From the first song to the third, where the words "no more" really mean a "yes" to what one expects from life, and then this one, where "yes" is really the only answer to living, Sugarland firmly place themselves in the context of the new 21st century country to be sure, but even more in the context of rock & roll's grand tradition of breaking out of the rut and inviting others to do the same thing.

It's always tempting to look at country records as collections of songs, with rare exceptions. *Enjoy the Ride*, like its predecessor, *Twice the Speed of Life*, is past the notion of "songs" as single entities. In fact, *Enjoy the Ride* is more cohesive, if anything, than the debut. The looped beats, synths, and organ lines at the beginning of "Everyday America" offer a slippery urban groove to the country mix. There's rhythm here that any soul singer could get behind, and the voices of Nettles and Bush entwine to take in the whole of what the words of that title mean—no matter how small the microcosmic glance at the scenery is. With those Steve Cropper-esque guitar fills, groove becomes the purveyor of poetry and listeners get the country connection to Stax/Volt. Get to the mid-tempo ballad of "These Are the Days," where the boy/girl duo can take on the world in the same way Doc Pomus and Dion DiMucci posed their protagonists against the night skyline of the Bronx; in every piano line playing that repetitive riff over and over again—joined by tambourines and drums, mandolins and guitars, or doo wop voices—it's the same portrait, the same situation. They become every stretched-to-the-point-of-fraying lover's story from pop music antiquity—and that's as it should be, because indeed in every story lies a moment when "These Are the Days."

While the summation of the album is in the track "Sugarland," where it ends properly, "One Blue Sky" is the place where that ending is defined: where disappearance, disappointment, and tragedy—in this case flood and natural disaster—create the notion of true American defiance. As the big popping tom-toms offer those electric six-strings something to really fly from, the voices of Nettles and Bush intersect with those left wanting and angry in the wake of Hurricane Katrina, those whose dreams disappeared in the fires of the West carried by the Santa Ana winds, and those across America whose small towns are what they have and so they dig in. Certainly Mellencamp, Seger, and Springsteen could have written or sung this one, but so could Melissa Etheridge and Patty Griffin, or any great soul and/or blues singer from Arthur Alexander to Muddy Waters to Sister Rosetta Tharpe.

What it all boils down to is that Sugarland, with or without the wonderfully gifted Kristen Hall, not only deliver on the promise of their debut, but further expand it. There is more country on *Enjoy the Ride*, but more rock & roll, too—check out the big blasting bass throb and smoking riff in "Mean Girls" (which could have been covered by a younger Chrissie Hynde). One can't forget that Jennifer Nettles came from blues, soul, R&B, and rock, and can sing anything she damn well pleases. When that attack blends into Kristian Bush's more rural and pastoral roots-oriented aesthetic, the result is magical. Traditions are damned so much as bridged. If Luke Lewis and his fine crew over at Mercury can wrap their heads around that, there should be no trouble in breaking this to mainstream rock & roll audiences as well. *Enjoy the Ride* may be the last great record of 2006, and ensures that Sugarland are no one-trick pony. They are a band whose promise is being revealed more with every offering and whose sense of song, drama, literate street sense, and integrity is straight-up, tough, and at times even wondrous.

Thom Jurek

Doug Supernaw

Red and Rio Grande
April 1993, BNA

Included is his initial mainstream country hits, "Reno," and the anthem for divorced fathers, "I Don't Call Him Daddy."
Michael McCall

Sweethearts of the Rodeo

Sweethearts of the Rodeo/One Time, One Night
November 2000, Collectables

This two-fer from Collectables features a pair of out of print Sweethearts of the Rodeo LPs: *Sweethearts of the Rodeo* and *One Time, One Night*, both originally issued on Columbia in 1986 and 1989. Highlights among the 22 tracks include "Midnight Girl/Sunset Town," "Hey Doll Baby," and "Satisfy You," which provide a perfect combination of country-rock and traditional bluegrass.

Al Campbell

Taylor Swift

Taylor Swift
October 2006, Big MacHine

All of 16 when she recorded this debut album, country-pop singer Taylor Swift's considerably strong voice straddles that precarious edge that both suggests experience far beyond her years and simultaneously leaves no doubt that she's still got a lot of life to live. It's a fresh, still girlish voice, full of hope and naïveté, but it's also a confident and mature one. That Swift is a talent to be reckoned with is never in doubt: her delivery on tracks like the up-tempo "The Outside," the spare acoustic ballad "Mary's Song (Oh My My My)," and especially the leadoff track, "Tim McGraw," which was the first single from the album, is that of a seasoned pro, despite Swift's newcomer status. "Tim McGraw" may also be the album's highlight—not a teenager's tribute to the country superstar, it instead uses McGraw as a marker in a lover's time line: "When you think Tim McGraw/I hope you think my favorite song." It's a device that's been used countless times in as many ways, that of associating a failed affair with items, places, and people, yet it works as a hook here and manages to come off as an original idea. Swift wrote or co-wrote every song on the record, a fairly remarkable feat considering the sophisticated manner in which she treats matters near and dear to the heart of one her age ("Now that I'm sitting here thinking it through/I've never been anywhere cold as you"). Producer/mentor Nathan Chapman has applied to some of Swift's songs a gloss that not all of them really require and in some cases would do better to shed. But Swift has no trouble overcoming any blandness taking place around her. She's come up with a commendable starter album that's as accomplished as any by a ten-year veteran who's seen a lot more road and felt a lot more emotion. Swift's young age may be a major point of interest in bringing listeners in, but by the end of the record she's succeeded in keeping them.

Jeff Tamarkin

Chalee Tennison

Chalee Tennison
June 1999, Elektra

Just about every one of Chalee Tennison's songs on her self-titled debut album, including her first release, "Someone Else's Turn to Cry," reek of heartbreak. From the effervescent "Handful of Water," the solemn "Just Because She Lives There," to the heartfelt "Leave It at That," one can tell this woman's had some experience with romances gone sour. But there's nothing sour about Tennison's first foray into country music. With so many country artists making the cross over to pop, Chalee Tennison reminds you of the reasons you started listening to country music in the first place.

Maria Konicki Dinoia

This Woman's Heart
October 2000, Asylum

Chalee Tennison doesn't have to worry about the sophomore jinx. Her self-titled debut album met with little more than critical acclaim, so one can only hope that album number two, *This Woman's Heart*, garners greater commercial success for this talented artist. Whether it's a ballad or a song with an upbeat tempo, Tennison sings it with wild abandon. Maybe there are too many female country artists on the charts to give Tennison her due, but what separates her from the pack is her own brand of country music—it's soulful and pure. Her voice is so appealing and original and it makes every one of her songs worth listening to. Whether she's singing about being a fool and making mistakes in "Yes I Was" or prayers that have been answered in "We Don't Have to Pray," she brings a welcome and refreshing sound to country music fans and, hopefully, finds herself in a welcome place on country radio and on the charts.

Maria Konicki Dinoia

Parading in the Rain
September 2003, DreamWorks

Chalee Tennison's third full-length (and first for DreamWorks) is firmly, proudly contemporary country—its hints of pedal steel and rootsy acoustic strum only surface in relation to lush, tasteful arrangements. But this straightforward sound is perfect for the husky-voiced Tennison, since her fiercely honest lyrics are *Parading in the Rain*'s true focus. In "Me and Mexico," she makes the country's simple pleasures proud accessories to a final breakup. "I bought a big sombrero and it made me laugh," "I drank some tequila/I said 'Who needs ya?'"—the electric feelings of freedom Tennison gives these lines is incredible. She's just as confident with slower, more introspective material. The brooding, largely acoustic "Mind of This Woman" is one of the album's emotional touchstones; in it, Tennison's detailed description of the painful piling up of everyday events and chores makes the memory of a brief romantic respite that much more heartening. Other highlights include the self-confident title track and the first single, "Lonesome Road," which lets Tennison loosen up with its rollicking banjo and fiddle. Contemporary and pop-country artists too often coast on easy elements of image and cliché, so it's refreshing to see Chalee Tennison building bridges between the bright footlights and the human heart.

Johnny Loftus

Texas Tornados

Texas Tornados
August 1990, Reprise

Predictably, this debut album by a sort of Tex-Mex Traveling Wilburys is a delight. Forty percent of the Sir Douglas Quintet—Doug Sahm and Augie Meyers—is represented, along with Freddy Fender and accordionist Flaco Jimenez. The album reflects the differing strains that each brings to the music, from the more pop/country approach of Sahm and Meyers to Fender's bluesy singing and Jimenez's Mexican playing. An all-star project that brings out the best in its members, *Texas Tornados* is a landmark Tex-Mex album. (The track "Soy de San Luis" won the 1990 Grammy Award for Best Mexican/American Performance.)

William Ruhlmann

Zone of Our Own
1991, Reprise

Even if the Texas Tornados had picked a different name, it would be pretty hard to imagine them coming from anywhere besides the Lone Star State; their high-spirited mixture of Tex-Mex, norteño, garage rock, blues, and hardcore honky tonk flavors brands them as proud sons of a place all these sounds and more happily co-exist on a regular basis. *Zone of Our Own*, the second album from the all-star quartet of Freddy Fender, Flaco Jimenez, Augie Meyers, and Doug Sahm, isn't quite up to the same level as their superb self-titled debut, but it sure doesn't miss by much. Sahm gets to rave up on Sir Doug-style rockers like "I Ain't That Kat Anymore," Fender sings sad and soulful on "Oh Holy One," Jimenez burns up the squeeze box on "La Mucura," and Meyers gets to show off his bluesy side on "Did I Tell You." For all the sonic diversity of the Texas Tornados, *Zone of Our Own* still sounds like it's all of a piece, like the play list of some blessedly eclectic radio station beaming out along the border, as the four frontmen bounce off each other with joyous aplomb. If you're looking for some aural seasoning for your next barbecue, *Zone of Our Own* is just the bottle of hot sauce you need.

Mark Deming

Cyndi Thomson

My World
July 2001, Capitol

At 24, Cyndi Thomson's deepest country music influence is current diva Trisha Yearwood, who herself was only a third-generation pop-country singer who transcended the genre's limitations with a rich voice and killer songs. But Thomson's youth shouldn't be held against her. For in the field of curtain-shirted rock & roll wannabes and Brooks & Dunn clones and Shania Twain-esque glamor queens who couldn't sing a lick if there weren't pitch levelers in recording studios, Thomson is a rarity. As a singer she posses a genuine slippery, smoky alto that reaches deep inside the heart for the lyric rather than in the trembling upper registers of her instrument. She has the songs too, given that her producer and co-writer is none other than Tommy James. Lastly, she's a country singer first and a pop singer second. *My World* will, hopefully, lay claim to a slot on the country chart near the top, which would mean there was hope for Nash Vegas (not a lot, but a smidge anyway—which is more than there is now). Sure, there are the requisite fiddles on her record, but there are also banjos and flat-picked guitars, as well as recorders, Hammond B-3s (as on the single "What I Really

Meant to Say"). The single is clearly meant to put the album in the hands and minds (not like they really have them, but we'll give them the benefit of the doubt on this set) of country music radio station programmers. Once said single charts, the label digs into the disc for further material, hopefully to the title track or "Hope You're Doing Fine," with its ringing mandolin and pedal steel whine. Ultimately, *My World* has some concessions to the pop market: it's slickly produced; there are some taut, pop sheeny arrangements and a few drum machines here and there. But compared to the absolute crap being cranked out of Nash Vegas, this is a bona fide country record in the same tradition as Thomson's mentor Yearwood. And there are a lot lower sights (especially now) to set your eyes on.

Thom Jurek

Pam Tillis

Put Yourself in My Place
1991, Arista

The album that established Pam Tillis as a performer in her own right has a traditional country base cut with bluegrass, folk, and rock. It all creates the same sort of mixed breed she sings about in "Melancholy Child": "You take a black Irish temper/Some solemn Cherokee/A Southern sense of humor/And you got someone like me." Her characters are the awkward dancers of "I've Seen Enough to Know": bruised, tentative, and needing to be cajoled back to love. Even the throwaway songs are of a high standard; the best ones ("Maybe It Was Memphis," "Don't Tell Me What to Do") are truly enticing.

Brian Mansfield

Homeward Looking Angel
1992, Arista

Pam Tillis had an enviable challenge with *Homeward Looking Angel*—topping the critically acclaimed and commercially viable *Put Yourself in My Place*, an album that spawned four Top Ten singles including "Don't Tell Me What to Do." Tillis' pure, full-bodied country voice can be both a boon and a burden. Some tracks on *Angel* seem cliché. On one cut, the retro "Do You Know Where Your Man Is," her genuinely throaty twang feels exaggerated to the point of annoyance. Yet other songs work seemingly effortless magic, including the sultry and sexy "Shake the Sugar Tree," and the wry and telling "Cleopatra, Queen of Denial." These songs, along with Gretchen Peters' ballad "Let That Pony Run" and the title cut—one of four written by Bob DiPiero—had no trouble finding their way to the chart heights of their predecessors and insuring Tillis another hit recording. While it may not be as flawless as *Put Yourself in My Place*, *Homeward Looking Angel* is a very solid—and at times even stellar—successor; it should be seriously considered by anyone who is curious about her music.

Roch Parisien & Thom Jurek

Sweetheart's Dance
April 1994, Arista

Producing herself for the first time (along with Steve Fishell), Tillis found the magic blend of Nashville Sound, California country-rock and post-Beatles pop. She released the heady "Spilled Perfume" as her first single, but the riches of *Sweethearts Dance* go much deeper: the Bo Diddley/Tejano rhythms of "Mi Vida Loca (My Crazy Life)," the lilting waltz of "In Between Dances," and a playfully romantic title cut. A charming album without a bad cut, *Sweethearts Dance* ranks with the best of Trisha Yearwood, Wynonna Judd and Carlene Carter.

Brian Mansfield

It's All Relative
September 2002, Epic/Lucky Dog

Best known as an engaging and often humorous performer, and secondarily as Nashville songbird Pam Tillis' father, Mel Tillis deserves greater recognition as one of country music's more enduring and consistent songwriters. This oversight is addressed in *It's All Relative*, as Pam joins with a cast of Music City luminaries to interpret some of his better-known works. Her performance is right on the money from start to finish. On up-tempo tracks, whether honky tonk excursions like "Unmitigated Gall" or a brisk rockabilly sprint with Ray Benson through "Honey (Open That Door)," she's expressive, though somewhat restrained. It's at slower tempos that her abilities are most evident, as she exploits the interpretive room that ballads allow. An exceptional harmony singer, she knows how to play off of the unique timbre and phrasing contributed by Dolly Parton on a lacelike rendition of "Violet and a Rose" and Emmylou Harris in a more Daniel Lanois-influenced treatment of "Heart Over Mind." On her own, Tillis is even stronger; she turns "Detroit City" into an intimate journal, with misty memories of home and the weary grind of life in the city made equally vivid by her reading. Yet on "Emotions," backed by jazz pianist Beegie Adair, Tillis eases smoothly into a torchier style that has nothing to do with rural idylls. The last track, "Come On and Sing," brings Dad into the picture, along with a gaggle of his grandkids; it's a predictable cameo, but irresistible nonetheless and a perfect dessert for this rich repast.

Robert L. Doerschuk

Aaron Tippin

You've Got to Stand for Something
1991, RCA

This exciting hardcore country comes from a man whose previous blue-collar experience as a farm hand, welder, pilot, and truck driver made him a publicist's dream. *You've Got to Stand for Something* includes the singles "You've Got to Stand for Something," "I Wonder How Far It Is over You," and "She Made a Memory out of Me."

Brian Mansfield

Greatest Hits . . . and Then Some
March 1997, RCA

Greatest Hits and Then Some contains all of Aaron Tippin's best-known songs and biggest hits from the early '90s, including "I Wouldn't Have It Any Other Way," "My Blue Angel," "Working Man's Ph.D.," "I Get It Honest," and the number one singles "You've Got to Stand for Something" and "That's As Close As I'll Get to Loving You."

Thom Owens

Trent Tomlinson

Country Is My Rock
February 2006, Lyric Street

Country Is My Rock—as in country is Trent Tomlinson's rock & roll, and that may be true since he certainly rocks country harder than any young country buck outside of such mavericks as Hank Williams III, who would rather kick up a storm with his metal band anyway. Tomlinson isn't that crazed—country may be his rock & roll, but it's also his rock as in the foundation of his music, and no matter how he cranks up the overdrive on the amps and boogies, he's still a country songwriter at heart, and a damn good one at that. Sometime his rock & roll act comes across as schtick, but like Hank Jr.—or Kid Rock for that matter—that sense of camp only enhances his persona, since he also has a knack for lean, hard, and melodic songs. Not everything here clicks—sometimes he gets a little silly (which is preferable to getting a little sappy), and sometimes his voice is just a shade too thin—but there are plenty of good, piledriving country-rockers and a handful of good barroom ballads, all performed with vigor and good humor, which makes this an excellent debut.

Stephen Thomas Erlewine

The Tractors

Farmers in a Changing World
November 1998, Arista

Four years after their acclaimed debut, the Tractors finally delivered their full-fledged follow-up, *Farmers in a Changing World*, in late 1998. (A holiday album, *Have Yourself a Tractors Christmas*, appeared in 1995, but that doesn't  count as a sequel to *The Tractors*). During that time, contemporary country became even more infatuated with the pop-country crossover, as the success of Shania Twain and Faith Hill proved. The title of the album hints at that situation, but the Tractors ignore such trends, choosing to synthesize a plethora of American roots musics into a distinctive sound—they're farmers in a changing world. Sure, they remain rooted in country, but they try a bunch of other things, including soul, New Orleans R&B, and rockabilly with "The Elvis Thing," backed by no less than Scotty Moore, James Burton, and DJ Fontana. What ties it all together is Steve Ripley's fine songwriting and the band's excellent taste in covers; the material is so good that the eclecticism doesn't seem jumbled—it makes sense. It may have taken a while for the album to have been recorded, but the wait was worth it.

Stephen Thomas Erlewine

Fast Girl
April 2001, Audium

A fine slab of NRBQ/Dave Edmunds-style country-inflected rock & roll, 2001's *Fast Girl* is another typically enjoyable album from the Tractors. Like their namesake farm equipment, the Tractors are never flashy, and they're built more for comfort than speed. Goofy rockers like "Babalou" (nothing to do with Desi Arnaz, of course), two-step ballads like "It's a Beautiful Thing," and honky tonk covers like the Tractors' version of Moon Mullican's classic "Don't Ever Take My Picture Down" blend into an eclectic but never scattershot blend of country, R&B, and early rock influences. In these surroundings, even stylistic experiments like the extended jam that closes the otherwise ultra-poppy "Ready to Cry" make perfect sense. *Fast Girl* is not the Tractors' best album, but coming as it did after a nearly four-year layoff, it shows that the group hadn't lost anything in its downtime.
Stewart Mason

Randy Travis

Always & Forever
1987, Warner Bros.

Randy Travis' first album, 1986's *Storms of Life* was one of those rare debuts that was nearly perfect: a confident, assured statement of purpose that set expectations for a follow-up almost too high. Remarkably, his second album *Always &* 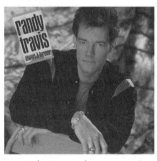 *Forever*—delivered just a year later—met those expectations and rivaled its predecessor in its quality. If there's just a slightly increased inclination to slick, radio-ready productions and an emphasis on ballads, the songs themselves are sturdy, classically styled country tunes, whether they're tales of heartache or devotion and they're grounded by Travis, whose nuanced baritone—bearing a definite Lefty Frizzell influence but possessing his own distinctive idiosyncrasies—cuts through whatever production glaze there is here. But that glaze is slight—it's just a hallmark of the era and when compared to other records in the charts in 1987, *Always & Forever* sounds positively lean—and the songs (including the chart-toppers "Forever and Ever, Amen," "I Won't Need You Anymore (Always and Forever)" and "Too Gone Too Long") are great, and through it all Travis proves that he's one of the great country singers of the '80s, if not the greatest.
Stephen Thomas Erlewine

Old 8x10
1988, Warner Bros.

Almost on a par with *Storms of Life*, Randy Travis' *Old 8x10* lacks the monster hits of his debut but wears just as well. When Travis sings of love, he doesn't mean romance; there's a permanence in his voice that sounds like settling down. The album contains "Honky Tonk Moon," "Deeper than the Holler," and "Is It Still Over?"
Brian Mansfield

No Holdin' Back
1989, Warner Bros.

Released in 1989, *No Holdin' Back* was an anomaly for a record coming from Nash Vegas at the turn of the decade: It's a very traditional country album. Period. Travis is a honky tonk singer who uses the entire scope of the music's history as his playground. He doesn't take a lot of chances, as this record proves, but then he doesn't need to. It's not about ambition on *No Holdin' Back*. Kyle Lehning's production is flawless, in that he allows Travis' big voice to be buoyed by his accompaniment. He sounds like he's dead center in the mix. The album begins with the Matraca Berg nugget "Mining for Coal," an elegiac love song. That's typical enough, but on the very next track, his cover of Melvin Endsley's "Singing the Blues," there is a straight-up honky tonk song complete with male backing chorus—à la the Jordanaires—vocals, plinky upright piano, harmonica, and a barroom tempo. But that's not all: Travis lets out a long Hank Williams-style yodel that will make the listener feel the master's ghostly presence. The single "He Walked on Water" by Allen Shamblin was a bad choice, though it sold well. It's a syrupy ballad that is so overly sentimental that there is no place in the song for Travis to go. The most notable cut on the set is Brook Benton's "It's Just a Matter of Time," and it should have been picked as the album's first single to radio and retail. First, coming almost in the middle, it's the hinge for the entire album. Secondly, this is Travis at his best, stretching to get to the heart of a music that has so little to do with country; like Ray Charles on the other side, he has to make this soul song his own. And he does. It's a country song like it was written that way. The other standout is "Hard Rock Bottom of Your Heart," a modern country shuffle reworked though the tradition. Travis goes after it like Merle Haggard would, slipping in under those verses to max out the emotion from the melody, and then driving that refrain home with a hammer as the pedal steel whines and the crisp drums accent the end of each beat. This is solid Travis, and it proves that at the end of the 1980s he was really just getting started.
Thom Jurek

Heroes and Friends
1990, Warner Bros.

This duets album includes the obvious influences (George Jones, Conway Twitty, Tammy Wynette) as well as a few surprises (B.B. King, Clint Eastwood). The Jones song, "A Few Ole Country Boys," and the title track were hit singles.
Brian Mansfield

High Lonesome
1991, Warner Bros.

High Lonesome is a mature record by a seasoned, forward-thinking country artist. Randy Travis, like George Strait and Alan Jackson, saw the new young bucks heading his way up the charts with a watered-down version of the country music 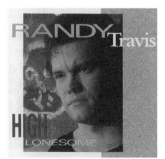 he held sacred. And Travis is a direct descendent of the greats like George Jones and Merle Haggard as well as Jim Reeves and Ernest Tubb. Travis wanted to articulate his vision of the music further and entrench it deeper in its roots, which were beginning to give way to the faux rock and pop styles of Garth Brooks and his dire ilk, who wore bachelor pad curtains for shirts. Travis co-wrote five of the album's ten tracks, including a trio with Jackson. Of those, "A Better Class of Losers" is the song that Brooks wishes he could have written. This is the angry side of the George Jones/Tammy Wynette version of "We're Not the Jet Set." Stinging dobros and pedal steels underline every one of Travis' indictments of yuppie culture. In addition, "I'd Surrender All" shows the pair digging deep into the territory Conway Twitty inhabited before he urbanized his sound, and their "Forever Together" is as fine a country love ballad as the 1990s produced; it's a song Hag would have been proud to record back in the day.

Another highlight is the mandolin and fiddle-driven waltz that comprises the title track. Written by the criminally undersung Gretchen Peters, it's the long, slow ballad with dobros ringing in the background that was made for Travis' amazing voice. He expresses without stretching; each phrase rings as true as the last. Kyle Lehning's production is unobtrusive and clean, setting Travis in perfect balance with a band that feels live. Not to be outclassed in the honky tonk department, "Allergic to the Blues" is a politically incorrect swinging barroom anthem written by Jackson and Jim McBride. Keeping a woman hostage because of an unwillingness to experience pain and rejection is hardly tasteful, but this is a country song and the tongue is firmly placed in cheek in Travis' read. The set closes with "I'm Gonna Have a Little Talk," an awesome a cappella duet with Take 6. It's country gospel elevated by the 6 to high tension rather than to differing versions of rural gospel. Take 6 is thoroughly modern, sophisticated, and glossy. Travis is so country he couldn't be city if he tried to buy it. This wouldn't have worked anywhere near as well if he had recorded the track with the Blind Boys of Alabama, but in this context, it puts a slick finishing touch on a fine album.

Thom Jurek

Full Circle
August 1996, Warner Bros.

Randy Travis' *Full Circle* is a return to form, of sorts. Although he never really left the country charts, his mid-'90s albums suffered from a tendency to sound a bit too similar too each other. *Full Circle* solves that problem by simultaneously reaching back into his hardcore honky tonk roots and moving toward more contemporary material, such as Mark Knopfler's "Are We in Trouble Now." Travis' exquisitely textured and weathered voice gives the new songs a gravity they might not have had if another vocalist had sung them. Furthermore, producer Kyle Lehning has once again assembled a top-notch backing band that manages to sound rootsy and professional simultaneously. With a fine band and an excellent set of material, Travis rises to the occasion with *Full Circle*, producing one of his finest albums of the '90s.

Thom Owens

A Man Ain't Made of Stone
September 1999, DreamWorks

Randy Travis has always been a traditionalist, which was fine in the late '80s, when he brought straight-up, hardcore country back into the charts, but a decade later, he was out of step with the charts. After spending his career at Warner, he switched to DreamWorks, adopting a new production team (James Stroud and Byron Gallimore) along the way.

Ironically, *You and You Alone*, his 1998 debut for the label, wasn't up to the standard of *Full Circle*, his last for Warner, and *A Man Ain't Made of Stone*, his second effort for DreamWorks, isn't either. Much like its predecessor, *A Man* is a sturdy, solid affair that takes a couple of chances that don't quite work, while offering several good, no-frills traditionalist numbers. All those are packed toward the front end of the album, and by the sixth song, "No Reason to Change," the record feels like a modest latter-day masterstroke. Things go a little haywire on the second half, beginning with "Where Can I Surrender," a turgid ballad with a gospel choir supporting him. From that point on, Travis isn't on secure ground, as even promising numbers are undone by weird quirks: the enjoyable rocker "I'll Be Right Here Loving You" is undone by a chanted litany of modern conveniences/hassles in the verse, "Once You've Heard the Truth" takes a weirdly anthemic turn in the chorus. Travis retains his dignity throughout it all, and the record is redeemed by the nice closer "Thirteen Mile Goodbye," but by that point, *A Man Ain't Made of Stone* has revealed itself as nothing new, simply a solid Randy Travis record. Much of it sounds fine, but it doesn't have the character of his earlier records, which proves that it's possible to stay traditionalist and still be memorable.

Stephen Thomas Erlewine

Trail of Memories: The Randy Travis Anthology
July 2002, Rhino

Trail of Memories: The Randy Travis Anthology is a welcome, needed addition to his catalog. Although he's had hits collections before, nothing has come close to offering as much music as this two-disc, 44-track collection, nor has anything else made as strong a case for his musical accomplishments—in this light, he truly sounds like the heir to such classic country singles as Merle Haggard, Lefty Frizzell, and George Jones. Part of the reason that might not have been apparent to some listeners during the '80s is that even a new traditionalist like Travis was recorded according to the state-of-the-art standards of the time. So, even his grittiest material has a clean, sparkling surface, big drums, and a lot of instrument separation, all the hallmarks of mainstream production in the '80s. Years later, it's easier to listen past the production and hear the songs and Travis' singing, which, as this collection proves, is remarkably sturdy and consistent throughout his career. And *Trail of Memories* touches on each aspect of his career, from his early hits like "Diggin' Up Bones" to his late-'90s recordings for DreamWorks. Throughout it all, what's surprising is how little Travis has changed—the best of his songs are always strong, simple, memorable, sung in a similar fashion, while dressed in pretty, clean production that disguises how close to classic late '50s/'60s hardcore country this really is. He was heralded as a keeper of the flame in the '80s, and in 2002, when this collection was released, his music sounds purer than ever. Needless to say, this is an essential cornerstone in any contemporary country collection.

Stephen Thomas Erlewine

Rick Trevino

In My Dreams
September 2003, Warner Bros.

Hispanic country crooner Rick Trevino's fourth English record is a brokenhearted love poem that radiates with Nashville polish. It was produced and co-written by Raul Malo, whose skills have been honed to perfection at his day job as the voice of the Mavericks. The ten songs on *In My Dreams* manage to sound both country ("Overnight Success") and Latino ("Have You Ever Really Loved a Woman") with an emphasis on Trevino's rich, honey voice. The title track is a lush, radio-ready lament, ripe with one of Malo's signature Roy Orbison-inspired choruses. As a whole, *In My Dreams* succeeds with its beautiful arrangements and Trevino's faultless vocals, making it a gem among music row's over-produced monthly quota of releases.

James Christopher Monger

Trick Pony

Trick Pony
March 2001, Warner Bros.

Elvis-style rock meets contemporary country music on Trick Pony's rollicking first single release, "Pour Me," from the band's self-titled debut. The song explodes right out of the starting gate and sets the stage for the rest of the 13-track disc, which is raucous country-rock music. Heidi Newfield, the trio's sassy lead singer, offers a powerhouse of a vocal delivery on *Trick Pony*, and her sound is reminiscent of Dolly Parton and Bonnie Raitt. Such songs as "Party of One" and "One in a Row," with its calypso-type flavor, offer up good old-fashioned bar fare. Elsewhere, anyone who has ever been broke before will truly appreciate the tongue in cheek "Spent," which genuinely describes the state of only having nickels and dimes as collateral. Johnny Cash and Waylon Jennings guest on the band's redo of Cash's "Big River." And the mid-tempo "Just What I Do," sung by bassist Ira Dean, and "Can't Say That on the Radio," sung by guitarist Keith Burns, have great pop-adult contemporary crossover potential, like many country artists have enjoyed in the early 21st century. While there a few ballads on the album, the most moving is the swaying "Stay in This Moment," which effectively captures the essence of wanting to stop time during a perfect instance shared between lovers. *Trick Pony* is an ideal listen for those who go to a bar to drink, dance, and forget about their problems. It's also a good pick for people who enjoy music that is real, carefree, sometimes melancholy, as well as rousing. What an impressive first effort by a group that promises to have more shots of whiskey and good songs up their sleeve.

Liana Jonas

On a Mission
November 2002, Warner Bros.

Performances are spirited, songs are catchy, and the good-time vibe is unavoidable throughout Trick Pony's sophomore release. What distinguishes this trio from their colleagues on the Music City assembly line are the rough edges they leave in their vocals. Even on their tightest harmonies they project a spontaneity that feels far more genuine than cultivated.

The material, most of which is their own, provides plenty of catchy hooks and down-home wordplay, though none of it leaves much of an aftertaste. Willie Nelson makes a predictably informal appearance in a cover of his old "Whiskey River" hit; its thrown-together quality feels pretty much like everything Nelson has done these past several decades.

Robert L. Doerschuk

R.I.D.E.
June 2005, Curb

Trick Pony was doing rough and rowdy long before Gretchen Wilson came along and flew the flag for redneck women, but their third album (and first for Curb), *R.I.D.E.*, proves that the trio sounds rougher and rowdier than Wilson. Trick Pony are a quintessential Southern bar band, nominally country but just as comfortable with rock & roll and blues. They'll also throw a little pop in the mix—as in "When I Fall," a bid for a crossover hit—but they're better off when they relax and kick out music that's the ideal soundtrack for a weekend. Heidi Newfield has a sexy, throaty growl that adds grit even to the slower songs and she's complimented by Keith Burns' clean swagger, and the combination of two lead vocalists helps give *R.I.D.E.* a welcome sense of variety. Sometimes, the trio can get a little silly and sometimes their material leans a little bit too close to the generic, but for the most part this is a lean, mean redneck country-rock album, one that promises and delivers a damn good time.

Stephen Thomas Erlewine

Trio

Trio
1987, Warner Bros.

Bringing together Emmylou Harris, Dolly Parton, and Linda Ronstadt for the album *Trio* was a truly inspired idea, and not simply because they were three of the finest voices in country and pop music at the time. While a gifted entertainer, Parton is also a business-savvy professional who will willingly set aside her gifts as a pure country singer if she thinks her audience would rather hear something like "Nine to Five." However, give her a stage for old-school country material, and she will always rise sublimely to the occasion. Similarly, some of Linda Ronstadt's finest work was on her early country-rock albums (especially *Heart Like a Wheel*), but she seems to operate best with strong collaborators; left to her own devices, she's just as likely to pick wrong-headed material in styles not comfortable to her, but in the right settings her gifts still dazzle. And while Emmylou Harris had as strong a track record as anyone in Nashville in the 1980s, it's obvious she loves to collaborate with others, and sings harmonies with the same rich and affecting beauty that she brings to her headlining gigs. So you take two gifted artists who need proper direction, team them up with an excellent collab-orative artist, and the results should fall neatly into place. In truth, that's a formula as likely as not to fail, but on *Trio* the experiment works brilliantly. The three vocalists display an obvious affinity and respect for one another's talents, inspiring superb performances in one another, and while they all shine in their solo spots, some of the album's most pleasurable moments are when the three harmonize, with their distinct but equally impressive voices melding into a whole that's more than the sum of its parts. Harris, Parton, and Ronstadt also make the most of a set of fine songs (certainly a better program than Parton or Ronstadt had taken on in the studio in a while), and producer George Massenburg lined up a wonderfully subtle and intuitive backing group, with Ry Cooder, David Lindley, and Albert Lee picking gloriously without calling undue attention to themselves. In short, *Trio* is that rare example of an all-star collaborative effort that truly shows everyone involved to their best advantage, and it ranks with the best of all three headliners' work.

Mark Deming

Trio II
November 1998, Elektra

Widely agreed upon as technically perfect, this five-year-in-the-making collaboration among these Oprytown divas should be a diamond—or three diamonds: a *Trio II* tiara. But this album, for all its harmonic, sopranic vibrato perfection, is not a glassy ride across the entire lake. Let Linda Ronstadt covet the tracks for her own album projects as much as she reportedly had—Dolly Parton walks all over this record in true Dollywood fashion, with Emmylou Harris and Ronstadt chirping deliciously behind her. There are plenty of exceptions to this, as "Feels Like Home" is really Ronstadt's, and Harris treats "You'll Never Be the Sun" with crystal, bitter prayer-book reverence. Even contributing fiddles and pedal-steel guitars drop by to accompany Parton without a flaw. It isn't her fault her voice, as distinct as the rarest and loudest bird in a forest populated by rare and loud birds, outsculpts the tone and impact of any song she sings with others. She and the gals score a soaring version of the old Carter Family classic "Lover's Return" in a heartbreaking three-parter; the baffling choice to include a Parton-heavy Neil Young standard about the survival and solitude of the dope-drenched '60s, "After the Gold Rush," is, well, baffling. Parton changes his lyrics to say, "I felt like I could cry," instead of voicing the song's former urge to procure some mind-altering substances. In general, a gem along the beautiful lines of cubic zirconium, from the most well-intended and loving of real-deal songbird girlfriends.

Becky Byrkit

Travis Tritt

Country Club
1990, Warner Bros.

Travis Tritt proclaimed his influences early with "Put Some Drive in Your Country," which paid homage not only to Roy Acuff and George Jones, but to Hank Williams, Jr. and Duane Allman as well. It was the lowest-charting single off Tritt's debut, but it sold him a ton of albums. Radio programmers preferred the ambitious "I'm Gonna Be Somebody" and the ballads "Help Me Hold On" and "Drift off to Dream."

Brian Mansfield

It's All About to Change
1991, Warner Bros.

Better production means ballads like "Anymore" sound bigger and rockers like "Bible Belt" (with Little Feat) and a cover of bluesman Buddy Guy's "Homesick" rock harder. Travis Tritt brought in Marty Stuart for a duet on "The Whiskey Ain't Workin'" and revived "Here's a Quarter (Call Someone Who Cares)" as a catch phrase.

Brian Mansfield

T-r-o-u-b-l-e
1992, Warner Bros.

On his third full-length, Travis Tritt's rollicking cover versions of Buddy Guy ("Leave My Girl Alone") and Elvis Presley ("T-R-O-U-B-L-E") are nice touches and show deeper roots than the Gary Rossington co-written tracks here ("Blue Collar Man"). This is also a very diverse collection that shows off a little (though not a lot) more of the singer and songwriter's depths as a performer as well. Tritt's abilities as an authentic showman come across on his recordings, and did even at this early stage of the game, establishing him as a top-flight entertainer and concert draw. Producer Gregg Brown plays to Tritt's strengths, by selecting freewheeling country tunes such as Marty Stuart's "A Hundred Years from Now," Troy Seals' "Lookin' Out for Number One," and Kostas' "Lord Have Mercy on the Working Man" for his moneymaker to sink that countrified voice into. That all said, *T-r-o-u-b-l-e* is also almost indistinguishable from *It's All About to Change*: a good novelty song masquerading as more, a couple of ballads with big flourishes, and a large helping of Southern rock strut is a good formula, granted, but it's still a formula. And for a guy who claimed he never played it safe, this was a bit to close to the net for posterity to bear.

Brian Mansfield & Thom Jurek

Ten Feet Tall and Bulletproof
1994, Warner Bros.

Travis Tritt's most personal album is the one in which he feels most comfortable with his Southern rock/outlaw mantle. ("Outlaws Like Us," in fact, features the voices of Hank Williams, Jr., and Waylon Jennings.) Tritt poked fun at his own foibles in the title track and co-wrote "Wishful Thinking" and "No Vacation from the Blues" with Lynyrd Skynyrd's Gary Rossington. "Wishful Thinking" and "Foolish Pride" are ballads that rival "Anymore" for power and Skynyrd and Bob Seger for production values.

Brian Mansfield

The Restless Kind
August 1996, Warner Bros.

Under the direction of Don Was, Travis Tritt turns in one of his leanest and easily his grittiest country record yet with *Restless Kind*. Cutting back the country-rock flourishes that have always distinguished his sound, Tritt opts for twangy guitars, wailing

fiddles, dobros, and unaffected guts vocals. Mirroring the stripped-down instrumentation, the song selection is straight-ahead honky tonk, rockabilly and traditional country. Tritt benefits immeasurably from this approach—he has never sounded so alive. Actually, he has never sounded so purely country.

Thom Owens

My Honky Tonk History
August 2004, Columbia

It's difficult to believe that Travis Tritt has been kicking it from Nash Vegas for nearly 15 years. For most of that time, Tritt has been remarkably consistent. He has espoused his own vision of outlaw country since the beginning. While marketed as one of the first "new traditionalists" and then refashioned as a progenitor of "young country," Tritt has followed his own redneck way throughout and for the most part made the records he wanted to make. *My Honky Tonk History*, is another chapter, though this one rocks pretty hard. Co-produced with Billy Joe Walker, Tritt assembled a stellar cast of pickers—including Reggie Young, Pat Buchanan, Brent Mason, Pig Robbins, and Eric Darken in a very large cast for this date—as well as some special guests. The title track opens the set with a rollicking firebrand and burning electric guitars all but covering a lone banjo that stands in for tradition. It's a juxtaposition that works, since Tritt's celebration of a hungry life of hustling is timeless. "Too Far to Turn Around," is a bluesy dobro-fueled ballad that is lean and mean, with Gretchen Wilson (one of the song's three writers) guesting on backing vocals. The intro to "What Say You," feels like a track off John Mellencamp's *Lonesome Jubilee*, but perhaps that's because Mellencamp duets with Tritt here on this working-class anthem. It's easily the best cut on the set, and the two singers are particularly suited to one another as electric guitars, mandolins, fiddles, a B-3, and Béla Fleck's banjo crisscross in a swirl of rocking country-soul. Honky tonk music proper enters the fray in Philip Claypool's "Circus Leaving Town," a modern take on the music that made the careers of George Jones and Ray Price. Texas R&B meets the country bar's sawdust floor in "Monkey Around," written by Delbert McClinton, Benmont Tench, and Gary Nicholson. It's greasy, raucous, and freewheeling with killer piano lines by Robbins. Of the ballads, slick as it is, Tritt and Marty Stuart's "We've Had It All," works well. Tritt brings the emotion in the tune right upfront and sings with conviction and grace, but the whining pedal steel in "Small Doses" makes the slow step of this low-down country tearjerker really stand out. Tritt's protagonist is a man on a barstool talking to himself, trying to buoy his courage to face the empty space left by a long-gone lover. In all, *My Honky Tonk History* is a solid, sure-voiced outing from an enduring and committed artist. Bravo.

Thom Jurek

The Very Best of Travis Tritt
January 2007, Rhino

Warner Brothers teamed with Rhino for *The Very Best of Travis Tritt*, the most comprehensive single-disc compilation of the rough-edged country singer's greatest hits to date. The two labels had teamed up in 2002 for a fine pair of Tritt collections—*The Rockin' Side* and *The Lovin' Side*, each of which includes 16 songs—but it's nice to have an all-encompassing single-disc collection like this one, especially for casual fans who don't want to buy two separate CDs. *The Very Best* includes the primary highlights from Tritt's Warner Brothers catalog, which began with *Country Club* (1990) and concluded with *No More Looking Over My Shoulder*

(1998). Furthermore, *The Very Best* includes a pair of songs from *Down the Road I Go* (2000), Tritt's debut album for Columbia: "It's a Great Day to Be Alive" and "Best of Intentions," which charted number two and one, respectively. Plus, there are a few non-album inclusions, namely "Take It Easy," from the Eagles tribute album *Common Thread* (1993); the "Single Version" of Steve Earle's "Sometimes She Forgets," from *Greatest Hits: From the Beginning* (1995); and "This One's Gonna Hurt You (For a Long, Long Time)," from Marty Stuart's *This One's Gonna Hurt You* (1992). The only minor complaint is that *The Very Best* isn't sequenced chronologically. But at least the sequencing is logical, for the most part alternating up-tempo songs with ballads. In the end, it's difficult to envision a better-compiled Warner Brothers-era single-disc collection of Tritt's music than *The Very Best*.

Jason Birchmeier

Josh Turner

Your Man
January 2006, MCA Nashville

Josh Turner's second album is deliberately steeped in country music tradition; at one point or another, he name-checks Johnny Cash, Loretta Lynn, Dolly Parton, Charley Pride, and Red Sovine; sings with John Anderson and Ralph Stanley; and borrows songs from Anderson and Don Williams. At a time when country music, as so often, was flirting with pop, Turner took a leaf from his main immediate influence, Randy Travis, and established a sort of neo-neo-traditionalist approach with his first significant hit, "Long Black Train," in 2003-2004. Although it topped out at only number 13 in *Billboard*'s country chart, the song established Turner, whose debut album, named after the single, went platinum. There isn't anything as arresting on this collection (the title song, an ordinary love ballad, inched into the country Top 20 prior to the album's release), but it is more consistent overall. Producer Frank Rogers constructs conventional country arrangements that do not draw any special attention to themselves, which is appropriate since all they need to do is serve as background to the real attraction, Turner's resonant bass baritone. It's that voice that matters, more than the music and more than the songs, although Turner and Rogers have put together a nicely balanced selection that includes a heartfelt ballad in "Angels Fall Sometimes" (one of five songs out of 11 that Turner wrote or co-wrote); the honky tonk duet "White Noise," a surprisingly successful pairing with Anderson; the dumb-but-no-doubt-sincere "Me and God," sung with Stanley; the rollicking novelty "Loretta Lynn's Lincoln" (a video waiting to happen); and the winning revival of Williams' 1977 hit "Lord Have Mercy on a Country Boy." Turner doesn't quite have the sense of wry humor necessary to make Anderson's (or songwriter Shawn Camp's) "Baby's Gone Home to Mama" his own—he's still a better technical singer than he is an interpreter—but he's still young, and improving.

William Ruhlmann

Shania Twain

Shania Twain
April 1993, Mercury

Shania Twain's eponymous debut album is a bland set of contemporary country that demonstrates her considerable vocal abilities but none of the spark that informs her breakthrough, *The Woman in Me*. Part of the problem is that none of the songs are well constructed and each leans toward soft rock instead of country or country-rock. By and large, the songs lack strong melodies, so they have to rely on Twain's vocal skills, and although she is impressive, she is too showy to make any of these mediocre songs stick. It's a promising debut, largely because it showcases her fine vocal skills, but it isn't engaging enough to be truly interesting outside of a historical context.

Thom Owens

The Woman in Me
1995, Mercury

Sometimes, all it takes for a singer to break it big is to have the right collaborator and nowhere is that truth more evident than with Shania Twain. After years of independent local releases and demo records, she released an OK major-label debut on Mercury in 1993—a record that was perfectly fine but not all that memorable. Not long after that, her path crossed with Robert John "Mutt" Lange's, the producer behind some of the greatest albums in hard rock history, including AC/DC's *Back in Black* and Def Leppard's *Hysteria*. Based on that, Lange didn't seem like an ideal match for Twain, but they turned out to be expertly matched collaborators—and romantic partners, too; they married as they were working on the material that became her second album, *The Woman in Me*. Together, they totally reworked Twain, turning her into a bold, brassy, sexy, sassy modern woman, singing songs that play like tongue-in-cheek empowerment anthems even when they're about heartbreak. She demands that "Any man of mine/better walk the line," tells a poor sap that "(If You're Not In It for Love) I'm Outta Here!" and when she confronts her lover asking "Whose Bed Have Your Boots Been Under?" it sounds like a threat, not a lament. All these songs are painted in big, broad strokes and Lange uses all the arena-filling tricks he's learned from Def Leppard, giving these steady rhythms and melodic hooks that are crushed only by the mammoth choruses which drill their way into permanent memory upon the first listen. That's not to say that *The Woman in Me* is nothing but heavy-handed pop/rockers dressed as country tunes—they are good at ballads like the title song, but they're even more impressive on "No One Needs to Know," as swinging slice of neo- Bakersfield country so good you'd swear that Dwight Yoakam is singing harmony. And that speaks to the skill of Lange as a producer—this is surely pop influenced, but he doesn't push it too far, for no matter how many rock tricks are in the production or how poppy the tunes are, they still feel like country songs, especially on "Any Man of Mine" and "Whose Bed Have Your Boots Been Under?" anthems for the post-"Boot Scootin' Boogie" era, when country slowly, steadily became the sound of middle-American adult pop. Garth Brooks started the ball rolling, but this is where the movement gained momentum, and although this isn't pure country, it *is* country in how it sounds and feels, particularly in how it captures the stance and attitude of the modern women, thanks in no small part to Twain who plays this part to a hilt. And, like all the best Lange productions, it's so exquisitely crafted from the songs to the sound that it's not only an instant pleasure, it's a sustaining one.

Stephen Thomas Erlewine

Come on Over
November 1997, Mercury

Shania Twain's second record, *The Woman in Me*, became a blockbuster, appealing as much to a pop audience as it did to the country audience. Part of the reason for its success was how producer Robert John "Mutt" Lange— best-known for his work with Def Leppard, the Cars, and AC/DC—steered Twain toward the big choruses and instrumentation that always was a signature of his speciality, AOR radio. *Come on Over*, the sequel to *The Woman in Me*, continues that approach, breaking from contemporary country conventions in a number of ways. Not only does the music lean toward rock, but its 16 songs and, as the cover proudly claims, "Hour of Music," break from the country tradition of cheap, short albums of ten songs that last about a half-hour. Furthermore, all 16 songs and Lange-Twain originals and Shania's sleek, sexy photos suggest a New York fashion model, not a honky tonker. And there isn't any honky tonk here, which is just as well, since the fiddles are processed to sound like synthesizers and talk boxes never sound good on down-home, gritty rave-ups. No, Shania sticks to what she does best, which is countrified mainstream pop. Purists will complain that there's little country here, and there really isn't. However, what is here is professionally crafted country-pop—even the filler (which there is, unfortunately, too much of) sounds good—which is delivered with conviction, if not style, by Shania, and that is enough to make it a thoroughly successful follow-up to the most successful country album by a female in history.

Stephen Thomas Erlewine

Up!
November 2002, Universal

When *Up!* was released in November 2002, Shania Twain revealed in one of many promotional interviews that she writes far more songs than can fit on her records and that she hides any personal, introspective songs she pens, not even playing them for her husband and collaborator Robert John "Mutt" Lange. Now, this is certainly a psychological quirk worth exploring, but it also suggests why Twain's albums are such brilliant pieces of mainstream pop. Anything that doesn't fit the mold is discarded, so the album can hum along on its big, polished, multipurpose hooks and big, sweeping emotions. This is Super-Size pop, as outsized and grandiose as good pop should be. And, unlike the work of most pop divas, where the subject matter is firmly about the singer, none of the songs on *Up!* are remotely about Shania Twain, the person—let's face it, she's never faced a situation like "Waiter! Bring Me Water!," where she's afraid her guy is going to be stolen away by their hot waitress. No, these songs have been crafted as universal anthems, so listeners can hear themselves within these tales. Just as cleverly, the songs are open-ended and mutable—always melodic, but never stuck in any particular style, so they can be subjected to any kind of mix and sound just as good. (Indeed, *Up!* was initially released in no less than *three* different mixes—the "Red" pop mix, the "Green" country mix, and the "Blue" international mix; sometimes the differences in mixes were so slight, it sounded like nothing was changed, but each mix revealed how sturdy and melodic the structure of each of the 19 songs was, and how they were designed to sound good in any setting.) True, the sheer length of the album could be seen as off-putting at first, since these 19 tracks don't necessarily flow as a whole. Then again, part of the genius of *Up!* is that it's designed as a collection of tracks, so the album is durable enough to withstand years on the charts, producing singles with different textures and moods every few months. Time revealed *Come on Over* as a stellar pop album, and the same principle works for *Up!*. Upon the first listen, singles seem indistinct, and it seems like too much to consume at once, but once you know the lay of the land, the hooks become indelible and the gargantuan glossiness of the production is irresistible. In other words, it's a more than worthy follow-up to the great mainstream pop album of the late '90s, and proof that when it comes to shiny, multipurpose pop, nobody does it better than Shania Twain.

Stephen Thomas Erlewine

Greatest Hits
November 2004, Mercury Nashville

Just like the albums her husband/producer Mutt Lange produced for Def Leppard, Shania Twain's albums are designed to generate hit singles for two or three years, which means that each of her blockbuster records—1995's *The Woman in Me*, 1997's *Come On Over*, 2002's *Up!*—already seem like greatest-hits records, since they're filled with huge hits. This makes assembling an actual greatest-hits album a little difficult, since not only is the material overly familiar, but there are so many hits that they're difficult to fit on a single-disc collection. Impressively, 2004's *Greatest Hits*—the first compilation Shania has released in her career—doesn't skimp in either the hits or its actual length. Weighing in at a whopping 21 tracks, it has every big hit from her career, bypassing just a handful of tracks (including anything from her eponymous 1993 debut, plus "God Bless the Child" from 1996 and "It Only Hurts When I'm Breathing" from 2004), none of which are greatly missed. The collection runs in reverse chronological order, beginning with the ballad "Forever and Always" from *Up!* then running through hits like "Man! I Feel Like a Woman!," "That Don' Impress Me Much," "You're Still the One," "Any Man of Mine"—all in their most familiar radio mixes, which means pop mixes alternate with country mixes according to the song—before ending with four new tracks (the gleefully goofy "Party for Two" is featured in two versions, a pop version with Sugar Ray's Mark McGrath and a country version with Billy Currington). Taken as a whole, this is a pretty impressive and consistent body of work—sure, her hits can be slick, glossy, and silly, but they're infectious, irresistibly catchy, impeccably crafted, and most importantly, still tremendous fun after hundreds of plays. This isn't straight country, but it never pretends that it is. Instead, Twain and Lange poached the catchiest elements from arena rock and adult contemporary pop, peppered it with '90s pop culture references—anything from bad hair days to Brad Pitt—and developed a glorious, supersized sound that defined mainstream pop and country for nearly a decade. And, as this wonderful collection proves, Shania's hits not only defined their time, but transcend them, as this *Greatest Hits* is as fun as pop music can get.

Stephen Thomas Erlewine

Carrie Underwood

Some Hearts
November 2005, Arista

Given the tightly controlled nature of *American Idol*, it's a wonder that the televised talent contest has never produced a winner who specialized in country music, since there's no segment of modern popular music that is controlled tighter than contemporary country. Maybe this thought was in the minds of Simon Fuller and the rest of *AmIdol*'s 19 management when they went into their fourth season in 2005, since as soon as fresh-faced Oklahoma blonde Carrie Underwood showed up in the audition rounds, the judges—alright, specifically Simon Cowell—pigeonholed her as a country singer, even if there was nothing specifically country about her sweet, friendly voice. From that point on, she was not only the frontrunner, but anointed as the show's first country winner, which apparently proved more enticing to the voters and the producers than the prospect of the show's first rock & roll winner in the guise of the Southern-fried hippie throwback Bo Bice. Which makes sense: cute, guileless young girls have a broader appeal than hairy 30-somethings. They're easier to sell and mold too, and Underwood proved particularly ideal in this regard since she was a blank slate, possessing a very good voice and an unthreatening prettiness that would be equally marketable and likeable in either country or pop. So, the powers that be decided that Underwood would be a contemporary country singer in the vein of Faith Hill—she'd sing anthemic country pop, ideal for either country or adult contemporary radio, with none of the delightful tackiness of Shania Twain. And her debut album, *Some Hearts*, not only hits this mark exactly, it's better than either album Hill has released since *Breathe* in 1999. Which isn't to say that Carrie Underwood is as compelling or as distinctive as a personality or vocalist as Faith Hill: Underwood is still developing her own style and, for as good a singer as she is, she doesn't have much of a persona beyond that of the girl next door made good. But that's enough to make *Some Hearts* work, since she's surrounded by professionals, headed by producers Mark Bright and Dann Huff, who know how to exploit that persona effectively. While some of the songs drift a little bit toward the generic, especially in regard to the adult contemporary ballads, most of the material is slick, sturdy, and memorable, delivered with conviction by Underwood. She sounds equally convincing on such sentimental fare as "Jesus, Take the Wheel" as on the soaring pop "Some Hearts," and even if she doesn't exactly sound tough on the strutting "Before He Cheats," she does growl with a fair amount of passion. In fact, the worst thing here is her chart-topping post-*American Idol* hit "Inside Your Heaven," which is as formulaic as the mainstream country-pop that comprises the rest of *Some Hearts*, but with one crucial difference: the formula doesn't work, the song is too sappy and transparent, the arrangement too cold. On the rest of *Some Hearts*, everything clicks—the production is warm, the tunes inoffensive but ingratiating, it straddles the country and pop worlds with ease, and most importantly, it's every bit as likeable as Carrie was on *American Idol*. Which means that even if she's not nearly as sassy or charismatic as Kelly Clarkson—she's not as spunky as *Nashville Star* finalist Miranda Lambert, for that matter—Carrie Underwood has delivered the best post-*AmIdol* record since Clarkson's debut.

Stephen Thomas Erlewine

Keith Urban

Ranch
1997, WEA

Technically, the Ranch is a country music trio consisting of Peter Clarke, Jerry Flowers, and Keith Urban, but in practice, it is a group of equals to about the extent that the Jimi Hendrix Experience was, which is to say, not at all. Clarke provides drums and percussion, Flowers plays bass and sings background vocals, and Urban does everything else. That means singing lead and background vocals and playing a variety of stringed instruments and keyboards, as well as taking co-writing credits on nine of the 12 tracks. The album is a showcase for Urban, the up-and-coming Down Under performer who moved to Nashville to be nearer the music he loved. Urban is a triple threat: he writes songs steeped in country traditions (yet not really traditionalist), he sings them with confidence, and, most impressively, picks a guitar authoritatively. His pop/country/rock sound occasionally recalls the 1980s style of Rodney Crowell, particularly on one of the songs he didn't write, "Just Some Love." His is an approach that takes the history of country into consideration, but looks forward. He may plead "Hank Don't Fail Me Now" in one song title, but he never really sounds like Hank Williams. He is perhaps most comfortable just picking fast, as he does on the instrumental "Clutterbilly," but the album reveals a budding talent not far from fully flowering. Not surprisingly, after the commercial failure of this release, the Ranch broke up and Urban went solo, breaking through to success shortly after.

William Ruhlmann

Keith Urban
October 1999, Capitol

Keith Urban's solo American debut for Capitol (after leaving the Ranch) may seem a bit quaint now that he's a superstar who is as well known for his production skills and songwriting as he is for his guitar slinging. But back in 1997 when this album was released, Urban looked like a fresh-faced kid who was entering the U.S. market a virtual unknown. Truth is, he made his recording debut in his native Australia in 1991 and had been on the radar of the Nash Vegas A&R men for a long time. This album proves why. There are four Urban originals here that showcase his knack for writing in numerous styles that all fit the expanding country radio format. He could marry a rock tune or a pop ballad to a country melody, set it off with just the right amount of heartfelt emotion and masterful production touches, whether it be playing the banjo or adding strings to the mix. He and co-producer Matt Rollings also selected a mostly winning combination of tunes to fill the remainder of the disc including Monty Powell's fiddle drenched barnstormer "It's a Love Thing," Charlotte Caffey's mid-tempo ballad "But for the Grace of God," and "Rollercoaster," which marks Urban's first signal towards the contemporary country community that he wasn't just a pretty face who could sing. The track is a guitar scorcher

from top to bottom with Urban playing guitar like he was Randy Scruggs' younger brother, flat picking his Stratocaster like it was another extremity he was born with. This and other such moments balance the slick and sometimes too-soft production on the record; as such, the album does mark the true root of his sound as a major artist wetting his feet.

Thom Jurek

Golden Road
October 2002, Capitol

Keith Urban's sophomore issue on Capitol is an early yet devastatingly original piece of work that pointed the way toward the album's *Be Here* and *Love, Pain & the Whole Crazy Thing* in 2004 and 2006, respectively. Urban is partially responsible for the diverse musical traditions that make their way into the contemporary country music scene of the 21st century. While others like Garth Brooks, Tim McGraw, Travis Tritt and the like modeled a sound that included Southern and '70s rock, Urban brought bluegrass, Top 40 pop stylings, and drum loops into the mix as well and made them all work in his own songs as well as those he covered. *Golden Road* is the first place listeners really get to hear the monster guitar slash and burn that he is well known for in his live performances. Urban and Dan Huff produced *Golden Road*. The album contains two Urban originals in the beautiful, lithe ballad "You're Not Alone Tonight," and the shuffling soft rocker "Song for Dad," that showcases the blend of sounds he would later employ as his own trademark mix. The set also contains a pair of excellent cuts by Rodney Crowell, which are particularly suitable, and perhaps were even tailor-made for Urban in "You Won" and "What About Me." The ballad "Raining on Sunday," was a single written by Darrell Brown as was the other single "You'll Think of Me." Tony Martin's "You Look Good in My Shirt," is a delightful stinging rocker, and Monty Powell's "Who Wouldn't Want to Be Me" is another, with Urban playing the strings off his banjo as well as electric guitar. While his later records were bigger hits, this one is consistent enough and full of such charm and personality that it's difficult to believe Urban didn't write everything here. That he owns these songs as if he did makes *Golden Road* a real lasting early achievement.

Thom Jurek

In the Ranch
February 2004, Capitol

Technically, the Ranch is a country music trio consisting of Peter Clarke, Jerry Flowers, and Keith Urban, but in practice, it is a group of equals to about the extent that the Jimi Hendrix Experience was, which is to say, not at all. Clarke provides drums and percussion, Flowers plays bass and sings background vocals, and Urban does everything else. That means singing lead and background vocals and playing a variety of stringed instruments and keyboards, as well as taking co-writing credits on nine of the 12 tracks. The album is a showcase for Urban, the up-and-coming Down Under performer who moved to Nashville to be nearer the music he loved. Urban is a triple threat: he writes songs steeped in country traditions (yet not really traditionalist), he sings them with confidence, and, most impressively, picks a guitar authoritatively. His pop/country/rock sound occasionally recalls the 1980s style of Rodney Crowell, particularly on one of the songs he didn't write, "Just Some Love." His is an approach that takes the history of country into consideration, but looks forward. He may plead "Hank Don't Fail Me Now" in one song title, but he never really sounds like Hank Williams. He is perhaps most comfortable just picking fast, as he does on the instrumental "Clutterbilly," but the album reveals a budding talent not far from fully flowering. Not surprisingly, after the commercial failure of this release, the Ranch broke up and Urban went solo, breaking through to success shortly after. [The 2004 reissue of the album adds two bonus tracks (a polite cover of the *Stealers Wheel* classic "Stuck in the Middle" and "Billy") as well as the videos for "Walkin' the Country" and "Clutterbilly".]

William Ruhlmann

Be Here
September 2004, Capitol

Keith Urban has been a consistent presence in the Top Ten of the country singles charts since 2000, scoring eight consecutive entries as of the release of his third U.S. solo album, *Be Here*, the eighth being the disc's leadoff track, "Days Go By." And there's plenty more where that came from. Unlike most other country artists, Urban doesn't restrict himself to ten selections from the Nashville songwriting establishment for his albums. This one contains 13 songs at a generous 55-minute running time, and Urban's name is on nine of them as a co-writer. Thus, the collection can be viewed as more of a singer/songwriter effort than the usual Music City product. From that point of view, the album has a distinct storytelling arc, beginning with the *carpe diem* sentiments of "Days Go By" and continuing into a series of songs that celebrate life and love, notably Rodney Crowell's unabashedly romantic "Making Memories of Us," which finds Urban doing his best Crowell imitation. Suggestions of struggle begin to intrude as of "God's Been Good to Me," however, and eight songs in Urban abruptly changes the sound and the mood with the piano-and-strings weeper "Tonight I Wanna Cry," a song this reformed drinker confesses in his press materials that his sponsor might not approve of. "She's Gotta Be" picks up the pace, if not the mood, and Matraca Berg and Jim Collins' "Nobody Drinks Alone" brings the singer to a sodden rock bottom before he changes the subject by covering Elton John's "Country Comfort" and finally overcomes adversity in "Live to Love Another Day," then rewrites the album's opening song to look forward again on the album-closing "These Are the Days." The album-length story of optimism and perseverance in the face of romantic turmoil and alcoholic temptation is told musically with Urban's usual collection of fast-picked string instruments, including electric and acoustic guitars, banjo, mandolin, and Dobro (the last played by Bruce Bouton). It's a muscular sound indebted at least as much to rock and

bluegrass as to traditional country, but it supports his light, flexible tenor and his essentially upbeat message.

William Ruhlmann

Days Go By
September 2005, EMI

Born in New Zealand but raised in Australia, Keith Urban established a base for himself in Nashville a decade or so ago, and while he certainly draws from country's long tradition in his music, he's infused it with a healthy dose of good old rock & roll attitude. This isn't something new in Nashville, mind you, but Urban also happens to be one heck of a guitar player and his seemingly boundless enthusiasm for what he does means his version of rocking country doesn't sound like a studied hybrid but instead appears as effortless and natural as the wind blowing down a freeway. Add to this Urban's refreshing optimism, and songs like "Days Go By," "Somebody Like You," and "Better Life" explode out of the speakers like joyous new beginnings. *Days Go By* combines most of the tracks from 2004's *Be Here* with a few from 2002's *Golden Road* to make what amounts to an introductory anthology of Urban's recent work for Capitol Records.

Steve Leggett

Love, Pain & the Whole Crazy Thing
November 2006, Capitol

Love, Pain & the Whole Crazy Thing was released on November 7, 2006, just after country singer and songwriter Keith Urban entered—of his own accord—into treatment for alcoholism. With Urban having married actress Nicole Kidman just months before, the timing couldn't be better. After all, Urban is trying to get well at the very peak of his life—thus far—personally and professionally. *Be Here*, his last album, is, at the time of this writing, at nearly the four-million mark in sales. As fine as that disc is, this one is another giant leap for Urban as an artist. *Love, Pain & the Whole Crazy Thing* is slicker than anything Urban has issued before, but that's because it's more ambitious as well. Urban is a rocking guitarist, a complete wildman on the electric six-string, and he can combine his tough, unhinged approach to playing guitar with pop songwriting and utterly brilliant production elements that layer strings, drum loops, fiddles, banjos, E-Bows, and Hammond B-3s. Add a songwriting style that touches on the classic elements of rock, country, and mainstream pop, and you have something that hasn't been heard in the country genre in this way before. That's right—the album is further proof of his ability to stretch the genre to the breaking point by bringing in more of modern pop's elements while remaining firmly within it.

This album feels, song by song, as if there isn't anything he can't do. Co-producing with Dan Huff, Urban wrote or co-wrote ten of the album's 13 cuts—there's a hidden track buried in the CD-ROM portion of the disc. The production is thoroughly modern, but feels like the country equivalent of George Martin. It's positively baroque in places, and there is so much packed in that it almost, ALMOST feels claustrophobic, but he makes it work beautifully. No record since Neil Diamond's brilliant *Beautiful Noise*—produced by the Band's Robbie Robertson—has sounded so regal and inviting. The album's first single, "Once in a Lifetime," opens the set; it entered the *Billboard* chart at number 17, the highest debuting single since the chart's inception. But the shock is simply that it's not the best track on the record. Urban has packed this disc with fine writing and excellent, even defining versions of the songs he chose to cover. There are a number of rockers, including "Faster Car," with its smoking, funky bassline and layered power chords on guitars and his "ganjo" that ring above the horn section, and "I Told You So," which uses acoustic guitars, fiddles, and the ganjo to usher in some twisting, minor-key electrics. Both songs are based on tight little hooks; both songs build to the breaking point and allow Urban's voice to soar above the instruments. On the latter tune, Uilleann pipes and bouzouki are layered into the mix in a melody that brings to bear Celtic cowboy lyric frames and tribal rhythms that just explode near the end when Urban cuts loose in a serious, distortion-laden guitar wrangle.

"Shine," which begins as a shimmering country-pop tune, is a another example, as a string section and his unhinged soloing style battle for dominance in the nearly unbearable climax. "I Can't Stop Loving You," written by Billy Nichols, is another big climax tune, but it becomes one of the great modern country love songs with its incessant reaching to its crescendo—provided by an army of strings and big power chords. "Used to the Pain," written with Darrell Brown, is a stealthy rocking love song that drips with emotion brought out by vocals that swirl all around the instrumental mix and huge drums. The down-home anthem "Raise the Barn," a duet with Ronnie Dunn, was written in reaction to the destruction done by Hurricane Katrina. Urban can write a shuffling country-rocker with the best of them. Urban didn't pen "God Made Woman," but his version makes the track his own. Beginning with a choir (somewhat smaller and yet reminiscent of the Rolling Stones on "You Can't Always Get What You Want"), the cut quickly becomes a loud and proud country-rock anthem that celebrates—not objectifies—women. "Tu Compañía" is a way funky country two-step love song driven by the ganjo. Yeah. Funky. The album's final cut, "Got It Right This Time," sounds like a homemade demo by the rest of the album's standards, with Urban handling drum machine and keyboard chores while singing. That said, it's far from substandard and certainly belongs here, as it showcases Urban's voice in all its unadorned grandeur and reveals the influence of soul music on his singing.

Those who wish to decry Urban as some kind of slick, formulaic songwriter and flavor of the country music moment are missing it. The man writes honest, beautifully crafted songs that are adult enough to ponder, tough enough to rock, and tender enough to pull—not tug—on the heartstrings. As previously stated, there's no better time to get well than when you are at the absolute top of your game. While Urban's previous records have had their moments and *Be Here* was his true arrival, *Love, Pain & the Whole Crazy Thing* is his mature pop masterpiece—and for all its wonder and expertise, it feels like it's just a taste of what he will offer in the future.

Thom Jurek

Ricky Van Shelton

Wild-Eyed Dream
1987, Columbia

This debut from this country hunk balladeer, with occasional thumpin' at the hop contains "Working Man Blues," "Crime of Passion, " and more.

Mark A. Humphrey

Loving Proof
1988, Columbia

Here are stabs at rockabilly alongside the ballads at which Shelton excels. Some of the songs on the album are "From a Jack to a King" and "Hole in My Pocket."

Mark A. Humphrey

RVS III
1990, Columbia

The third album puts out more sounds in the winning Shelton formula, such as "I Still Love You," "I've Cried My Last Tear for You," "Oh Pretty Woman," and more.

Mark A. Humphrey

Backroads
1991, Collectables

When he's not trying to be Roy Orbison (as he did on 1990's *RVS 3*), it's easy to see that Van Shelton's a fine singer. And this is a fine record—so fine it's tempting to hunt for signs of listener manipulation. But Van Shelton balances the self-pity of songs like "After the Lights Go Out" with the up-tempo punch of stuff like "Call Me Up." So even though Van Shelton recycles "Rockin' Years," the duet from Dolly Parton's *Eagle When She Flies*, just call it good taste, sit back, and enjoy.

Brian Mansfield

16 Biggest Hits
February 1999, Columbia/Legacy

Ricky Van Shelton scored 16 Top Ten country solo hits between 1987 and 1993, and they are all on this appropriately named compilation, which is sequenced in hit order: first the ten number ones, then the three number twos, and so on. Van Shelton came  in on the neo-traditionalist wave of the mid-'80s, and his hits spotlight such veteran country songwriters as Harlan Howard, Roger Miller, and Boudleaux and Felice Bryant and include revivals of standards like "From a Jack to a King." They also exhibit the sentiment and wordplay typical of the country songwriting craft on such newly composed works as the philosophical "Keep It Between the Lines" and the romantic twist of "I Meant Every Word He Said." As country veered toward pop in the Garth-and-Shania era of the '90s, sturdy talents like Van Shelton struggled, but this thorough collection of his most popular material confirms his veneration of traditional country and his status as one of its latter day masters.

William Ruhlmann

Phil Vassar

Phil Vassar
February 2000, Arista Nashville

Phil Vassar established himself as a top country songwriter by penning vigorous, rock-influenced romps for Tim McGraw and Jo Dee Messina. On his own, Vassar is an enthusiastic vocalist, a skilled pianist, and a gifted composer of spirited, nostalgic tales. Like Tom T. Hall, Vassar has a talent for chronological storytelling, squeezing big emotions out of small-town details. The boisterous "Carlene," an immediate hit, details the rediscovery of a high school valedictorian who blossomed into a fashion model. "Joe & Rosalita" follows a similar blueprint, commemorating the journey of two childhood sweethearts from senior prom to domestic bliss. Subsequent hits like "Just Another Day in Paradise" and "That's When I Love You" benefited from the album's good-time piano and vibe, and launched Vassar as a distinctive recording artist. Various country music awards may have solidified his reputation among his peers, but no accolade validates Vassar's talent more than a song like "Didn't You Know She's Gone," in which Vassar speaks through various inanimate objects before admitting the truth to himself. As the dialogue progresses, echoes of '60s pop give way to heartbreaking guitar until his revelation surmounts poetic denial. It is one of many highlights on *Phil Vassar*, an imaginative debut that suggests he has a wealth of future material for himself and others.

Vince Ripol

American Child
July 2002, Arista Nashville

What makes Phil Vassar a true find in today's Nashville climate is his rock-solid ability to pen a convincing song and then turn around and sing it in an equally convincing manner. His writing has been embraced by everyone from Alan Jackson to Cledus T. Judd to Engelbert Humperdinck. Vassar's sophomore album on Arista Records, *American Child*, is exactly what he wants it to be: 12 songs that he had a hand in writing and knew he could convey to his audience. That translates into some catchy lines, a few unconventional choruses, and Vassar's fervent belief in every note. The album offers both powerful ballads like "I Thought I Never Would Forget" and "Stand Still" tempered with the humor of "Athens Grease," the story of a Georgia mechanic Vassar dubs the "redneck Picasso of the manual transmission." The title cut is probably some of Vassar's best songwriting, with plenty of good ole' American imagery. On the downside, some of the cuts just don't merit space on this album. That's no slap to Vassar's songwriting; the best of the best can't write top quality every time they pick up the pen. Here, it's more a question of weeding out and replacing tunes such as the generically bland "I'll Be the One" that ends the album or the confusing "Forgettin's So Long." That said, *American Child* is a solid, enjoyable effort with a few flaws.

Rick Cohoon

Shaken Not Stirred
September 2004, Arista Nashville

Phil Vassar had his breakthrough in 2002 with his second album, *American Child*, a mature set of contemporary country-pop that established that the former professional songwriter had the chops to be a performing star in his own right. For its 2004 follow-up, *Shaken Not Stirred*, Vassar loosens things up a little bit, borrowing a little from Kenny Chesney's laidback party-ready style. While he never indulges in the Jimmy Buffett worship of the island-obsessed Chesney, he does share a similar fondness for '70s arena rock and singer/songwriters, and he's injected *Shaken Not Stirred* with a heavy dose of

humor and good times that only rarely surfaced on *American Child*. Unfortunately, this can veer close to novelty territory, at least on "What Happens in Vegas" and "I'll Take That as a Yes (The Hot Tub Song)," which arrive way too early on this album and nearly ground its momentum to a halt. Significantly, these are the only two songs that Vassar didn't have a hand in writing on this album, and the rest of the record is much more assured, clever, and affecting than these two tunes. Vassar benefits from a looser vibe, since it not only results in livelier performances and funnier jokes, but the sentimental ballads resonate more in this context. Perhaps the record is a little heavy on mid-tempo cuts and the production may be a little slicker than it needs to be, but the polish is appealing, the performances strong, and the songs are, by and large, sturdy and memorable, making *Shaken Not Stirred* Vassar's best record to date.

Stephen Thomas Erlewine

Clay Walker

Clay Walker
1993, Giant

Clay Walker is another country music product from Beaumont, TX (others include George Jones, Mark Chestnut, Doug Supernaw, and Tracy Bird) who has broken into the Nashville music scene. Walker has a high-energy voice and a growl that reminds you of Conway Twitty. The highlights of his first album include "What's It to You?," his first number one hit, and "Live Until I Die." Other featured songs include "The Silence Speaks for Itself" and "White Palace."

Larry Powell

Greatest Hits [Giant]
June 1998, Giant

Clay Walker's *Greatest Hits* collection includes all the key hits from his first four albums—*Clay Walker* (1993), *If I Could Make a Living* (1994), *Hypnotize the Moon* (1995), *Rumor Has It* (1997)—and it also tacks on two new songs ("Ordinary People," "You're Beginning to Get to Me") for good measure. *Clay Walker* is represented by four songs ("What's It to You," "Live Until I Die," "Dreaming with My Eyes Open," "Where Do I Fit in the Picture"), *If I Could Make a Living* by two ("This Woman and This Man," "If I Could Make a Living"), *Hypnotize the Moon* by three ("Hypnotize the Moon," "Only on Days that End in 'Y'," "Who Needs You Baby"), and *Rumor Has It* by three ("Rumor Has It," "Then What," "Watch This"). Many of these songs were number one country hits, and those that weren't chart-toppers were popular nonetheless. In fact, every song here was a major hit for Walker, even the newly recorded songs, and since his hitmaking slowed in the years that followed the 1998 release of *Greatest Hits*, you won't find a better one-disc summary of his prime.

Jason Birchmeier

Steve Wariner

Greatest Hits
September 1987, RCA

Many of Steve Wariner's best moments were his singles and *Greatest Hits* contains many of his best and biggest hits, including the number ones "Some Fools Never Learn," "You Can Dream of Me," and "Life's Highway."

Thom Owens

The Warren Brothers

Barely Famous Hits
August 2005, BNA

The Warren Brothers have a lean and clean rootsy sound, craft solid songs, harmonize sweetly, and have an appealingly self-deprecating sense of humor. They're even engaging on TV, where they have their own reality series, *Barely Famous*, on CMT and have judged on *Nashville Star*. So why aren't they more compelling on record? It's the same problem that plagues many Music City behind-the-scenes pros—they have the skills and talent, but they don't have the presence that makes them recording stars. BNA/RCA Records tried to make the duo into stars at the turn of the millennium, but the public wasn't biting, as their singles and albums stalled in the middle of the charts. The label responded by dumping the brothers, but Nashville survivors that they are, they soldiered on, eventually scoring the TV gigs in the mid-2000s that helped turn them into country stars and, in turn, prompted the summer 2005 release of *Barely Famous Hits*, a compilation of 12 highlights from their three albums released between 1998 and 2004. Not all their charting singles are here, nor are all the good moments from their full-lengths, but most of the good stuff is here—enough to be a representative compilation, a good introduction to the duo, one that will satisfy fans of the TV series. But for those who aren't familiar with *Barely Famous*, this cash-in comp—which admittedly is one of the few times a cash-in is truly warranted—is kind of puzzling. It's good, sturdy contemporary country, well-constructed, slickly played, occasionally pretty funny (as on "Sell a Lot of Beer," the best tune here), but it never is gripping. These are songs and performances that beg to be delivered by somebody with true on-record charisma—somebody like Warren Brothers friend Tim McGraw, or even Dierks Bentley. Without that kind of forceful singer, the Warren Brothers' music is pleasant, but a little flat—which may explain why they didn't have hits prior to being on TV, as well as explaining why their new fans are more forgiving of these polished, well-made, and rather predictable recordings. After all, now that the Warren Brothers are nearly famous, they're familiar, and fans are much more likely to accept such straight-ahead, nearly generic stuff like this from an act they already know. So, *Nashville Star* doesn't just work for the contestants, it works for the judges too! Just don't think that this is anywhere near as good as Miranda Lambert's *Kerosene*.

Stephen Thomas Erlewine

Dale Watson

Cheatin' Heart Attack
1995, Hightone

Watson's hearty, down-to-earth honky tonk makes *Cheatin' Heart Attack* one of the most exciting country debuts this side of Junior Brown's *12 Shades of Brown*. Watson and his band Lone Star burn through 14 no-nonsense songs that prove the genre can be vital and fun at the same time. Watson's voice is pure, deep, and strong, and his songs feature guitar and pedal steel prominently. He's a veteran of the Texas honky tonk circuit, which shows in his sharp arrangements on songs

like "List of Reasons," "Holes in the Wall," and "Nashville Rash" — the latter mixing heartfelt commentary on the current country market with a smart sense of humor.

Kurt Wolff

Blessed or Damned
1996, Hightone

Blessed or Damned pretty much picks up where Watson's 1995 debut, *Cheatin' Heart Attack*, left off. He pines for "A Real Country Song" on modern radio, sings praises for his adopted state on "That's What I Like About Texas" (a good-natured duet with Johnny "Whiskey River" Bush), and wonders at the fate of his chosen musical genre on the moving title track. Watson may have no surprise ace in the hole on *Blessed or Damned*, but it's nonetheless a solid hand of fresh, invigorating material.

Kurt Wolff

The Best of the Hightone Years
January 2002, Hightone

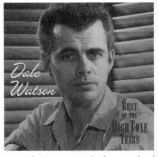

It might deem strange to place country singer and songwriter Dale Watson in the context of contemporary country. Surely, Watson is more than the spiritual heir of Merle and Buck— his music has all the dim lights and beer mugs of the best honky tonk. This compilation creams the best work of his three Hightone discs, all of which sound as if they should have been recorded in the '50s or '60s rather than the '90s; if there ever was a man out of time, it's Dale Watson. He can write some classic cheating songs like "Caught" and truckers' anthems such as "Hey Driver" and "Truckstop in La Grange" (which might be the only song to celebrate La Grange, KY, and romanticize I-71), and condemn modern country on "Nashville Rash," which also pays tribute to his heroes. His deep voice and style (which can easily become a sing-speak) owe plenty to Merle Haggard and a little to George Jones, while his players, including the great Jerry Donahue, can twang like there's no tomorrow. That said, the only place where it comes unstuck is on "Blessed or Damned," which tries to step outside the musical and lyrical boundaries where he is comfortable. This is also the place, amid all of these others, that Watson appeals—at least on CMT and GAC—to listeners of the more pop-oriented country music of the late 20th and early 21st centuries. Truth is, they still appreciate the real thing, especially when it's played by a guitar-slingin' no-nonsense redneck son of a gun. Watson's penchant for stripped-down rockabilly riffs—even if they do come by way of Bakersfield—are still rock & roll roots music. So, if you think honky tonk died when Jones and Hag fell off the charts, or appreciate hard, beer-drinking, hell-raising music, then you need this, quite simply. It's not alt-country or neo-traditionalist country (whatever those things are); it's nothing but dyed-in-the-wool heartbreak diesel, although you need to bring your own beer to cry into. If you get a hankering for that classic country sound, placed in a contemporary context of American music (Watson calls it "Ameripolitan"), then Dale Watson's your man.

Chris Nickson & Thom Jurek

Bryan White

Greatest Hits [Elektra]
October 2000, Elektra

As demonstrated on this compilation, which contains his ten biggest hits and two new tracks, Bryan White never made really compelling country music. In fact, the music is only country-flavored pop, the real antecedents for which lie in early '70s folk-rock. When White performs a ballad like "I'm Not Supposed to Love You," it sounds like the Eagles doing "Desperado"; when he turns to a rhythm song like "So Much for Pretending," it recalls Stephen Stills' "Love the One You're With." Clearly, White is more pop than country, and he has paid the price by apparently becoming a has-been before his 25th birthday. The two new songs, "How Long" and "The Way You Look at Me," are typically pleasant, but they don't sound like what's needed to turn things around. As it stands, *Greatest Hits*, which manages to encapsulate all of White's popular material without including anything from his 1999 album *How Lucky I Am*, sums up a representative career in the pop-oriented country music of the '90s with no indication that that career will flourish in the future.

William Ruhlmann

Lari White

Lead Me Not
April 1993, RCA

White's ambitious debut covered a lot of musical territory, from straight country ("Where the Lights Are Low") to torch ballad ("Just Thinking"), from Latin-flavored pop ("Made to Be Broken") to fervid gospel ("Good Good Love"). The breadth of her talent turned out to be something of a problem. Since nobody could get a handle on her, none of the album's three singles ("What a Woman Wants," "Lead Me Not," and "Lay Around and Love on You") broke the Top 40.

Brian Mansfield

Wishes
June 1994, RCA

Wishes was Lari White's breakthrough release, and it's easy to hear why. Besides the infectious, small-town summer crush feel of lead single "That's My Baby," there's the spectacular chorus harmonies of "That's How You Know (When You're in Love)" (featuring Hal Ketchum), the gospel-tinged "When It Rains," and the brassy "Go On," which could almost be the fiery heart of a feisty insurgent country artist's next project for Bloodshot. Tracks like this showcase White's torchy vocal, which is a combination of Trisha Yearwood's brassiness with a bit of Patsy Cline. Then there's White's band, who give each track a ground-level feel that's often missing from top-line Nashville releases. Instead of relying

on the comfortably bland, they grit up "Somebody's Fool" and "Now I Know" with honest hooks and touches of slide guitar. *Wishes* is a solid home run of an album with much more to offer than simply its singles.

Johnny Loftus

Stepping Stone
July 1998, Hollywood

Lari White has one of the finest voices in popular music. Her ability to bring the strength of her gospel background to anything she sings makes her talent a real treasure. Sadly, she has been misused and abused by the factory system in Music City and has not attained the success she should have. But quality can't be overlooked; like cream, it rises to the top. And while most of the material on this project is not worthy of her talent, she still makes a good showing all across the board. Perhaps the most stunning performance this time out is "You Can't Go Home Again," a traditional tune that allows White to show off the prowess in her vocal style. Just as good is the Deborah Allen-Chuck Jones tune "On a Night Like This," which showcases White's ability to rock. The thing about Lari White is that no matter the caliber of material, for better or worse, she makes you believe every word she sings.

Jana Pendragon

Green Eyed Soul
May 2004, Skinny WhiteGirl

Lari White's first American album of the new millennium (her last, *Stepping Stone*, was issued in 1998) was released in the United Kingdom in June of 2004 on the Mesmerizing label. *Green Eyed Soul*, produced by White, comes to us courtesy of her own Skinny White Girl label. Having established herself in the '90s as a pop-country artist, this set is going to be a change-up for some as the title offers a sleek peek toward what she's going for. White's aim is slick, chart-ready R&B, and nu-soul. It's also a given with White's voice, and that this disc was made in Nash Vegas, her roots sound cannot be covered entirely. But what's most startling is her use of loops and even breaks alongside her studio band. Her love of Southern soul and Motown is everywhere evident, but with the use of technology alongside horns and strings—check "Right Here Right Now"—the effect is startling. There are trip-hop beats, turntables, and samplers flitting through the mix and creating rhythms. The country-R&B of "Eden Before the Fall" is driven by slow, electric slide guitar, but ambient sounds and shimmering backdrop electronics color and texture the tune displacing its center. "Because I'm a Woman" is a tight little groover that's part slow-funk anthem, part country song, and part soul rave-up, with a killer refrain. The strutting B-sharp on "High," is pure silk and groove (think Al Green or Ron Isley) albeit it in a thoroughly modern context. White's voice shines throughout; her pitch, phrasing, and emotional involvement in her songs is not only credible but worth celebrating. Make no mistake, this is a very smooth, slick record; but its depth cannot be denied and as a pop record, one of the majors could have scored big with it. Highly recommended.

Thom Jurek

Keith Whitley

Don't Close Your Eyes
1988, RCA

Don't You Close Your Eyes was more successful than Keith Whitley's two previous albums and it's easy to see why. Though the record still suffered from a handful of mediocre songs and a slightly soft production, the overall album was leaner and more direct than Whitley's earlier solo work, showcasing his talent for heartfelt honky tonk singing and his skill for crafting excellent barroom ballads. "Don't Close Your Eyes," "When You Say Nothing At All," and "I'm No Stranger to the Rain" were the hits, but there's a wealth of excellent material here, including a haunting version of Lefty Frizzell's "I Never Go Around Mirrors." The sheer strength of the best numbers make the handful of weaker songs perfectly excusable. After all, country in the late '80s rarely got better than *Don't You Close Your Eyes* at its best.

Thom Owens

I Wonder Do You Think of Me
1989, RCA

Though Keith Whitley displayed his immense talents on his previous albums, it was only in small measures. It wasn't until *I Wonder Do You Think of Me*, his fourth and final album, that he truly came into his own. The difference between this album and its predecessors is focus. The essential style remains the same, but Whitley has decided to concentrate only on a heart-tugging, gritty honky tonk and to give the record an appropriately straightforward, simple production. The direct approach gives more weight to the sad tales of lost love and drinking and when Whitely died shortly before the record's release, these songs gained even more gravity. Still, *I Wonder Do You Think of Me* stands as an excellent testament—songs like "It Ain't Nothin'," "I'm Over You," and the title track only begin to suggest the depth and appeal of this album.

Thom Owens

Greatest Hits
1990, RCA

Assembled and released shortly after Keith Whitley's death, *Greatest Hits* contains nine of his biggest songs—including the Top Ten singles "Ten Feet Away," "Don't Close Your Eyes," "When You Say Nothing at All," "I'm No Stranger to the Rain," "I Wonder Do You Think of Me," "It Ain't Nothing," and "I'm Over You"—plus two unreleased songs: a duet with wife Lorrie Morgan on "'Til a Tear Becomes a Rose" and a demo of "Tell Lorrie I Love Her." It's an excellent compilation, but it is a bit unbalanced, drawing almost entirely from *Don't Close Your Eyes* and *I Wonder Do You Think of Me*. Granted, those are his two best albums, but it would have been nice to have collected highlights from his first two uneven solo records. Nevertheless, *Greatest Hits* is a fine last will and testament to a tremendously gifted artist

who set a template for contemporary country, even as he was faithful to its long history and lineage. Whitley's voice was one of pain and quiet passion, its grain an instantly recognizable trademark. Sure, *Greatest Hits* is for those fans who just want the big singles, but this collection is also a stellar—even classic—introduction to his work.

Thom Owens & Thom Jurek

Kentucky Bluebird
1991, RCA

Kentucky Bluebird is a posthumous album of unreleased Keith Whitley material that was issued a year after his 1989 death. This is a documentary of sorts, including Whitley's early appearance on *The Buddy Starcher Show*, a duet recorded with Earl Thomas Conley called "Brotherly Love," and live versions of favorites like "I Never Go Around Mirrors" and the title track. Especially interesting for dedicated fans are the interview segments included throughout. This is definitely not a first-purchase disc, but a recommended curio.

Al Campbell

RCA Country Legends
March 2002, RCA

This is an enjoyable sampler from one of the leaders of the new traditionalist movement, Keith Whitley. The 16 tracks stem from his mid- to late-'80s RCA material, including the hits "When You Say Nothing at All," "I'm No Stranger to the Rain," and "Ten Feet Away." Whitley's widow, Lorrie Morgan, appears on "Til a Tear Becomes a Rose," which was released posthumously following Whitley's accidental death from alcohol poisoning in 1989.

Al Campbell

Hank Williams, Jr.

Family Tradition
1979, Curb

Family Tradition followed *The New South* by a couple of years and delved deeper into Hank Williams Jr.'s spirit of adventure in reinventing his music to fit him as an individual. Far from giving a damn about what Nash Vegas thought of him at this point, Williams worked with three different producers on this set: Jimmy Bowen, Ray Ruff, and Phil Gernhard. While it's true that this set doesn't have the grit that *Hank Williams, Jr. & Friends* or *The New South* had, it does showcase Williams as a singer of real distinction and his love of soul and R&B music. An example of how willing he was to experiment was on the opening track, where he covers the Bee Gees' "To Love Somebody" with a chorus of backing vocalists. And he pulls it off in spades. It's moving, it swings, and it has that gospel feel that the hint of this song always contained but which had never been brought out before. He follows the R&B tip on "Old Flame, New Fire," an Oskar Soloman song that fuses country and Memphis-style R&B—again, with the female chorus raining down all around him. On Steve Young's dark and tenuous love song "Always Loving You," Charlie Daniels fiddles his way through the background in his inimitable style and Reggie Young's electric guitar can be heard trading fills with Brad Felton's steel. A notable cover on the set is a funky-butt read of Bobby Fuller's "I Fought the Law." There's a country feel in the phrasing, but that was there in the original tune; Williams brings a popping bass and honky tonk piano to the proceedings. It's not the best version of the tune, but it is an interesting one. The latter half of the set is chock-full of Hank Jr. compositions, with the notable exception of Ivy J. Bryant's "Only Daddy That'll Walk the Line," a song closely associated with Waylon Jennings. But Williams' version rocks harder than any other on record. Williams' own personal outlaw anthem is present as well, the infamous and wonderful "Family Tradition," with Daniels laying out a laid-back but gorgeous fiddle solo in the bridge. There's also the redneck manifesto "I've Got Right" and the killer "Paying on Time." In all, this is a slick, over-the-top-production album, but the quality of the songs and the arrangements, along with Williams' dynamite singing voice, make this set a necessity.

Thom Jurek

Major Moves
1984, Curb

Williams topped the country charts with this album, largely on the strength of the raucous "All My Rowdy Friends Are Coming over Tonight," though the title track and the caustic "Attitude Adjustment" were also hits.

William Ruhlmann

Born to Boogie
1987, Curb

Born to Boogie is Hank Williams, Jr. claiming his reign as elder statesman over the burgeoning young-country movement of the late '80s. This is heavy on uptempo rock tunes, including the title cut, the Rolling Stones' "Honky Tonk Women," and "Keep Your Hands to Yourself," originally by the Georgia Satellites. The album's centerpiece is the anthemic "Young Country," in which Williams and his like-minded musicians/friends (including Highway 101, T. Graham Brown, and Marty Stuart) engage in a singalong declaring their love for not only the classic country of Hank Williams, but equal admiration for the Rolling Stones, ZZ Top, and Van Halen.

Al Campbell

America (The Way I See It)
1990, Curb

Williams plays political commentator on this, a collection of his best revenge fantasies, reasons for America's problems, and the theme from Monday Night Football. The album includes the survivalist anthem "A Country Boy Can Survive" and "Don't Give Us a Reason," an open letter to Saddam Hussein.

Brian Mansfield

The Bocephus Box [Curb]
August 2000, Curb

The years covered on Curb's *The Bocephus Box (1979-1999)* are the 20 years where Hank Jr. was an American icon, the

larger-than-life rowdy man of country. His rise began in the early '80s, when he hit upon a terrific blend of honky tonk, Southern rock, blues, and country that appealed to rock and country audiences alike—rednecks of all persuasions, as less charitable critics would say. Throughout the '80s, he ruled the country charts, as every single one of his new albums went gold. For some observers, he slipped into self-parody halfway through that reign, but as this three-disc box set proves, the best of his music was remarkably consistent. Yes, the individual albums sagged somewhat (especially in the mid-'90s), but he remained true to his vision and had a good choice of material, whether it was newly written songs or rock covers. Early on in *The Bocephus Box*, it dawns on you that while some have replicated his style—and while he has spent a long time working the same ground—nobody really did this rowdy, rockin' country before Hank, and nobody has done it better since. Country purists may deny it, but he was a distinctive stylist, and while he got a little silly even when he was good, he usually delivered, especially in a concentrated setting like this. During those two decades, he released an album almost every year, which were distilled to 65 songs and three discs with almost no duds—which means he must have been doing something right. For doubters and fans alike, this is the place to really absorb Hank Jr. at the height of his powers.

Stephen Thomas Erlewine

The Almeria Club Recordings
January 2002, Curb

The words self, parody, and Hank Williams, Jr. have been inextricably tied for such a long time—nowhere more so than in his 1999 album, *Stormy*, where he seemed like he was auditioning for a sketch comedy, competing with Bob Odenkirk's send-up on *Mr. Show*—that the spare, gritty, compelling 2002 release, *The Almeria Club Recordings*, comes as a bracing surprise. It's not that Williams Jr. has left all of his silly self-mythologizing behind, or that he's now developed a disdain for the ridiculous—witness "Big Top Women," who "sure do bounce around," or how he's decided that he's "X-Treme Country," or how he mentions hanging with Kid Rock and Hank III on "The 'F' Word"—but all that is part of his character, and it's much more acceptable now that he's reclaimed the other thing that's defined him—namely, a talent for raw, hardcore honky tonk that's genuine, so genuine that it gives the rockers passion and the ballads a real melancholy streak. This, according to the man himself, may have been inspired by the location of the recording—*The Almeria Club*, allegedly the site where a Hank Williams Sr. performance was interrupted by a gun-toting man looking for his cheating wife—and if that's so, he should continue to record there, because he hasn't sounded this committed, this alive, in years. Even when the album gets silly, which it does frequently, it's buttressed by a crackerjack band at the top of their game and a set of really good songs. More than that, Williams Jr. clearly has some emotional stake in the songs, whether it's his salute to dead friends "Cross on the Highway," the post-September 11, 2001 "America Will Survive," "Last Pork Chop," the second of two tributes to Kansas City Chiefs linebacker Derrick Thomas here, or "Tee Tot Song," dedicated to the man who taught Hank Williams Sr. how to play guitar. The end result is a stripped-down, fun, gutsy, and even moving album that offers a welcome musical reminder that Hank Williams, Jr. is indeed his father's son (something that he's never stopped reminding us verbally throughout the years).

Stephen Thomas Erlewine

Hank Williams III

Risin' Outlaw
September 1999, Curb

Hank Williams III's debut album *Risin' Outlaw* presents 13 tracks that show Williams' affection for authentic, rough around the edges country. From the catchy, driving album opener "I Don't Know" to his honky tonk vocals on "You're the Reason," Hank III blends his famous heritage with his own musical outlook. Ballads like "Lonesome for You" and up-tempo tracks like "If the Shoe Fits" show off Williams' ability to be purely country as well as original.

Heather Phares

Straight to Hell
March 2006, Bruc

Anyone hoping that Hank Williams III's "Hellbilly" metal band Assjack would finally make it onto one of his albums is still out of luck, but Hank III's third solo effort *Straight to Hell* comes close to getting their no-quarter spirit onto plastic, if not their sound. Taking the no-frills hard-country sound of 2002's *Lovesick, Broke & Driftin'* as a starting point, *Straight to Hell* pumps a good bit more darkness into the mix; mostly recorded at home on a digital portastudio, *Straight to Hell* begins with a sample of the Louvin Brothers' "Satan Is Real" interrupted by a burst of demonic laughter, which then segues into the title tune, a testimony to a life of cheap thrills and dangerous living that sounds like a classic string band rounding the corners at 90-miles-an-hour with empty bottles of bourbon propping open the windows. A similar mix of old-school country and chemically-fueled rebellion run through songs like "Pills I Took" and "Smoke and Wine," and even the less menacing tunes like "My Drinking Problem" and "Angel of Sin" boast too much swagger and grit to fit comfortably on the radio next to Toby Keith or Gretchen Wilson. While Hank III's self-mythologizing outlaw stance is not entirely unlike that of his father, there's a crazier and more sinister energy to *Straight to Hell* than Bocephus has ever conjured up on record, and numbers like "Country Heroes" and "D. Ray White" eloquently testify to his notion that bad craziness is a long and rich tradition along the margins of Nashville. (He also has a few things to say about Hank Jr. hanging out with Kid Rock on "Not Everybody Likes Us" to confirm he's most certainly not turning into his dad.) The album's most extreme departure point, however, is the bonus audio collage "Louisiana Stripes," which combines a handful of high-lonesome tunes with layers of ambient noise, bits of found dialogue, dub-wise echo and reverb effects, stray telephone messages, and sound effects ranging from thunderstorms to gurgling bong water. There's a pure and soulful musical vision at the heart of *Straight to Hell* no matter how much Hank III lashes out against the confines of current country music and messes with the form, and that's what makes him most valuable as an outlaw—there's lots of long-haired dope-smoking rednecks out there, but not many that can tap into the sweet and dirty heart of American music

the way Hank III does, and *Straight to Hell* proves he's got a whole lot to say on that particular subject.

Mark Deming

Kelly Willis

Well Travelled Love
1990, MCA

On her debut, this Austin country-rocker sings Texas-steel tunes and roisterous rockers with spirited assurance, but there's a natural tremble in her voice that makes her sound dangerous yet vulnerable. Willis is one of the few country singers with the disarming beauty to become a true sex symbol, and if she's the feminine response to all the hat acts, that's fine.

Brian Mansfield

Bang Bang
1991, MCA

Willis's idea of country comes from female rockabillys like Janis Martin and Wanda Jackson and from the blues-influenced Texas crowd she runs with in Austin. *Bang Bang* reflects that influence in the blistering tempos of "Too Much to Ask" and "Standing by the River," the Tex-Mex groove of "The Heart That Love Forgot," and an absolutely incendiary version of Joe Ely's "Settle for Love."

Brian Mansfield

Kelly Willis
1993, MCA

You just have to feel bad for Kelly Willis. Gorgeous and rambunctious, with a voice featuring both traits in equal measure, Willis spent the early '90s issuing well-appointed country-rock collections that went curiously, damnably unnoticed. 1993's eponymous effort was no different. Produced by Don Was, the album accessed the same smart sound that made Dwight Yoakam a star, but all it did for Willis was get her dropped from MCA. Fortunately, by decade's end, persistence, patience, and a streak of good old stubborn pride had helped land her a new deal with Ryko, and a good bit of the attention she'd always deserved. Willis presaged all of this with one of the slower burning tracks on the 1993 release. "There's so much to take for granted when life is going well," she sings on "I Know Better Now." "When the tides will turn no one can tell." The song's touches of mandolin and warm Hammond organ are typical of the album's sound, which is just as comfortable with the raggedy guitar and hoochie coo of "Take It All Out on You" as it is with the wistful, mature pop of "Get Real" (a song that helped write the sonic blueprint for the later crossover success of Faith Hill). Willis' vocal style is like granules of sand in a clear mountain stream, or a torn T-shirt in the back row of church—as pretty as it can be, her voice never quite loses the signature of her youthful turn as a barroom belter. In retrospect, it's nearly impossible to see how *Kelly Willis* wasn't a success. But she seemed to take it all in stride. Her sighing duet with Kevin Welch on his "That'll Be Me" applies well to the two singers' country outsider status. "You and I were gypsies born under the same sign," Welch croons over a dusty pedal steel guitar. But by the time Willis joins him on the title line, you've stopped feeling bad for Willis' run of fool's gold and started seeing a diamond in the rough.

Johnny Loftus

What I Deserve
February 1999, Rykodisc

This effort from country singer Kelly Willis has a number of important things going for it. First of all, there's her voice, which is an almost archetypally perfect blend of sweetness and grit. Then there are her backing musicians—in particular guitarist Mark Spencer, who makes a recognizably country sound without overdoing it or descending into bathos and stereotype. Last, and very importantly, there's producer Dave McNair, who has crafted a beautifully balanced and full-bodied sound for the album without allowing things to get too slick and prettified. What's lacking, for the most part, are melodies strong enough to grab your interest and hold it. There are some hooks—"Take Me Down" is quite singable, and there's a great version of Nick Drake's "Time Has Told Me"—but they're relatively few and far between, and scarcity of hooks can be death for a country album. In this case the lack is far from fatal, but it's noticeable. Recommended with reservations.

Rick Anderson

One More Time: The MCA Recordings
September 2000, MCA Nashville

MCA Nashville's *One More Time: The MCA Recordings* was released on the heels of the independent success Kelly Willis enjoyed in 1999 with *What I Deserve*. Though it may have appeared after a success, the compilation isn't really a cash in. It's really quite useful, as a matter of fact, since it summarizes her three MCA albums—1990's *Well Travelled Love*, 1991's *Bang Bang*, and 1993's *Kelly Willis*—while adding "Little Honey," her contribution to the *Thelma & Louise* soundtrack. For anyone looking to catch-up after *What I Deserve*, this is an excellent place to go (especially since two of her three MCA albums were out of print at the time of *One More Time*'s release), and it's a satisfying listen in its own right.

Stephen Thomas Erlewine

Easy
August 2002, Rykodisc

Austin, TX, sure has it good—a lot of amazing musicians are calling it home: Shawn Colvin, Patty Griffin, and the Dixie Chicks, to name a few. Add Kelly Willis to the list, because with *Easy* she has earned, or at least kept, her place in amazing-ville. Funny thing is, Willis is almost the perfect synthesis of the above-mentioned artists. She has a tender, romantic way in her songcrafting not at all unlike Colvin. Her voice has an rich, expressive ache, as does Griffin's. And she incorporates the best of country and bluegrass music into her own sonic foundry à la the Dixie Chicks (it certainly doesn't hurt much that she and Dixie Chick Emily Robison are sisters-in-law via the Robison brothers, Bruce and Charlie). With *Easy*, Willis offers up a half-dozen original compositions and a few very tasteful covers that are, well, easy— easy on the ear, easy on the heart, easy on the mind. She's one of those gals who can say she was country when country wasn't cool, if only

for her dignified and much-appreciated adherence to a real, organic, rooted sound that's as much Americana as anything else. This framework suits her well. The record would have been great without them, but it should also be noted that some very talented folks contributed a little something along the way. Alison Krauss, Chris Thile, Vince Gill, Dan Tyminski, and Ian McLagan all get a tip of the hat on this one, too.

Kelly McCartney

Translated from Love
June 2007, Rykodisc

Translated from Love is Kelly Willis' seventh album and her first (aside from a Christmas set in 2006) in five years. It was produced by Chuck Prophet with a small group of musicians that rotates a bit but is more or less a unit: Prophet, Greg Leisz, Marc Pisapia, John Ludwick, and Michael Ramos. Guests include Willis' husband Bruce Robison, the Tosca String Quartet, and Jules Shear (who wrote or co-wrote a couple of tunes here). Prophet, Willis and Shear take on the lion's share of writing credits here, often in combinations. Willis is the darling of alt country fans and NPR listeners, and each recording has received more platitudes than the one before. It will be interesting to see what they make of *Translated*. This is, in many ways, as slick as her MCA records, though it is punchier, rocks a little harder, and feels like it was geared for more open-minded country radio stations. The music is full of keyboards featured as prominently as guitars, tight arrangements, clipped harmonies, and bona fide rock riffs in places; what's more, the tracks accent the jumpier side of Willis' voice. Think Carlene Carter's 1980 album *Musical Shapes* (produced by Nick Lowe) (and yeah, it *is* a good thing).

Alt country, Americana or, as some are now calling it, "Ameripolitan" has become a ghetto of generic artists, sounds, and utterly forgettable songs that rely more on lyrical imagery than on their crafted melodies to get them across. Willis, who has played this game her way since leaving MCA in the '90s, knows what she's doing. Prophet's a perfect producer for getting what an artist wants out of a tune. "Nobody Wants to Go to the Moon Anymore" opens the set with its jaunty, popping 21st century rockabilly. It's got a shuffling, crisp blend of acoustic and electric guitars, and solid snare pop driving the thing. "Don't Know Why," with its Wurlitzer and B-3, carries a kind of '80s roots country feel: it's got a solid, hooky melody in a beautiful mid-tempo pop-love song written by Willis, Prophet and Shear. If there are any questions about the early rock & roll influence on this disc, go no further than "Teddy Boys," with its modified Chuck Berry lick. It's modified by Ramos playing a big fat Moog as part of the melody line. There are those young and middle-aged men (many of them critics who are projecting their own fantasies) who will write all these songs off as sell-outs, as "merely" recordings by female artists, unless their titles are drenched in a slavish vulnerability they perceive as "honesty." Willis offers a twist on these themes in "Losing You," with its banjo lines featured prominently, the tempo in the middle, and her expressive Virginia drawl drenched in strings and pedal steel.

"Too Much to Lose" puts Robison's vocals in the mix, and is also laden with strings. It's a slow, simple tune, but Willis sings with great authority. The longing in her voice and in her lyrics never sacrifices her dignity. The '60s rock harmonies that introduce "The More That I'm Around You" are offset by the cheesy synth lines. This is one of Shear's great pop songs and Willis does it justice, as does Leisz's Rickenbacker 12-string. The great cover of David Bowie's "Success" is simply a riot. It's all loose and ranging, driven by Ramos playing a Vox Continental organ and shouted backing vocals by the Gourds. There's a stolid country ballad in "Stone's Throw Away," a gorgeous song that plays more to Willis' recognizable past (so it may be big with the males mentioned above). The big fat rock & roll guitars in "I Must Be Lucky" accented by dobro and organ, make it one of the best cuts on the set, before the album's taken out by the minimally dressed acoustic title track with the sweet tinges of Shear's backing vocal and Ramos' accordion. In all, it's a winner, a solid, consistently crafted "new country" record that wears rock & roll proudly on its sleeve. And don't be surprised if the contemporary country stations or CMT and GAC pick up on it.

Thom Jurek

Trent Willmon

Trent Willmon
October 2004, Columbia

Trent Willmon's self-titled debut album is a fairly typical piece of Nashville product. Decked out in the *de rigueur* cowboy hat, the West Texas native sings in a matter-of-fact low tenor, indulging in perhaps one too many mannered groans more reminiscent of Britney Spears than Merle Haggard, but his voice is an efficient delivery device for the songs, which are played in what passes for standard country in the early 21st century, arrangements that feature more electric guitar and a heavier beat than traditional country, but mix in fiddle and pedal steel guitar to make the style unmistakable. In fact, one track, "All Day Long," even has echoes of Western swing. Co-writing eight of the 11 tracks in the company of 11 other writers, Willmon drenches his lyrics in alcohol and romantic regret, starting with the leadoff track, a statement of purpose if there is one, called "Beer Man." "Home Sweet Holiday Inn" is sung by a divorced father to the child with whom he has visitation rights spent in a motel. Other songs address a departed lover whose reasons for leaving are never explained; rather, the songwriters focus on gimmicks, such as the city-limits sign in "Population 81" (it used to say "Population 82," you see) and the flat West Texas plains that keep the ex-girlfriend's getaway car in sight "All Day Long." Of course, with all this romantic discord, liquor gets drunk throughout the album—six of 11 songs refer to alcohol. But Willmon's protagonist doesn't drink because he's unhappy in love; he just drinks. This is made clear in "Every Now and Then," in which a man whose romance is in order nevertheless goes out for a

few rounds occasionally with no better excuse than "I just do it every now and then to remind myself why I just do it every now and then." Alcoholics Anonymous wouldn't approve, of course, but country fans in honky tonks around the country will understand that sentiment perfectly.

William Ruhlmann

A Little More Livin'
June 2006, Columbia

All is not lost. You can still get a butane lighter for 99 cents and bait a hook while drinking Shiner. It's still cool to name your dog after a color, and completing a full work week is still a valid excuse to drown and smoke your mind on the weekend. So in spite of whatever may be wrong in your life—it's all good. Or at least that's what Trent Willmon would have you believe in "Good One Comin' On," the first track on his incredibly good-natured release *A Little More Livin'*. It wouldn't be a gamble to say Willmon's sophomore album will surely help him rise to an even brighter stardom. It's the ideal album for listening to when everything just, well, sucks. It's lighthearted, often humorous, and clever. Whether Willmon's getting ready for a night of binge drinkin' or losing his wife to his best friend after a night of sadomasochistic endeavors in "Surprise" (only to get his buddy's wife and high-rise apartment in return)—nothing's bad enough to make him give up. He's got all he needs—his guitar, his truck, his cooler full of ice, and so on. His songs are ideal for blue-collar weekend warriors. Willmon is a contemporary country artist, and *A Little More Livin'* is proof of this—the album has absolutely no rawness about it. It's produced to a tee. Which could be a good thing, depending on how you feel about that level of perfection. But while it might sound a little too over-produced to some country fans, Willmon's songwriting talents, as well as his musicianship, cannot go overlooked. The charm of *A Little More Livin'* isn't necessarily found in Willmon's voice, or the music (both of which are just fine, by the way), but rather in the album's attitude. It's non-pretentious and embraces life's simple pleasures: fishing, ropin' cattle, playing poker 'til dawn, and being broke as a joke but in love. The preeminent love song on the album is "So Am I," also certain to be one of the most popular singles. It's a sweet, sugary ballad, penned in part by Willmon himself (as were six of the album's 11 songs). With the fiddle in the forefront, Willmon sings, "But she loves the life we're livin'/Barefoot dancin' in the kitchen/While I'm pickin' with one string missin'/But she don't seem to mind." *A Little More Livin'* might not be a very diverse release, but with the screamin' electric blues solo on "Louisiana Rain," the humorous country-rock number "Surprise," and sentimental love ballads like "Island," it keeps the album from becoming too monotonous. Willmon is one of those success stories of a country boy who had a dream to make it in Nashville—and actually did, all without having to show up with a lot of money or sell his soul.

Megan Frye

Mark Wills

Permanently
January 2000, Polygram

With a reputation for music and songs that speak to people's hearts, Mark Wills' *Permanently* doesn't disappoint. With songs like "In My Arms" about being a dad to a brand-new baby daughter (a tribute to his little girl) and "Rich Man" about being rich in love, Wills' has a penchant for appealing to fans' sensitive sides. But whether he's singing about love, loss, fear, joy, or hope, Wills delivers a rock-solid third album with ease and confidence. No doubt that comes from working with producer Carson Chamberlain for the third time and singing about the things he knows best. Mixing things up just a bit, Wills recorded "Almost Doesn't Count," a song made popular by pop star Brandy, with his very own brand of soulful country.

Maria Konicki Dinoia

Greatest Hits
November 2002, Mercury

Mark Wills' *Greatest Hits* collects 11 of the earnest country crooner's biggest hits and best songs. He has been a fixture near the top of the country singles and album charts since the beginning of his career. The disc kicks off with two songs from Wills' 1997 self-titled debut record: "Jacob's Ladder," a number six country hit, and "Places I've Never Been," a number five hit. Four tunes from his 1998 hit album follow and are all chart smashes: the number one "Wish You Were Here," the number twos "I Do (Cherish You)" and "Don't Laugh at Me," and the number seven "She's in Love." 2000's *Permanently* was another huge success for Wills, spawning the hits singles "Back at One" and "Almost Doesn't Count." Around this time Wills' sound began to get a little more glossy and pop-oriented, though strangely his songs didn't do as well in the charts. "I'm Not Going to Do Anything Without You," his duet with Jamie O'Neal from 2001's *Loving Every Minute* album, only reached number 31. The two new songs Wills recorded for this hits collection, the sentimental rocker "Somethin'" and the ballad "When You Think of Me," are solid country-pop tunes that also failed to catch fire with country audiences. Still, fans of Wills need to pick up the disc to get these two songs, and fans of solid, earnest country who want to check Wills out will find this the best place to start.

Tim Sendra

And the Crowd Goes Wild
October 2003, Mercury

Putting forth an impressive effort to dispel the myth that he is "the sad guy," *And the Crowd Goes Wild* is a collection of enjoyable songs that let us know that maybe Wills does have something to smile about. The title track is a get-out-of-your-seat rocker that's bound to inspire; "He's a Cowboy" is a toe-tapper about fun-loving cowboys; "Married in Mexico" is a bouncy song about a proposal, to name a few. But lest we forget, there are several ballads on the album that remind us why we first fell in love with Wills' warm baritone wrapped around a sad story-song. "What Hurts the Most" is an ode to a failed relationship. "I Just Close My Eyes" is about the pain of a long-distance relationship. And deserving an honorable mention is "Prisoner of the Highway," a duet with one of Wills' heroes, Ronnie Milsap, on Milsap's 1984 hit.

Maria Konicki Dinoia

Gretchen Wilson

Here for the Party
May 2004, Epic

Taking its cues from her hit single "Redneck Woman," *Here for the Party*'s opening title track introduces Gretchen Wilson in no uncertain terms. "I'm here for the beer and the ball-bustin' band," she sings over its emphatic kick drum beat and barroom twang. "I may not be a ten, but the boys say I clean

up good." The vocalist's brassy delivery—not to mention her brazen honesty—differs considerably from the songbirds that often surround her on country radio in 2004. In fact, she's closer to the leather pants and poppy honky tonk of Tanya Tucker's 1978 effort *T.N.T.* Tucker is referenced in the aforementioned "Redneck Woman," as are Hank Williams, Jr. and Kid Rock, who also seem like primary sources for Wilson's mix of traditional country, pop accessibility, and uncut rock & roll attitude. Though she happily belts out the harder edges of "Homewrecker" and the hometown tribute "Pocahontas Proud," Wilson is also convincing on the ballad "When I Think About Cheatin'," and the softer tones of "What Happened." These tracks give *Party* some welcome depth, playing off its more rowdy material nicely and proving that Wilson isn't just a loudmouth novelty. Sure, that mud on her jeans in the back cover photo is real. But so is the sentiment in "Holdin' You," when she declares that "Holdin' you/Holds me together." Gretchen Wilson may be a redneck woman, but she has a heart of gold.

Johnny Loftus

All Jacked Up
September 2005, Epic

Gretchen Wilson uses the title of her second album as a euphemism for wasted. "Next thing you know, the bartender's pou-rin'/Shots a flow-in', got me stoned and. . . ."—the moral of the story is, don't pick fights or start trucks when you're "All Jacked Up." But the phrase is broadly applicable, too. "All jacked up" describes a malfunctioning engine as effectively as the roughshod look of an ill-advised one-night stand. Of course it's also a rallying cry for the blue-collar zeitgeist, like Larry the Cable Guy's "Git-R-Done" or the title of Wilson's breakthrough single, "Redneck Woman," and it's that constituency *All Jacked Up* sings to proudly. It's not its music that makes an impression—this record was rushed after the phenomenal success of her debut, *Here for the Party*, with writing and recording squeezed in between continued promotion and performance, and while Wilson's always refreshingly brash as a vocalist, the arrangements are only satisfactory. No, *All Jacked Up*'s lyrics, attitude, and message are its most important parts. In "California Girls" Wilson thumbs her nose at Hollywood excess and body image. "Ain't you glad there's still a few of us left?" she asks, "[Who] ain't afraid to eat fried chicken and dance to Merle?" Haggard himself guests on "Politically Uncorrect," a tribute to the soldiers, single mothers, third-shifters, and believers—any group you can think of that's been marginalized and/or politicized in the culture war. And in the terrifically unapologetic honky tonk "Skoal Ring," Wilson "don't want a bunch of bling-bling," because the "berry blend on his lips still turns me on." *All Jacked Up* just keeps building on the themes of *Here for the Party*, swaggering boldly and nodding to the legacy of George Jones along the way. Wilson is pushing back against the weird plastic and flashbulb "norms" of American popular media with mud on her hands and simple pleasures on her mind. In "One Bud Wiser" she finds solace from a bad break-up in a cold sip of beer, while "Not Bad for a Bartender" is the sequel to *Here for the Party*'s "Pocahontas Proud," with

Wilson reflecting on her rise to fame with an air of thanks, amazement, and "it could happen to you" homespun encouragement. We're all in this together, she's trying to say; so let's get some drinks and celebrate the New Redneck.

Johnny Loftus

One of the Boys
May 2007, Columbia Nashville

Gretchen Wilson set the country music charts on fire with her smash single "Redneck Woman" and her debut album, *Here for the Party* (2004). The track—though composed by colleague John Rich (of Big & Rich)—became an anthem for women all over America.

Written especially for Wilson, it is from-the-gut, working-class feminism for the post-feminist age, straightforwardly sung with a celebratory vengeance. As a slice-of-life singer who embodied and brought to life each cut on the album, she became an "overnight sensation." Her follow-up, *All Jacked Up* (2005), was recorded and rushed out by Sony a year later. Certainly the marketing department wanted to capture Wilsonmania, since her debut sold five-million copies. During the process, Wilson fought for the songs she wanted and got her way, and she co-produced with Rich and Mark Wright. Once more, she didn't write a single track on the set, but made her own song choices. The problem was (and remains true for virtually any artist) that following a debut phenomenon like *Here for the Party* is not only difficult, it's all but impossible. It went platinum, and concert tours sold out everywhere she played, but didn't hit the same mark despite being a better album song for song. Since 2005, Wilson has written a book—named for her first single—and absorbed the whirlwind of her life in the studio and as an internationally renowned celebrity. Rather than follow formulas, Wilson decided to do everything her way on *One of the Boys*, and that meant change. Once again producing with aid from Rich and Wright, Wilson shines this time out as a songwriter as well as a singer. She co-wrote nine of the album's 11 songs with Rich, longtime collaborator Vicky McGehee, and Rivers Rutherford. She says in the small note in the booklet that this is the most important recording she's ever made; it's her diary set to music. She's telling the truth. While there are excellent rockers on this set, there are also poignant ballads. *One of the Boys* (the title track is a great song with an intentionally misleading title) is a true country album. It has steel guitars, fiddles, and mandolins everywhere. It touches the heart of the tradition deeply from the opening cut, particularly in the ballads. Wilson is following her own muse, the one that comes from the lineage of Haggard, Parton, Lynn, and Strait as much as it does Hank Jr., Daniels, Skynyrd, and Kid Rock. The former side of her inspiration comes through loud and clear without sacrificing the persona her fans have come to know and love. This means one thing: that Wilson is the real deal: 100 percent authentic. She has become an artist without compromise, and it's obvious from the first note of "The Girl I Am," the set's opening cut. Fiddles and electric guitars announce her lyrics and it's in the final verse that she lays

it out bare: "Sometimes I know there's somethin' missing/ Sometimes I want to start again/Sometimes I scream and no one listens/Sometimes I feel like givin' in." There's confession and self-doubt here, but in the refrain she states: "And I never make apologies, 'cause I don't give a damn/I guess I'll always be the girl I am." The end result: she expresses the complexities of being human and claims radical self-acceptance. The artist who revealed herself early on is speaking from the other side, from her femininity and vulnerability, but there's great strength here, too, as the Don Rich-style guitars spit and roll, with a whining pedal steel, and the fiddle accents every line.

This track is followed by the gorgeous "Come to Bed" (the album's first single written by Rich and McGehee). Wilson owns it in her delivery. It's a ballad that lays out the truth in any genuine romantic relationship: that some disagreements, problems, and knock-down drag-out battles can only be equaled by the communication of physical intimacy, the kind expressed by the equality of the lovers' bed. It's quietly dynamic and poignant, yet it's only a small hint of the great treasures to be found here. The title track, a mid-tempo shuffle, reveals the truth in the misleading title. To an acoustic guitar and mandolin led by a popping electric six-string, the rowdy hell-raiser reveals: "But I still got this little girl inside of me/That likes to be treated like a queen/I know I don't act much like a lady/But I still need to be somebody's baby/You might find me makin' too much noise/But I'm more than just one of the boys." She claims her acumen in playing pool, drinking, and in general raising Cain, but reveals a true vulnerability in wanting to be known in total— as a woman who is made of paradoxes, as a complex being. Though its beat is solid 4/4, and it shuffles and choogles with drums rumbling to a pumping bassline, this is one of the most naked tracks on this set disguised by the music that contains it. Wilson's rockers follow in "You Don't Have to Go Home," about the desperation, party-killing bummer that is closing time at the local bar. It roils and coils; it's thunderous and hilarious, though true. The killer "There's a Pain in the Whiskey" is an unruly Lynyrd Skynyrd-esque blues-rocker that holds within it a burning truth. "There Goes the Neighborhood" is a modern-day rollicking honky tonk two-stepper, with the roots rocking fiddle and pedal steel-driven "Good Ole Boy" and the hysterically sarcastic "If You Want a Mother" vehicles for Wilson to lay out her strengths. She can write these beer-swillers with the best of them and they are not scored as crowd-pleasers, but as a genuine aspect of the songwriter's—and singer's—aesthetic and personal being. These are good-time tracks that offer the side of Wilson listeners know and love.

Yet it's in the haunting and utterly moving ballads that Wilson's bounteous gift is unwrapped in full. "Heaven Help Me" is a prayer sent in a place of solitude and the hope for deliverance. It's a confession and a plea: "I have wounded those who love me/And refused to take the blame/I have hidden all my demons/But I cannot hide my shame. . . ." Requesting faith, wisdom, and assistance, she pleads: "Heaven help me, because I can't help myself." This is the most nakedly confessional song ever recorded by Wilson. With its interweaving of acoustic instruments and pedal steel, it's a ballad for the ages. It's a prayer for anyone who desires to be set free by heaven from the bondage of self-sabotaging character defects. Likewise, "Pain Killer," a cut Haggard himself wishes he could have written, is a slow barroom weeper. Wilson sings of knowing of only one thing that will eliminate her loneliness and suffering: "I need a pain killer/Just one night of sin/Someone who will hold me tight/And get me over him/ And it'll taste bitter/But stranger set me free/I need a pain killer/ Before this pain kills me." Not simply a request for sex, it's a plea that rips the skin off the singer's body and gets to the sinew, blood, and bone of the truth, which is need and escape—if only for a moment—from a pain that isn't dissipating anytime soon. Her soulful voice is underscored by a high lonesome steel and snare-drum shuffle—this kind of vulnerability is so well hidden by everyday life, the revelation deepens the wound.

The album's final cut, "To Tell You the Truth," is simply devastating. Introduced by a shimmering acoustic guitar, it speaks from the well of secrets—the human heart, cracked, broken, and bleeding—as the protagonist is being torn apart by the lie she relives every day. The music is uncasy; it swells, thunders, whispers, and intones, struggling with itself as the singer struggles with the breaking of each morning. Guitars and drums collide in the refrains, as the bassline keeps it on the ground; each of the instruments, from keyboards to fiddle and mandolin, convict the singer as much has her words do: "It all comes up with the morning sun/It all comes down to the said and done/You know sometimes I pray for rain/I think somehow it hides my pain/To tell you the truth would set me free/I'm livin' a lie, and it's killing me/What I really wanna do/ Is just talk this thing through/But it'd hurt you/To tell you the truth." The band crashes into the final verse when the truth comes out: that she won't be able to do things any differently on this day, but who knows about tomorrow? The sheer craftsmanship in this song is a feat of inspiration. Everything in it tries so hard to hold a line as hard as the singer does. But there's a tempest inside them both and the music reveals that pressure. It ends the album with a series of questions that aren't answered. The double is the metaphor on *One of the Boys*: the private versus public persona; the sinner who wishes to repent and become, if not a saint, then at least someone she can live inside without shame; the woman who can drink, smoke, swear, and game like a man—though "the feminine" needs to be fed, caressed, nurtured, and recognized. Then, at the end there's the liar, the one who hurts desperately; she knows the truth and wants to tell it because it would set her free, but she doesn't for fear of damning the other to the pain she knows it would cause. *One of the Boys* isn't only the most diverse record from Wilson thus far, it's her most adventurous. It reveals so much, yet leaves the listener yearning to know more because it asks profound questions. Its songs are tight and wonderfully produced; these songs embrace the modern guise of the current country scene, even as the writing and singing put her squarely inside the music's grand tradition. She's offering the listener so much more of herself than she has before by admitting that she's still trying to find her way in truly dark times as well as joyous ones. This is a portrait of an artist who arrives here fully mature, with a clear vision and an uncompromising sense of direction. *One of the Boys* is the record Gretchen Wilson has been waiting to deliver since she came to Nashville, maybe since she dreamed of becoming a country singer and songwriter. We all benefit from her restlessness and her relentless pursuit of excellence. This is as good as it gets right now; it'll be the country album to beat in 2007.

Thom Jurek

Lee Ann Womack

Some Things I Know
September 1998, Decca

On Lee Ann Womack's self-titled debut album, she moved effortlessly from traditional country balladry to honky tonk to country-pop, but on this second effort, her varied styles have melded into a prosaic Nashville sound for the '90s. To be sure, Womack's voice, an achingly sweet instrument not unlike Dolly Parton's, is still one of the best in country music, but stylistically, there's little here to hold the listener's interest. "A Little Past Little Rock" is a prime example. Lyrically, the song is predictable: "I'm a little past Little Rock and a long way from over you." The strings from the Nashville String Machine and the "ooh"s and "ah"s in the background contribute to the blandness of the track, and even such studio stars as Brent Mason on electric guitar and Jelly Roll Johnson on harmonica only play tastefully and without inspiration. The album's hilarious highlight, "I'll Think of a Reason Later," sounds like anything else on the radio in the late '90s, but on this album it stands out from the too laid-back sound of the rest of the songs. It seems that producer Mark Wright has made an effort to soften Womack's sound to make it more palatable to country radio, but in the process he has removed the soul of her music. Hopefully, next time out they'll return to the style that brought her a CMA Female Vocalist of the Year nomination in 1998.

Brian Wahlert

I Hope You Dance
May 2000, MCA Nashville

After a platinum-selling self-titled debut and a gold follow-up with *Some Things I Know*, Lee Ann Womack just keeps getting better. *Billboard* calls it "a career record." *I Hope You Dance* is one of the finest albums to hit country music post Shania Twain. Womack possesses such a sweet, melodious voice and its distinctiveness graces every one of the 12 tracks like they were chosen just for her vocals. But it's the album's title track, a dedication to Womack's daughters (and featuring the Sons of the Desert) that will leave you feeling swept away. (Her daughters, Aubrie and Anna Lise, who were ages 9 and 1 [respectively] at the time, appear in the video with her.) "Don't let some hardened heart leave you bitter/When you come close to selling out, reconsider/Give the heavens above more than a passing glance/And when you get the choice to sit it out or dance, I hope you dance." Listeners will undoubtedly dance to *I Hope You Dance*.

Maria Konicki Dinoia

Something Worth Leaving Behind
August 2002, MCA Nashville

Lee Ann Womack scored her contemporary country music critical breakthrough with *I Hope You Dance* in 2000. Almost universally acclaimed, it showcased the singer's exceptionally wide range. While her platinum-selling self-titled debut made the critics take notice—as usual in this genre, only underscoring what country music programmers, DJs, and listeners already knew—and her sophomore issue, *Some Things I Know*, multiplied her fan base, *I Hope You Dance* was cited as a "career album," meaning that it wouldn't get much better. The pundits were wrong. *Something Worth*

Leaving Behind cemented Womack's place in the country music pantheon by pushing her own boundaries as an artist further than ever before. Her seemingly effortless cruise through honky tonk, country-pop ballads, and searing mid-tempo "message" numbers serves her well on this wildly adventurous collection of songs. Stepping into the producer's chair for the first time—along with longtime producers Mark Wright and Frank Liddell and newcomers Matt Serletic and Mike McCarthy—Womack fills the album with some off-center, nearly alt-country cuts by Bruce Robison (the gorgeous ballad "Blame It on Me") and a pair by the now reclusive Julie Miller (the poignant "Orphan Train" and rollicking funky gospel tune "I Need You"), who also sings backup on the set. Added to this are tracks by mainstream successes Monty Powell ("When You Gonna Run to Me"), Gretchen Peters (the stellar and anthemic "I Saw Your Light"), and Brett Beavers (two versions of the title track)—who accounted for the singles here. But it isn't just the mix of tunes. It's the performers themselves. Producer and guitar ace Kenny Greenberg handled the arrangements; former Joe Ely and John Mellencamp guitar slinger David Grissom is here and also contributed a tune; another former Mellencamp ace turned country session musician Kenny Aronoff mans the drum kit; and Greg Leisz, master of lap steel, pedal steel, and Dobro (or anything with strings called a guitar) is here as well—as are many others. Womack nailed it on *Something Worth Leaving Behind*. It may not have sold quite as well as her previous offerings, but record biz folks were happy just the same, and it achieved an even higher level of acclaim than any of her preceding records, eking out a place in the CD collections of fans of rock, pop, and even adult alternative music in the process. Finally, more than any of her previous recordings, *Something Worth Leaving Behind* gave her the confidence and authority necessary to record her masterpiece, 2005's *There's More Where That Came From*.

Thom Jurek

There's More Where That Came From
February 2005, MCA Nashville

Lee Ann Womack has always been more comfortable with country-pop than hardcore country, sounding relaxed and assured in smoother surroundings. That friendliness helped Womack become one of the most popular country singers of the late '90s, and it's what made her albums enjoyable even when they were a little bit too slick or relied on material that was just this side of generic. *There's More Where That Came From*, her fifth proper studio album and first after her 2004 *Greatest Hits* compilation, is still firmly within the country-pop confines, but there's a notable difference—as the rather brilliant cover art suggests, this hearkens back to the sound and style of early '70s country-pop albums from the likes of Barbara Mandrell, Loretta Lynn, and Dolly Parton. Not that this is a retro effort, or anything like a stab at neo-traditionalist country. Instead, Womack takes her inspiration from these records, crafting a record that's laid-back but never lazy, smooth but never too slick, tuneful without being cloying. While it's not far removed from her earlier albums, *There's*

More Where That Came From has a warmer feel, a textured, colorful production, and, best of all, a strong set of songs that may be highlighted by the cheater's anthem of the title track, but has 11 songs of equally high quality. All this adds up to an album that's not only the best album that Lee Ann Womack has yet made, but one that does suggest that there is indeed more where this came from.

Stephen Thomas Erlewine

The Wreckers

Stand Still, Look Pretty
May 2006, Maverick

Sometime between the release of her second album *Hotel Paper* in 2003 and the birth of her first child in 2005, Michelle Branch decided that she was tired of following the adult alternative career path that she'd been pursuing since her 2001 debut *Spirit Room*. She made no bones about her frustration, memorably posting on her website in late 2005 that she was "tired of sucking * * * * *" to get my music heard" in the course of an inspired rant in which she vented her frustration at the music biz and everything that surrounded it. It was a ballsy move, but it did accomplish its desired effect of loosening the log-jam that stalled her career, particularly her plans to release a duet album with her friend and collaborator Jessica Harp under the name the Wreckers. Branch received resistance from her label, not just because she wanted to trade in her solo career for life in a group, but because the Wreckers were a country duo, and the shift in sound was as risky as the decision to be part of a band. At least it must have seemed that way on paper, but in practice, the duo's debut *Stand Still, Look Pretty* doesn't seem like a radical departure from Branch's solo albums. Sure, there are fiddles, acoustic guitars, and twangy Telecasters instead of layers of synths, but the album is pitched halfway between Sheryl Crow and the Dixie Chicks, spiked with enough mainstream country-pop sheen to have it fit comfortably next to Miranda Lambert on the airwaves, but not enough to change the overall feeling that this record is a rootsy AAA record at its heart—not far from Crow and the Dixie Chicks. It's a subtle change from Branch's previous work, but it does pay off significant dividends in a number of ways. First off all, Branch sounds at ease as part of a duo, and this truly is an equal partnership; in fact, Harp bears more songwriting credits than Branch does here, including two cuts that are hers alone ("Tennessee" and "Cigarettes"). Second, the clean-but-natural production is better suited to Branch's strengths than the stilted glossy sound of *Hotel Paper*, letting her songs stand on their own merits. And if she sounded a little tentative and fuzzy on her sophomore solo effort, she sounds focused here, thanks in large part to working with Harp, who helps draw out the earnest likeability that made *Spirit Room* appealing. It also helps that the Wreckers, in true country fashion, also cut a few professionally written tunes, such as the glittering opening cut "Leave the Pieces," that help keep this cohesive and entertaining. Not that there isn't a stumble or two along the way—the anti-fame ruminations of the title track is too navel-gazing for country both in its topic and its moody dirge—but the great majority of *Stand Still, Look Pretty* is tuneful, tastefully rootsy, and quite engaging country-pop. Based on this enjoyable album, if Branch decides to ditch her solo career to devote herself full-time to the Wreckers, it'd be a smart decision.

Stephen Thomas Erlewine

Chely Wright

Let Me In
September 1997, MCA Nashville

For her third album, Chely Wright switched record labels and teamed up with producer Tony Brown, who helmed the boards for records by George Strait and Reba McEntire, among others. Brown stripped Wright's music down to the core—for much of *Let Me In*, she's singing over clean acoustic arrangements; only a few cuts are adorned with pop-rock instrumentation. Wright benefits from the spare arrangements, which only emphasize her lovely voice and charisma. The result is her most accomplished and arguably best album to date.

Thom Owens

Single White Female
May 1999, MCA Nashville

Chely Wright reunited with producer Tony Brown—the man behind hit records by George Strait and Reba McEntire, as well as Wright's own *Let Me In*—for her fourth album, *Single White Female*. The record picks up where its predecessor left off, offering a selection of ten songs with clean, tasteful arrangements that place Wright in the forefront. If the songs aren't always immediately grabbing, they're all classy, well-written tunes that slowly work their way into memory. Even when Wright and Brown shoot for the charts, such as on the big chorus of "The Love That We Lost," they pull it off, since Chely never oversings and the instrumentation is never bombastic. She still sounds her best on ballads, but her up-tempo numbers—including the clever title track and "The Fire"— are equally convincing, which is one of the main reasons that *Single White Female* is a welcome addition to an already impressive catalog.

Stephen Thomas Erlewine

The Metropolitan Hotel
February 2005, Dualtone

Chely Wright wasn't the only female country vocalist to straddle the line between neo-traditional country and slick modern country-pop, but she was one of the best of her kind, thanks in large part to her earthy tenor, which gave even the poppiest songs a rooting in real country. In 1999 she had a breakthrough with *Single White Female*, whose title track not only topped the country charts but cracked the pop Top 40, but she had a hard time capitalizing on its success, stumbling with its 2001 sequel, *Never Love You Enough*, which may have charted higher than its predecessor, but that was only due to momentum. It not only didn't produce a big hit, it led to a separation from her major label, MCA. When she re-emerged nearly four years later on the indie Dualtone, she was part of a wave of artists from the '90s who turned toward indies after being abandoned by the majors, a movement that resulted in a bunch of interesting records that found artists who played the Nashville game for the better part of ten years finding their true voice nearly a decade into their career. Sometimes the results were uneven, but they were always interesting and often were quite good, sometimes resulting in the riskiest and best work of an artist's career, as is the case with Wright's 2005 album, *The Metropolitan Hotel*. For the first time, Wright wrote or co-wrote the majority of the material—eight of the 12 songs bear a writing credit for her—and produced the entire record herself (five songs were co-produced with Jeff Huskins, one was co-produced with Stephony Smith). While she hasn't completely abandoned the sound of contemporary country-pop—many of the songs could comfortably slip onto the radio—the sound is stripped-back and direct, as is the emotion, which gives *The Metropolitan Hotel* an affecting immediacy. Not that all of it works—the cloying "The Bumper of My S.U.V." is well-intentioned but is one of the more awkward Iraqi war songs—but those missteps only enhance the feeling that this album is a personal work for Wright, and that she's willing to make mistakes along the way. Even if this is riskier than her previous albums, this album is still a hybrid of melodic, catchy contemporary country and the gutsy spirit of such '70s trailblazers as Loretta Lynn and Dolly Parton, and for every confessional like "Between a Mother and a Child" there are two or three engaging open-ended tales of love. And that's what makes *The Metropolitan Hotel* such a success—it's the sound of a professional musician finding the right blend of personal of universal in her writing and the right blend of country and pop in her production, resulting in a record that's fully realized and multi-dimensional, easily her best and most complete album to date.

Stephen Thomas Erlewine

Michelle Wright

Now & Then
1992, Arista

Wright made a mainstream move with *Now & Then*, downplaying the R&B and remaking herself as a sleek, sultry version of Lorrie Morgan. It paid off, too: she had her first real hits in the U.S. with "Take It Like a Man" and "He Would Be 16," a tear-jerking ballad dealing with the regrets of giving an illegitimate child up for adoption. Her Nudie jackets and black bodysuits made her a video favorite, too. The music's not as distinctive here as on *Michelle Wright*, but the hits hold up nicely.

Brian Mansfield

For Me It's You
August 1996, Arista

For Me It's You continues Michelle Wright's streak of winning albums. Featuring songs from writers as gifted as Rodney Crowell and Pam Tillis, the album has a rich selection of material that is alternately gritty and soulful and always powerful. Wright blesses each song with her powerful pipes, singing the songs with conviction—even when the songs border on lightweight country-pop, she sings them as if they were pure country. The result is a terrific little album, one that makes you wonder why Wright isn't a star in America like she is in her native Canada.

Thom Owens

Trisha Yearwood

Trisha Yearwood
1991, MCA

Hindsight being 20/20, when Trisha Yearwood's eponymous debut was issued in 1991, it was obvious a star had been born. From the choice of players, to Garth Fundis' snappy crisp production, to the songs written by the cream of the crop of Nashville's new generation—including a pair by Garth Brooks, Pat McLaughlin, Carl Jackson, and one by Kostas and Hal Ketchum. What set Yearwood apart is her enormous voice; coming from Georgia, there is no lilt in it—she can go from a whisper to a full-throated wail in a second, and her pitch is spot on every time. Fundis and MCA chose the kinds of songs Yearwood sings better than almost any of her peers—working-class love songs, from the opener, the simple mid-tempo rocker "She's in Love with the Boy," to the ballads such as "Like We Had a Broken Heart," written by Brooks with Pat Alger. Brooks sings backup here, and the pace of the song is slow. Its poetry is in the emotion her voice conveys rather than the lyrics, which aren't bad; they just aren't special. But it's "Fools Like Me" (by Kostas and Ketchum), where Yearwood lets every bit of what's inside of her out. A slow rocker with a Hammond B-3 swirling gently in the background played by Al Kooper, this is the broken love song at its best. When Yearwood sings, "You go your way baby, and I'll go mine/I'll go crazy like the wind," the entire track just comes apart before she reaches the end of the verse. The vision of a goodbye said in some motel parking lot or suburban driveway is almost unbearable. Yearwood was the first female country singer of her generation that didn't try to be a sex symbol, and she didn't try to project anything other than the fact that she was a good singer. And she was and is a fine singer, and this is a very classy debut that stands the test of time.

Thom Jurek

Hearts in Armor
September 1992, MCA

The leap Trisha Yearwood made as an artist between her debut in 1991 and *Hearts in Armor* in 1993 is remarkable. It remains one of her highest achievements. In addition, this one was wrought from conflict; it was released just after divorce and the record feels like an exorcism. As with her debut, producer Garth Fundis and Yearwood selected songs from the cream of Nashville's hit producers; "Wrong Side of Memphis," a tough, near spitting rocker tempered by honky tonk fiddles was written by Matraca Berg and Gary Harrison, opened the disc and may have thrown fans of her ballad style. But fears would have been unfounded as "Harrison's Nearest Distant Shore" was all ballad and then some. There's the R&B-flavored "You Say You Will," by Beth Neilsen Chapman, that's sassy and tough, full of funky piano and a killer acoustic guitar solo by Billy Walker Jr. and a killer backing vocal by Raul Malo (before anyone knew who the Mavericks were). Chapman also contributes a stunning ballad to this set, "Down on My Knees," that is wrenching in its pure intent. "Walkaway Joe" features a harmony vocal

by Don Henley and Dobro ace Jerry Douglass. Yearwood's telling the story she tells best, working-class love gone bad. But the finest moment on *Hearts in Armor* is Yearwood's cover of Emmylou Harris' "Woman Walk the Line," with Harris singing backup with Stuart Duncan on fiddle and Sam Bush on mandolin along with Yearwood's band; this is the ultimate testament about being woman cheated on who goes out to have a drink to hear some music and walk the line between marriage and dissolution. It's searing in its heartbreak and full of the tension that comes with the territory of loving someone who needs by his very nature to cheat. It's devastating, helped in part by Harris' unobtrusive but emotionally loaded backing vocal to Yearwood's open-throated wail. Henley also guests on the closer, which is the title track. If there is any speculation about whether Yearwood was airing her dirty laundry on the album, it becomes obvious in this song, that this is about her dealing with her own emotions, her own issues. Blame is useless in this ballad, there's nothing left but heartbreak and emptiness and the challenge of rebuilding a life haunted by the ghosts of another. *Hearts in Armor* is stunning; it's one of the best heartbreak records country music delivered in the '80s and '90s.

Thom Jurek

The Song Remembers When
1993, MCA

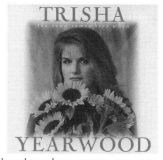

1995's *The Song Remembers When* is another chapter in the ongoing collaboration between Trisha Yearwood and producer Garth Fundis. Where 1993's *Hearts in Armor* was a cathartic masterpiece that broke Yearwood worldwide, this record is straighter down the contemporary country lane. As usual, the material is top-notch no matter where the pair get it from. Whether the tunes come from stalwarts like Kostas, Rodney Crowell, and Willie Nelson, or relative unknowns like the phenomenal Kimmie Rhodes, this ten-song set delivers the same drama and tension with glorious, transcendent singing from Yearwood. The title-cut opener is a reverie of innocent love gone bad, recalled at a retail store counter while receiving change. Mid-tempo ballads are a Yearwood strength, and she delivers tough and true. Next, "Better Your Heart Than Mine," written by almost-country-chanteuse Lisa Angelle and pop washout Andrew Gold, is a beautiful twining of Bonnie Raitt-styled R&B, roots rock, and neo-traditionalist country with some killer guitar playing by the great Steuart Smith. Rodney Crowell backs Yearwood on his "I Don't Fall in Love So Easy"; it's one of those beautiful country songs that almost isn't. Crowell has always been able to walk the pop-country borderline, and in Yearwood's voice he has found the perfect vocalist to execute his vision. She sings the hell out of a slick little downtempo rocker by making it sound like it's the easiest song in the world to deliver honestly. Nelson not only contributes a tune here, but he guests both in duet and backing vocalist capacities on his own "One in a Row" and Rhodes' "Hard Promises to Keep." His presence adds real depth and dimension here because his thin, reedy voice stands in such sharp contrast to Yearwood's full-throated one. "Here Comes Temptation" by

Kostas is one of those groovy little pop numbers that touches on the kind of '60s pop that came from Doc Pomus and Phil Spector crossed through the heart by a contemporary Nash Vegas feel; its glitzy surface covered by a sheen of sweet soul even if it is accompanied by a pedal steel. The disc closes with Matraca Berg's "Lying to the Moon." Accompanied only by her band, Yearwood takes a pop song and turns it into a country song with the ripped-up heart that comes in the grain of her voice. It's poetry, this combination of singer and song. She couldn't sing it any better if she'd written it; the accents create tension and drama and images from every betrayed-lover's movie from the '40s on, washing through the mix. Only a real singer can deliver the image from the heart of the song. Yearwood here is the heart of the song itself.

Thom Jurek

Thinkin' About You
1995, MCA

Although there are a couple of high points on *Thinkin' About You*, the record is weighed down with mediocre material and slick, commercially oriented production. Occasionally, Trisha Yearwood's vocals save the day, but there are times where she oversings the songs, giving them emotion they don't deserve. In all, it's one of the few Yearwood albums that can be called a disappointment.

Thom Owens

Everybody Knows
August 1996, MCA

Trisha Yearwood firmly enters middle-age with *Everybody Knows*, a collection of ballads and country-pop. Even when she kicks the tempo into high-gear, Yearwood and her band lay back, easing the beat along instead of pushing it. Similarly, the country-pop is engaging and relaxed, gently winning you over. But the heart of the album lies in her ballads, which are appropriately theatrical and grandiose—it's big music with big melodies. The quality of the songs are a little uneven, but Yearwood continues to improve as a singer, which means she brings conviction even to the lackluster material on *Everybody Knows*.

Thom Owens

Where Your Road Leads
July 1998, MCA Nashville

Trisha Yearwood is a pop diva who knows how to play her instrument: her voice. Perhaps one of the most gifted contemporary pop vocalists, Yearwood continues to explore the vast expanses of her talent. Displaying only traces of her early work as a country music artist, she sings with yearning on songs like "Powerful Thing." Buddy Miller's backing vocals on "Bring Me All Your Lovin'" are a highlight of this project. Yearwood's brilliance is adequately displayed on "I Don't Want to Be the One" and "I'll Still Love You More" (the latter a Diane Warren composition). She is at her best when she inhabits the world of emotional ballads and snappy, up-tempo tunes about the emotional life of modern women. While she is no country singer by any stretch of the imagination, she is still an important element in pop music.

Jana Pendragon

Real Live Woman
March 2000, MCA Nashville

Once an artist like Trisha Yearwood enters her second decade of recording, it's easy to take her for granted. Why? Well,

consistency doesn't make for quite as dramatic a story as dramatic swings between brilliance and failure. That may be unfair, but that's the way it is. Yearwood has never swung between such extremes. She has released some exceptional albums, plus a couple of sub-par efforts, but for the most part, she has remained an artist that is reliable—you pay your money, and you know you'll get something satisfactory. *Real Live Woman* is one of those records; it may not rock your world, but it will hardly disappoint. A little more mature and straight-ahead than even her latter-day efforts, *Real Live Woman* is a measured, deliberate record in the best possible sense. The tempo never gets too heated, but the songs never drift into laziness, either. The tunes are always melodic and always well-chosen. They don't just play to Yearwood's strengths, but they're solid songs in their own right, whether it's a new Matraca Berg and Al Anderson song ("I'm Still Alive"), an overlooked Springsteen tune ("Sad Eyes") or a Linda Ronstadt chestnut ("Try Me Again"). Yes, there are a couple of moments where the momentum drags ever so slightly, but as soon as they occur, the album perks back up with the next song. *Real Live Woman* isn't significantly better or worse than the average Trisha Yearwood album, but that's not a bad thing, since few people do this mainstream country—meaning, by late '90s/early 2000s standards, country music that still sounds country but is also melodic enough for pop—quite as well as this.

Stephen Thomas Erlewine

Inside Out
June 2001, MCA Nashville

Trisha Yearwood's full of a whole lotta love. Five of the album's 12 tracks have "love" in the title, and the seven others that don't are about love and relationships. But whatever Yearwood's singing about, she still manages to dazzle listeners even ten years and ten albums into her career. She's an artist who blossoms with every album and just keeps getting better. She's even managed to arrange a superior list of musical collaborators, including Don Henley (back for more after "Walkaway Joe") on the rhythmic title track; Roseanne Cash harmonizing on the classic song she originally composed, "Seven Year Ache"; and even Vince Gill lending his vocal talents to the blazing "I Don't Paint Myself Into Corners." With praiseworthy songs too numerous to mention, *Inside Out* is bound to inspire fans and fellow artists alike. Simply put, Trisha Yearwood is timeless.

Maria Konicki Dinoia

Jasper County
September 2005, MCA Nashville

Trisha Yearwood took an unprecedented four years between her eighth album, 2001's *Inside Out*, and its 2005 follow-up, *Jasper County*. There was a variety of reasons for the extended hiatus—it was one part creative, one part personal, as Yearwood weathered the storm of going public with her relationship with Garth Brooks (as of the release of *Jasper County*, the couple was engaged to be married)—but the long wait proved worthwhile since *Jasper County* is one of her very best records, an album that stretches further musically than most of her albums while being more cohesive than most of her records as well. Reuniting with longtime producer Garth Fundis, with whom she's done most of her best work (he did not helm *Inside Out*), Yearwood's picked a set of 11 songs that aren't just uniformly strong, but are quite diverse. While there's a strong bluesy undercurrent here, highlighted by the slow-churning opener "Who Invented the Wheel" and the Bobbie Gentry-styled Southern country-soul of "Sweet Love," this is firmly a country album, with few concessions to pop crossover. The tracks that do have a lush, slick surface do tend to be the big ballads, such as "Standing out in a Crowd," but those do tend to be grounded with acoustic guitars and Yearwood's impassioned delivery. Plus, even those sweeping slow tunes are offset by such excellent ballads as the heartbroken "Trying to Love You" and the epic "Georgia Rain," which are pure country and lend the overall album a sweet, reflective quality. Even if the album does tend toward relaxed, meditative tunes, *Jasper County* works because instead of maintaining that introspective vibe throughout the album, Yearwood and Fundis bring in not just those bluesy, soulful songs for balance, but they find two rip-roaring Al Anderson songs—the white-hot "Pistol" and the old-fashioned honky tonk anthem "It's Alright"—to give this more country grit than has been heard on any Yearwood album in a long time. At a mere 38 minutes, the album moves along briskly, not just because of the short running time, but because the album is paced well, moving gracefully between ballads, blues like "River of You," and rollicking up-tempo tunes. The end result is an album that's not just one of Yearwood's most entertaining albums, but one of her richest records, in both musical and emotional terms as well.

Stephen Thomas Erlewine

Dwight Yoakam

Guitars, Cadillacs, Etc., Etc.
1986, Reprise

Dwight Yoakam's *Guitars, Cadillacs, Etc., Etc.* began as an EP issued on the California Oak label. When Reprise signed him, they added four more tracks to the mix to round it out as an album. Yoakam, a Kentuckian, brought country music back into its own medium by reviving the classic Bakersfield sound with the help of his producer and lead guitarist, former Detroiter Pete Anderson. As a result, the "new traditionalist" movement was born, but Yoakam was always a cut or three above the rest, as this album displays in spades. *Guitars, Cadillacs, Etc., Etc.* kicks off with a smoking cover of Johnny Horton's "Honky Tonk Man," a song now so closely associated with Yoakam, the original has all but been forgotten. But this is only the beginning. Yoakam's own songs such as "Bury Me," a duet with Maria McKee, and "South of Cincinnati" reference both the pastoral and dark sides of his native state.

"South of Cincinnati" is a paean to those who left Kentucky for Ohio in search of jobs, and "Bury Me" celebrates the land itself. In addition, the title track, with Anderson's Don Rich-influenced guitar style, walks the Buck Owens line until the line extends to Yoakam. With fiddles and backing vocals, Yoakam's street poetry is both poignant and profound, built into a barroom anthem. In addition to this there is the gorgeous "Miner's Prayer," an acoustic number powered by dobro (courtesy of David Mansfield), flat-picked guitar, and Yoakam's singing of his grandfather and generations like him who lived and died in the mines of Kentucky. Here Bill Monroe meets Ralph Stanley meets Bob Dylan. In the grain of Yoakam's voice there isn't one hint of irony, only empathy and raw emotion. Yoakam also does a more than acceptable version of June Carter's "Ring of Fire," the "Cherokee" of country music—meaning that if you can play it and pull it off, you're taken seriously by the veterans. The album closes with the Harlan Howard classic "Heartaches by the Number." Because of Ed Black's steel playing, Brantley Kearns' fiddle, and Anderson's guitar, the accompaniment is stronger and far edgier than the Ray Price version, but from Yoakam's throat comes an entirely different story than Price's. In Price's case the song was a plea; in Yoakam's it's a statement of fact. An astonishing debut, *Guitars, Cadillacs, Etc., Etc.* changed the face of country music single-handedly and remains one hell of a party record.

Thom Jurek

Hillbilly Deluxe
1987, Reprise

Hillbilly Deluxe proves beyond the shadow of a doubt that Dwight Yoakam's *Guitars, Cadillacs, Etc., Etc.* was no fluke. There's no sophomore slump here, and while *Hillbilly Deluxe* may be seen as an extension of his debut, repetition 'taint necessarily a bad thing. In fact, it can be heard and viewed as Yokam and producer/guitarist Pete Anderson cementing the commitment to Bakersfield-styled honky tonk music. Yoakam's voice is a dead cross of Merle Haggard's early voice and Lefty Frizzell's—a fine cover of the latter's "Always Late (With Your Kisses)" is included here—and as such, it is one of the purest, most soulful voices in the music of this era. But as displayed on his debut, Yoakam is one hell of a songwriter as well. Cuts like "Little Ways," the album's first single, "Readin' Writin'," "Rt. 23," and the amazing "Throughout All Time," with its dancing fiddles and lap steel guitars entwined with Anderson's lead, are worthy of serious consideration as among the finest country songs written in the preceding five years. An added bonus is a killer version of Doc Pomus's classic "Little Sister" that rivals Elvis Presley's—yeah, that's right—and blows Ry Cooder's tepid cover of it away. The only other cover here is the classic "Smoke Along the Track" by Alan Rose and Dan Helms, and in true hardcore troubadour fashion, Yoakam makes it his own, swinging it in the best Johnny Cash and Tennessee Three fashion rhythmically and with Haggard's winsome railroad vocal that he took from Jimmie Rodgers. While there can be no doubt about Yoakam's "hillbilly" roots in Kentucky, this disc is deluxe in virtually every way.

Thom Jurek

Buenas Noches from a Lonely Room
1988, Reprise

The third effort from Kentucky's Dwight Yoakam shows the first signs of beginning to stretch out and be comfortable with his unique approach to hard honky tonk music,

Bakersfield-style. *Buenos Noches From a Lonely Room* features a number of variations on the themes Yoakam explores in his songs—mainly heartache. Not since Leon Payne has anyone gone from love that is so obsessive it cares not a whit for the most basic of life's needs ("I Got You"), to a murderous jealousy ("What I Don't Know"), to homicide ("Buenos Noches From a Lonely Room [She Wore Red Dresses]") in the first five songs. In addition, Yoakam and producer/guitarist Pete Anderson are exploring the colorations of other instruments in their mix such as the addition of the legendary Flaco Jimenez's accordion on the title track. The transition tracks between these three facets of human meltdown are the stunning melody in "One More Name" and a radical cover of Johnny Cash's "Home of the Blues." In addition, there's a read of J.D. Miller's "I Hear You Knockin" as an alternate ending, though it's still plenty dark. After the murder in the title track, the cycle is complete, and the album shifts gears radically. It kicks off with a balladic elegy to a worn-out drunk called "I Sang Dixie," full of lilting fiddle and subtle singing leads from Anderson. It's a tearjerker in classic country fashion, its tone almost reverential. Track two is a duet with Yoakam's hero, Buck Owens, who came out of retirement—briefly—to record this song and a new album. There's only one song the pair could sing together, the anthem of lost but proud down-and-out ramblers, and that's Homer Joy's "Streets of Bakersfield." The other cover here is Hank Locklin's beautiful love song "Send Me the Pillow" with a return by Maria McKee on backing vocals (she sang a duet on "Bury Me" with Yoakam on *Guitars, Cadillacs, Etc., Etc.*). The pair are as natural together as Gram Parsons and Emmylou Harris were, though far more traditional in their approach. As chapter three in the Dwight Yoakam restoration of honky tonk music project, this is the best yet.

Thom Jurek

Just Lookin' for a Hit
1989, Reprise

Released in 1989 just three years after his debut, *Just Lookin' for a Hit* may have been a bit premature for a greatest-hits album, but it did the trick and sold better than any album Dwight Yoakam had thus far issued. This set is chock-full of the definitive Dwight—at the time—from the opener, a hard rocking version of the Dave Alvin & the Blasters' "Long White Cadillac," to his self-penned honky tonk soul jam "Little Ways," before moving into hardcore barroom twang with Johnny Horton's "Honky Tonk Man" and the rockabilly country kicker "I Got You." Just how closely Yoakam walked the line between hard country and soulful rockabilly is nowhere more evident than it is on his cover of Doc Pomus' "Little Sister." Thankfully his theme "Guitars, Cadillacs" is here as is his duet with k.d. lang on Gram Parsons' "Sin City." Add "I Sang Dixie," "Please, Please Baby," and his duet with Buck Owens on "Steets of Bakersfield." When one considers that these are merely highlights—and some of them arguable choices—from his first three records, the true value of Yoakam as a recording artist who single-handedly revitalized traditional country music becomes evident. This is a smoking hits collection but is only a taste of the treasures that lie within the individual albums themselves.

Thom Jurek

If There Was a Way
1990, Reprise

If There Was a Way from 1990 is the first full display of Dwight Yoakam's doppelgänger on record. From the mid-

tempo honky tonk of "The Distance Between You and Me" and the classic Bakersfield balladry of "The Heart That You Own" to the balls-out live 21st century rockabilly "It Takes a Lot to Rock You Baby," Yoakam shows his fragmented musical personality that somehow remains inside the framework of his own brand of country. Fans of the old heroes such as Ernest Tubb, Merle Haggard, George Jones, Buck Owens, Hank Thompson, Loretta Lynn, and so on dig Yoakam because he knows how to write and sing a good old country song. The kids and pop audiences love him because he seems to speak to them as much with his swagger as his electricity—guitarist Pete Anderson is like Don Rich, only from the rock side of the country music fence. "Nothing's Changed Here," written by Yoakam and master songwriter Kostas, is a nod to Tubb in that it refers to the master's "Walkin' the Floor Over You" in "Nothing's Changed Here," a barroom stroller with a gorgeous fiddle solo by Don Reed and a splendid use of reverb by Anderson. "Since I Started Drinkin' Again" is a bluegrass sh*tkicker, but it is one hell of a self-destructive broken-heart song that features some awesome fiddlework by Scott Joss and mandolin and backing vocals by Tim O'Brien. The bluesy, doo-woppy, Doc Pomus-inspired rock balladry of the title track is another move toward the margins for Yoakam—especially with the shimmering B-3 work by Skip Edwards. "It Only Hurts Me When I Cry," Yoakam's co-write with Roger Miller, who sings backing vocals on the track, is another rocker à la early Conway Twitty. Ultimately the duet with Patty Loveless on Kostas and Kathy Louvin's "Send a Message to My Heart" is a wrought and deeply moving love song. Loveless is the best of her generation. Not even Martina McBride with all her emotion and range can match the soul in the grain of her voice, nor does anyone possess as pure a country voice with the exception of Emmylou Harris perhaps. The bravest moment on the record is also its most fun. The closer is a truly hillbilly deluxe version of Wilbert Harrison's anthem "Let's Work Together." Anderson tears this mother up, raw and wooly, and Yoakam proves himself as fine a R&B singer as he is a country crooner. Here again the rock side of country, the soul side of rock, and the country side of soul are all wrapped here in Yokam's voice backed by a band who have a complete understanding of the tune. Highly recommended.

Thom Jurek

This Time
1993, Reprise

Six years after his monumental debut recording, *Guitars, Cadillacs, Etc., Etc.*, Dwight Yoakam is still delivering the goods. After inadvertently (and unwillingly) being credited with creating the new traditionalist movement, Yoakam takes his hard-edged country influences from Buck Owens, Johnny Horton, Ray Price, and Merle Haggard and expands them to include new instruments and textures as well as voices—one can hear in these broken love songs the voice of Gene Pitney as well—and come up with something new again. *This Time* is not a party record in the way his first pair of albums were.

Take the first half of *Buenos Noches From a Lonely Room* and add a marvelously played Hammond B-3 courtesy of Skip Edwards and keep the downer flow going and you got it. Buck Owens' spirit appears on "This Time," a song that, while deep in the Bakerfield groove, has a more elegiac tone thanks to Yoakam's songwriting collaboration with country songsmith legend Kostas (who first worked with Yoakam on *If There Was a Way*); they wrote half the album together. Kostas' lush approach to melody is not alien to Yoakam's as demonstrated by the tunes Dwight penned himself—"Pocket of a Clown" (with a doo wop backing chorus in swing harmony) and the devastating ballads "A Thousand Miles From Nowhere" and "Home for Sale," among others. But in Kostas Yoakam found a writer as interested in textures as in unique ways to use his voice. "Two Doors Down" is a stunning example, as is the lone cover on the disc, by Kostas and James House, "Ain't That Lonely Yet," where Yoakam moves into Roy Orbison territory with strings and lush backdrops that meld Bakerfield with Pitney's conceptual mini-soundtracks and the arrangements on Jim Reeves' best records. With production help from Dusty Wakeman (Lucinda Williams' self-titled and *Sweet Old World* albums), Pete Anderson was able to add depth and dimension to an already full sound. The echoes of early rock and soul entwine the honky tonk tempos and instruments and become something wholly other. This album is a welcome addition to Yoakam's formidable catalog. *This Time* is no sell out; it's a new way to present the timelessness of hard, torn, wasted-love country love songs with less reckless sentimentality and more honest emotion.

Thom Jurek

Gone
November 1995, Reprise

1995's *Gone* is a startling moment in Dwight Yoakam's career. It's been a decade since the California Oaks six-track EP version of *Guitars, Cadillacs, Etc., Etc.* had been released (before Warner picked it up, added four cuts, and issued it as an album in 1986). It's been a helluva run thus far, and *Gone* marks it as a milestone. Given that record companies don't nurture artists over their first two or three albums anymore, Yoakam has managed ten years on the charts and a decade's worth of fine albums—with a couple of masterpieces among them. *Gone* fully integrates the early '60s grooving rock and R&B of Doc Pomus and Lieber and Stoller with the hard honky tonk of the Bakersfield sound with regional touches that have become so prevalent on his records (example: note the opening track here, "Sorry You Asked?," with its mariachi horns in the refrains and bridge). Yes, and sometimes they all occur in the same song such as on the title track here where the Farfisa sound of Tex-Mex, Doug Sahm-style rock meets Chuck Berry's guitar riffing meets Buck Owens country, and all of it is Yoakam. Then there's "Gone" with its Hammond B-3 and string section that could be an early rock anthem from the New York street corners if it weren't for Yoakam's restless Kentucky voice crooning in the swinging Texas wind. Even the straight rock & roll of "Never Hold You," with its psychedelic guitar fills before its "C.C. Rider"—à la Mitch Ryder not Charlie Rich—refrain turns on a country-rock dime. Pete Anderson is a guitar slinger maximus who may have been schooled in the Buckaroos' Don Rich's style, but he plays with the razor-sharp intensity of the Detroit rocker he is. While it's true that those who long for Yoakam's pure honky tonk style may be lost a bit here, with a few spins they'll get it. Yoakam's music has been a thrill to witness as it has developed. *Gone* is the work of a singular talent with input from many different sources, from instrumentalists and horn and string sections to a dozen backing vocalists all used on different tracks. As the album closes with "Heart of

Stone," a co-write with Kostas, you hear Yoakam go back to where modern country music came from in the first place: In the cascading strings that fall over the face of the mix, the band slide in behind them and the ghosts of Jim Reeves and Patsy Cline enter the singer and intone the kind heartbreak that can only be voiced in a country song. Chalk up another winner for Yoakam.

Thom Jurek

Under the Covers
July 1997, Reprise

Given how easily Dwight Yoakam makes the songs of others his own, including classics like "Sin City" and "Streets of Bakersfield" as well as the Doc Pomus nugget "Little Sister," it's a wonder it took him 11 years to record an album of covers. Yoakam had nothing left to prove as a songwriter, penning hit after hit and album after album of constantly evolving country music that remained true to the honky tonk tradition while stretching it sonically—without revisionism. Here, Yoakam interprets everyone from Roy Orbison to the Clash to the Beatles to Danny O'Keefe, often radically reworking these genuine enduring classics of popular music to bring out the hidden meanings rather than remake them in his own image, the near bluegrass version of "Train in Vain" being a prime example. The Orbison tune that opens the album, "Claudette," rocks with a country swagger the original never had and feels like more of a celebratory tone to a third party than it does a love song. The Kinks tune "Tired of Waiting for You" is as far from a country song as can be with a full horn section—and this cut works the least—and is an oddity but entertaining when heard once. O'Keefe's "Good Time Charlie's Got the Blues" is less melodic than the writer's version, but it is far more desolate and haunting. The duet on Sonny Bono's "Baby Don't Go" with Sheryl Crow doesn't really work either, because Crow is not a country singer and there's enough countrypolitan in Yoakam's read that the two singers seem cold and at odds with each other. The lush, funky version of Jimmy Webb's "Wichita Lineman" may not replace Glen Campbell's, but it is a credible, even fine read with all of its textural embellishments (Pete Anderson, Yoakam's guitarist and producer is a genius), a B-3, layers of guitars, double-timed drums . . . awesome. "Here Comes the Night," with its ringing electric 12-string guitars and faux Caribbean rhythm is stunningly beautiful, and the Beatles' "Things We Said Today" is a psychedelic country jewel. While this set is not perfect, it's still damn fine and warrants repeated listens to come to grips with Yoakam's visionary ambition.

Thom Jurek

Last Chance for a Thousand Years: Greatest Hits from the 90's
May 1999, Reprise

During the '90s, Dwight Yoakam settled into a weird role. No longer a representative of the cutting edge, the way he was in the '80s, he was nevertheless far too restless and young to become an elder statesman. Instead, he followed his own path, which resulted in a series of albums that were (arguably) every bit

as rewarding as his '80s efforts. And, like his '80s recordings, his '90s albums stood as cohesive, individual entities that nevertheless boasted several great singles apiece. Which is a roundabout way of saying that Yoakam was as much a singles artist as he was an album artist, and that's why his second compilation, *Last Chance for a Thousand Years: Greatest Hits from the '90s*, is every bit as entertaining and revelatory as *Just Lookin' for a Hit*. It is true that the hits didn't arrive as fast and furious in the latter half of the '90s as they did in the first, but the quality of the singles didn't dip at all, as this terrific disc proves. All of the 11 singles—including "Turn It On, Turn It Up, Turn Me Loose," "It Only Hurts When I Cry," "A Thousand Miles from Nowhere," "Ain't That Lonely Yet," "Fast As You," "Sorry You Asked"—sound like modern classics, and the two previously unreleased cuts ("Thinking About Leaving," "I'll Go Back to Her"), plus his cover of Queen's stab at rockabilly, "Crazy Little Thing Called Love," nearly match that standard. And if it is true that country artists can be judged by their singles comps, as some have alleged over the years, then *Last Chance for a Thousand Miles* proves that Yoakam is one of the greats of the '80s and '90s.

Stephen Thomas Erlewine

Tomorrow's Sounds Today
October 2000, Reprise

The title has to be a goof because this album, as well as Dwight Yoakam's entire catalog, should be dubbed "Yesterday's Sounds Today." The only connection Yoakam retains to the slick, cross-over, big hat crowd is the big hat, and these 14 tracks prove that even as country music continually evolves into glossy pop, this artist has entrenched himself in all things retro. The crying steel guitars, jaunty mandolins, and plaintive fiddles that drive this rootsy country & western could have been recorded in the 1950s, and only the tasty electric guitar licks of longtime producer/cohort Pete Anderson bring the music up to date. Further cementing his connection with the classic Bakersfield sound, Yoakam invites founding father Buck Owens to join the fold once more (their 1988 collaboration produced a number one C&W hit with "The Streets of Bakersfield") and the resulting three tracks yield results just as winning. Yoakam goes the Hank Williams Sr. route on "A Promise You Can't Keep" and especially "The Heartaches Are Free," which sounds so similar to a Hank Sr. tune in melody and vocal inflection, you'll find yourself double checking the liner notes to be sure it's a Yoakam original. The singer dips into his '70s classic rock roots again too, as he follows up his wildly successful Queen remake with a cover of Cheap Trick's "I Want You to Want Me." Like his interpretation of "Crazy Little Thing Called Love," he makes it sound like an obscure barnstorming country track instead of the power pop nugget it is. Ten of the album's 14 tunes are self-penned and song titles like "A World of Blue," "A Place to Cry," "The Sad Side of Town," and "Time Spent Missing You" show that Yoakam is still drenched in the spilt tears, heartbroken brand of country that has proven to be so lucrative, artistically and commercially, in the past. Best of all, he makes it seems easy. Even though there's little stylistic maturation in his approach since his first release in 1986, Yoakam's songwriting craft keeps improving, and any track from this album could be a hit single. With *Tomorrow's Sounds Today*, Dwight Yoakam has fashioned a contemporary roots-conscious country album whose qualities, like the artist's distinctive style, are timeless.

Hal Horowit

Population Me
June 2003, Audium

Dwight Yoakam returns on a new label with his first album proper in three years—the soundtrack to his directorial film debut, *South of Heaven, West of Hell* is just that, not an album of songs. And while one might wonder if *Population Me* is more of the same brand of Bakersfield-styled honky tonk blues from Yoakam and be right, there are two arguments as to why it's a necessary purchase. First and foremost, the quality of Yoakam's material is the most consistent in country music since the outlaws of the mid-'70s. Arguably, Yoakam has never released a shoddy album, and this one is no exception. Most importantly are the surprises, of which there are plenty. On the opener, "The Late Great Golden State," written by Mike Stinson, Yoakam does his best Jackson Browne-Eagles—and actually reveals why the L.A. drugstore cowboy sound is timeless when done right. Eagles bassist Timothy B. Schmidt lends a hand on the backing vocals and gives it a solid "take it easy" rollicking roll. Elsewhere, as on the title track driven by guitar ace Pete Anderson and pedal steel, banjo, and dobro king Gary Morse, Yoakam weaves a perfect blend of driving rockabilly, Chuck Berry, and honky tonk. On a banjo-drenched cover of Burt Bacharach's "Trains and Boats and Planes," Yoakam sings his skinny butt off, while Anderson rides the mandolin down into the lost wail of Scott Joss' fiddle. They transform the pop song into a traditional country shuffle graced with the high lonesome sound of Earl Scruggs' electrifying banjo work, punching the fills and turnarounds with grease and grit. "If Teardrops Were Diamonds" is one of Yoakam's most beautiful ballads. Willie Nelson performs a duet with him, adding a gorgeous pop sensibility to Yoakam's hillbilly moan. Through the rest, Yoakam's songwriting continues to grow and transform itself into an accurate reflection of American culture as felt through the poetic heart of a country musician. The songs are right there: lean, tough, raw, and drenched with hooks as well as emotions—check out the honky tonk stroll of "I'd Avoid Me Too." This is stellar, kickin' impure country.

Thom Jurek

Dwight's Used Records
June 2004, Koch

Few if any major country artists of the 1980s and '90s had as consistent a run of strong recordings as Dwight Yoakam, and this compilation proves that even the material he gave away was better than what most of his peers were sending out as top-shelf product. *Dwight's Used Records* features cuts Yoakam contributed to several tribute compilations, duets that appeared on other artists' albums, and a few unreleased covers, and while the results aren't quite as cohesive as a proper album, nearly everything here would have fit the bill on a "real" Dwight Yoakam album. His duets with Deana Carter and Heather Myles show what a generous vocal partner he can be, while his turns with Ralph Stanley and the Nitty Gritty Dirt Band add some new layers of depth to his traditionalist approach. Yoakam's covers of "I'm Bad,

I'm Nationwide" and "Mercury Blues" are sly and witty but never descend into self-parody, and he sure does right by Johnny Cash and Webb Pierce as he tackles their songs. The album's only real flaw would be the two back-to-back versions of John Prine's "Paradise"; both performances are worthwhile, but over ten minutes of the song gets to be a bit much. Baring that, *Dwight's Used Records* is a thoroughly enjoyable collection of odds and ends that congeals into some solid listening—but how come his superb version of Merle Haggard's "Holding Things Together" from the *Tulare Dust* album didn't make the cut?

Mark Deming

Blame the Vain
June 2005, New West

When Dwight Yoakam burst onto the charts with his first album in 1986, he was the young honky tonk firebrand who set out to remind Nashville of its noble past and celebrate the accomplishments of Bakersfield heroes such as Buck Owens and Merle Haggard. The irony is that nearly 20 years later, Yoakam is in pretty much the same boat as the artists he championed in the 1980s—he's a respected veteran of the country scene who still has a loyal audience but lost the interest of the major labels and isn't drawing the attention he used to get. But if any of this troubles him, you'd never guess to listen to 2005's *Blame the Vain*, which is his sharpest and liveliest set in some time. With Yoakam producing himself for a change without the help of longtime studio partner Pete Anderson, *Blame the Vain* also finds him fronting a new band anchored by guitarist Keith Gattis, and the new blood seems to have done wonders for Yoakam—while he wasn't exactly in a slump, *Blame the Vain* boasts a sharper and more energetic approach than his last several efforts, with "Just Passin' Time," "Three Good Reasons," and the title cut revealing that Yoakam is still a honky tonk man supreme. Elsewhere, the whacked-out intro to "She'll Remember" and the ad-libbed final rant on "Intentional Heartache" show Yoakam's firmly in touch with his inner goofball weirdo, the songwriting is both literate and down-home in the manner of his best work, and he sings up a storm from front to back. Two decades into his career, Dwight Yoakam is still the man who is too country for Nashville, and on *Blame the Vain* he shows he's got too much strength and soul to let anyone hold him down—this is inspired stuff from a rebel who still has plenty to offer.

Mark Deming

Chris Young

Chris Young
October 2006, RCA

Here it is: the debut album by the winner of 2005's *Nashville Star* competition. His prize was a contract with RCA Nashville. Given the music biz hype surrounding the show, it's no secret that his first single "Drinkin' Me Lonely," was a hit and garnered lots of interest at radio. But there's another reason for that, too: it's a great tune—and it was self-penned. But that's really just the beginning. Chris Young has one of those classic country voices that is memorable after one hears it the first time, like Keith Whitley, George Strait, Clint Black, and Ronnie Milsap. The record opens with "Beer or Gasoline," a loud country rocker, and slips effortlessly into "You're Gonna Love Me," a straightforward up-tempo country love song. By the time "Drinkin' Me Lonely'" comes up on the player, the album is in full swing. It's a song Merle Haggard would have been proud to write. Other notable cuts here include the rollicking wildness of "Lay It on Me," and the slippery love song "Center of My World." There are plenty of bad boy rockers to accompany the ballads, which makes for an auspicious debut. The only complaint is Buddy Cannon's production. It's so huge and compressed it makes the album sound generic even if the songs aren't—fiddles sound more like synths, the guitars all sound like they were recorded the late '70s, and the drums all have so much reverb on them, they sound more like programmed beats than an actual drumkit. The production will date this record instead of making it sound timeless like the great country albums that Young seems to adore given his classic writing style. Still, it's a first record, and Young is the real thing. It's no fluke he won the competition, and from the sound of this set, he's in it for the long haul.

Thom Jurek

PLAYLISTS

Drinking Songs

Toby Keith: "I Love This Bar"
Alan Jackson: "It's Five O'Clock Somewhere"
Dwight Yoakam: "This Drinkin' Will Kill Me"
Travis Tritt: "If I Were a Drinker"
Garth Brooks: "Friends in Low Places"
Alan Jackson: "I Don't Need the Booze (to Get a Buzz On)"
Clint Black: "Killin' Time"
John Anderson: "Brown Liquor"
Dwight Yoakam: "Since I Started Drinkin' Again"
Martina McBride: "Two More Bottles of Wine"
Garth Brooks: "Longneck Bottle"
Alan Jackson: "Designated Drinker"
Brad Paisley: "Alcohol"
Trick Pony: "Pour Me"
Tracy Byrd: "Drinkin' Bone"
Kenny Chesney: "Being Drunk's a lot like Loving You"
Big & Rich: "Drinkin' About You"
Montgomery Gentry: "I Got Drunk"
Blake Shelton: "I Drink"
Toby Keith: "Get Drunk and Be Somebody"

Beer Run

Garth Brooks: "Beer Run"
Kenny Chesney: "Beer in Mexico"
Trent Wilmon: "Beer Man"
Brooks & Dunn: "Beer Thirty"
Phil Vassar: "Six-Pack Summer"
Aaron Tippin: "Many, Many, Many Beers Ago"
John Michael Montgomery: "Beer and Bones"
Toby Keith: "Beer for My Horses"
Kevin Fowler: "Beer, Bait and Ammo"
Chris Young: "Beer or Gasoline"

Whiskey Rivers and Lullabies

Travis Tritt: "Whiskey Ain't Workin"
Brooks & Dunn: "Whiskey Under the Bridge"
Chris Cagle: "Who Needs the Whiskey"
Patty Loveless: "Cheap Whiskey"
Pat Green: "Whiskey"
Trick Pony: "Whiskey River"
Trick Pony: "Ain't Wastin' Good Whiskey on You"
Jon Randall: "Whiskey Lullaby"
Terri Clark: "I Wish He'd Been Drinkin' Whiskey"
Toby Keith: "Whiskey Girl"
Martina McBride: "Cheap Whiskey"
Dierks Bentley: "Whiskey Tears"
Brad Paisley: "Whiskey Lullaby"

Tequila and Margarita Time

John Anderson: "Straight Tequila Time"
Alan Jackson: "Margaritaville"
Tim McGraw: "Senorita Margarita"
Tracy Byrd: "Ten Rounds with Jose Cuervo"
Lonestar: "Tequila Talkin'"
Terri Clark: "Not Enough Tequila"
Kenny Chesney: "Tequila Loves Me"
Big & Rich: "20 Margaritas"
Garth Brooks: "Two Pina Coladas"

Party Songs

Gretchen Wilson: "Here for the Party"
Big & Rich: "Comin' to Your City"
Hank Williams, Jr.: "All My Rowdy Friends Are Comin' Over Tonight"
Brooks & Dunn: "Boot Scootin' Boogie"
Alan Jackson: "Chattahoochee"
Billy Ray Cyrus: "Achy Breaky Heart"
Joe Diffie: "Third Rock from the Sun"
Garth Brooks: "Ain't Going Down ('Til the Sun Comes Up)"
Travis Tritt: "Ten Feet Tall and Bulletproof"
Shania Twain: "That Don't Impress Me Much"
Dwight Yoakam: "Fast as You"
Dixie Chicks: "Sin Wagon"
Toby Keith: "How Do You Like Me Now?"
Tracy Byrd: "How'd I Wind Up in Jamaica"
Kenny Chesney: "When the Sun Goes Down"
Sammy Kershaw: "National Working Woman's Holiday"
Miranda Lambert: "Kerosene"
Tracy Byrd: "The Truth About Men"
LeAnn Rimes: "Big Deal"

Love Songs

Shania Twain: "Nobody Needs to Know"
Shania Twain: "Forever and Always"
Martina McBride: "When You Love Me"
Alabama: "Closer You Get"
Toby Keith: "Huckleberry"
Kenny Rogers: "Islands in the Stream"
Trisha Yearwood: "She's in Love with the Boy"
Mary Chapin Carpenter: "Passionate Kisses"
Tim McGraw: "You Turn Me On"
Faith Hill: "This Kiss"
Faith Hill: "Just to Hear You Say You Love Me"
Sammy Kershaw: "She Don't Know She's Beautiful"
Faith Hill: "Breathe"
Faith Hill: "The Way You Love Me"
Vince Gill: "Let's Make Sure We Kiss Goodbye"
Sara Evans: "Every Little Kiss"
Shania Twain: "You're Still the One"
John Michael Montgomery: "I Don't Want to Miss a Thing"

Novelty Tunes
Joe Nichols: "Tequila Makes Her Clothes Fall Off"
Big & Rich: "Save a Horse, Ride a Cowboy"
Cowboy Troy: "I Play Chicken with the Train"
George Strait: "Hollywood Squares"
Brad Paisley: "Ticks"
Trace Adkins: "Honky Tonk Badonkadonk"
Travis Tritt: "Here's a Quarter (Call Someone Who Cares)"

Heartache Songs
Roseanne Cash: "Seven Year Ache"
George Strait: "You Sure Got This Old Redneck Feelin' Blue"
Reba McEntire: "Whoever's in New England"
Randy Travis: "Diggin' Up Bones"
Keith Whitley: "I Wonder Do You Think of Me"
Kathy Mattea: "Lonesome Standard Time"
Lyle Lovett: "She's Already Made Up Her Mind"
Martina McBride: "Independence Day"
Toby Keith: "We Were in Love"
LeAnn Rimes: "Blue"
Dixie Chicks: "You Were Mine"
Chely Wright: "Just Another Heartache"
Brooks & Dunn & Reba McEntire: "If You See Him, If You See Her"
Dwight Yoakam: "Thousand Miles from Nowhere"
Lee Ann Womack: "I Hope You Dance"

Covers of Country Classics
George Strait: "Right or Wrong" (originally by Bob Wills)
Dwight Yoakam: "Honky Tonk Man" (originally by Johnny Horton)
k.d. lang: "Three Cigarettes in an Ashtray" (originally by Patsy Cline)
Lyle Lovett: "Stand by Your Man" (originally by Tammy Wynette)
Rodney Crowell: "Above and Beyond (the Call of Love)" (originally by Buck Owens)
Travis Tritt: "T-R-O-U-B-L-E" (originally by Elvis Presley)
Mark Chesnutt: "Who Will the Next Fool Be?" (originally by Charlie Rich)
Dwight Yoakam: "Always Late with Your Kisses" (originally by Lefty Frizzell)
k.d. lang: "Don't Let the Stars Get in Your Eyes" (originally by Skeets McDonald)
BR5-49: "Honky Tonk Song" (originally by Webb Pierce)
Ricky Van Shelton: "From a Jack to a King" (originally by Ned Miller)
Collin Raye: "Big River" (originally by Johnny Cash)
Alan Jackson: "Little Bitty" (originally by Tom T. Hall)
Martina McBride: "Swingin' Doors" (originally by Merle Haggard)

BR5-49: "Crazy Arms" (originally by Jerry Lee Lewis)
Tracy Byrd: "(Don't Take Her) She's All I Got" (originally by Johnny Paycheck)
Sawyer Brown: "Six Days on the Road" (originally by Dave Dudley)
George Strait: "If You Ain't Lovin', You Ain't Livin'" (originally by Faron Young)
Brooks & Dunn: "Husbands and Wives" (originally by Roger Miller)
Sara Evans: "I've Got a Tiger by the Tail" (originally by Buck Owens)
Alan Jackson: "Pop a Top" (originally by Jim Ed Brown)
LeAnn Rimes: "Crazy" (originally by Patsy Cline)
Suzy Bogguss: "In the Jailhouse Now" (originally by Webb Pierce)
Dwight Yoakam: "Streets of Bakersfield" (originally by Buck Owens)
Daryle Singletary: "I Never Go Around Mirrors" (originally by Lefty Frizzell)
Mark Chesnutt: "Honky Tonk Heroes" (originally by Waylon Jennings)
Martina McBride: "Pick Me Up on Your Way Down" (originally by Charlie Walker)
Alan Jackson: "Tall, Tall Trees" (originally by George Jones)
George Strait: "Deep Water" (originally by Bob Wills)

Texas Tunes
Keith Whitley: "Talk to Me About Texas"
George Strait: "All My Ex's Live in Texas"
Lyle Lovett: "That's Right (You're Not from Texas)"
Nanci Griffith: "Lone Star State of Mind"
Little Texas: "God Blessed Texas"
Dale Watson: "That's What I Like About Texas"
Tracy Lawrence: "Stars Over Texas"
Foster & Lloyd: "Texas in 1880"
Lyle Lovett: "Long Tall Texan"
Mark Chesnutt: "Blame It on Texas"
Brooks & Dunn: "Texas and Norma Jean"
David Ball: "Texas Echo"
Blake Shelton: "Austin"
Pat Green: "Texas on My Mind"
Phil Vassar: "Houston"
Trace Adkins: "There's a Girl in Texas"
Trick Pony: "Stand in the Middle of Texas"
George Strait: "Somewhere Down in Texas"
Clint Black: "I'll Take Texas"

Songs About Memphis
Rodney Crowell: "Rose of Memphis"
Lyle Lovett: "I've Been to Memphis"
Tim McGraw: "Don't Mention Memphis"
Trisha Yearwood: "Wrong Side of Memphis"
Lonestar: "Walkin' in Memphis"

Cowboys

Toby Keith: "Should've Been a Cowboy"
Marty Brown: "Cherokee Boogie"
Trace Adkins: "All Hat, No Cattle"
Tim McGraw: "Cowboy in Me"
Randy Travis: "Cowboy Boogie"
Dale Watson: "Cowboy Lloyd Cross"
Brooks & Dunn: "Good Cowboy"

Songs About Mexico

David Ball: "She Always Talked About Mexico"
Garth Brooks: "Rodeo or Mexico"
Tim McGraw: "That's Why God Made Mexico"
Toby Keith: "Good to Go to Mexico"
Chalee Tennison: "Me and Mexico"
Mark Willis: "Married in Mexico"
George Strait: "Seashores of Old Mexico"
Montgomery Gentry: "All I Know About Mexico"
Clint Black: "Gulf of Mexico"
Kenny Chesney: "Beer in Mexico"
Reba McEntire: "Till it Snows in Mexico"
Brooks & Dunn: "Mexican Minutes"
Texas Tornados: "Adios Mexico"

Neon Blues

George Strait: "Beyond the Blue Neon"
Terri Clark: "Neon Flame"
Brooks & Dunn: "Neon Moon"
Mavericks: "Neon Blues"
Sammy Kershaw: "Neon Leon"
George Strait: "Neon Row"
Alan Jackson: "Chasin' That Neon Rainbow"

Rocking the Jukebox

Mark Chesnutt: "Brother Jukebox"
Alan Jackson: "Don't Rock the Jukebox"
Travis Tritt: "If Hell Had a Jukebox"
Mark Chesnutt: "Bubba Shot the Jukebox"
Joe Diffie: "Prop Me Up Beside the Jukebox (If I Die)"
Doug Stone: "Jukebox with a Country Song"
Mark Chesnutt: "Numbers on the Jukebox"

Honky Tonk Heaven

Tracy Lawrence: "I Hope Heaven Has a Honky Tonk"
Marty Brown: "Honky Tonk Special"
Randy Travis: "Honky Tonk Side of Town"
Joe Diffie: "Honky Tonk Attitude"
Doug Supernaw: "Honky Tonkin' Fool"

Garth Brooks: "American Honky-Tonk Bar Association"
Dale Watson: "Honkiest Tonkiest Beer Joint"
BR 549: "Honky Tonk Song"
Mark Chesnutt: "Hello Honky Tonk"
Brooks & Dunn: "Little Miss Honky Tonk"
Kenny Chesney: "From Hillbilly Heaven to Honky Tonk Hell"
Marty Brown: "No Honky Tonkin' Tonight"
Randy Travis: "Honky Tonk Moon"
George Strait: "Honkytonkville"
Marty Stuart: "Honky Tonk Crowd"
Brooks & Dunn: "You Can't Take the Honky Tonk Out of the Girl"
Travis Tritt: "Honky Tonk History"
Alan Jackson: "Burnin' the Honky Tonks Down"
Mark Chesnutt: "Somebody Save the Honky Tonks"
Toby Keith: "Honky Tonk U"
Trent Tomlinson: "Cheatin' on My Honky Tonk"

Hillbillies, Rednecks, and Working Men

Kenny Chesney: "From Hillbilly Heaven to Honky Tonk Hell"
Marty Stuart: "Hillbilly Rock"
Montgomery Gentry: "Hillbilly Shoes"
Alan Jackson: "It's Alright to Be a Redneck"
Marty Brown: "I'd Rather Fish Than Fight"
Confederate Railroad: "White Trash with Money"
Blake Shelton: "Asphalt Cowboy"
Sammy Kershaw: "Beer, Bait and Ammo"
Andy Griggs: "Hillbilly Band"
Trick Pony: "Hillbilly Rich"
Montgomery Gentry: "Hillbilly Shoes"
Brooks & Dunn: "Hillbilly Deluxe"
Gretchen Wilson: "Skoal Ring"
Billy Currington: "I Wanna Be a Hillbilly"
Travis Tritt: "Blue Collar Man"
George Strait: 'You Sure Got This Old Redneck Feelin' Blue"
Alabama: "Mountain Music"
Travis Tritt: "Lord Have Mercy on the Working Man"
Gretchen Wilson: "Redneck Woman"
Aaron Tippin: "Working Man's PhD"
Sammy Kershaw: "Queen of My Double Wide Trailer Park"
Judds: "John Deere Tractor"
Kenny Chesney: "She Thinks My Tractor's Sexy"
Joe Diffie: "John Deere Green"
Dierks Bentley: "Cab of My Truck"

YEAR BY YEAR

1989

k.d. lang: *Absolute Torch and Twang*
Alan Jackson: *Here in the Real World*
Vince Gill: *When I Call Your Name*
Keith Whitley: *I Wonder Do You Think of Me*
Lyle Lovett: *Lyle Lovett and His Large Band*
Lorrie Morgan: *Leave the Light On*
Kentucky Headhunters: *Pickin' on Nashville*
Faster & Lloyd: *Faster and Llouder*
Clint Black: *Killin' Time*
Marty Stuart: *Hillbilly Rock*
George Strait: *Beyond the Blue Neon*
Garth Brooks: *Garth Brooks*

1990

KT Oslin: *Love in a Small Town*
Mary Chapin Carpenter: *Shooting Straight in the Dark*
Dwight Yoakam: *If There Was a Way*
Mark Collie: *Hardin County Line*
Rosanne Cash: *Interiors*
Mark Chesnutt: *Too Cold at Home*
Garth Brooks: *No Fences*
Texas Tornados: *Texas Tornados*

1991

Vince Gill: *Pocket Full of Gold*
Trisha Yearwood: *Trisha Yearwood*
Kelly Willis: *Bang Bang*
Travis Tritt: *It's All About to Change*
Randy Travis: *High Lonesome*
Aaron Tippin: *You've Got to Stand for Something*
Reba McEntire: *For My Broken Heart*
Hal Ketchum: *Past the Point of Rescue*
Brooks & Dunn: *Brand New Man*
Marty Brown: *High and Dry*
Suzy Bogguss: *Aces*
Marty Stuart: *Tempted*
Garth Brooks: *Ropin' the Wind*

1992

Wynonna Judd: *Wynonna*
Alan Jackson: *A Lot About Livin' (And a Little 'bout Love)*
Mary Chapin Carpenter: *Come On Come On*
Sawyer Brown: *Cafe on the Corner*
Kathy Mattea: *Lonesome Standard Time*
Billy Ray Cyrus: *Some Gave All*
Mark Chesnutt: *Longnecks and Short Stories*
Clint Black: *Hard Way*
John Anderson: *Seminole Wind*
Marty Stuart: *This One's Gonna Hurt You*

Joe Diffie: *Regular Joe*
Lyle Lovett: *Joshua Judges Ruth*
Rodney Crowell: *Life Is Messy*
Marty Stuart: *Let There Be Country*
Vince Gill: *I Still Believe in You*
Trisha Yearwood: *Hearts in Armor*
Garth Brooks: *The Chase*

1993

Garth Brooks: *In Pieces*
Nanci Griffith: *Other Voices, Other Rooms*
Dwight Yoakam: *This Time*
Willie Nelson: *Across the Borderline*
Sammy Kershaw: *Haunted Heart*
Junior Brown: *12 Shades of Brown*
Toby Keith: *Toby Keith*
Martina McBride: *The Way That I Am*
Kelly Willis: *Kelly Willis*
George Strait: *Easy Come, Easy Go*
Clay Walker: *Clay Walker*
Kathy Mattea: *Good News*
Mark Collie: *Mark Collie*
Carlene Carter: *Little Love Letters*
Marty Brown: *Wild Kentucky Skies*
Rosanne Cash: *The Wheel*
Patty Loveless: *Only What I Feel*
Doug Supernaw: *Red and Rio Grande*
Wynonna Judd: *Tell Me Why*
Kathy Mattea: *Walking Away a Winner*

1994

Alan Jackson: *Who I Am*
Tracy Byrd: *No Ordinary Man*
Vince Gill: *When Love Finds You*
Mavericks: *What a Crying Shame*
Joe Diffie: *Third Rock from the Sun*
Travis Tritt: *Ten Feet Tall and Bulletproof*
Colin Raye: *Extremes*
Brooks & Dunn: *Waitin' on Sundown*
David Ball: *Thinkin' Problem*
Faith Hill: *Take Me as I Am*
Mary Chapin Carpenter: *Stones in the Road*
Little Texas: *Kick a Little*
Patty Loveless: *When Fallen Angels Fly*
Hal Ketchum: *Every Little Word*
Marty Brown: *Cryin', Lovin', Leavin'*
Johnny Cash: *American Recordings*
Tim McGraw: *Not a Moment Too Soon*
Pam Tillis: *Sweetheart's Dance*
Reba McEntire: *Read My Mind*
Lari White: *Wishes*
Lyle Lovett: *I Love Everybody*

1995

Shania Twain: *The Woman in Me*
Deana Carter: *Did I Shave My Legs for This?*
Alison Krauss: *Now That I've Found You: A Collection*
Ty England: *Ty England*
Terri Clark: *Terri Clark*
Faith Hill: *It Matters to Me*
Confederate Railroad: *When and Where*
Trisha Yearwood: *Thinkin' About You*
Colin Raye: *I Think About You*
Kenny Chesney: *All I Need to Know*
Blackhawk: *Strong Enough*
Tim McGraw: *All I Want*
Mrtina McBride: *Wild Angels*
Mavericks: *Music for All Occasions*
Dwight Yoakam: *Gone*
Vince Gill: *Souvenirs*
Garth Brooks: *Fresh Horses*
Joe Diffie: *Life's So Funny*

1996

LeAnn Rimes: *Blue*
Mandy Barnett: *Mandy Barnett*
Dale Watson: *Blessed or Damned*
Wynonna Judd: *Revelations*
Kenny Chesney: *Me and You*
Tracy Lawrence: *Time Marches On*
Mindy McCready: *Ten Thousand Angels*
JoDee Messina: *JoDee Messina*
George Strait: *Blue Clear Sky*
Lyle Lovett: *The Road to Ensenada*
Trace Adkins: *Dreamin' Out Loud*
Marty Stuart: *Honky Tonkin's What I Do Best*
Randy Travis: *Full Circle*
Ty Herndon: *Living in a Moment*
Travis Tritt: *Restless Kind*
BR5-49: *BR5-49*
Ty England: *Two Ways to Fall*
Tracy Byrd: *Big Love*
Alan Jackson: *Everything I love*
Terri Clark: *Just the Same*
Johnny Cash: *Unchained*

1997

Shania Twain: *Come on Over*
Garth Brooks: *Sevens*
Alison Krauss: *So Long So Wrong*
Tracy Lawrence: *Coast Is Clear*
Nanci Griffith: *Blue Roses from the Moon*
Liittle Texas: *Little Texas*
Tim McGraw: *Everywhere*
Anita Cochran: *Back to You*
Toby Keith: *Dream Walkin'*
Sara Evans: *Three Chords and the Truth*
Kenny Chesney: *I Will Stand*
Martina McBride: *Evolution*
Chely Wright: *Let Me In*
Mark Chesnutt: *Thank God for Believers*

Matraca Berg: *Sunday Morning to Saturday*
Patty Loveless: *Long Stretch of Lonesome*
Mindy McCready: *If I Don't Stay the Night*

1998

Dixie Chicks: *Wide Open Spaces*
Alan Jackson: *High Mileage*
Mavericks: *Trampoline*
Sara Evans: *No Place That Far*
JoDee Messina: *I'm Alright*
Faith Hill: *Faith*
George Strait: *One Step at a Time*
Tracy Byrd: *I'm from the Country*
Terri Clark: *How I Feel*
Trisha Yearwood: *Where Your Road Leads*
Lari White: *Stepping Stone*
Vince Gill: *Key*
Brady Seals: *Brady Seals*
Lorrie Morgan: *Secret Love*
Deana Carter: *Everything's Gonna Be Alright*
Tractors: *Farmers in a Changing World*

1999

Tim McGraw: *Place in the Sun*
Dixie Chicks: *Fly*
Brad Paisley: *Who Needs Pictures*
Toby Keith: *How Do You Like Me Now?!*
Faith Hill: *Breathe*
Chely Wright: *Single White Female*
Alan Jackson: *Under the Influence*
Mark Chesnutt: *I Don't Want to Miss a Thing*
Kelly Willis: *What I Deserve*
Sara Evans: *Girls Night Out*
Montgomery Gentry: *Tattoos and Scars*
Mandy Barnett: *I've Got a Right to Cry*
Mindy McCready: *I'm Not so Tough*
Martina McBride: *Emotion*
Brooks & Dunn: *Tight Rope*
John Berry: *Wildest Dreams*
Shedaisy: *Whole Shebang*
Keith Urban: *Keith Urban*
Trace Adkins: *More*
Tracy Byrd: *It's About Time*
Reba McEntire: *So Good Together*

2000

Sara Evans: *Born to Fly*
Alan Jackson: *When Somebody Loves You*
Wynnona Judd: *New Day Dawning*
Lee Ann Womack: *I Hope You Dance*
Vince Gill: *Let's Make Sure We Kiss Goodbye*
Phil Vassar: *Phil Vassar*
Trisha Yearwood: *Real Live Woman*
Rascal Flatts: *Rascal Flatts*
Jo Dee Messina: *Burn*
Patty Loveless: *Strong Arm*
Terri Clark: *Fearless*
Chalee Tennison: *This Woman's Heart*
Mark Willis: *Permanently*
Chris Cagle: *Play It Loud*

2001

Tim McGraw: *Set This Circus Down*
Brad Paisley: *Part Two*
Blake Shelton: *Blake Shelton*
Toby Keith: *Pull My Chain*
Garth Brooks: *Scarecrow*
Gretchen Peters: *Gretchen Peters*
Rodney Crowell: *Houston Kid*
Trick Pony: *Trick Pony*
Brooks & Dunn: *Streets and Stripes*
Mary Chapin Carpenter: *Time Sex Love*
Trisha Yearwood: *Inside Out*
David Ball: *Amigo*
Tracy Byrd: *Ten Rounds*

2002

Alan Jackson: *Drive*
Kenny Chesney: *No Shoes, No Shirt, No Problems*
Andy Griggs: *Freedom*
Shania Twain: *Up!*
Phil Vassar: *American Child*
Toby Keith: *Unleashed*
Lee Ann Womack: *Something Worth Leaving Behind*
Dixie Chicks: *Home*
Kelly Willis: *Easy*
Montgomery Gentry: *My Town*
Keith Urban: *Golden Road*
Shedaisy: *Knock on the Sky*
Faith Hill: *Cry*
Rascal Flatts: *Melt*
Tim McGraw: *Tim McGraw and the Dancehall Doctors*

2003

Toby Keith: *Shock'N Y'All*
Trace Adkins: *Comin' on Strong*
Tracy Byrd: *Truth About Men*
Brooks & Dunn: *Red Dirt Road*
Brad Paisley: *Mud on the Tires*
Sara Evans: *Restless*
Dierks Bently: *Dierks Bentley*
Martina McBride: *Martina*
Blake Shelton: *Dreamer*
Vince Gill: *Next Big Thing*
Craig Morgan: *I Love It*
Terri Clark: *Pain to Kill*
George Strait: *Honkytonkville*
Rick Trevino: *In My dreams*
Patty Loveless: *On Your Way Home*

2004

Kenny Chensey: *When the Sun Goes Down*
Big & Rich: *Horse of a Different Color*
Gretchen Wilson: *Here for the Party*
Tim McGraw: *Live Like You Were Dying*
Alan Jackson: *What I Do*
Montgomery Gentry: *You Do Your Thing*
Phil Vassar: *Shaken Not Stirred*
Blake Shelton: *Blake Shelton's Barn & Grill*

Sugarland: *Twice the Speed of Life*
Lonestar: *Let's Be Us Again*
Julie Roberts: *Julie Roberts*
The Notorious Cherry Bombs: *The Notorious Cherry Bombs*
Keith Urban: *Be Here*
Rascal Flatts: *Feels Like Today*
Lari White: *Green Eyed Soul*
Trent Wilmon: *Trent Wilmon*
Pat Green: *Lucky Ones*

2005

Kenny Chesney: *Be as You Are (Songs From an Old Blue Chair)*
Lee Ann Womack: *There's More Where That Came From*
Dierks Bently: *Modern Day Drifter*
Toby Keith: *Honkytonk University*
Miranda Lambert: *Kerosene*
Big & Rich: *Comin' to Your City*
Carrie Underwood: *Some Hearts*
Gretchen Wilson: *All Jacked Up*
Little Big Town: *Road to Here*
Sara Evans: *Real Fine Place*
Trace Adkins: *Songs About Me*
Jo Dee Messina: *Delicious Surprise*
Kenny Chesney: *Road and the Radio*
Bobby Pinson: *Man Like Me*
Patty Loveless: *Dreamin' My Dreams*
Sawyer Brown: *Mission Temple Fireworks*
Brooks & Dunn: *Hillbilly Deluxe*
Trisha Yearwood: *Jasper County*
Keith Urban: *Days Go By*
Martina McBride: *Timeless*
Billy Currington: *Doin' Something Right*
Joe Nichols: *III*
Jace Everett: *Jace Everett*
LeAnn Rimes: *This Woman*
Terri Clark: *Life Goes On*
Montgomery Gentry: *Something to Be Proud Of*

2006

Toby Keith: *White Trash with Money*
Taylor Swift: *Taylor Swift*
Rascal Flatts: *Me and My Gang*
Dierks Bentley: *Long Trip Alone*
Montgomery Gentry: *Some People Change*
Vince Gill: *These Days*
Sugarland: *Enjoy the Ride*
Keith Urban: *Love, Pain & the Whole Crazy Thing*
Shooter Jennings: *Electric Rodeo*
Dixie Chicks: *Taking the Long Way*
Trent Wilmon: *Little More Livin'*
Ronnie Milsap: *My Life*
Emerson Drive: *Countrified*
Trent Tomlinson: *Country Is My Rock*
Alan Jackson: *Like Red on a Rose*
George Strait: *It Just Comes Natural*

2007

Miranda Lambert: *Crazy Ex-Girlfriend*
Brad Paisley: *5th Gear*
Elizabeth Cook: *Balls*
John Anderson: *Easy Money*
Gretchen Wilson: *One of the Boys*

Toby Keith: *Big Dog Daddy*
Tim McGraw: *Let It Go*
Martina McBride: *Waking Up Laughing*
Ty Herndon: *Right About Now*
Mary Chapin Carpenter: *Calling*
Blake Shelton: *Pure BS*